Parliamentary Con Policy Process

This book sheds new light on the often shadowy, but essential role of committees, which exist in modern parliaments around the globe, and it questions the conventional notion that the 'real' work of parliament happens in committees.

Renowned country specialists take a close look at what goes on in committees and how it matters for policy-making. While committees are seen as the central place where policy is made, their sessions are often closed to the public and calls for transparency are growing. To understand this 'black box' it is necessary to look within but also beyond the walls of the committee rooms and parliament buildings. Bringing together formal and informal aspects, rules and practices shows that committees are not a paradise of policy-making. They have great relevance nonetheless: as crystallization points in the policy networks, as drivers for division of labour and for socialization and the integration of MPs.

The new insights presented in this book will be of interest to scholars, students and professionals in parliamentary affairs, legislative studies, government, and comparative politics. They are also relevant for political analysts, journalists, and policymakers.

Sven T. Siefken is professor pro tempore of political science at the Martin-Luther-University Halle-Wittenberg, Germany.

Hilmar Rommetvedt is research professor of political science at NORCE Norwegian Research Centre in Stavanger, Norway.

Library of Legislative Studies
Series Editor: Lord Philip Norton of Louth, *University of Hull, UK*

Parliamentary Communication in EU Affairs
Connecting with the Electorate?
Edited by Katrin Auel and Tapio Raunio

Government-Opposition in Southern European Countries during the Economic Crisis
Great Recession, Great Cooperation?
Edited by Elisabetta De Giorgi and Catherine Moury

The Legislature of Brazil
An Analysis of Its Policy-making and Public Engagement Roles
Edited by Cristiane Brum Bernardes, Cristina Leston-Bandeira and Ricardo de João Braga

Regional Parliaments
Effective Actors in EU Policy-making?
Edited by Gabriele Abels and Anna-Lena Hogenauer

The Iberian Legislatures in Comparative Perspective
Edited by Jorge M. Fernandes and Cristina Leston-Bandeira

The Impact of Legislatures
A Quarter-Century of The Journal of Legislative Studies
Edited by Philip Norton

Parliaments and Post-Legislative Scrutiny
Edited by Franklin De Vrieze and Philip Norton

Parliamentary Committees in the Policy Process
Edited by Sven T. Siefken and Hilmar Rommetvedt

Parliamentary Committees in the Policy Process

Edited by
Sven T. Siefken and Hilmar Rommetvedt

Routledge
Taylor & Francis Group
LONDON AND NEW YORK

First published 2022
by Routledge
2 Park Square, Milton Park, Abingdon, Oxon OX14 4RN

and by Routledge
605 Third Avenue, New York, NY 10158

Routledge is an imprint of the Taylor & Francis Group, an informa business

© 2022 selection and editorial matter, Sven T. Siefken and Hilmar Rommetvedt; individual chapters, the contributors

The right of Sven T. Siefken and Hilmar Rommetvedt to be identified as the authors of the editorial material, and of the authors for their individual chapters, has been asserted in accordance with sections 77 and 78 of the Copyright, Designs and Patents Act 1988.

All rights reserved. No part of this book may be reprinted or reproduced or utilised in any form or by any electronic, mechanical, or other means, now known or hereafter invented, including photocopying and recording, or in any information storage or retrieval system, without permission in writing from the publishers.

Trademark notice: Product or corporate names may be trademarks or registered trademarks, and are used only for identification and explanation without intent to infringe.

British Library Cataloguing-in-Publication Data
A catalogue record for this book is available from the British Library

Library of Congress Cataloging-in-Publication Data
A catalog record has been requested for this book

ISBN: 978-0-367-61788-2 (hbk)
ISBN: 978-0-367-61795-0 (pbk)
ISBN: 978-1-003-10657-9 (ebk)

DOI: 10.4324/9781003106579

Typeset in Times New Roman
by Newgen Publishing UK

Contents

List of figures	viii
List of tables	ix
List of contributors	xi
Preface	xvi

1 Investigating the role of parliamentary committees in the policy process   1
SVEN T. SIEFKEN AND HILMAR ROMMETVEDT

2 A black box that deserves more light: comparative findings on parliamentary committees in the policy process   9
SVEN T. SIEFKEN AND HILMAR ROMMETVEDT

3 Assess in order to assist: a preliminary analysis of committees in Arab Parliaments   38
ALI SAWI

4 The role of parliamentary committees and legislative agreements in party bargaining during minority government in Denmark   61
FLEMMING JUUL CHRISTIANSEN AND HENRIK JENSEN

5 Committees in the Finnish Eduskunta: cross-party cooperation and legislative scrutiny behind closed doors   79
TAPIO RAUNIO

6 Twenty years of attempts at reforming committees: a tale of reforms missing the mark in the French National Assembly   98
CLAIRE BLOQUET

7 No paradise of policy-making: the role of parliamentary
   committees in the German Bundestag   116
   SVEN T. SIEFKEN

8 From 'a rubber stamp' to influencing policy: a critical
   view of committees in the Parliament of Ghana   137
   ERNEST DARFOUR

9 Parliamentary committees in the Hungarian
   Parliament: instruments of political parties and
   government agenda control   159
   CSABA NIKOLENYI

10 Strength and weakness: legislative and oversight powers
   of the parliamentary committee system in Israel   177
   CHEN FRIEDBERG

11 Japan's unusual but interesting parliamentary committees:
   an arena and transformative model?   189
   KUNIAKI NEMOTO AND ELLIS S. KRAUSS

12 Exploring the gap between theory and practice in
   law-making and oversight by committees of the
   Nigerian National Assembly   206
   BENJAMIN EKEYI

13 Norwegian parliamentary committees: split and
   sidelined in the policy process   224
   HILMAR ROMMETVEDT

14 Committees in a party-dominated parliament: the
   Spanish Congreso de los Diputados   244
   PABLO OÑATE AND BERNABÉ ALDEGUER

15 Parliamentary committees in the Grand National
   Assembly of Turkey (2002–2020)   263
   ÖMER FARUK GENÇKAYA

16 The role of legislative committees in the policy
   process: the case of the Ukrainian Parliament   287
   IRINA KHMELKO, OLEKSII BRUSLYK AND
   LIUDMYLA VASYLIEVA

17 Still deviant? The development and reform of the UK
   House of Commons committee system (1979 to present) 302
   STEPHEN HOLDEN BATES, LOUISE THOMPSON,
   MARK GOODWIN, AND STEPHEN MCKAY

18 'Specially commissioned minorities': committee
   governance and political parties in the United States
   Congress 320
   ANNE MARIE CAMMISA

Appendix 344
Index 347

Figures

2.1	Policy formulation in the legislative process	27
7.1	Number of investigating committees in the Bundestag (1949–2021)	119
7.2	Committees in the Bundestag (2018)	120
7.3	Committee meetings in the Bundestag open to the public	122
7.4	Public committee hearings in the Bundestag	123
7.5	Committee reports and recommendations in the Bundestag	129
8.1	The legislative process in Ghana	150
11.1	Public observers attending committees in Japan	192
13.1	Parliamentary committees dealing with bills, reports and budget chapters from each of the ministries (2018–2019)	230
14.1	Development of oral questions to the government in committees of Congreso de los Diputados (1979–2019)	257
15.1	Flow of law-making in the committees in Turkey (since July 2018)	273

Tables

2.1	Typology of parliamentary committees	11
2.2	Committee systems and committee sizes compared	14
2.3	Transparency of parliamentary committees	17
2.4	Competencies of committees in legislation	29
3.1	Composition of the survey in Arab parliaments	39
3.2	Committee tools for oversight in Arab parliaments	47
3.3	Ways to strengthen committees in policy-making in Arab parliaments	55
6.1	Percentage of non-broadcasted meetings per committee in France	106
7.1	Committee size in the Bundestag (1990–2017)	121
8.1	Examples of ad hoc committees in Ghana	140
8.2	Standing committees of the Parliament of Ghana	141
8.3	Select committees of the Parliament of Ghana	142
8.4	MPs' professions and committee membership in Ghana	144
8.5	Types of parliamentary business in Ghana	148
8.6	Success rate of government bills introduced to the Parliament of Ghana (1993–2017)	152
8.7	Amendments of selected legislation in Ghana	154
9.1	Legislative standing committees and subcommittees in the Hungarian Parliament (1990–2018)	165
9.2	The representation of the governing coalition on Hungary's standing committees	168
9.3	Investigative Committees in the Hungarian Parliament (1990–2018)	169
9.4	Legislative activity of Hungarian standing committees (1998–2018)	171
9.5	Legislative initiative by standing committees in Hungary	171
9.6	Submission and rejection of private members' bills by committees in Hungary	173
11.1	Standing committees in the Diet of Japan and their sizes	191
12.1	Number of committees in the National Assembly of Nigeria	211
13.1	The standing committees of the Norwegian Parliament	229

x   List of tables

13.2	MPs and committee chairs by party in Norway (2017–2021)	232
13.3	Percentage of MPs that were reelected to the same committee as at the start of the previous election period (four years earlier) in Norway	232
13.4	MPs judgement about formal committee meetings in Norway	233
13.5	Committee members' contact with interest groups and NGOs in Norway	235
13.6	Committee recommendations with dissenting remarks in Norway, percentage (budget recommendations excluded)	237
13.7	Where are the real decisions made (in Norway during minority government)? Percentage of MPs	238
13.8	MPs' assessments of various groups and institutions' decision-making influence in Norway	240
14.1	Government and private members' bills and their success rates in Spain	246
14.2	Distribution (government-opposition) of committee chairs and committee board majority in legislative standing committees in Spain (1977–2020)	255
15.1	Relationships between standing committees and ministries in Turkey	265
15.2	Average turnover in committees' membership by party origin in Turkey (2002–2020)	267
15.3	Distribution of standing committee members by party groups in Turkey	268
15.4	Meetings and law-making activities of the standing committees in Turkey	271
15.5	Practices of guillotine and omnibus law methods in Turkey	277
15.6	Motions of parliamentary supervision in Turkey	280
16.1	Number of legislative committees in Rada of Ukraine	288
16.2	Committees of the Verkhovna Rada of Ukraine of the 9th convocation	291
16.3	Draft laws submitted and not voted on in Ukraine by initiator	298
16.4	Committee decisions on substantive amendments in Ukraine by initiator	298
16.5	Support of majority coalition and committee decision in Ukraine	299
18.1	Committees in the 116th United States Congress (2019–2020)	330
18.2	Legislative jurisdiction of the US House Committee on Education and Labor	331
18.3	Sources of authority for selected aspects of committee governance in the US House of Representatives, 116th Congress (2019–2020)	332

Contributors

Bernabé Aldeguer is lecturer of political science at the University of Valencia, Spain. He has published on political institutions and public administration, being the author of a number of journal articles and book chapters on these topics. His PhD is on regional parliamentarian elites in Spain from a gender perspective.

Stephen Holden Bates is a senior lecturer in political science at the University of Birmingham, UK. His current research interests are in the areas of parliamentary committees and parliamentary roles, He is the co-convenor of the UK Political Studies Association's Parliaments specialist group.

Claire Bloquet is a PhD candidate in the department of political science at the University of Paris 1 Panthéon-Sorbonne (France). Her research focuses on the substantive representation of women and on the role of MPs in the legislative process in the French Parliament.

Oleksii Bruslyk holds a Candidate of Science degree in legal studies. He is a Ukrainian researcher and an expert on Ukrainian public policy and politics. He also works as head of the legal department for the territorial control of the Kharkiv municipal council.

Anne Marie Cammisa is the Director of the MA program in American Government at Georgetown University in Washington, D.C., where she also teaches in the Government Department and the McCourt School of Public Policy. Dr. Cammisa is President of the New England Political Science Association, and has been an APSA Congressional Fellow. Her research interests revolve around American legislative process; she is interested in the American system in comparative perspective. She has published four books as well as numerous scholarly chapters and articles.

Flemming Juul Christiansen is an associate professor in politics and public administration at Roskilde University, Denmark. He received his PhD from Aarhus University (2008) with a thesis on legislative bargaining. He has published primarily on parliamentary politics and political parties. He is President of the Nordic Political Science Association (since 2017) and Secretary of the ECPR Standing Group for Parliaments (since 2018).

Ernest Darfour is an assistant parliamentary clerk at the Parliament of Ghana and the director of research and training at the Centre for Legislative and Parliamentary Research in Accra, Ghana. He received his PhD in legislative studies from the University of Hull in 2017. He researches on African legislatures, comparative legislative systems and parliamentary rules and procedures. His recent publication is on *'Ghana Legislative System: the history, procedure and practice of the Parliament of Ghana'*.

Benjamin Ekeyi is a full-time independent consultant, trainer and researcher with expertise in legislative strengthening and legislative policy analysis, public financial management, governance/development and security sector reforms. His research has focused on parliamentary practices and procedures, legislative policy analysis, parliament and public financial management as well as governance.

Chen Friedberg is a senior lecturer in the Department of Middle Eastern Studies and Political Science at Ariel University and a research fellow at the Israel Democracy Institute. Her areas of expertise are parliamentary oversight and legislation, parliamentary committees, Israeli politics and women in parliament. She has published articles and chapters in those fields and co-authored a book on the reforms that are needed in the Israeli political system.

Ömer F. Gençkaya is a full-time professor of political science and public administration at Marmara University in Turkey. He is a member of RCLS of IPSA (since 1994) and of the Core Group of Experts at OSCE-ODIHR (since 2012). He served as a country evaluator at COE-GRECO (2008–2016). He was a visiting researcher at the University of Oslo, Duke University, and Roanoke College (VA, USA). His publications include books, chapters, and articles on constitutional politics, parliament, political funding, and governance.

Mark Goodwin is a lecturer in politics in the School of Humanities, Coventry University. His research focuses on the UK Parliament and British public policy.

Henrik Jensen is an associate professor in political science at the University of Copenhagen. After serving as a secretary to legislative committees of the Danish Parliament, he received his PhD from Aarhus University (1995), and a doctorate (Dr.scient.pol.) from the University of Copenhagen (2005). He has published several highly recognized monographs (in Danish) on the workings of Danish legislative committees, party groups, and ministries, and is published in international journals.

List of contributors xiii

Dylan Johnson is a PhD student at the University of Hamburg. He served as editorial assistant for the preparation of this volume.

Irina Khmelko is a UC Foundation Professor at the University of Tennessee, Chattanooga, USA. She has also served as an associate, contractor, and invited guest speaker for developmental organizations, including the US Agency for International Development and the World Bank. Her research interests lie in the field of legislative studies, democratic institution-building, and democratization in post-authoritarian societies.

Ellis S. Krauss (PhD, Stanford University) is professor emeritus at the School of Global Policy and Strategy, UCSD. The author of nine books and over 80 articles about Japanese politics and US–Japanese relations, he most recently co-authored the book *Reluctant Warriors: Germany, Japan and their US Alliance Dilemma* (Brookings Institution Press, 2019) comparing the two countries' military intervention policies. He is co-author of a recent book on comparative elections, political parties, and committee assignments (Oxford University Press, 2021). In 2018 Krauss received the Order of the Rising Sun, 3rd class with Gold Leaves and Neck Ribbon from the Emperor and government of Japan for his professional work.

Stephen McKay is Distinguished Professor in social research at the University of Lincoln, UK. He conducts quantitative research on a range of topics, including the career paths of politicians and their interactions with parliamentary committees.

Kuniaki Nemoto is professor at Musashi University, Japan. He specializes in electoral systems, parties and party systems, and legislative politics with a regional focus on Asia-Pacific. His articles have appeared in the *British Journal of Political Science*, *Comparative Political Studies*, *Electoral Studies*, and *Party Politics*, among others.

Csaba Nikolenyi is professor of political science and director of the Azrieli Institute of Israel Studies at Concordia University. His research focuses on the comparative study of political parties, electoral systems, and legislatures in post-communist democracies, as well as on the political systems of Israel and India. Nikolenyi has published extensively in comparative political journals and has authored two books: *Minority Government in India* (Routledge 2010) and *Institutional Design and Party Government in Post-Communist Democracies* (Oxford University Press, 2014).

Pablo Oñate is professor of political science at the University of Valencia, Spain. He has published extensively on the Spanish political system, multi-level politics, political parties and party systems, parliaments and parliamentarian elites, and electoral quotas and their impact. He also works as a consultant for political institutions.

Tapio Raunio is professor of political science at Tampere University, Finland. His research interests cover legislatures and political parties, the European Union, semi-presidentialism, and the Finnish political system. Recent publications include two special issues co-edited with Wolfgang Wagner, *Challenging Executive Dominance: Legislatures and Foreign Affairs* (West European Politics, 2017) and *Political Parties and Foreign Policy* (Foreign Policy Analysis, 2020), as well as the book *Semi-Presidential Policy-Making in Europe: Executive Coordination and Political Leadership* (2020), co-authored with Thomas Sedelius.

Hilmar Rommetvedt is dr. polit. and research professor at NORCE Norwegian Research Centre in Stavanger, Norway. He has published numerous books and articles on parliament, the executive, and interest groups, as well as the formulation and implementation of public policies within areas such as the environment, agriculture, international trade, sport and culture, health and welfare services.

Ali Sawi is professor of political science at Cairo University, Egypt. He holds a PhD from the University of Vienna, Austria, and concluded peace studies at the American University in Washington, DC. He has taught comparative government and constitutional law, and supervised theses on parliamentary development in Arab countries. Sawi conducts consultancies for Arab parliaments in bill drafting, committee development, assessing the cost of legislation, and reforming parliamentary administration. In 2001, he founded the Center on Parliamentary Research at Cairo University. He has published over 20 books in Arabic, a series of contributions in English, and contributed to the first Global Parliamentary Report of UNDP/IPU.

Kevin W. Settles is a master's student at the Martin-Luther-University Halle-Wittenberg. He served as editorial assistant for the preparation of this volume.

Sven T. Siefken is professor of political science pro tempore at the Martin-Luther-University Halle-Wittenberg, Germany, and visiting professor at Colorado College, USA. Recent publications deal with parliamentary control and representation in comparative perspective, and with parliaments in the pandemic. He is a member of the editorial board of the German Journal of Parliamentary Affairs (*Zeitschrift für Parlamentsfragen*) and serves on the advisory board for the Third Global Parliamentary Report of IPU/UNDP on parliamentary public engagment.

Louise Thompson is senior lecturer in politics at the University of Manchester. She researches political parties and the legislative process in the UK Parliament.

Liudmyla Vasylieva is pursuing an LLM degree at the University of Oslo, Norway. She holds an MA degree in parliamentary procedures and legislative drafting, and a BA degree in law from the National University 'Odesa Law Academy', Ukraine. She was a short-term researcher at the Center for European Studies, University of Florida, USA. Her research interests are legislative process, ICT law, and privacy.

Preface

The role of committees is a central topic in the analysis of parliaments and parliamentary democracy. It has been a long-lasting interest of members of the Research Committee 08 – Legislative Specialists (RCLS) of the International Political Science Association (IPSA). This volume is another milestone in an ongoing process endorsed by the RCLS. Earlier milestones were an international conference on 'The Changing Roles of Parliamentary Committees' that was held in Budapest, Hungary, in 1996. Its results were subsequently published as *The New Roles of Parliamentary Committees* in 1998. Twenty years later, in 2018, the RCLS organized a panel on 'The New Roles of Parliamentary Committees Revisited' at the IPSA World Congress in Brisbane, Australia. The need for a deeper investigation became apparent – as political practices had changed over the decades and academic understanding had developed. Thus it was decided to investigate the topic anew and take a closer look at the role of parliamentary committees in the policy process. In response to a global open call for contributions, scholars met for a fruitful workshop in Valencia, Spain, in the autumn of 2019. Later, more academics joined the group, and this volume is the outcome – so far.

We would like to thank all the contributors for the preparation of their insightful chapters in this volume, and for their patience and speed in responding to the editors' questions and suggestions. In particular, we thank Pablo Oñate, University of Valencia, for his efforts in organizing the workshop in 2019. We also extend our gratitude to the Valencian Regional Government and the University of Valencia for funding and hosting the meeting where the contributions for this book were first discussed. Very special thanks go to Dylan Johnson and Kevin W. Settles for their excellent editorial assistance in the preparation of the manuscript for publication. We thank Philip Norton, Lord Norton of Louth, for the opportunity to have our results published in the Library of Legislative Studies series and two anonymous reviewers for their helpful comments. The publishing team at Routledge under the leadership of Andrew Taylor has been very helpful and professional in moving this book to and then through production. Finally, we thank our own institutions, the Martin-Luther-University Halle-Wittenberg and NORCE Norwegian Research Centre, for their support.

Hilmar Rommetvedt and Sven T. Siefken
Stavanger / Mannheim, May 2021

1 Investigating the role of parliamentary committees in the policy process

Sven T. Siefken and Hilmar Rommetvedt

Parliamentary committees – where the real work takes place?

Committees – with large or limited decision-making competencies – exist within most modern parliaments. This is true all over the world and in political systems that are liberal democracies or not, in developed and developing countries, in presidential, semi-presidential and parliamentary systems, and in parliaments that are big or small. Committees are often seen as the central organizational units of parliaments, especially with regard to policy-making. In his landmark study from 1892, political scientist Woodrow Wilson – who later became president of the United States of America – wrote a classic line that has been often quoted: 'Congress in session is Congress on public exhibition, whilst Congress in its committee rooms is Congress at work' (Wilson 2006 [1892]: 69). It is still a common argument today, formulated by journalistic observers and practitioners – and political scientists, too – that the committees are the heart of parliamentary activities, 'the engine room of democracy' (Alexander 2009) or the 'work horses of legislatures' (Mickler 2017: 6).

In this book, we question these assumptions and assume that a more complex picture is required. In our understanding of established democracies, committees cannot be seen as collective actors or even as central fora for policy-making. In established democracies with a strong party system, these activities happen elsewhere: in the specific policy communities, in the parliamentary party groups, among individual MPs, and in the executive governments. But this does not mean that committees are irrelevant. Their very existence does influence the functioning of both parliaments and policy-making. The question is how?

Committees and the classification of parliaments

The role of committees has been part of overarching classifications in parliamentary studies.[1] Winfried Steffani used it to distinguish two types: a 'debating parliament' serves as a showroom, where the prime minister and the opposition leader meet and present their positions. Committees in this

DOI: 10.4324/9781003106579-1

model are 'second-rate support institutions' while the plenary assembly is the 'central forum for action' (Steffani 1979: 96). This is different in a 'working parliament' where 'power and work have been decisively transferred into the committees. Not the grand orator, but the knowledgeable expert for details ... is the most important parliamentary figure' there (Steffani 1979: 96). The differentiation between arena and transformative parliaments by Nelson Polsby is similar. Arena parliaments 'serve as formalized settings for the interplay of significant political forces in the life of a political system' (Polsby 1990 [1975]: 129–130). In other words, they help to put on exhibit what has been decided already; for example, in the government executive, in party systems, or elsewhere in a societal stratarchy. An arena is equivalent to a debating parliament – the primary role is in informing the public about the 'pros and cons' on policy topics and about the final decision taken by the majority. On the other end of the spectrum is a transformative parliament. It has 'the independent capacity ... to mould and transform proposals from whatever source into laws' (Polsby 1990 [1975]: 129). As the name suggests, the focus here is on parliaments' opportunity to independently draft or amend bills in the legislative process. This influence is exercised largely in the committees and thus they are deemed to be the focal point for studying transformative parliaments (Polsby 1990 [1975]: 140).

Committees and their changing roles

In 1969, following a call from the Political Studies Association, international scholars held a conference in London on the role of committees and their comparative study. In close coordination of research and after two more conferences, the findings of that effort were published in an edited volume – ten years later. It contained detailed descriptions of eight country cases: the United States of America, Italy, West Germany, the Philippines, Canada, the United Kingdom, India, and Japan (Lees & Shaw 1979). That book remains instructive over 40 years later, especially its comparative conclusion is worth re-reading (Shaw 1979). Yet obviously, much has changed since then.

Roughly 30 years later, in 1996, an international conference was held in Budapest on 'the changing roles of parliamentary committees' around the world. The conference was organized by the Research Committee of Legislative Specialists (RCLS) of the International Political Science Association (IPSA). The contributions were first published in a working paper series (Longley & Ágh 1997), and a revised selection was compiled in a special issue of the *Journal of Legislative Studies* on 'The New Roles of Parliamentary Committees'. Based on the research included in that issue, the editors noted in their opening article that 'parliaments have, in the past three decades, become more influential bodies globally, and this has been due particularly to their newly created or revived committee system' (Longley & Davidson 1998: 5). In that issue, Kaare Strøm (1998: 47) provided a comprehensive overview of 'Committees in [18] European Democracies' and concluded that they are 'by broad consensus, among the most significant organizational features of modern parliaments'.[2] He also claimed that 'strong committees, it appears, are at least a necessary condition for effective parliamentary influence in the policy-making process'. In the same issue Hilmar Rommetvedt (1998: 81) questioned that assumption and showed that the Norwegian Parliament had increased its relevance while the role of standing committees declined. This conclusion was later supported based on broader data from 17 West European parliaments (Damgaard & Mattson 2004: 139).

A quarter of a century has passed since these topics were raised. Parliaments have met new challenges and adapted to them worldwide. So it is time to ask: do influential parliaments (still) go hand in hand with vital committees? 'Yes', is the answer according to a recent chapter in the *Oxford Handbook of Legislative Studies*: 'Today, the conventional notion is that a strong system of committees, however defined, is a necessary if not sufficient condition for the legislature to operate effectively, not least in terms of influencing the content of legislation and holding the executive accountable' (Martin 2014: 352). Yet when looking beyond this widespread assumption, quite a few interesting questions about the underlying mechanisms remain unanswered: what actually happens in committees? How does it relate to policy-making and to the influence on policy? And what does that mean for the strength of parliament?

To conclusively investigate these questions, it is necessary to look beyond the formal institutions and official announcements by parliamentary PR departments. This may reveal that parliamentary committees are not the policy-making paradise that they are often portrayed to be. However, this should not be confused with claiming that committees are completely irrelevant. In their day-to-day work, neither arguing nor bargaining approaches to policy-making may prevail, and they might have a more preparatory role for the plenary debate. They may also serve communicative functions, if not to a broad audience, then perhaps to the more targeted one in the policy subsystems.

The fact that parliament installs committees can lead to the policy specialization of MPs – at least for a certain time period. By nominating rapporteurs, committees – or rather the parliamentary parties – assign them clear tasks and responsibility. Those MPs conduct their policy-making in many places: as members of their party working group, members of their parliamentary party, in the network of the respective policy domain, and with regard to government and the executive. Parliamentary committees may also serve as an important place for the socialization and specialization of MPs, teaching them how to work in a parliamentary way, how to interact with each other, and how to understand specific policy fields. Thus, committees may be neither central *actors* in the process, nor the most important forum for *deliberation*. But their very existence can influence how the political process works even though their functions may be different from the conventional and often communicated views.

Requirements for a deeper understanding – and the way towards it

Surprisingly, political science has so far only gained a limited understanding of what is going on inside parliamentary committees and what substantial role they actually play in policy-making. Scholars have come to the conclusion, time and again, that 'a greater understanding of committees is crucial to more fully understand the functioning of legislatures' (Martin 2014: 353) and that they 'do play an underappreciated role in European parliaments both with regard to policy-making and to monitoring the behaviour of different executive actors' (Sieberer & Höhmann 2017: 318). What Kaare Strøm formulated 20 years ago is still to be repeated today: 'The analytical literature has only scratched the surface of [committees] and ... many of the critical questions concerning parliamentary committees have not yet been asked, much less answered' (Strøm 1998: 55). And while quite some effort has been made to shed light on who gets to sit on which committee (Chiru 2019; Fernandes, Riera, & Cantú 2019; Gschwend & Zittel 2018; Shugart et al. 2021), what a recent article calls 'the post-assignment phase' is largely left in the dark, even though it comprises 'the actual decision-making processes' (Martin & Mickler 2019: 92). This lack of knowledge is due to a number of reasons:

- First and foremost, committees by their own choosing or by the rules of parliament often do not hold their sessions in public. Access to data on formalities may be easy, but it is more difficult to capture political realities.
- Second, there is a large variety of institutional settings in which committees operate. If committees exist in such different environments, their role is likely to differ, too.
- Third, not only the external institutions may differ, but the internal ones, too: the rules for committees and their work inside parliament can be manifold. This variety of external and internal settings makes it difficult to come to conclusions in a comparative perspective.
- Fourth, for this reason, both academic and journalistic observers have trouble gathering information about what happens in committees.
- Fifth, political science itself has differentiated itself into subfields; parliamentary studies and policy analysis are quite separate. For the United States it has been suggested that 'a focus on committees as arenas for policy-making could facilitate efforts to incorporate policy content into empirical studies of Congress' (Evans 2013: 419). Yet for the moment, many studies of committees have only applied an intra-parliamentary perspective.

In the meantime, as demands for a higher transparency and stronger accountability have grown, changes have been adopted in many countries;

some even speak of a 'reform wave of the committee rules' (Mickler 2017: 10). For example, almost all committee and subcommittee sessions in the US Congress have been open to the public since the 'sunshine' rules in the mid-1970s (Patterson 1990: 266). The Assemblée nationale has (slightly) diversified its committee system and the number of committee sessions that are open to the public in the German Bundestag has strongly increased in recent years (Siefken 2018: 787). In the Norwegian Storting, committee hearings are now held in public, but ordinary meetings and negotiations still take place behind closed doors. Some parliaments stream their public committee meetings regularly on the internet or via television. Not only their accessibility varies, but also committee competencies. In some countries, committees can initiate laws or make final decisions in place of the plenary. Based on data from over a quarter of a century ago Strøm (1998: 48) noted that 'there is considerable variation in committee powers'. Has this variation been reduced since? And what effect do recent democratic backlashes have in some transition countries? These questions deserve to be answered, too.

Comparing parliamentary committees through country case studies

In light of these three facts – the assumed importance of committees, gaps in their understanding and changes in proceedings – the RCLS organized a panel on 'The New Roles of Parliamentary Committees Revisited' at the IPSA World Congress 2018 in Brisbane, Australia. It brought together scholars working on parliamentary committees around the globe; the renewed interest and need for academic debate on the topic became apparent. Thus, we decided to investigate the role of committees anew and look more closely at their role in policy-making. To this end, parliamentary scholars were invited to contribute their insights in a workshop at the University of Valencia, Spain, in October 2019. The aim was to tackle this fundamental question: what roles do parliamentary committees have in the policy process?

The present volume is the result of this fruitful meeting and the concluding exchange and discussion via email and video conferences in the pandemic year of 2020. In order to gain a broad understanding, the study is not limited to liberal or Western democracies as many other have been before. It includes contributions from researchers on the Arab countries, Denmark, Finland, France, Germany, Ghana, Hungary, Israel, Japan, Nigeria, Norway, Spain, Turkey, Ukraine, the United Kingdom, and the United States. Among these countries are liberal democracies and systems that are in a transition. The selection includes countries with a majoritarian approach to politics as well as countries from a consociational tradition. It has parliamentary systems that are closer to an arena parliament and also examples that are more transformative. And it includes young and older political systems. In other words, there is huge variety among the underlying cases. The idea of this rather open approach is to use an analytical perspective that is far broader than the usual one for studying parliamentary committees: first, to look at different types of committees, second to include more than their legislative and control functions, third to encompass the complete policy cycle, and fourth to move beyond liberal western democracies.

To come to common conclusions, a simple research framework has been developed to guide the analysis. It served as an inspiration for the authors of the country case investigations. This was not meant to be a mechanical exercise and the authors were encouraged to apply different methods and to stress specialties and particularities of their respective parliaments in their analyses. In this way, the present volume is as much an explorative endeavour as it is a comparative exercise. As common starting points, three simple research frameworks were employed: actor-centred institutionalism, the policy cycle, and parliamentary functions. From them, we derived a list of 32 questions to be addressed by the country specialists (see Appendix). To avoid overlaps, we have decided to integrate the description of our research framework with the comparative findings (see chapter 2).

The overview has shown that parliamentary committees deserve more scholarly attention than they have received so far. To find out whether they are indeed the central working units of a modern and strong parliament or not, a comprehensive study is necessary. The present discussion based on the literature and some of the empirical data and analyses presented in this volume leads to the following preliminary assessment: parties rather than committees are the most important actors within parliaments. Nowadays, parliamentary committees are not always the places of policy-making through negotiation. And today, it is incomplete to judge them only based on their contribution to the legislative function of parliament: the control function is also of high importance for evaluating committees, as is – and may be increasingly so – the communication function. In this regard, there may have been significant changes over the last decades. It will be a challenge – but a worthy one – to try and uncover them. Because one puzzle is obvious: if parliamentary committees are not the engine rooms, why do they exist everywhere?

Bringing together experts on a large variety of political systems to discuss the country cases and relevant questions about the role of committees, is a first step in this endeavour. It will help to focus the presented framework and possibly to extend it. At the same time, this volume wants to help identify topics with regard to parliamentary committees in the policy process that have not been taken into account so far.

Notes

1 Some ideas and arguments in this chapter are based on Siefken (2018).
2 In a more recent chapter, Saalfeld and Strøm (2014: 372) argue that committees and parties in parliament are 'the most important component of legislative organization and preference aggregation'.

References

Alexander, R. (2009). Im Maschinenraum der Demokratie: Die Welt. Retrieved from www.welt.de/welt_print/politik/article5331987/Im-Maschinenraum-der-Demokratie.htm (access: 20.02.2020).

Chiru, M. (2019). Low-cost policy specialisation, district characteristics and gender. Patterns of committee assignment in Romania. *Journal of Legislative Studies*, 25(3), 375–393.

Damgaard, E., & Mattson, I. (2004). Conflict and Consensus in Committees. In H. Döring & M. Hallerberg (eds.), *Patterns of parliamentary behaviour: Passage of legislation across Western Europe* (113–140). Aldershot: Ashgate.

Evans, C.L. (2013). Committees. In E. Schickler & F.E. Lee (eds.), *The Oxford Handbook of the American Congress* (396–425). Oxford: Oxford University Press.

Fernandes, J.M., Riera, P., & Cantú, F. (2019). The Politics of Committee Chairs Assignment in Ireland and Spain. *Parliamentary Affairs*, 72(1), 182–201.

Gschwend, T., & Zittel, T. (2018). Who brings home the pork? Parties and the role of localness in committee assignments in mixed-member proportional systems. *Party Politics*, 24(5), 488–500.

Lees, J.D., & Shaw, M. (eds.) (1979). *Committees in legislatures: A comparative analysis*. Oxford: Martin Robertson.

Longley, L.D., & Ágh, A. (eds.) (1997). *Working papers in comparative legislative studies: Vol. 2. The Changing Roles of Parliamentary Committees: Ipsa RCLS Working Papers on Comparative Legislative Studies*. Appleton: Lawrence University.

Longley, L.D., & Davidson, R.H. (1998). Parliamentary Committees: Changing Perspectives on Changing Institutions. In L.D. Longley & R.H. Davidson (eds.), *The New Roles of Parliamentary Committees* (1–20). London: Frank Cass.

Martin, S. (2014). Committees. In S. Martin, T. Saalfeld, & K.W. Strøm (eds.), *The Oxford Handbook of Legislative Studies* (1st ed., 352–368). Oxford: Oxford University Press.

Martin, S., & Mickler, T.A. (2019). Committee Assignments: Theories, Causes and Consequences. *Parliamentary Affairs*, 72(1), 77–98.

Mickler, T.A. (2017). Parliamentary Committees in a Party-Centred Context: Structure, Composition, Functioning. University of Leiden: PhD thesis.

Patterson, S.C. (1990). Parties and Committees in Congress. In U. Thaysen, R.H. Davidson, & R.G. Livingston (eds.), *The U.S. Congress and the German Bundestag: Comparisons of democratic processes* (249–271). Boulder: Westview Press.

Polsby, N.W. (1990 [1975]). Legislatures. In P. Norton (ed.), *Oxford readings in politics and government. Legislatures* (127–148). Oxford: Oxford University Press.

Rommetvedt, H. (1998). Norwegian Parliamentary Committees: Performance, Structural Change and External Relations. *Journal of Legislative Studies*, 4(1), 60–84.

Saalfeld, T., & Strøm, K.W. (2014). Political Parties and Legislators. In S. Martin, T. Saalfeld, & K.W. Strøm (eds.), *The Oxford Handbook of Legislative Studies* (1st ed., 371–398). Oxford: Oxford University Press.

Shaw, M. (1979). Conclusion. In J.D. Lees & M. Shaw (eds.), *Committees in legislatures: A comparative analysis* (361–434). Oxford: Martin Robertson.

Shugart, M., Bergman, M.E., Struthers, C.L., Krauss, E., & Pekkanen, R. (eds.) (2021). *Party Personnel Strategies: Electoral Systems and Parliamentary Committee Assignments*. Oxford: Oxford University Press.

Sieberer, U., & Höhmann, D. (2017). Shadow Chairs as Monitoring Device? A Comparative Analysis of Committee Chair Powers in Western European Parliaments. *Journal of Legislative Studies*, 23(3), 301–325.

Siefken, S.T. (2018). 'Plenum im Kleinen' oder Ort der Verhandlung? Verständnisse und Forschungsbedarf zu den Fachausschüssen des Deutschen Bundestages. *Zeitschrift für Parlamentsfragen*, 49(4), 777–792.

Steffani, W. (1979). Das präsidentielle System der USA und die parlamentarischen Systeme Großbritanniens und Deutschlands im Vergleich. In W. Steffani (ed.), *Parlamentarische und präsidentielle Demokratie: Strukturelle Aspekte westlicher Demokratien* (61–104). Opladen: Westdeutscher Verlag.

Strøm, K. (1998). Parliamentary Committees in European Democracies. *Journal of Legislative Studies*, 4(1), 21–59.

Wilson, W. (2006 [1892]). *Congressional Government: A Study in American Politics* (9th ed.). Mineola: Dover Publications.

2 A black box that deserves more light

Comparative findings on parliamentary committees in the policy process

Sven T. Siefken and Hilmar Rommetvedt

Analysing three dimensions of politics to understand the role of committees

Academic understanding of parliamentary committees has taken up many ideas and findings from studying the United States Congress and tried to transfer them to other parliaments.[1] These can be grouped into five approaches, all (loosely) based on rational choice (Martin 2014: 352–360): (1) Distributional theory looks at the electoral advantages from committee work for the individual MP; for example, by investigating the linkage between gains for the district ('pork') and the committee specialization of an MP. (2) Informational theory studies the use of individual expertise of MPs for the whole parliament – or for the parties. (3) Models following party cartel theory look at political parties and their respective checks in coalition government and (4) bicameral–rivalry–theory focuses on inter-institutional relations between the two chambers. (5) The latter two have been developed into the 'keeping tabs argument' (André et al. 2016: 109) to stress that committees may play a role in checking and balancing between coalition partners (Martin & Vanberg 2011).

We suggest that a broader perspective is helpful for understanding the role of parliamentary committees in policy-making and in fulfilling the functions of parliament. It must take up findings in those five perspectives and integrate them with formal and informal processes of governance. Comparative overviews of parliamentary committees have largely focused on formal institutions (Strøm 1998) and the 'structural features' (Mickler 2017: 68–98). As parliaments are ever evolving, such studies need to be updated because there have been many changes in parliamentary rules over the last decades – and some with regard to digitalization are still underway, accelerated by the global pandemic crisis in 2020 and 2021. But for a full understanding of the institutional setting of committee work, it is necessary to look at more than only formal rules in constitutions, laws, rules of procedure (RoP) or standing orders. Such formalities serve as a necessary starting point, but established parliamentary customs have to be considered as well. Institutions provide both opportunities and restrictions for politicians, but they do not fully

DOI: 10.4324/9781003106579-2

determine their behaviour. Consequently, a renewed look at 'parliamentarians in committees' is needed; a perspective established by Richard E. Fenno (1973) but then sidelined over the decades. Thus, we suggest, for one, to study the microcosm of political actors in committees. But the overarching interest of our endeavour is not to explain committees as a set of rules or a group of people – we want to discover what roles committees play in the policy-making process. To do that, it is necessary not only to 'zoom in' and see what goes on inside committees, but also to 'zoom out', moving beyond the walls of the parliament building and look at the relevant governance processes in the respective policy networks. It needs to be determined where committees are within the political systems and how relevant they are. In other words, we approach parliamentary committees in three steps: committees as institutions, MPs in committees, and committees in the policy process.

This book follows a broad approach not only by integrating those three perspectives, but also by looking at very different political systems. Many long-established democracies are included, as are some countries undergoing transitions as political systems – not necessarily towards liberal democracies, but sometimes away from it. The country cases included here are neither based on a random nor on a systematic sampling. Yet, they share a common framework that the editors and contributors have discussed and applied. By engaging political scientists with a practice-oriented perspective from around the world, we have sought not only to assemble academic knowledge about the state of committees, but also to generate relevant questions for future research. Accordingly, the country case studies move from the readily available rules and the easily counted facts (such as the format and fragmentation of the committee system), to informal aspects of the nonpublic interactions and parliamentary customs and areas that require interpretative analysis. To take a closer look at committees as important units of parliamentary organization is not only an academic exercise – it is also highly relevant for political practice.

Committee institutions

Types of parliamentary committees

Committees are established as a subgroup of parliament to deal with a specific set of issues and make recommendations about them. They are related to the functions parliaments fulfil in a political system – election, legislation, oversight, and communication – aimed at achieving the overarching goal of democratic representation. Combining this functional perspective with the temporal dimension allows us to order all committee types (see Table 2.1). How committees contribute to these core functions is a bit varied – but not very much. Usually, legislation and oversight are performed by the same permanent committees, while investigating committees and commissions of inquiry are set up ad hoc. But in the UK, legislation is handled by the public

Table 2.1 Typology of parliamentary committees

Function	Permanent	Ad hoc
management	usually steering, elections, immunity committees	-
legislation	usually permanent committees, based on ministerial portfolios or policy areas	public bill committees (UK), ad hoc legislative committees (France) subcommittees of the respective committees (Turkey, Spain, Nigeria)
finance	usually budget committee sometimes finance committee (Germany) sometimes appropriations committee (US, Nigeria)	-
inquiry	often fulfilled by permanent committees	sometimes special commissions of inquiry (Germany, Spain), sometimes fact-finding committees (Egypt)
oversight	usually integrated with legislative committees sometimes subcommittees to check implementation (Hungary) sometimes subcommittees for oversight (US) sometimes one or more dedicated oversight committees (US., Norway, Japan)	
scrutiny	sometimes integrated with oversight (US)	often investigating committees
petitions	sometimes petitions committees sometimes ombudspeople	-

bill committees, while select committees are active in oversight and investigation. Committees in the US Congress fulfil all three: legislation, oversight, and investigation. How the allocation of committee functions determines their activity and their level of influence is yet to be determined and a worthy endeavour for future research. Usually, a budget committee exercises the 'power of the purse' as a classic parliamentary right – although sometimes other committees are also involved in financial affairs. And it is common to have formal committees for keeping parliament running; they are necessary units for its efficient organization. Malcolm Shaw (1979) called them housekeeping committees; we suggest the broader term of management committees. This does not mean, though, that all management of parliament is only done there. The 'presidium' (Norway, Israel) or the 'council of elders' (Ältestenrat, Germany) are not formal committees but very important for this task.

In most parliaments, legislative business is conducted in permanent committees. Ad hoc committees for legislation are used only in few parliaments, where a committee is set up for each important bill. The public bill committees in the UK (previously standing committees) are the most notable example of this. Similarly, in France special committees (*commissions spéciales*) can be set up ad hoc to deal with a particular piece of legislation – but it is used much less frequently and only for very politicized topics.[2] In similar fashion, in Spain, special subcommittees are installed for each important bill. In Turkey, this is also practiced. While most other parliaments use integrated committees of legislation and control, the internal organization of committee work varies considerably across parliaments. For all parliaments analysed in this volume the division of labour goes beyond and below the committee level. In some, it is instituted formally in many permanent (USA) or ad-hoc subcommittees (Spain) or in working groups within committees (Finland). Others have a higher differentiation on the committee level (Nigeria). Elsewhere, the division of labour happens within committees through a system of 'rapporteur governance' (Germany, France, Turkey).

Rapporteur structures are semi-formal and create their own challenges for visibility and accountability. Actually, the original role of committee rapporteurs is not readily compatible with political parties in modern parliaments. Traditionally, a rapporteur will report to the plenary on behalf of the whole committee. This is still practised in France, where an official rapporteur is usually selected from the PPG that initiated a particular piece of legislation. But in many parliaments today, all parties often set up their own rapporteurs who connect committees both to the PPG and the plenary (e.g. in Germany). Sometimes the term rapporteur is used for this role; in other parliaments they are called party spokesperson (Finland) – and in yet others (France) this is an informal internal practice of PPGs. Investigating these processes comparatively, it is necessary to be aware that those terms vary between parliaments.

There is more variation between parliamentary committees and the control function than those related to legislation. Oversight, scrutiny, and control are often used interchangeably (Harris 1964: 9; Olson 2008: 324), also throughout this volume. In Table 2.1, we differentiate the broader term of control into three perspectives (based on Siefken 2018: 109): (1) Inquiry refers to gathering information and taking in demands in an ex-ante perspective. (2) Oversight is used for processes that are accompanying the policy process, both with regard to policy-making and to implementation. (3) Scrutiny happens ex post: it is usually applied after something has gone wrong or has been scandalized, for example by setting up parliamentary investigations.

Many parliaments give extensive competencies to the regular committees in all three of these control activities. Some parliaments use separate institutions for certain aspects; for example, ad hoc investigating committees for ex-post scrutiny. Other parliaments (Norway, Japan, USA) also have one or more dedicated committees for accompanying government oversight, while the permanent committees are often also active in overseeing 'their' agencies (USA).

Committees for petitions or ombudspeople are related to both the control and the communication function. Such committees can be part of parliamentary oversight and scrutiny, but their logic is particular and they exist in only few parliaments studied here (Germany, Turkey, Spain) and are newly established in the UK in 2015. Others have integrated petitions through their website (Kuwait, Tunisia) or deal with them in the general committees (France, Denmark, Ghana). Petition committees provide a way of direct communication from the citizens into parliament – yet the effectiveness of this path is sometimes questioned (Germany, Spain). What stands out is that there are no other dedicated committees conducting communication, public engagement, and outreach.

The main focus of this volume is on the legislation and oversight committees. Financial committees which are involved in the classic parliamentary 'power of the purse' are also worthy of closer investigation (Stapenhurst et al. 2008). But with their separate processes they were beyond what could be achieved here in a systematic fashion. The same goes for the management committees. However, those two committee types are included in the general descriptions below, as long as they are formal committees.

Format of the committee system

Committees may be mandated by the constitution, in full (as in France) or in part (as in Finland and Germany). In France, the Constitution now allows for a maximum of eight standing committees and the committee of European affairs – two management committees are added. In Germany, a few committees are mentioned in the Constitution and thus have to be established: defence, budget, petitions, and European affairs. In Israel, the system of 12 permanent committees is established 'automatically' after each election to the Knesset (which can add or abolish individual committees). But in most countries, how many committees are set up is up to each parliament to decide.

Table 2.2 shows that there is quite some variation among the cases in this volume with a maximum of 109 committees in the National Assembly of Nigeria and a minimum of eight in the French Assemblée nationale. If those two extreme cases are excluded, there are 22 committees on average. A relationship to the size of parliament is not straightforward as noted before (NDI 1996: 11): Some big parliaments have a relatively small number of committees (Turkey, France) and some small parliaments have many committees (Denmark). Whether a parliament is in a liberal democracy or in a transition country seems to have no direct effect on the number of committees – but the cases of Ukraine and Nigeria demonstrate that in transitioning countries committee membership can fulfil many other more individualized functions for MPs: giving status, additional salaries or better access to resources, and serving clientelist demands.

14 Sven T. Siefken and Hilmar Rommetvedt

Table 2.2 Committee systems and committee sizes compared

Country	Parliament (1st chamber)	Total MPs	Total Permanent Committees	Total MPs/ Committees	Committee Members
France	Assemblée nationale	577	8 + 3 [I]	72.1	70 – 73
Israel	Knesset	120	12	10.0	<= 15 [II]
Norway	Stortinget	169	12 [III]	14.1	9 – 20
Finland	Eduskunta	200	17	11.8	11 – 25
Hungary	Országgyűlés	199	17	11.7	6 – 39
Turkey	Grand National Assembly	600	19	31.6	17 – 35
USA	House of Representatives	435	20	21.8	10 – 60
Ukraine	Verkhovna Rada	450	23	19.6	5 – 34
Germany	Deutscher Bundestag	709	24	30.8	14 – 49
Egypt	Magles en-Nowwab	596	26	22.9	9 – 45
Japan	House of Representatives	465	17	27.4	20 – 50
Denmark	Folketinget	179	26	6.9	(17 –)29 [IV]
Spain	Congreso de los Diputados	350	30 [V]	11.7	34 – 50
UK	House of Commons	650	30 [VI]	21.7	11 – 16
Ghana	Parliament of Ghana	275	31	8.9	18 – 25
Nigeria	House of Representatives	360	109	3.3	11 – 51
Average		396	26.6	19.0	
Average	(without France, Nigeria)	385	21.8	17.8	

Note: The numbers reflect the current situation in 2020; committee numbers and sizes vary over time in most parliaments. For details see the country chapters in this volume.

I There are eight permanent committees in France that have 70 to 73 members and conduct the parliamentary business. The committee on the EU (48 members) has limited competencies and there are two management committees (each 15 members). Each MP can be member in one of the eight committees.
II Not more than 15 members in most committees, in two not more than 17; the actual size is often smaller and depends on the coalition format.
III Numbers refer to standing committees, committees for internal management, and consultations with the government not included.
IV 21 of the 26 committees have 29 members.
V In Spain, there are 21 permanent legislative committees, nine permanent non-legislative committees, and seven permanent Congreso-Senado joint committees.
VI 20 departmental select committees and 10 cross-cutting select committees; additionally there are six cross-cutting joint committees.

If each MP served in one – and only one – committee (which is the case in France and with a few exceptions in Norway), we would find a statistical average size of 18 MPs per committee across the parliaments included in this volume. But the actual committee size is usually larger. In our case studies, the smallest committees can be found in Israel and the UK, the largest in France and the USA. And there is a wide variation of their size within parliaments; future research should investigate this more closely: for example, by comparing sizes and policy portfolios. The information compiled indicates that prestigious or important committees (see below) are bigger, while parliamentary management committees are often smaller.

Committee structure and portfolio allocation

The formal freedom to establish committees in whatever way fits does not lead to endless debates about the portfolio allocation at the beginning of a newly elected parliament. Clearly, parliaments do not start 'from zero' after a new election but follow established routes from the past. Committees have a high degree of permanence across legislative periods. Comparative studies have formulated the expectation that committees can be more effective if their jurisdiction is synchronized with the bureaucratic structure (Mattson & Strøm 1995: 251). It is assumed that this increases their strength in legislation and control. Accordingly, each committee ideally has one government ministry to deal with. Nowadays, it has become a common assumption that committees mirror the bureaucratic structure and largely follow ministerial portfolio allocation. Most authors of the case studies assembled here do report that there is such a relationship. Looking more closely at the structure of both committees and ministries reveals that there are five types of correspondence:

(1) the 'perfect mirror' with one committee for each ministry (Spain);
(2) one committee may deal with several ministries (France, Ghana);
(3) one ministry is 'mirrored' by several committees (Hungary);
(4) there is a mix of the above (Germany, Finland, Norway, Israel) and
(5) committee structure is set independently of executive bureaucracy (USA, Egypt).

There have been specific and deliberate changes with regard to correspondence. For example, in Norway, all references to specific ministries were removed from the RoP in 1993 to reduce the potential influence of special interests and give committees a more holistic perspective on policies. The Diet of Japan employs a rotation system and regularly reassigns MPs to new committees, following a similar practice in the cabinet and in political parties.

Committee structure may in part be explained by path dependency – once established, it is unlikely that a committee ceases to exist. For example, the sports committee in the German Bundestag was originally established as an ad hoc committee to prepare the Olympic Games of 1972 – and it is still around today. Likewise, parliament may install committees to deal with 'new policies' before the executive has done it. This may start with a subcommittee or an ad hoc committee. Thus, parliamentary committee structure can be relevant for the 'birth' of new policy areas, as has recently been the case for issues such as integration, digitalization, or climate change. This is another important link between the analysis of public policy and parliamentary affairs.

Transparency of committees

A central topic of committee design is whether they hold their sessions in private or in public. Public meetings are often seen as moving political decision-making from backroom deals to centre stage, enhancing 'throughput legitimacy' in the political process (Schmidt 2013). The argument goes that if everybody can see what MPs do, this will create better accountability, too, and a higher motivation for responsive MP behaviour. On the other hand, private meetings are favoured for three theoretical expectations: (1) deliberative advantages, (2) better bargaining and (3) reduced external influence. The classic rationale for non-public meetings stems from thoughts on deliberation. Accordingly, a meeting behind closed doors facilitates meaningful exchange, where better arguments can win and compromise can be found, because 'a small interacting, face-to-face group' (Sartori 1987: 228) helps build trust among their members who can find solutions through arguing and convincing each other. Modern-day rationalists see advantages of committee work, because bargaining will be much easier if 'logrolling' and 'pork barrelling' are not transparent to the outside. A third argument against openness is related to external influences; PPG leadership can better 'monitor the performance of committee members' (Strøm 1998: 42) in open sessions while closed ones may help MPs to focus on policy matters; the same is true for lobbyists, NGOs, and even supporters or potential voters in MPs' districts. Comparative studies, however, show that in parliamentary systems the party discipline in committees is strong, irrespective of public or non-public sessions (Ismayr 2008: 34). Committee work in closed sessions is also expected to have an influence on the style of interaction: 'Rational choices and/or social norms will lead to integrative ... decision making in committees' (Damgaard & Mattson 2004: 117). Indeed, a lower level of conflict has been found in private than in public committee meetings (Damgaard & Mattson 2004: 124).

An older compilation looking at the (then) EU member countries observed that in about half of the parliaments, committee sessions were public by default (Schüttemeyer & Siefken 2008: 498). These countries were mostly those with newly introduced parliamentary systems, while the older democracies conducted non-public meetings. The case studies in this volume also show a balance with regard to committee openness (see Table 2.3). In less than half of the parliaments, openness is the default; the others hold private sessions by default. A clear pattern of system characteristics is not apparent: There are old and young democracies in both groups.

But a closer look at the country chapters assembled here shows that committee transparency is not adequately answered by 'yes' or 'no'. First of all, the precise meaning of 'open' differs from country to country. Some

Table 2.3 Transparency of parliamentary committees

Country	Parliament (1st chamber)	Open by default	Share of open sessions*	Public hearings	Frequency of public hearings*
Denmark	Folketinget	--	low	X	low
Egypt	Magles en-Nowwab	--	very low	X	low
Finland	Eduskunta	--	very low	X	low
France	Assemblée nationale	X	very high	X	high
Germany	Deutscher Bundestag	--	low	X	high
Ghana	Parliament of Ghana	--	very low	--	--
Hungary	Országgyűlés	X	very high	X	low
Israel	Knesset	X	very high	--	--
Japan	House of Representatives	--	n/a	X	low
Nigeria	House of Representatives	--	very low	X	high
Norway	Stortinget	--	none	X	high
Spain	Congreso de los Diputados	X	very high	X	medium – high
Turkey	Grand National Assembly	X	low	X	low
UK	House of Commons	X	high	X	high
Ukraine	Verkhovna Rada	--	very high	X	high
US Congress	House of Representatives	X	very high	X	high

X = yes, -- = no
* the frequency/share reported is based on the qualitative assessments of the country case specialists.

committees grant access only to the press (Spain), while others also invite the interested public, and still others completely televise or livestream their sessions. And most parliaments can open their sessions by committee decision even if closed ones are the default. Such practice has strongly grown in recent years, for example in Germany. And some parliaments decide for certain committees to always be public – in Ghana that has been the case for the public accounts committee, the appointments committee and the government assurances committee. Such a decision can also be made in the reverse direction when certain meetings are held in private – or even under secrecy, typically for issues of national or international security.

For a full picture, the analysis of institutional rules about committee transparency needs to be complemented by information on practice. Surprisingly, such information is hard to come by and often needs to be compiled, because such committee-specific data are not aggregated and reported by parliaments. And there may again be a huge variation between the different committees within one parliament. In Hungary, for example, ten out of 16 committees held all their sessions in public while the remaining six varied between

24 percent and 76 percent. It may be possible to find policy-specific patterns across parliaments that influence openness of committee sessions.

Apart from the regular committee sessions, almost all parliaments in our study have special provisions for conducting public hearings or evidence sessions. Academic experts, interest groups or representatives of civil society are invited to testify before a committee and answer questions of MPs open to public view. This can be done in the course of a concrete piece of legislation (Spain), but also independent from it. Some parliaments have had this institution for a long time (since the 19th century in the US, Germany since 1951), others have introduced it more recently: Belgium in 1985, Sweden in 1989, Finland in 1991 (Strøm 1998: 54). Today, most parliaments can hold such public hearings – an overview showed that out of 83 parliaments only in three cases did this option not exist (Pelizzo & Stapenhurst 2008: 10–12). A recent survey of parliaments across the globe found that out of 68 participating parliaments, 72 percent reported that they were holding legislative hearings and 65 percent reported to conduct oversight hearings (IPU 2021). It is surprisingly difficult to find reliable data on the actual use and – even more challenging: the effects of this instrument. From the cases in this volume, we do see that about half of the parliaments frequently make use of it and public hearings have become a standard in policy-making. In most others, however, it is not employed much. There is also recent experimentation with new formats: In 2009, the Danish Folketing introduced open consultations with ministers for the committees which have overtaken such sessions in a closed format. And quite a few parliaments have started to conduct 'field hearings' for direct citizen contact (IPU 2021). Israel is another special case: while the Knesset does not formally have public hearings, some committee chairs decide to hold special committee sessions and call them hearings anyway. It is obvious: these instruments and their functions in policy-making deserve closer attention. They may be relevant for information gathering and processing, but they may also serve as a tool for parliamentary communication and outreach.

MPs in committees

Committee size

Structuring a decision-making body into several subgroups helps to increase efficiency because these groups can work in parallel (Strøm 1998: 24). The specialization for a policy field that comes with committee assignment also eases coordination because MPs do not need to start 'from zero' but can build on previous and acquired knowledge. Too much turnover in the committee membership may disturb this. As was shown above, a number of theoretical advantages of work in committees have been mentioned: specialization, deliberation, bargaining, and independence. What exactly constitutes an optimal size for such group work is hard to determine. Some scholars say not more than 15 (Pfetsch 1987: 256), some speculate '12–15, perhaps' (Gaines et al. 2019b: 332), others set the maximum size at 30 (Sartori 1987: 228).

As Table 2.2 shows, parliamentary committees are often much larger than that. There is also a policy-specific pattern: the more important, the more prestigious a committee, the larger it tends to be. For example, the committee of the economy in the German Bundestag has 49 members, the budget committee in the House of Representatives in Japan has 50 and the transportation committee in the US House of Representatives has 60 members. From a negotiation perspective, that is a paradox: more relevant topics should require more intense negotiations – which would be facilitated by smaller groups. But this may already be an indicator that the theoretical understanding of committees as places of negotiation is wrong.

How exactly this committee size is determined in practice remains unclear. A few parliaments impose a certain maximum size; for example, in Israel and Finland and in the UK for departmental select committees. This seems to be the only safe way to keep them small. Other parliaments have more flexible rules and adjust the number of seats in order to include small parties; in Spain every PPG is to have at least one seat in every committee, other seats are then calculated to secure proportionality to their mandate share in parliament. It may be useful to look at how committee size and the portfolio are related in order to see if the respective policy – or its prestige – can explain it. To find patterns, it would be worth investigating the average committee size in relation to parliament size, its fragmentation and policy variables, too.

Committee membership

Commonly, committee seats are assigned in proportion to the strength of each party in parliament – which creates its own challenges if there is a very dynamic party system (Hungary) or high fragmentation (Spain) or both (Ukraine). But how exactly an individual MP is chosen to serve on a particular committee is difficult to disentangle (Martin & Mickler 2019). It is clear that the PPGs and their leaderships always play an important role in this, and that they often have to balance the individual expertise, district requirements and wishes of MPs, along with regional demands and requirements. Thus, committee assignment is an important leadership challenge often fulfilled informally in the PPGs – and sometimes with formal election by the entire PPG assemblys on who gets to sit on which committee as a last resort. Analyses about committee composition have been conducted in numerous quantitative and comparative studies (most recently, Shugart et al. 2021). An investigation of committee assignments in a comparative study on Germany, Ireland, and the Netherlands showed that there is 'no general guideline for the allocation of committee seats in the three analysed legislatures' (Mickler 2017: 183). Its mechanisms remain unclear and can hardly be qualified as a simple 'choice' by MPs, a fact that had been stressed in the interview-based study on parliamentary roles (Searing 1994: 62) and also through more formal approaches (Cox & McCubbins: 1993) before.

While both MP wishes and leadership decisions play a role in committee assignment, their balance can differ. For example, in the case of Ghana it is reported that MPs have no say in the process, in Spain the PPG leadership can even remove MPs from committees, in Hungary the PPG leadership has full control but MPs (in some of the parties) may articulate their wishes. In Finland, however, there can be a vote of the entire PPG assembly if there is no other way to find consensus. And in the UK, formal elections do routinely take place by the party caucuses for the Commons select committees. Thus, committee assignments are best understood as a continuum: on one end is the election by the PPG assembly, on the other the pure decision – including those for recall – by the PPG leadership. Practice in most parliaments falls somewhere in between.

In many parliaments, members can serve on more than one committee and for smaller parties, this may be necessary to adequately cover all policies in parliament. MPs in Spain are typically assigned to two or three, in Israel to three on average – which actually creates its own challenges for participation, as many of the meetings take place at the same time. In Denmark the number of committee memberships is between three and five – and in Japan, the average committee membership of MPs is 2.2 with over 10 percent of MPs even serving on four committees. Likewise, in Nigeria a typical MP is a member of three to five committees.

The temporal perspective needs to be looked at as well. In most parliaments, committees are set up – and members assigned – for the entire legislative period, but some parliaments make these assignments annually (France, Ghana). Potentially, this leads to larger turnover and higher influence of the PPG leadership. In Japan, committee membership even rotates every year. In the UK, there is large turnover in select committee membership – even though assignments are for the entire legislative period (Bates et al. 2017). Turnover in committee membership can also be analysed across legislative terms. For example, in Spain less than one-third of MPs served in the same committee in two consecutive terms, in Hungary the number is around 50 to 60 percent, in Turkey the average turnover is 43 percent, in Norway around 20 percent of committee members are reassigned to the same committee at the beginning of the following election period, and in Finland, only around 11 percent of MPs serve in the same committee for more than two electoral terms. But these data show different aspects of committee turnover and, even though this is a technically simple task, it has surprisingly not been analysed for many parliaments.

But it is safe to say that turnover in committee membership is higher than of other actors in the relevant policy networks such as interest groups, civil society organizations (CSOs), and executive agencies and departments. In part, this is a logical arithmetical consequence of high turnover in parliamentary membership combined with the parliamentary career paths. But it indicates that policy expertise by MPs may often not be a long-term project. In reverse and with the direct electoral connection of MPs, this facilitates their innovation function. Yet again, there is need for closer study of membership turnover in committees, its influences, the consequences it may have, and what the typical career paths are for MPs.

This finding does insinuate, however, that the expected nexus between previous training and work experience of MPs and their committee assignment is not as strong as often expected. But as our own discussions have shown as well, even if the data on committee turnover were readily available for comparative studies (which they are not), to determine what exactly is a low and a high turnover can be debated.

Committees as places of specialization and socialization

This leads to a question of causal attribution: Are MPs policy experts because they are members of a committee or are they members of a (particular) committee because they are policy experts? All contributors for the country cases in this volume have trouble answering this question and stress that policy expertise is among the criteria relevant for committee assignment but is certainly not the single determining factor (Oñate & Ortega 2019: 405). In summary, their estimate is that, more often than not, the committee makes the expert, rather than the expertise making the committee – at least if there is some duration of assignments. Through this committee assignment, MPs receive a certain responsibility and are tasked with becoming specialists in the subject matter. In reverse, they also receive 'property rights' (Mickler 2017: 13) for this issue of their specialization. Strong socialization effects can also be at play here: in committee work, new members (can) learn how to be MPs, how to coordinate with their PPG, and how to prepare and debate the issues (Sarcinelli 1989: 400). As a consequence, MPs can become active players in the policy network, in the working groups of their own party, and in dealings with interest groups, the media, and the broader public outside the committee. The rotation system in Japan increases MP exposure to different policy fields and gives them more opportunity for 'credit claiming' in their constituencies. But MPs may also repeatedly return to a special policy area and eventually become '*seisaku zoku*', experts in a 'policy tribe' noted for their deep contacts with interest groups and bureaucrats in the relevant ministries. This can help their career in party and parliament and eventually lead to becoming a government minister.[3]

Richard Fenno (1965; 1973) provided early scholarship for this perspective on committees and stressed their integration function in the US Congress. Role theory has also touched upon committee activity and seen MPs in the subrole of the 'policy advocate' who 'aim, through their committee work, to influence government policy' (Searing 1994: 59) or focus on the role of 'subject-matter expert' (Wahlke 1962: 14). Role theory can also help distinguish different MP positional roles, notably the committee chair, the party speakers, and the rapporteurs for a particular topic or piece of legislation. Of particular relevance are leadership positions of committee chair and vice-chairs. Their task is to organize the meetings and conduct the business, often with the help of committee staff. The contributors to this volume see the chairs more as managers of keeping business running rather than exercising policy influence – so they have more of an institutional role. This is contrary to what research on the topic has recently assumed (Fernandes et al. 2019: 183; Krauss et al. 2021). In parliamentary customs, the policy influence of committee chairs seems stronger in some (e.g. the UK and Israel) and weaker in other parliaments (e.g. Japan, Germany, Denmark).

Interactions in committees

Looking at the micro-level of interactions requires researchers to open the 'black box' and see what goes on in committees. A study of Western European parliaments in the 1980s found that, contrary to expectations, committees were not removing conflict from political issues (Damgaard & Mattson 2004: 120), indicating that interactions may be different than previously thought. Based on MP interviews, it was shown that in the Norwegian Parliament, formal committee meetings usually deal with practical and administrative matters and that there were hardly any deliberations or negotiations at all in the committee meetings. Policy compromises are negotiated among committee members from government parties and selected opposition parties, but outside the full committee. Most of the country specialists in this volume report similar findings: there may be discussion and debate in committees and it is often a bit different – more constructive, less contentious – than in the plenary. But real 'deliberation' or negotiation does not take place in committees. If it happens, it happens elsewhere: within – and among – the parliamentary party groups or in smaller circles of involved MPs; for example, the subcommittees in Spain or the meetings of policy rapporteurs from different parties in exchange with the executive.

Committees are assemblies of human beings and, thus, the concept of organizational culture may help understand the informal dimension of interaction. Some committees are more conflict-oriented, others more consensual, as Fenno (1973: xiii) found: 'Congressional committees differ'. Many explanations for such variation are plausible. The most immediate has to do with the issues at hand. Some committees deal with topics more ideological in nature than others and it can be expected that this coincides with the level of conflict. In Japan, defence was a contested topic during the Cold War – consequently, in the 1960s, security-related committees like the foreign affairs committee 'tended to be conflictual and even chaotic, with violence and physical obstruction of voting fairly widely seen'.[4] But for the same type of committees – in another time and country – it has been argued that they have an outward focus and a more consensual character, in Finland (Raunio 2016: 323).

Other characteristics may explain how 'policy determines politics' (Lowi 1972: 299) in committees. A higher level of conflict can be expected for redistributive policy than for distributive policy and for constituent policy than for regulative policy. Interviews showed that in the German Bundestag there is indeed quite some variation between committees; for example, the level of conflict and of formal proceedings is quite high in the agriculture committee (Siefken 2018: 398). The same has been found for the US Congress (Evans 2013: 399). But while some country experts report 'significant variation in style among committees'[5] (UK), for other countries such as Nigeria and Spain it is reported that variation between them is rather small. Apparently, the variation varies.

The level of conflict in various countries in general, and parliamentary committees in particular, may also change over time. In the case of Norway from 1945 to the beginning of 1970s, dissenting remarks from one or more party representatives were found in approximately 15 percent of the committee recommendations. From 2001 to 2013, this occurred in more than 70 percent of the reports. In Finland, dissenting votes in committee reports have meanwhile declined from 30 percent in the early 1970s to 20 percent more recently. In Turkey, dissenting opinions depend on the coalition format. But for many parliaments such information has not yet been analysed.

Composition characteristics can also influence the style of interaction as certain committees assemble more junior MPs, and others more senior ones. The same is true for gender variation and professional backgrounds. Finally, a personal perspective can explain variation: committee chairs may have a strong influence on the interaction style because of their leadership position, but the ranking members may also be relevant there, as was noted for Germany and the US.

Not only MPs are relevant actors in committees, but also those they interact with – during and outside committee sessions. Two groups stand out: government officials and representatives of interest groups. Government ministers may have access to committee sessions and, in some cases, even have the right to be heard (France, Spain). In most other parliaments, committees can – and do – invite government representatives to attend. The old British saying that 'parliament knows only the minister' does not apply broadly. In Finland, for example, the executive is usually represented by civil servants, in Germany this task is also fulfilled by the parliamentary undersecretaries, and in Spain junior ministers represent the executive in committees while ministers do the same in the plenary. In Hungary, senior government officials often delegate the task to junior ones 'who may not have the expertise or the competence to answer the questions'.[6] In Denmark since recently it is no longer possible for civil servants to appear in committees without the presence of 'their' minister – in order to avoid any blurred responsibility.

Committees also take in positions from NGOs or academic institutions and think tanks as experts or witnesses in committee sessions. In some countries the relationship between the members of a specific committee and interest groups and NGOs within the same policy area may be a close one. Labels such as 'segmented state' and 'iron triangles', 'sub-government' and 'policy communities' (Egeberg et al. 1978; Hernes 1983; König 1998) have been used to characterize tight connections between a specific parliamentary committee, the corresponding government ministry, and interest groups and experts within the sector or community. They are assumed to share important values and attitudes related to the policy field they represent. However, in the case of Norway, parliamentary committee members were contacted by a variety of interest groups, not just the ones engaged in the same policy area as their committee (Rommetvedt 1998). Specific studies on these relationships are missing for most countries – but it is clear that there are certain, yet not exclusive relations with particular groups. In this volume it was reported only for Japan that committees have a minor role for interest groups – because in the political system dominated by the Liberal Democratic Party, they gear their efforts prior to parliamentary processes towards its Policy Affairs Research Council. In other countries (like Germany) the main focus of lobbying activities is the ministerial bureaucracy.

Committees in the policy process

To examine parliamentary committees' role in policy-making, the analytic perspective needs to be extended beyond the traditional perspectives of parliamentary studies. These approaches can be fruitfully combined with broader frameworks, models, and theories of public policy-making. Obviously, 'the relationship between politics and the policy processes, and the new roles of committees in this synthesis, is complex' (Longley & Davidson 1998: 16). At the most general level, the input and output dimensions can be distinguished (Easton 1965). Parliament is a subsystem of the political administrative system and committees are subsystems of parliament. They receive input in the form of concrete demands (and general support) and transform it into output in the form of draft laws, recommendations, or other statements. The policy cycle can help take a closer look at this process. Based on a simple phase approach to understanding the political 'decision process' (Lasswell 1956), it progresses from identifying a problem, via looking at different options for action, to making a decision, and then implementing it, in order to solve the problem (Jann & Wegrich 2007). The cycle metaphor stresses that policies often do not finish. Indeed, termination of policy is the exception. More often, policies stay in place and are amended or changed according to new developments or a better understanding after feedback from the environment is taken in (Easton 1965: 28).

The cycle and phase approaches have been criticized for applying an overly simplistic and rationalistic perspective to public policy-making. But they can serve as a good starting point to integrate parliamentary research and the public policy perspectives. Parliaments and parliamentary committees can play a role throughout the entire policy cycle – not as collective actors, but rather in relation to the individual MPs and the PPGs. For Norway, case studies of decision-making related to environmental issues show that interest groups and other actors lobbied parliament in all phases of the policy cycle, from initiation to implementation (Rommetvedt 2003: 168).

Problem definition and agenda-setting

In the early phases of the policy cycle, a problem is defined and described by involved interests and actors who try to put it on the political agenda. Problem definition and agenda-setting are not possible without framing processes. They may be used intentionally by political actors when they try to give a particular 'spin' to an issue, but they can also occur unintentionally as part of the human condition (Tversky & Kahnemann 1981). Parliamentary actors, individual MPs, party groups, and parliamentary committees can play a role in problem definition and agenda-setting – both inside parliament and outside. Through general statements in their reports, committees may define problems that were previously not perceived. In this way, they can help draw attention to relevant topics and, thereby, channel societal wants and demands as inputs into the political process (Easton 1965: 37).

But even without this official competence, committees may play an indirect role in agenda-setting because their members can take part in the expert discussions of an active policy network. Originating in media studies (Scheufele & Tewksbury 2007), interest in agenda-setting has moved into public policy research. Any seasoned politician knows that the early phases of the policy cycle are highly relevant for the subsequent steps. Thus, an MP who is passionate about a topic or has a particular interest in it will try to influence the problem definition and have a say in it. Being active as a committee member in the relevant policy community may bring about great influence. To be sure, this is not a formal influence, but an informal struggle, and committee membership does not guarantee influence. The involved actors may be policy entrepreneurs, 'willing to invest their resources in return for future policies they favour' (Kingdon 1995: 211). In this mechanism, it is not the committee as a whole that exercises influence, but (some of) its individual members who are interested experts in the field. In a now classic study of political agenda-setting in the United States, the questions were asked from members of Congress and representatives of the administration: 'What are you dealing with right now and why?' Congress was seen as very important in setting the political agenda (Kingdon 1995: 37, 224). This perspective of looking at parliamentary actors in the policy networks should be brought more into policy studies.

Committees may have more or less influence on their own agenda, too. The internal perspective of the parliamentary agenda has been studied as 'agenda control' (Bräuninger & Debus 2009; Döring 2001). In many systems, committees can only react to bills that have been forwarded to them by the plenary, but they may prioritize some topics over others, thereby moving them up on the agenda. In reverse, they can delay topics or – in some cases – even 'kill a bill' (see below). Committees are also sometimes able to set up issues on their own, either by introducing bills or by asking for reports on a certain topic. In Hungary, for example, they do have the right to legislative initiative – but in reality, rarely use it. Three committees in Israel are entitled to initiate bills on special topics within their own domains and actually do so.[7] Committees in other parliaments have the right to legislative initiative as well: Estonia, Austria, Poland, and Sweden (Schüttemeyer & Siefken 2008). But a meaningful study of committees' role in agenda-setting has to follow a broader approach that is not limited to parliamentary agenda control.

Policy formulation

In policy formulation, committees usually make neither first nor final decisions on the draft bills and topics they deal with. Instead, they write up reports with recommendations as a base for a final decision in the plenary. The question is how far reaching their influence is on the policy matters at hand.

Figure 2.1 shows the important and universal elements regarding the role of parliamentary committees in the policy process. It should be underlined that there are many variations among the countries represented in this volume regarding the details of it.

(1) The first idea – or demand – for legislative action can originate in many places, usually in the relevant policy networks. This was mentioned before in the discussion of problem definition and agenda-setting. Civil society, interest groups, the media, political parties, academic experts, the government itself may all be relevant here.
(2) A formal legislative initiative can be brought into parliament by different groups that are less diverse. Parliament itself always has the right to legislative initiative – in some parliaments, individual MPs, in others only groups meeting a certain quorum can start the legislative process (for example, 15 MPs in Spain or 5 percent of MPs in Germany). In parliamentary systems, the government also has the right to legislative initiative. Such government bills may be the result of forthgoing processes including proposals for new policies developed by commissions, appointed by the government and including experts and interest group representatives. In some countries, committees themselves hold the formal right to legislative initiative (for example, in Egypt, Hungary, Japan).
(3) A first reading usually just assigns the bill to one or more committees. In some countries, a first debate can take place in the plenary before submission to the relevant committee(s), but based on the cases in this volume, such a debate is the exception and only held for very relevant or politicized topics.
(4) In a formal meeting the full committee organizes its work. In some cases, a deadline for the committee phase is set by the president of the parliament.
(5) The full committee may organize hearings and deliberate on the issue, which may be long lasting or short. In France and Norway, there are

Parliamentary committees compared 27

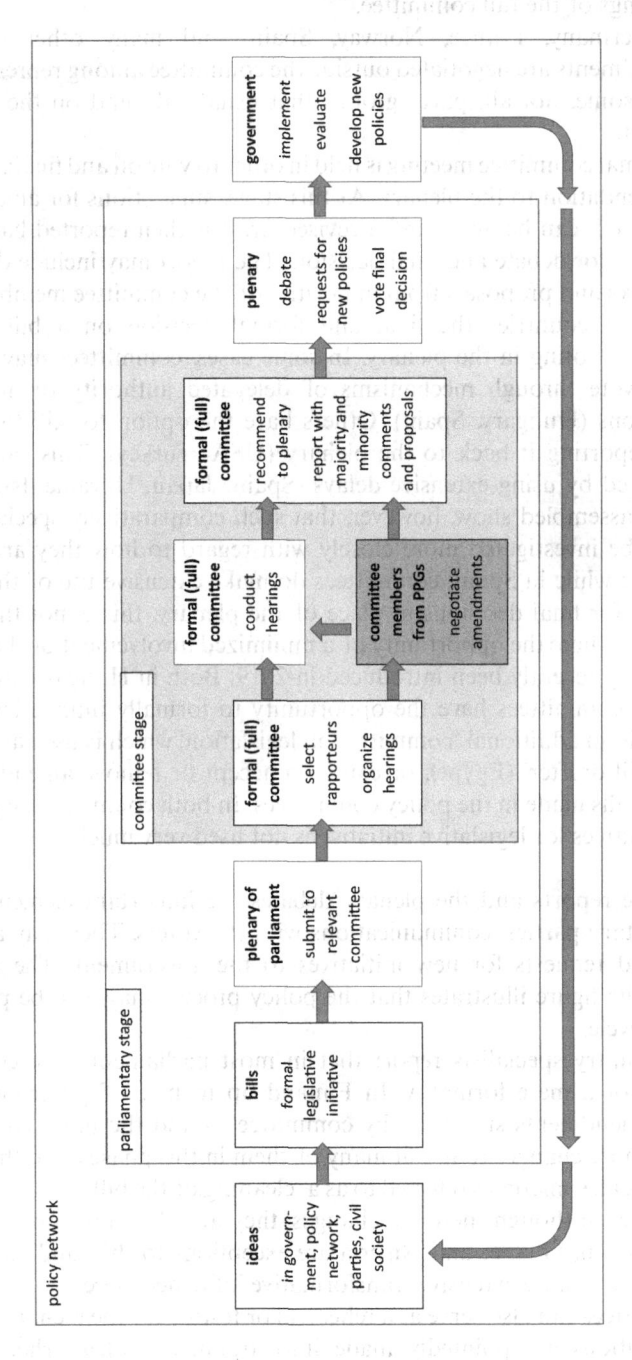

Figure 2.1 Policy formulation in the legislative process.

hardly any 'real' deliberations on the content of the bill in the formal meetings of the full committee.
(6) In Germany, France, Norway, Spain, and many other countries, amendments are negotiated outside the committee among representatives from some, not all, party groups that usually depend on the coalition format.
(7) A formal committee meeting is held in order to vote on and finalize the recommendation to the plenary. At this stage, suggestions for amendments to the bill can be made and a revised draft is then reported back to the plenary for debate and final decision. The report may include dissenting remarks and proposals from minorities of the committee members.
(8) In most countries the final and formal decision on a bill is made through voting in the plenary. In some cases, committees may have the final vote through mechanisms of delegated authority to make final decisions (Hungary, Spain). Others have the option to 'kill the bill' by not reporting it back to the plenary (USA, Turkey). This can also be achieved by using extensive delays (Spain, Japan, Ukraine, Israel). The cases assembled show, however, that such comparatively special powers must be investigated more closely with regard to how they are used in reality: while in Spain, committees do make extensive use of the opportunity for final decisions in place of the plenary, this is not the case in France where the opportunity of a minimized involvement of the plenary has only recently been introduced in 2019. Both in Hungary and Egypt, where committees have the opportunity to formally initiate legislation, there is an additional 'committee on legislation' which is used as the 'central bill drafter' (Egypt), or can even accept or remove amendments to draft bills made in the policy committees. In both countries, the power of committees for legislative initiative is not used very much.

Committee reports and the plenary debates are important elements in the parliamentary parties' communications with the voters. They may also send signals and requests for new initiatives to the government. The feedback arrow in the figure illustrates that the policy process may also be portrayed as policy cycle.

The country specialists report that in most parliaments, the committee phase is not a mere formality. In Finland up to half of government bills include amendments suggested by committees – and the more complex an issue the more changes to it, but many of them in this phase are rather minor and technical, sometimes referred to as a 'cleaning of the bill' – a last check for errors. So even though there are changes, they are often not transformative. The US, Spain, Ghana, and Nigeria are exceptions to this, and committees seem to have a more extensive transformative influence there.

Committees can also serve as a rehearsal or testing for the plenary meeting. Here, positions are pointedly made into arguments, ideas, rhetoric, and narratives are tested. But in the end, the majority will usually push through its position by vote. However, minority factions of the committees may present alternative proposals and arguments in the committee report. In that view, committee deliberation would have more of an internal role: testing, cleaning, preparation – while committee reports also have an external function in presenting alternative viewpoints to the public (see Table 2.4).

Developing a differentiated view by moving away from viewing committees as collective actors or arenas for political actors, scholars have argued that it is not the committees as actors, but the 'committee stage' in the process which is of central relevance for policy-making (Longley & Davidson 1998: 2; Mattson & Strøm 1995: 274). During this stage, the relevant coordination may happen elsewhere: within the parliamentary parties or in negotiations between selected parties, within the executive administration, or in the policy networks. Models about policy learning may help structure this investigation and it will be helpful to differentiate important from unimportant legislation or politicized topics from others that are dealt with more routinely.

Yet the very fact that policy-specific committees exist can lead to the anticipation of criticism there and an increased willingness of ministries to cooperate with the parliamentary parties on policy details. This is hard to

Table 2.4 Competencies of committees in legislation

Country	Parliament (1st chamber)	initiate bill	amend bill [I]	kill bill	report on bill	adopt law
Denmark	Folketinget	--	X	--	X	--
Egypt	Magles en-Nowwab	X	X	--	X	--
Finland	Eduskunta	--	X	--	X	--
France	Assemblée nationale	--	X	--	X	--
Germany	Deutscher Bundestag	--	X	--	X	--
Ghana	Parliament of Ghana	--	X	X[II]	X	--
Hungary	Országgyűlés	X	X	X	X	X
Israel	Knesset	X	X	X[II]	X	--
Japan	House of Representatives	X	X	X[II]	X	--
Nigeria	House of Representatives	--	X	X	X	--
Norway	Stortinget	--	X	--	X	--
Spain	Congreso de los Diputados	--	X	X[II]	X	X
Turkey	Grand National Assembly	--	X	X	X	--
UK	House of Commons	--	X	--	X	--
Ukraine	Verkhovna Rada	--	X	X[II]	X	--
USA	House of Representatives	--	X	X	X	---

X = yes, -- = no
I whether committees actually make amendments or only propose amendments varies.
II factually 'kill a bill' by delaying it indefinitely is possible.

'measure', but the mechanisms should not be written off: 'Private discussions between the government and its supporters in the legislature may lead the government to modify its proposals before submission to the legislature in order to mollify party dissidents' (Mezey 1990 [1975]: 154). In Norway, both majority and minority governments frequently consult their PPG before they finalize a bill and submit it to the parliament (Heidar and Rommetvedt 2020). Such consultations are difficult to observe, and even harder to discover is anticipation: 'Anticipated opposition in the legislature may lead the government to postpone a potentially controversial proposal until the climate of opinion is more favorable, or it may lead it to phrase its proposals in such a way as to ameliorate anticipated objections' (Mezey 1990 [1975]: 155). This is an eternal challenge in studying modern political systems. Parliamentary influence must be measured not only by what happens, but also what does not but may have happened otherwise.

Implementation and evaluation

At first sight, the implementation of policies seems unrelated to parliamentary committees, and they do rarely have a formal say in it. After all, in a classic perspective, policy implementation is the domain of public administration. But what has been shown in public policy studies (Pressman & Wildavsky 1973) is also known by political practitioners: the fact that a law has been passed does not mean that it is implemented properly. Public administration, after all, is not a computer programmed through legislation, but an actor with its own motives, interests and shortcomings. So the traditional perspective that the job of parliament is done by passing a law is outdated. That is why parliamentary committees may follow up: they can ask ministers in their committee meetings about the implementation status, they may invite administrative heads for a question-and-answer session, or they may request regular reports. In some cases, committees even make such progress reports mandatory in the original legislation. Even though reporting requirements may be addressed to the whole House, according to customs they are often dealt with by the relevant committee.

In some parliaments, special committees deal with the task of government oversight (USA, Norway). In Hungary, special subcommittees are set up to check the implementation of laws. In the Japanese Diet, the Cabinet Committee is responsible for the oversight of the 15 bureaucratic agencies, commissions, councils, and offices connected to the Cabinet Office. They cover a broad range of activities such as the fair trade and the public safety commissions. In Japan, there is also a special committee to conduct parliamentary question time. But in most parliaments, the function of oversight is conducted in the regular permanent committees. Generally, they 'can maintain vigilance of the many post- and non-legislative activities of individual ministers' (André et al. 2016: 110). While all contributors stress that committees do have an eye on implementation, this is usually not done in a formalized way – beyond reporting requirements. That an explicit oversight strategy or plan is developed by committees in a separate document has been reported only for a few transformation countries (Ghana and Nigeria) – which may indeed be a consequence of international parliamentary development processes. Committees in the established democracies still follow the model of 'fire alarm' rather than 'police patrol' in their control activities (McCubbins & Schwartz 1984).

To formally evaluate policies is a rather modern approach. Sometimes, an evaluation after a certain time is even mandated by the original legislation itself, which is fairly common in Switzerland, for example. The US is another example where original legislation often includes provisions for reporting and evaluation. Such studies check whether a policy has had the desired effects. Parliamentary actors in committees have long been factually active in policy evaluation, when they check if a policy is working and bringing about the expected results. In rare cases, the evaluation may lead to terminating a policy. This can also be achieved through sunset rules (Ranchordás 2015), which is only common in a few political systems. But the usual way of terminating a policy requires a new legislative process to change the original laws. The role of committees in that does not vary from policy formulation.

Committees and the parliamentary functions

Throughout the policy cycle, different functions of parliament come to the fore: the communication function during problem formulation and agenda-setting, the legislative function during policy formulation, and the control function during implementation and evaluation. Committees are often judged in the context of their legislative output, and less so by their contribution to control and oversight. But what was stressed over 30 years ago for the US is true for many parliaments today that 'the work of ... committees goes well beyond law-making' (Patterson 1990: 266). Indeed, 'policy relevance need not be confined to how committees matter in the passage of new legislation' (Gaines et al. 2019b: 333). The case studies assembled in this volume have clearly demonstrated this: parliamentary committees are active in both of these activities: legislation and oversight. These are usually integrated in the permanent policy-specific committees and even in the rare cases of separate committees for oversight, deeper analyses have shown how they are also active in the legislative process. To avoid misunderstanding, it may thus be helpful not to use the term 'legislative committees' as a synonym for all parliamentary committees because – intentionally, or not – it narrows down the perspective to this one function of law-making.

Studying committees in the context of these two functions may not be sufficient. Committees can also be understood as places of parliamentary communication and outreach. It has become apparent, for example, that the function of parliamentary hearings may be less relevant for gathering new information but more for communication within the policy network and the broader public. Committees may travel around the country for site inspections or field hearings, and the committee work itself can also achieve significant visibility in the news media, as has been shown for Spain and for the select committees in the UK (Gaines et al. 2019a: 427). Individual committee members may use their public expert status when speaking to the news media. The fact that committees have opened up their proceedings in many countries to be at least partly accessible to the public, is another indicator of the increased communicative role of committees. In countries where committee meetings are held in private, committee reports are sometimes published and thus communicate the views and priorities of different members and parties to the voters. In many countries, they now have individual websites and report their membership, agendas, and proceedings – in France, each committee even has its own Twitter account. Maybe committees, traditionally seen as the workhorses of parliaments, are slowly turning into showhorses?

The role and functions of committees in the policy process

The organization into committees as subgroups characterizes parliaments all across the globe. Committee systems vary in the number of committees and members as well as in their authority and power. Usually, they include management committees, committees for legislation, and oversight at the core and a few more specialized committees. Strong committees were claimed to be a necessary, if not sufficient, precondition for a strong parliament. Measuring the role of committees (and parliaments) in policy-making is a complicated mission. What has become clear is that one cannot rely on formalities to describe the 'real' role of parliamentary committees in the policy process. There are many issues for future systematic comparative studies, but also for deeper analysis of single cases. This is not only required for a better academic understanding but also to help improve public perceptions of parliaments by making it more accurate and closing the gap between the presentation of politics and the production of policy. Such investigation can help in 'uncovering the consequences of committee design' (Martin 2014: 366) and provide practical advice to parliaments on how their institutions should be adjusted with respect to appropriate committee size, strategies for small parties regarding committee membership, or the ever-debated openness of committee work.

In some parliaments, committees meet behind closed doors and it is quite obvious that we somehow need to have a look into this 'black box'. In other parliaments, committee meetings are open to the public, which apparently changes their dynamic. But even those closed committee meetings are usually neither an arena for bargaining, nor the forum for deliberation among party groups and MPs. The 'real' negotiations on policies usually take place somewhere else, out of sight for both observers and the public. Nowadays, parliamentary committees are inadequately described as places of policy-making through negotiation in small, interacting groups – if they ever were shall be investigated by historians. It is certainly incomplete to judge committees based only on their contribution to the legislative function: the control function is of high importance for evaluating committees, as is – and maybe increasingly so – their contribution to the communication function. In this regard, there may have been significant changes over the last decades. It will be a challenge – but a worthy one – to try and uncover them.

In most parliaments, the political parties or groups of MPs are the important actors and decision-makers not the committees. We should not, however, jump to the conclusion that committees do not matter. Summarizing the studies in this volume, we conclude that committees do have an important function, but it is not the committees as actors; it is the division and specialization of work, and the subsequent increase in parliamentary capacity. Modern parliaments have to deal with and make decisions regarding a significant amount of complex issues. They would not be able to accomplish much if MPs were expected to deal with all the relevant issues at once. What parliaments do, then, is to use committee assignment as as a mechanism for division and allocation of work.

Suppose for the sake of argument that parliaments did not establish committee systems. What would other organizations do in order to specialize and increase their working capacity? A private company would establish specialized departments with different functions, and then assign employees to them. Companies might also choose a regional, or geographic, logic for distributing their work. Parliaments use committee assignments as a functional equivalent for specialization and allocation of tasks to be performed by various 'departments' – both with regard to policy content and to functions. The geographic representation is fulfilled by all MPs simultaneously as they – in most parliaments – are representatives of their 'home' district or their parties – or most often, both. Without committees, the integration of policy perspectives in parliament would likely not work very well. MPs might look out only for their own district, for their own party, or for their own reelection chances – which may lead to the danger of 'collective irresponsibility' (Bogdanor 1986: 300). On the other hand, committee specialization may lead to sectorization and coordination problems across policy areas.

The role of committees for policy-making must be judged not only by their immediate effect. Committee assignments strongly structure the division of labour inside and outside parliaments. The allocation of a policy specialization to individual MPs through their committee membership is an organizing principle that spills over into the parliamentary parties, where it defines the necessary linkage between individual MP behaviour as district representative and party rapporteur or spokesperson for a policy. This also gives MPs much say in the relevant policy network – at least potentially. So, committee assignment can lead to a shifted role of the individual MP in the parliamentary party group and in the policy network and thus affect their behaviour as representatives of the people.

In other words, the installation of committees increases the policy-making capacity of parliaments and puts political actors into a field of complex tensions. Committee members have to specialize and navigate in a policy network, but also among potentially conflicting interests of their parliamentary party groups – and the demands from their district. Seen in this way, parliamentary committees are not just an efficient mechanism for the division of labour but also for the internal separation of powers. As it is with every tool: whether it functions well depends on how it is used.

So yes, parliamentary committees are very important units of modern parliaments. But that is not as places of negotiation or deliberation. It is because they bring about specialization and the socialization of MPs and help fulfil the function of integrating different perspectives and demands, making committees an important crystallization points in the policy networks. Thus, research on parliamentary committees can help bring parliamentary studies and public policy research together which will open new theoretical paths in both subdisciplines – and help sharpen their relevance for political practice, too.

Notes

1 For a detailed and critical overview of literature on Congressional committees in the United States see Evans (2013) and, somewhat dated, Deering and Smith (1997). See Mickler (2017, 35–38) for a detailed discussion about the usefulness of Congressional theories for the study of parliaments.
2 Claire Bloquet, communication with the authors, March 2021.
3 Ellis Krauss, communication with the authors, February 2021.
4 Tapio Raunio, Committees Checklist Finland, communication with the authors, June 1, 2020.
5 Stephen Holden Bates, Committees Checklist The United Kingdom, communication with the authors, June 30, 2020.
6 Csaba Nikolenyi, Committees Checklist Hungary, communication with the authors, May 28, 2020.
7 The House Committee, the Constitution, Law and Justice Committee, and the State Control Committee are entitled to initiate bills on topics such as Basic Laws; the Knesset; members of the Knesset; the elections; political parties; party financing; and the State Comptroller. In the last decade (2009–2019) these committees initiated 36 laws (seven in the 17th and the 18th Knessets, two in the short-termed 19th Knesset, and 20 in the 20th Knesset). Source: Chen Friedberg, communication with the authors, March 2021.

References

André, A., Depauw, S. & Martin, S. (2016). Trust is good, control is better. *Political Research Quarterly*, 69(1): 108–120.
Bates, S., Goodwin, M., & McKay, S. (2017). Do UK MPs engage more with Select Committees since the Wright Reforms? An interrupted time series analysis, 1979–2016. *Parliamentary Affairs*, 70(4), 780–800.

Bogdanor, V. (1986). Conclusion. In V. Bogdanor (ed.) *Representatives of the people? Parliamentarians and constituents in western democracies*. Aldershot: Gower, pp. 293–301.
Bräuninger, T. & Debus, M. (2009). Legislative agenda setting in parliamentary democracies. *European Journal of Political Research*, 48(6): 804–839.
Cox, G.W. & McCubbins, M.D. (1993). *Legislative leviathan: Party government in the House*. Berkeley: University of California Press.
Damgaard, E. & Mattson, I. (2004). Conflict and consensus in committees. In H. Döring & M. Hallerberg (eds.) *Patterns of parliamentary behaviour: Passage of legislation across Western Europe*. Aldershot: Ashgate, 113–140.
Deering, C.J. & Smith, S.S. (1997). *Committees in Congress*. Washington, D.C.: CQ Press.
Döring, H. (2001). Parliamentary agenda control and legislative outcomes in Western Europe. *Legislative Studies Quarterly*, 26(1): 145–165.
Easton, D. (1965). *A systems analysis of political life*. New York: Wiley.
Egeberg, M., Olsen, J.P. & Sætren, H. (1978). Organisasjonssamfunnet og den segmenterte stat. In J.P. Olsen (ed.) *Politisk organisering: Organisasjonsteoretiske synspunkt på folkestyre og politisk ulikhet*. Bergen: Universitetsforl, 115–143.
Evans, C.L. (2013). Committees. In E. Schickler & F.E. Lee (eds.) *The Oxford Handbook of the American Congress*. Oxford: Oxford University Press, 396–425.
Fenno, R.F. (1965). *The power of the purse: Appropriations politics in Congress*. Boston: Little Brown and Company.
Fenno, R.F. (1973). *Congressmen in committees*. Boston: Little Brown and Company.
Fernandes, J.M., Riera, P., & Cantú, F. (2019). The politics of committee chairs assignment in Ireland and Spain. *Parliamentary Affairs*, 72(1), 182–201.
Gaines, B.J., Goodwin, M., Holden Bates, S. & Sin, G. (2019a). A bouncy house? UK select committee newsworthiness, 2005–18. *Journal of Legislative Studies*, 25(3): 409–433.
Gaines, B.J., Goodwin, M., Holden Bates, S. & Sin, G. (2019b). The study of legislative committees. *Journal of Legislative Studies*, 25(3): 331–339.
Harris, J.P. (1964) *Congressional control of administration*. Washington, D.C.: The Brookings Institution.
Heidar, K. & Rommetvedt, H. (2020). Er fagkomiteene eller partigruppene Stortingets "politiske verksteder"? In J. Bergh, A.H. Haugsgjerd & R. Karlsen (eds.) *Valg og politikk siden 1945. Velgere, institusjoner og kritiske hendelser i norsk politisk historie*. Oslo: Cappelen Damm, 140–153.
Hernes, G. (1983). *Makt og styring. Det moderne Norge*. Oslo: Gylendal.
IPU (2021). Global Parliamentary Report 2021. Parliamentary Public Engagement and Outreach. Geneva: Inter-Parliamentary Union and United Nations Development Programme.
Ismayr, W. (2008). Gesetzgebung in den Staaten der Europäischen Union im Vergleich. In W. Ismayr (ed.) *Gesetzgebung in Westeuropa: EU-Staaten und Europäische Union*. Opladen: VS Verlag, 9–64.
Jann, W. & Wegrich, K. (2007). Theories of the policy cycle. In F. Fischer, G.J. Miller & M.S. Sidney (eds.) *Handbook of public policy analysis: Theory, politics, and methods*. Boca Raton: Taylor & Francis, 43–62.
Kingdon, J.W. (1995). *Agendas, alternatives, and public policies*. New York: Harper Collins.

König, T. (1998). Modeling policy networks. *Journal of Theoretical Politics*, 10(4): 387–388.
Krauss, S., Praprotnik, K., & Thürk, M. (2021). Extra-coalitional policy bargaining: investigating the power of committee chairs. *Journal of Legislative Studies*, 27(1), 93–111.
Kreppel, A. (2020). Legislatures. In D. Caramani (ed.) *Comparative politics*. London: Oxford University Press, 119–138.
Lasswell, H.D. (1956). *The decision process: Seven categories of functional analysis*. College Park: University of Maryland Press.
Longley, L.D. & Davidson, R.H. (1998). Parliamentary committees: Changing perspectives on changing institutions. In L.D. Longley & R.H. Davidson (eds.) *The new roles of parliamentary committees*. London: Frank Cass, 1–20.
Lowi, T.J. (1972). Four systems of policy, politics and choice. *Public Administration Review*, 33(4): 298–310.
Martin, L.W. & Vanberg, G. (2011). *Parliaments and coalitions: The role of legislative institutions in multiparty governance*. Oxford: Oxford University Press.
Martin, S. (2014). Committees. In S. Martin, T. Saalfeld & K.W. Strøm (eds.) *The Oxford Handbook of legislative studies*. Oxford: Oxford University Press, 352–368.
Martin, S. & Mickler, T.A. (2019). Committee assignments: Theories, causes and consequences. *Parliamentary Affairs*, 72(1): 77–98.
Mattson, I. & Strøm, K. (1995). Parliamentary committees. In H. Döring (ed.) *Parliaments and majority rule in Western Europe*. Frankfurt am Main: Campus, 249–307.
McCubbins, M.D. & Schwartz, T. (1984). Congressional oversight overlooked: Police patrols versus fire alarms. *American Journal of Political Science*, 28(1): 165–179.
Mezey, M. (1990 [1975]). Classifying legislatures. In P. Norton (ed.) *Legislatures*. Oxford: Oxford University Press, 149–176.
Mickler, T.A. (2017). Parliamentary committees in a party-centred context: Structure, composition, functioning. University of Leiden: PhD thesis.
NDI (1996). *Committees in Legislatures. A Division of Labor*. Washington, D.C.: National Democratic Institute for International Affairs.
Olson, D.M. (2008). Legislatures and administration in oversight and budgets: Constraints, means, and executives. In R. Stapenhurst, F. Pelizzo, D.M. Olson & L. von Trapp (eds.) *Legislative oversight and budgeting: A world perspective*. Washington, D.C.: World Bank Institute, 323–331.
Oñate, P. & Ortega, C. (2019). Committee parliamentary specialization index. Explaining MPs' specialization in the Spanish Congreso de los Diputados. *Journal of Legislative Studies*, 25(3), 394–408
Patterson, S.C. (1990). Parties and committees in Congress. In U. Thaysen, R.H. Davidson & R.G. Livingston (eds.) *The U.S. Congress and the German Bundestag: Comparisons of democratic processes*. Boulder: Westview Press, 249–271.
Pelizzo, R. & Stapenhurst, R. (2008). Tools for legislative oversight: An empirical investigation. In R. Stapenhurst, F. Pelizzo, D.M. Olson & L. von Trapp (eds.) *Legislative oversight and budgeting: A world perspective*. Washington, D.C.: World Bank Institute, 9–28.
Pfetsch, F. (1987). Politische Theorie der Entscheidung in Gremien. *Journal für Sozialforschung* 27(3/4): 253–275.
Pressman, J.L. & Wildavsky, A.B. (1973). *Implementation. How great expectations in Washington are dashed in Oakland*. Berkeley: University of California Press.

Ranchordás, S. (2015). *Constitutional sunsets and experimental legislation: A comparative perspective*. Cheltenham: Edward Elgar Publishing.
Raunio, T. (2016). Refusing to be sidelined: The engagement of the Finnish Eduskunta in foreign affairs. *Scandinavian Political Studies*, 39(4): 312–332.
Rommetvedt, H. (1998). Norwegian parliamentary committees: Performance, structural change and external relations. *Journal of Legislative Studies*, 4(1): 60–84.
Rommetvedt, H. (2003). *The rise of the Norwegian Parliament*. London: Frank Cass.
Sarcinelli, U. (1989). Parlamentarische Sozialisation in der Bundesrepublik Deutschland. Zwischen politischer "Sonderkultur" und Basislegitimation. *Zeitschrift für Parlamentsfragen*, 20(3), 388–408.
Sartori, G. (1987). *The theory of democracy revisited*. Chatham: Chatham House.
Scheufele, D. & Tewksbury, D. (2007). Framing, agenda setting, and priming: The evolution of three media effects models. *Journal of Communication*, 57(1): 9–20.
Schmidt, V. A. (2013). Democracy and legitimacy in the European Union revisited: input, output and 'throughput'. *Political Studies*, 61(1): 2–22.
Schüttemeyer, S.S. & Siefken, S.T. (2008). Parlamente in der EU: Gesetzgebung und Repräsentation. In O.W. Gabriel & S. Kropp (eds.) *Die EU-Staaten im Vergleich: Strukturen, Prozesse, Politikinhalte*. Wiesbaden: VS Verlag, 482–513.
Searing, D.D. (1994). *Westminster's world: Understanding political roles*. Cambridge: Harvard University Press.
Shaw, M. (1979). Conclusion. In J.D. Lees & M. Shaw (eds.) *Committees in legislatures: A comparative analysis*. Oxford: Martin Robertson, 361–434.
Shugart, M., Bergman, M.E., Struthers, C.L., Krauss, E. & Pekkanen, R. (eds.) (2021). *Party personnel strategies: Electoral systems and parliamentary committee assignments*. Oxford: Oxford University Press.
Siefken, S.T. (2018). *Parlamentarische Kontrolle im Wandel: Theorie und Praxis des Deutschen Bundestages*. Baden-Baden: Nomos.
Stapenhurst, R., Pelizzo, R., Olson, D.M. & von Trapp, L. (eds.) (2008). *Legislative oversight and budgeting: A world perspective*. Washington, D.C.: World Bank Institute.
Strøm, K. (1998). Parliamentary committees in European democracies. *Journal of Legislative Studies*, 4(1): 21–59.
Tversky, A. & Kahnemann, D. (1981). The framing of decisions and the psychology of choice. *Science*, 211(4481): 453–458.
Wahlke, J.C. (1962). Theory. A Framework for Analysis. In J.C. Wahlke, H. Eulau, W. Buchanan, & L. Ferguson (eds.), *The Legislative System: Explorations in Legislative Behavior*. (3–28). New York, NY: Wiley.

3 Assess in order to assist
A preliminary analysis of committees in Arab Parliaments

Ali Sawi

In the 22 Arab states,[1] parliaments are formed in various ways: via both direct and indirect elections, and appointment. The role of Arab committees in policy-making depends on the power of parliament. In some countries, constitutions provide for parliament's legislative authority, while elsewhere they are assigned only a consultative role. Yet members in such *consultative* councils (e.g. Saudi Arabia, Qatar, the UAE) may still influence policy-making even without formal legislative powers. This ranges from debating on matters in committees and in plenary sessions to utilizing oversight tools to discuss issues with the 'government', along with proposing legislative amendments and examining bills introduced by the government. They may also use these platforms to reach out to the public and share their views via media, constituency offices, traditional gatherings at the local level, and other avenues.

This chapter highlights similarities and differences between Arab parliaments. Arab states are highly variable and societies differ in their political culture and level of economic development. Here parliaments are assessed and assisted together, rather than in single-case descriptions. There are three reasons for that approach: the high level of exchange of experiences among them, the specific nature of legislating and legal drafting in Arabic, and the will to sustain a common parliamentary culture as marked in the establishment of the Arab Parliament.[2]

After a short introduction of the employed methodology, the chapter is structured around four main parts. The first part provides an overview of the regulatory framework of parliamentary committees; the second part reviews present committee structures, mandates, and membership; the third part analyses the capacities of committees in policy-making and the technical assistance available for members, in particular the roles of staffers, and collaboration with civil society; and finally, part four presents findings and ideas to enhance the role of committees in policy-making in the Arab states, and looks into the potential for effective international assistance.

DOI: 10.4324/9781003106579-3

Methodology

This chapter is based on the premise that despite the tight political realities in Arab states, the legal framework enables parliament to engage more effectively in policy-making if given appropriate support and technical assistance. There is hardly a parliament that is totally helpless if members wish to contribute to policy-making and practise its power. Some parliaments seem determined to reach out and communicate better and more frequently with the general public, including at the constituency level. In this way, they may raise public awareness and engage civil society in policy debates, and social media provides tools for more open space for the public to engage in policy-making and evaluate parliamentary functioning. The overall development in the region indicates a growing attention for parliaments in public opinion as well as the pressures on Arab countries to empower their parliaments relative to the executive.

To analyse the regulatory framework of Arab councils, this chapter relies on a comprehensive review of national constitutions or basic laws, laws of parliament, and rules of procedures. In addition, an expert survey asked parliamentary practitioners about the composition, institutional setup, and functioning of committees.[3] It was administered via questionnaire to a sample of 80 MPs and experts and covered a variety of Arab parliaments (16 out of 22 countries), i.e. monarchies and republics, with unicameral and bicameral parliaments, comprising elected and appointed MPs[4] (see Table 3.1).

Although the sample was small and is not representative, responses help understand the dynamics in real-world contexts, especially as respondents were insiders who have been in parliament and dealing with committees for a long time. But one needs to be cautious in reading the differences in responses, as they reflect different practices in Arab parliaments. Additionally, the analysis rests upon accumulated knowledge of the author delivering training programmes and providing consultation for Arab parliaments over the last three decades.

Like most parliaments, Arab counsels exercise their powers and functions through plenary sessions, the work of standing committees, and special committees. To understand how committees work, it is crucial to examine

Table 3.1 Composition of the survey in Arab parliaments

Parliament	No. of participants	Parliament	No. of participants
Saudi Arabia	4	Morocco	6
Oman	5	Algeria	5
Emirates	4	Tunisia	4
Bahrain	5	Sudan	6
Qatar	4	Egypt	5
Kuwait	4	Palestine	5
Lebanon	5	Syria	2
Jordan	6	Iraq	10

Source: survey of 80 MPs / experts by the author.

the way they are constituted, their organization, their membership, and the support resources they have (Leston-Bandeira & Norton 2017: 37).

Regulatory framework of parliaments and their committees

Arab parliaments are constitutionally independent bodies. The majority are unicameral (UAE, Qatar, Kuwait, Iraq, Syria, Palestine, Lebanon, Egypt, Tunisia, Saudi Arabia, Comoros Islands, Djibouti, Mauritania, and Libya), while eight parliaments are bicameral (Yemen, Oman, Bahrain, Jordan, Sudan, Algeria, Morocco, and Somalia).[5] Their names differ according to national cultures and political context. They are often called 'council' or 'assembly' (*majles*, e.g. Iraq, Lebanon, Tunisia, Egypt), but also union (*ittihad*, e.g. Comoros Island), house (Somalia), and national authority (*hai'aa quameyya*, e.g. Sudan). So, the preferred title is often not 'parliament' and the meaning of 'representative body' is often replaced by 'consultative council'. However, Arab literature uses the term 'parliament' in writing and speaking (*barlaman*), and the recently created legislative body of the Arab League is called the Arab Parliament (*al barlaman al' araby*). In this chapter, the terms 'council' and 'parliament' are used interchangeably.

There are 29 chambers in the 22 Arab states, with around 5,000 members, ranging in size between 40 members in Bahrain and the UAE to 596 in Egypt, thus showing an average of about 170 MPs per chamber, which is lower than the global average of 240 MPs per chamber.[6] About 90 percent of Arab MPs are elected, usually directly by the eligible voters. Twenty percent of the total number of MPs are women, and two councils are currently chaired by women.[7] Most of those bodies have constitutional mandates, e.g. legislative and oversight, and many are entitled to interrogate ministers and public officials, override the executive's veto powers, and, in some cases, hold not only the head of government accountable but can also indict the head of state, e.g. Egypt's Constitution.

In Arab states, regulatory frameworks for parliaments derive from national constitutions, law of parliament, rules of procedure (RoP), or standing orders. The difference between RoP and standing orders is important, as 'the constraints on how rules are set up and changed differ considerably' (Leston-Bandeira & Norton, 2017: 30). This chapter uses the term RoP to combine the two Arabic titles of regulatory frameworks of parliaments, which are similar in essence, i.e. *la'eha dakheleya* in Kuwait, Egypt, and Oman, and *nezam dakhely*, as in Iraq and Tunisia.

However, the substantial difference lies in the legal status, not the title. Arab RoP are either internal regulations that concern only parliament or are issued as a law binding to all. There are examples of RoP that have been recently enforced as laws (like in Bahrain and Morocco), or drafted by parliaments and enforced as law (like in Egypt since 2015, and Iraq as per law issued in 2018). In addition, the constitution of Comoros Islands provides that the Assembly of the Union drafts its own rules of procedure, and that before their application, the constitutional court shall review them for constitutional conformity. The Jordanian constitution provides that the Senate and the Chamber of Deputies each make the internal regulations for the control and organization of their own proceedings, which is then submitted to the king for ratification. The RoP of the Syrian People's Assembly assures their mandatory effect. The RoP of the Tunisian Parliament provides that the Assembly shall issue a special law which must define the mandate of committees vis-à-vis all other agencies and institutions of the state. On the other end, some countries empower the parliament to issue its own RoP by discretion (e.g. Oman),[8] yet as such they are neither binding to others nor do they have legal effect vis-à-vis the government, thus resulting in recurring conflicts between committees and respective ministries regarding access to information.

That regulatory framework provides for the power of each committee to scrutinize all policy sectors which fall under its jurisdiction. Most RoP detail the scope of work of each of the standing committees and reassure the principle of exclusive mandate for each one, sometimes even in repetitive articulations, e.g. 'the committee shall deal with all matters related to its specialization'. This explains why the majority of respondents confirmed that committees have the formal authority to function as 'policy-kitchen'. In reality, however, only a few cases show that committees initiate investigations on issues under their jurisdiction (e.g. in Iraq, Kuwait, and Tunisia). On the question 'How would committees decide to investigate an issue?' the majority (75 percent) stated that a committee can commence work on an issue only if the plenary decides to refer the issue to the committee. Sometimes the plenary would assign an issue of high importance not to the directly concerned committee, but rather to a special committee or a joint committee for political reasons, e.g. to avoid opposition and carry the matter without difficulty.

Committee structures

Good practices show that every committee should be an image of the whole House (Delcamp 2018: 22), i.e. it should represent the political and partisan diversity of its members. In Arab councils, the number, title, size, and mandate of committees are set out in the RoP. This gives parliament flexibility to modify its committee structure as needed but may also be politicized. Partisan politics and personal preferences of parliamentary leaders may also result in changes to the committee structure.

Parliamentary practices show that stability of committee structure is vital for members and staff to accumulate knowledge, no matter the titles of cabinet ministers. A the same time committees can always form subcommittees (and other types such as ad hoc, select, and joint committees) to deal with specific issues without creating new standing committees. That said, Arab committee systems seem to face a common structural difficulty. There are around 500 standing committees in Arab councils, leaving aside special, ad hoc, and joint committees.

According to the RoP in the Arab parliaments, the number of standing committees per chamber ranges from five (24 percent), ten (16 percent), to more than 20 (8 percent). Asked their judgement on the organization of their respective councils, most respondents to the expert survey (85 percent) stated that the current number is reasonable. Only 7 percent said that it is less than needed, and 8 percent said that that it is more than necessary. Comparing the number of (standing) committees to the size of parliament does not reveal a pattern. The Iraqi Parliament consists of 229 MPs and has 24 committees; the one of Egypt has almost the same number of committees but is much bigger (596 MPs).

Unified criteria as to when and how committee structure is to be modified do not exist. Sometimes it is adjusted in response to changes in cabinet ministers, e.g. creating a new committee to specialize in a newly established ministry. At other times parliament forms a new committee to respond to a new priority of the head of state, e.g. committees for Africa, National Happiness, Widows and Victims of War against Terrorism, etc. In both cases it is the executive that actually drives the modification process of committee structure. Committee structure may also recognize partisan balances (e.g. in Tunisia, where chapter 60 of the Constitution assigns chairmanship of the financial committee to the opposition in addition to its right to form and chair investigative commissions every year). In a few cases, the number of committees is fixed (e.g. five standing committees in Bahrain). Parliament often generates a variety of special, ad hoc, sub-, and interim committees to handle legal restrictions or procedural difficulties of amending the structure of standing committees.

Although there is no clear relationship between the number of committees and the number of parliamentarians (Delcamp 2018: 5), the size of the committees might account for their effectiveness. Some researchers argue that 'if committees are very large their usefulness as a smaller forum of work is lost' (Leston-Bandeira & Norton 2017: 30). On the other hand, small parliaments often have greater difficulties operating as compared to larger ones simply 'because of the small number of members available to participate in the full range of committees'.[9] Smaller committees may be challenged to fulfil their participation quora and thus have to cancel sessions. Also, an MP cannot belong to more than one committee, or exceptionally two.[10] This is said to preserve the effectiveness of the system and prevent absenteeism and consequently facilitate reaching quorum. Parliaments are keen to keep small committees functioning if not meeting quora, and might apply one of the following tactics: borrowing members from other committees to attend,[11] having the speaker/deputy attend and chair the meeting, or, allowing enough members to sign up for a second/additional committee. More so, other parliaments tend to offer special status to specific committees to help them adjust the practice of quorum, while others link financial rewards or sanctions to the attendance of committee meetings (e.g. in Tunisia).

Committee chairs are formally elected by committee members themselves. However, 85 percent of the respondents point out the role of party affiliations, tribal balances, and rapport with the government as key factors in designating leadership of committees. The professional background of committee members come second in the nomination of committee chairs, e.g. a physician for the health committee or a lawyer for the legal committee. But government intervention may lead to unexpected results, such as a businessman in his 70s chairing the youth committee, or a police officer chairing the human rights committee. Most respondents (78 percent) believed that committee chairs are selected to serve political and partisan or even personal interests and are not freely elected on the basis of their professional background – they see them as nominated by major party leaders (e.g. Iraq, Tunisia, Lebanon), backed by the government (e.g. Saudi Arabia, Bahrain), and using personal assets to mobilize supporters to get elected. Basically, committee chairs serve for the whole term, although reelected each legislative year. Some contend that stability of the membership and quality of legislation could be a strong argument in favour of the independence of committees. However, this becomes a challenge when partisan and personal factors affect nomination of chair persons that might lack professional background or commitment to committee work. Continuous service as committee chair can help when exchanging favours with respective government offices.

Names of committees are a topic that remains a grey zone in parliamentary practices. The majority of respondents (77 percent) considered titles of the committees in Arab parliaments to be relevant to their actual mandates. However, names of committees often do not correspond to respective ministries and government agencies. In fact, it is not the mere names of committees that matter, but rather how those names are perceived by members. When members and staff seem not to share an understanding regarding division of labour in parliament, names of committees may be interpreted in different ways. Such overlapping committee portfolios can create confusion over the terms of oversight responsibilities.

Although the RoP enable committees to function as autonomous bodies, reality shows that the workings of committees are substantially affected by the personalities of the speaker and the committee chair, as well as the chemistry between the two. Good practices suggest that it is vital for parliaments to develop instruments of coordination and association of committees in the general management of the House (Delcamp 2018: 34–36), yet Arab parliamentary practices show that the agenda of the plenary is generally set by the Speaker and the secretary-general (El-Mikawy 2000). This affects the referral of issues to committees, as well as the enrolment of committee reports in the business order of the plenary. It is not surprising, then, to observe critical comments from committees for not including their reports, or for moving forward without waiting for their reports.

Working methods of committees are generally unified and their outcomes are standardized (e.g. the format and structure of reports). The majority of respondents (70 percent) viewed the current methods as appropriate. It is noteworthy that in response to political and constitutional changes, several parliaments have reviewed their internal procedures over the last few years. The majority of respondents (77 percent) argued that committees have recently been restructured, yet their working methods have not. Very few committees have developed tools to work effectively. For example, only 5 percent of the respondents reported that committees have standard operating procedures (SoPs), 12 percent said committees have strategic plans, 12 percent mentioned that committees have annual action plans, 35 percent claimed that committees have manuals for newcomer members, and, 22 percent stated that committees have websites. The analysis also shows that in the few cases where committees have a strategic plan, 65 percent of the respondents said that the plans were developed by the committee staff, while 12 percent stated that they were developed by external consultants. In general, committee plans have to be approved by the council (mostly by the house bureau, and rarely in the plenary).

As a rule, committee meetings are held in camera and their records are not publishable. Both the law and the RoP prohibit committee members from disclosing committee deliberations. Yet, it is up to the committee chair to allow reporters into the meetings and issue a press release as necessary.

Role of committees in regulating public policies

The policy-making process starts with the forming of government. Parliament regulates policies and monitors their implementation. In some Arab states, parliament has the power to vote on the cabinet (collectively like in Morocco, Lebanon, and Egypt, or on each and every minister as in Iraq), while in other cases (e.g. Bahrain, Syria, Kuwait, Saudi Arabia, UAE, and Oman) ministers are appointed by sole decree of the head of state. In both cases, according to most Arab constitutions, the executive is obliged to put together an annual statement, known as the government statement[12] that describes policy initiatives, accompanied by a budget proposal.[13] While these policies are to reflect the views and will of the head of state, government and parliament can influence the articulation and programming of policy implementation.

In most countries, the parliament forms a special commission to review and assess the government statement, and present a report to the plenary. The special commission reviews standing committees' reports on their respective sectors of public policies, as well as individual contributions of MPs. The Speaker or their deputy chairs the commission, which comprises standing committee chairs, party whips, and representatives from minorities and independents. More so, it holds calls upon most ministers to review respective policies, work out disputes, reach compromises, and finalize the collective report. One can hardly observe dissent in such 'macro/all the house' special committees, as they show to the public that government and parliament can work out required policies. However, it is worth noting that committee reports provide for general framework, leaving it to the government to articulate as it sees fit, and then initiate related bills to parliament to be processed. Hence, the significance of such grand committees seems to be political more than legislative.

Parliament debates with the government on public policies and the development agenda. The debate results in a set of policy declarations known in the Arab context as 'government promises' to parliament. Parliament then votes on government policy as a package. Committees are part of these dynamics. They would then focus on their respective policy sectors, hold meetings with ministers and ministerial senior administrators to elaborate on specific policy details and programmes. They also pave the way for negotiations and compromises between MPs and ministers, and influence the plenary debate on government policies. Parliament then allocates necessary funds for the policy implementation by approving the annual state budget.

The government submits bills related to the implementation of public policies. The majority of legislation considered by Arab parliaments is introduced by the governments. Although most Arab constitutions empower parliaments to reject, amend, and approve bills,[14] rejecting a government bill in parliament rarely occurs, given that the majority is pro/or backed by government, and that most parliaments might be dissolved at will of the head of state. A few cases (like Kuwait, Lebanon, Tunisia, and Iraq) provide examples of Arab parliaments rejecting a government bill, and ones which are able to negotiate with government in order to reach compromise on legislative proposals. As the 'policy kitchen', committees ought to have a legislative policy and agenda. Committees can also play an important role in scrutinizing the provisions of bills before the parliament. Usually, a bill will be referred to a committee for 'inquiry and report'. Based on the evidence it has heard, the committee may recommend that certain changes be made to the bill; however, there is no requirement for parliament to implement the recommendations of the committee.

The imperative challenge is that government does not really submit a specific annual legislative plan to parliament, and consequently neither parliament nor its committees can develop a concrete legislative agenda. Government argues that the government statement is sufficient for MPs to be aware of legislative needs to implement policies that parliament has approved, and that government bill proposals react to changing development needs as they arise. The problem is that parliament cannot predict legislative intentions of government, and sometimes is taken by surprise and asked to review and vote on bills. According to some RoP, parliament should vote on a bill within a time limit of 15 to 45 days, otherwise the bill will be considered approved (e.g. Oman). This problem also hampers efficient legislative work in committees. Arab parliaments generally seem to live with that, despite a few opposition and independent MPs who urge parliament to request a full annual legislative plan from the government.

Arab RoP provide that the legislative process usually starts with the minister's speech in which the principles and purposes of the bill are outlined.

Parliament considers it in a first reading and gives in-principle approval, then debates take place during the second (in detail) reading. The House refers the bill to relevant committees and tasks them to prepare a report as the basis for debate. Committees mainly rely on the 'bill essentials' provided by the government to assess the bill. In the absence of a clear government legislative agenda, committees often consider each bill as if it were disconnected from other related bills and respective policies.

Legislative initiatives of members may be rejected by government or confused with government bills. In most RoP, a bill proposal by members would be considered as an amendment to a related government bill, thus the committee at work shall review the government bill first, then see into members' proposals for amendments. Sometimes the government rushes to interrupt committee work by submitting a bill related to the member's bill if it sees the bill is crucial and would attain public gains for the member or party, and thus government tries to take the lead on the matter. This may frustrate members who invested their political capital and worked hard on the proposal to be ready for committee review (i.e. technical drafting, mobilizing peers to support, consulting with civil society to fine-tune the draft).

Finally, the plenary debates the bill article by article, and in totality. Upon approval, parliament forwards it to the head of state for issuance and promulgation. Some Arab constitutions empower MPs to suggest amendments to the bill during plenary debates (e.g. Iraq, Tunisia, and, Egypt) while others require government consent to any proposed amendment (e.g. Bahrain, Oman, and UAE).

A good legislative process assumes that law-makers have perspective on the *impact* of law and criteria for assessing the provisions, as well as skills to articulate them. So, committee members would need a reference while discussing a bill. Some members work hard to relate a proposed bill to the government statement (often independent/opposition members), ask staffers to conduct necessary research, and request expert opinion to enlighten them on the wider impact of the bill on public policies (hearings, field visits, meetings with ministers, etc.).

With regards to consultation with relevant stakeholders in the course of legislation, most parliaments make bills available to the public after the first reading. Committees take evidence from officials, experts or social groups when considering a bill. Some parliaments are more open to consultations (e.g. Lebanon, Iraq, Tunisia, and Morocco) than others. Some have modernized their websites to give access to the public to share their comments/petitions (e.g. Kuwait, Tunisia, while the Palestinian Council created a department[15] to review and formalize citizens' proposals in order to be forwarded to the House and the Cabinet). However, it is not clear how parliaments deal with such petitions.

Most Arab RoP permit public committee hearings but they rarely assist their members and staff in training for and conducting them. But topics such as how to set the agenda and formulate questions, identify participants, keep records, and prepare reports are not self-evident.

Arab states have approved various international conventions and treaties pertinent to addressing corruption, illegal immigration, gender equality, anti-discrimination, child protection, human trafficking, environmental protection, etc. These obligations should be considered when designing public policies, reviewing related legislative proposals, and undertaking oversight work of parliament. Most Arab parliaments have created specialized committees to deal with some of these major obligations and put them on the policy priorities of the government.[16] However, Arab parliaments continue to face a significant challenge in ensuring the incorporation of such a perspective in their work. Namely, the lack of sufficient tools and mechanisms including adequate information and technical assistance hinders the ability of committees to scrutinize bills for their consistency with relevant constitutional and international obligations, and monitor the implementation of laws on the ground. There is no systematic evaluation of the extent to which legislative goals have been achieved, and ministries do not specifically report to parliament on the progress of implementation of legislation.

Oversight role of committees

The role of committees in policy-making depends greatly on their capacity to monitor policy implementation. Arab parliamentary committees are legally entitled to use a set of tools to exercise their oversight authority. This includes meetings with government officials, holding public hearings, conducting consultations with stakeholders, and proposing policy recommendations. That said, the overarching challenge lies in the lack of relevant research and technical assistance available for committee members to scrutinize policy implementation. Answering the question 'How do committees hold government accountable for its performance?', respondents answered as shown in Table 3.2:

In reality, the oversight work of the committees over the ministries, state-owned companies, and entities under their purview relies to a large extent on the annual administrative reports received from these institutions. Yet,

Table 3.2 Committee tools for oversight in Arab parliaments

	Yes
Apply specific indicators developed for that purpose	5%
Through open discussion on respective public policy sector	75%
Uses reports of specialized agencies (official, civil society, academic)	45%
Through direct interaction with government officials	55%
Uses public opinion surveys to question government officials	12%
Meetings with experts to assess government performance	35%

Source: survey of 80 MPs / experts by the author (see Table 3.1).

in many instances, institutions do not submit regular reports. Moreover, the quality of the reports is often uneven. There is therefore a need for government to adopt a consistent and parliament-sensitive structure and methodology in preparing reports for parliament.

Committees often practise oversight in meetings with government officials. Staff and advisors prepare questions, develop background papers, and collect written submissions from MPs to enhance oversight. Committees also interact with stakeholders (e.g. civil society, experts, media, social groups) and hold consultations, share comments, and receive petitions. Yet, the consultation process is largely limited to those known to committee chairs and key members. It would be useful for each committee to develop a comprehensive database of relevant experts, stakeholders and the beneficiaries of the public service sector under the committee's jurisdiction to call upon for written submissions or in-person participation at the hearing.[17]

One of the tools commonly used by committees conducting oversight is policy recommendations. Usually, committee reports include recommendations, which, if adopted by the House, are then directed to the relevant government minister, who is expected to report back to the House on how the ministry will deal with them. Such a response is sent to the Speaker, who refers it to the relevant committee or tables it on the business order for plenary debate. This should facilitate monitoring of government's compliance to the laws and dedication to approved public policies.

But, more important, is how committees follow through to ensure their recommendations are acted upon. One may come across numerous committee recommendations based on their inquiry work, yet the use of these recommendations in government policy is rarely evident. On the one hand, government officials describe many recommendations as plain wishes which do not help improve policy-making, that they reflect MPs' wishes for local services and personal favours, and sometimes MPs abuse their oversight power to get what they want. It is also said that some recommendations are irrelevant, vague, and not feasible (e.g. that 'government must alleviate poverty', 'subsidize basic goods', 'modernize infrastructures'). In some cases, recommendations are provided to the government after the budget is approved, thus, budgetary limitations hinder their implementation. In other cases, committees may even produce conflicting recommendations directed to the same ministry; for some reason, these contradictory recommendations are in turn endorsed by the plenary, even though all those concerned realize that they are not actionable recommendations. Thus, government attitude often lacks seriousness, reflected in statements such as 'we will take it into consideration in the next budget', 'if resources are available', 'laws need to be amended', 'we are already working on it'.

Responding to this criticism, MPs argue that they are doing the best they can given the prevailing state of affairs, such as a committee's lack of access to necessary information that can enable members to examine public accounts and financial issues, and assess whether a policy is carried out efficiently, effectively, and economically, and whether expenditure conforms to the authority which governs it. Access to information can be restricted under different guises. The easiest way ministers could deny parliament adequate information is to claim that the information is 'confidential', 'secret', or 'top secret'. MPs also argue that lack of sufficient cooperation by ministers impedes the ability of committees to carry out their work effectively; most ministers attend few committee meetings, where they provide statements and leave hastily.

Political dynamics

Political dynamics affect the working of committees and their actual role in policy-making. They include personality factors, partisan politics, political culture, and social traditions, as well as the relationship between government officials and MPs.

Committee structures are constant, and do not change much during the term. Although this might help to accumulate experience, it can result in stagnation when major problems are not resolved. The analysis of the expert interviews shows that 60 percent of respondents believe that members of committees are often elected to sit on the same committee for the whole term, while others report that members are to be reelected to their committees every year (40 percent). The same applies to committee chairs. Although most constitutions and RoP allow yearly reelections of all parliamentary leadership positions (e.g. Speaker, committee chairs, caucuses and whips), there is a tradition to keep persons in post for the whole term, for the sake of stability. Some scholars would also argue that continuity of MPs serving in each committee is useful, as it allows for enhanced quality of work (Leston-Bandeira & Norton 2017: 28). Interviewed experts argue that as for the staff, they generally stay even longer in the same committee over consecutive terms, as well as advisors and consultants who even continue to serve the same committees for more than one parliament.

To the question 'Who might influence the working of committees?', respondents offered varied responses: some point out the leading role of the Speaker (23 percent), leading parties/blocs (45 percent), the committee chairs (13 percent), certain prominent members of committees (9 percent), and, the government (10 percent). These responses may explain why the majority (87 percent) of respondents also believed that committees have varying powers when it comes to shaping policy. The closer the committee to the government the greater input it might have on policy-making. In general, the most influential committees are said to be legislative, finance/budget, security, and foreign relations.

The role of the Speaker seems to be the most important reference for committees, for various reasons. A limited awareness of the legal frameworks among members leaves them dependent on the Speaker's interpretation. The lack of legal awareness renders customs more important than regulations – often, the Speaker is seen as 'the boss' of the institution. As the government usually influences the selection of the speakers and backs them, and all interaction between committees and government agencies must go through the Speaker, they can therefore strongly influence committee work and its oversight role over respective ministries.

Regarding the actual mandate of their committees, 24 percent of the respondents believed that MPs were aware of the mandate of the committees compared to 82 percent with regard to staffers. This is not unexpected, and can be explained by the high turnover of members serving on committees compared to the limited turnover of staff. In this regard, the issue of significance is how both groups interact and work together. When members believe that they know better and look down at their technical support staff, and if the latter see themselves the only professionals in committee work, then the spirit of teamwork and productivity becomes uncertain. Moreover, members of the legislative committee may tend to see themselves as the exclusive drafters of all regulations and bills, a matter that bothers members of other committees, which in fact have the same legislative mandate.

Assessing technical assistance for committees

Members are mostly generalists rather than specialists; they are not expected to be fully qualified and capable of scrutinizing all subjects considered in parliament or on the committee. They require the support of parliamentary staffers. As one MP said:

> There is a pressing need to provide committees with competent advisors and skilful staff, as members of the committees would not have the capacity, energy and objectivity to put together reports assessing government performance and recommending workable solutions ... this is the area of professionals, then comes the duty of MPs to review, improve, and consider possible decisions for the plenary ... unfortunately most committees fall short of such expertise.
> (Rachid Lemdower, MP, Moroccan House of Representatives)

An effective parliament requires an efficient administration, but it in some Arab states, observers recognize an efficient secretariat-general serving mediocre MPs. Committees require support of experts with specialized policy knowledge and an understanding of parliamentary procedures, law, and legal drafting. Such services can also be outsourced, as is the practice in the Gulf States.

Arab parliaments look like massive machines, operated by a large number of individuals of various backgrounds and specializations. They differ in size (from 40 members in Bahrain and the UAE to around 600 in Egypt) and the average is around ten staffers per one member. Approximately 20,000 staff personnel are employed to serve the standing committees. This is an average of four to five staffers per committee member. However, committees seem to be understaffed, given the fact that a considerable number of the entire staff are not political advisors – rather logistical, administrative, IT specialists, accountants, handworkers, maintenance, and security. A group of qualified technical staff serves exclusively the speaker, deputies, party leaders, the secretary-general, and committee chairs. In sum, those serving in committee technical work constitute around a quarter of the entire parliamentary staff.

Recruitment policies of committee staffers is another area of concern. Staffers should serve all members equally; they should be neutral, impartial and avoid any appearance of bias or partisanship; upon receiving tailored training, they should also be able to serve any committee. It clearly follows that recruitment needs to follow special strategies and procedures, as parliamentary jobs require special characteristics, which are different for those of other administrative jobs. Respondents mentioned that staffers are hired in accordance with the civil service code (30 percent), by discretion of the Speaker (31 percent), or the secretary-general (39 percent). This brings attention to the personal factors in selecting staff, which is particularly concerning as they are hired as permanent employees.

Respondents do say that technical assistance and facilities available for committees are sufficient to perform energetically in policy-making but MPs do often complain that they do not get the required quality of technical assistance, in particular to assess government policies and propose workable recommendations. Hence, the fastest and easiest way for parliamentarians is to seek funds to hire more of their own political staff.

The issue on the working relationship between MPs and their staff here is threefold: how staff are treated by members, how they view their status in committee work dealing with policy-making, and how this relationship affects staff productivity and quality of service.[18] Staffers work closely with the chair, and sometimes directly with committee members, but they report to their administrative supervisors. While members expect staff to follow their guidance (i.e. what to do and how to do it), it is the administrative supervisor who directly manages the staff workload and assesses their technical performance. Committee staffers criticize that MPs mix the function of a committee researcher with that of a personal aide. Members may tell staffers to fetch and deliver packages, escort their guests, write personal papers, etc. More so, members may convey their needs to the committee staff and ignore the administration, thus disputes are likely to arise between committee members and the parliament administration/committee chief clerk. In both cases, staffers are caught in the middle.

The debates around the job titling and competencies of staff and administrative leadership of parliament, however implicit, do not preclude us from considering the issue and its implications in reality. When MPs belittle the role of the technical staff or fail to utilize their professional skills, staff morale may decline, putting the entire working environment at risk. In fact, the statements of work (SoW) and job descriptions of committee staffers in almost all Arab parliaments are written in the internal procedures, but in reality, are rarely followed.

Arab parliaments' secretariats-general mostly include three assistant general secretariats which are further differentiated into divisions, sections and units. Managers at the lower levels (i.e. unit managers) are required to seek the authorization of the higher-level managers (i.e. divisional and sectional managers) in order to proceed with almost anything. This naturally has a debilitating effect on leadership at the lower levels, as well as on productivity and job satisfaction in the parliamentary support structure as a whole (Germanos 2019).

Arab RoP formally require that both the secretary-general, and staffers be non-partisan and committed to serve all members equally. Yet, the work of the general secretariat is affected by their degree and quality of professional autonomy. This is questionable in many Arab cases. In some parliaments, the secretary-general is appointed by the discretionary decision of the Speaker (e.g. Egypt, Algeria, and the Sudan), or approved by the House Bureau (e.g. Iraq). In other cases, he is appointed by a decree issued by the head of the state (e.g. Oman, Bahrain, and the UAE).

Regarding the status and thus the ability to lead the entire staff of the parliament, the secretary-general may be granted a 'special rank' (e.g. Iraq), the position of 'under-secretary of state' (e.g. Bahrain, Egypt), or that of 'general manager' (e.g. Syria). In Saudi Arabia, the rank and titles of the secretary-general are set by royal decree. In almost all cases, the secretary-general is seen as a political post rather than a professional manager of parliament business. With a few exceptions (e.g. Lebanon), they are recruited from outside the institution. A new secretary-general will often redeploy committee staffers to satisfy committees and incentivize staffers (moving a committee's staffer from a regular committee to a key one, or promoting a staffer by moving him/her from administrative job to committee staff, and vice versa). Evidently, the committee work is affected by the changes in administrative leadership, for good or bad. Respondents asserted that the secretary-general plays a key role in influencing the technical performance of committee staffers (65 percent), compared to the influence of the committee chair (12 percent), and the Speaker (10 percent).

There is no specialized agency designed to build the capacity and raise the skills of parliamentary staffers in Arab states. For instance, universities do not offer degrees in parliamentary affairs, nor do they organize practical training in committee-specific expertise, such as legal drafting, report writing for committees, budget analysis, oversight and inquiry and the like. Upon starting work for a legislative committee, fresh law school graduates are often told: 'Forget what you learnt at university, which is all academic and theoretical; start all over here – you must just learn how we do it'. In other cases, a newcomer will be assigned to a serious legislative job, yet left to navigate through unchartered territory on their own, learning through trial and error.[19]

Building capacity of parliamentary research, in particular at the committee level, is an ongoing effort even in well-established democracies. Unfortunately, none has proved sustainable in Arab experiences so far. Arab councils currently tend to launch research units within their organizational structure (i.e. part of the general secretariat, as in Egypt, Iraq, and Lebanon). However, these institutional initiatives still face major challenges, including poor coordination between the two chambers, lack of sufficient funding and qualified trainers, and sensitivity about learning from foreign experiences and lessons of other countries.

Challenges to be addressed by Arab parliaments

In order for Arab committees to become more engaged in policy-making, five major challenges need to be addressed, both at strategic and instrumental levels.

First: promote collaboration between government and parliament

In Arab states, there is a critical need for developing new procedures for cooperation and communication between parliament and government. Since government officials draft bills upon receiving directives or the "green light" from the head of state and the cabinet, legislative initiatives remain, to a large extent, unknown to parliament. Thus, when committees seek to develop their work plans, they mostly include generic items or await government to introduce bills and the Speaker to assign a bill to a committee to commence working on it. Committees may draw their plans as they wish, but those may not show up on the business of the plenary until the government supports them. On the other hand, if the government submits a comprehensible legislative agenda, parliament will be able to anticipate future workload and enhance the capacities of committees.

Most Arab governments have a minister for parliamentary affairs, who is constitutionally empowered not only to represent government views in parliament but also to facilitate cooperation between government and parliament in policy-making. Under this arrangement, the competent minister must be able to share technical experiences between government and parliament, raise awareness of MPs of dynamics of policy implementation, and thus help parliament conduct well-informed debates and objective assessment of public policies. In other cases, parliament assigns MPs to liaise with respective ministries or allows committee chairs to join ministerial workgroups on strategies and policy-making. Parliament may also encourage committee staffers to build trust and develop direct contacts with their counterparts at respective ministries. It is therefore useful to consider at least one annual plenary debate on how to improve the work of the committees and empower their oversight role. The need for government to 'help' parliament might be seen as recipe for government domination over parliament. In fact, governments are the centre of power in Arab states, but also control sources of information. Parliaments would not be able to examine, assess, and improve public policies without relevant data and reliable information, let alone the required technical assistance to enable members to process information and reflect on policy-making functions. It is not surprising to see MPs from most parliaments who point out the need for governmental information, not the least in parliamentary governments, i.e. elected by parliament, as in Lebanon. Numerous members use their own sources of information (aides, civil society, media, etc.) in their debates. However, government will generally underestimate this information and challenge it by unveiling 'official' records. It is therefore for the benefit of all parties and stakeholders that government smoothly 'releases' data to parliament and provides needed technical expertise to help parliament assess public policies.

Second: improve the legislative capability of committees

The role of parliament is evident throughout the legislative process, and especially in committees. But the legislative performance of committees depends, among other factors, on their technical bill drafting and amending capacities. MPs need to have adequate capacity for it, analyse their likely practical impact, and financial viability. Parliaments need to be more effectively engaged in consultations with stakeholders. In many Arab states, legislative proposals are uploaded on the parliament website for discussion and comments (e.g. Iraq, Kuwait, Syria, Tunisia, and Jordan), yet public hearings and field visits would help committees get a deeper sense of possible impact of legislation and a more comprehensive view of how it should be implemented.

The first source of information that MPs rely on for reviewing proposed legislation is the explanatory memo,[20] which is prepared by the government. In practice, however, these memos rarely include the essentials of the proposal, rather they focus on the general political imperatives for the proposed legislation. More so, it is also very rare that government provides any cost assessment of a bill.

Effective committees require the availability of efficient support. International best practice requires parliament to have its own dedicated parliamentary research unit with the professional staff to answer questions of MPs and committees as they arise, including on legislation under review (De Vrieze 2014). This calls for making available tailored training for committee staff on legislative drafting, impact assessment, and policy evaluation. Some parliaments prefer to create a completely separate entity that reports directly to the senior executive management of the parliament. Under such a model, the research service may have a more direct and visible connection with the secretary-general. In this regard, it is noticeable that some Arab parliaments have established a properly staffed research unit (e.g. Egypt, Kuwait, Oman, UAE, and Saudi Arabia). However, compared with the government technical capacity in drafting legislations, Arab parliaments still have a long way to go.

A precondition of an in-depth legislative review is the availability of a central registry of legislation in force. In many Arab states, the laws are consolidated and are readily available digitally on the website of the ministry of legal affairs, the constitutional court, the cabinet, and the government print house. Some parliaments (like UAE and Kuwait) have developed legislative information systems to help standardize the legislative process, speed up the publication of legislations, and assist with the consolidation of bills during committee debates. Other parliaments need assistance to do that. All parliaments, however, need to have access to the implementing regulations of laws (i.e. secondary legislations, issued by the executive).

Third: reinforce the oversight function of committees

In principle, all Arab parliaments have an oversight mandate, along with sets of tools, that range from request for information, providing recommendations on governments reports (Saudi Arabia, Oman, the UAE, Qatar), tabling questions, to forming inquiry and fact-finding commissions, voting down the cabinet (Tunisia, Iraq), and bringing the head of state to trial (Egypt). In practice, the impact of oversight on public policies is hard to assess. And limited access to relevant sources of information still poses a challenge to committees, despite recent freedom of information legal reforms (e.g. Jordan, Tunisia). But the need to train (newcomer) MPs on oversight and evidence-making is definite. It is also important to encourage cooperation between government and parliament to provide adequate information and data relevant to objective oversight.

Table 3.3 Ways to strengthen committees in policy-making in Arab parliaments

	Yes
Governments should assume responsibility for providing committees with data and information	85%
Ministers and their representatives should commit to attend committee meetings	75%
Modernize system of the House to enable committees' access to information	85%
Prepare orientation kit for new MPs at the beginning of every term	88%
Review the RoP to enhance the committees' mandate	35%
Modernize the organizational structure of committees	24%
Review SoW of committee staffers to be more realistic	75%
Link the incentive structure to the evaluation of committee staffers	82%
Provide staffers with advanced training in research and report writing	75%
Provide committees with financial support to conduct field visits and meet with stakeholders	24%

Source: survey of 80 MPs / experts by the author (see Table 3.1).

Fourth: support institutional capacity

In almost all modernization plans the committees' work occupies a major concern. Table 3.3 illustrates respondents' tendencies as gleaned from answers to the following question: 'Do you agree with the following suggestions for enhancing the role of committees in policy-making?'.

The results show the importance of information for members and the need to capacitate them with the *know-how and how-to* skills in order to perform their functions, as well as the need to improve human resource development of committee staffers, all of which are essential inputs for enhancing the role of committees in policy analysis. It is therefore recommended that Arab councils work on the following areas:

a) To conduct a mapping exercise to determine the capacity needs for improving the committee management and performance and how to monitor government policies.
b) To review RoP in a way that should strengthen the oversight role of committees.
c) To revise the seniority system that is less sensitive to performance and move towards merit-based assessment of the staff.
d) To review the organizational structures of the general secretariat to make it more conducive to parliamentary functions and committee needs.
e) To develop data bases for stakeholders (CSOs, experts, think tanks, etc.), and systematically engage respective stakeholders in committee work.

Fifth: invest in human resources

Improving staff organization and management is a key to strengthening the institutional capacity of Arab parliaments. Professional development and career structures within parliaments to retain staff, and to foster their role as a source of independent advice and guidance for MPs, are important in ensuring some degree of continuity and institutional memory in parliaments (SCD, 2015, p. 18). In Arab parliaments, staff salaries are rarely affected by the level of performance, rather they are monthly fixed payments. However, there is a need to reward active committee staffers and encourage those with low performance to improve.

Concluding remarks and the way forward

I have worked on parliamentary development in Arab states for many years, conducting research, designing and delivering training programmes and providing consultancies to most of the Arab councils. One of the challenging questions that often arise is: 'Do we really have parliaments?' Many observers believe that policy-making in Arab states is still in the sole hands of 'ultimate rulers'. The question becomes even more challenging when one tries to investigate the role of parliamentary committees in policy-making. What makes analysis of committee engagement in policy-making an edgy task is the fact that there are many issues to tackle in politics and parliaments, and almost every aspect of development is deeply connected with another. However, one needs to reflect on recent developments in the region, i.e. the Arab Uprising, and rephrase the question to read: How much of a role can Arab parliaments possibly play in policy-making, and how to enable and assist MPs to effectively realize their functions?

Democracy assistance gained a lot of interest during the 'Arab Spring', but the problem facing parliamentary projects is twofold: first, key donors eventually direct bigger portions of their funds to other areas (e.g. civil society) and less to parliamentary institution capacity projects, although in many cases the composition of parliament has been changed due to new groups joining parliament, in particular youth activists; and second, more political parties and groups have entered parliament with little experience in how to work together.

In Arab states, several donors have been active in providing capacity-building support for MPs and their support staff, with a focus on those on standing committees. Many democracy assistance projects focus on key committees (e.g., budget, decentralization, gender, human rights, reconciliation) to build leverage and lead others. More so, immense amounts of resources and time have been allocated to enhance community participation in parliamentary work and give citizens voice in the public policy-making process, i.e. civil society groups, political parties, the media, and civic education for the public to support transformation to democracy. However, the parliamentary establishment seems hesitant, sometimes suspicious, towards foreign interventions; while CSOs and think tanks are more willing to cooperate, they face barriers in reaching out to members and staffers. More so, government officials claim that parliament is not short on funds, and argue that affordable and voluntary local experts are numerous, and national interests and sovereignty must be secured from potential interference or foreign initiatives that do not consider sensitivity of national parliaments or might cause internal splits among MPs.

Respondents recognized the political sensitivity surrounding active collaboration with foreign assistance. In fact, in most cases, those providing the democracy assistance and the support were the same actors who were propping up the authoritarian regimes. Hence, democracy assistance initiatives did not deliver much impact.

Democracy assistance initiatives for Arab parliaments need to:

- Enhance the committee system as a whole; not focus only on a few committees.
- Assess the needs of committees to identify priorities, e.g., orientation/induction programmes for new MPs, develop committees' strategic plans,

design SOPs for committee workings, and assist members to articulate sustainable development goals (SDGs) into committee policy-making efforts.
- Adopt creative ways for committee development such as twinning with peers, organizing study tours to examine working methods of other parliaments on the ground, and utilizing networks to share experiences.
- Select and train local teams implementing activities on the ground to assure quality of assistance and adherence to standards set by project experts.
- Focus on tools to sustain development assistance and on institutionalizing a process for continued institutional development.

Arab parliaments must contribute to assistance projects, in kind and/or in funds. They have their own budgets, and most of them are wealthy. Arab parliaments should also help each other in the area of capacity building as they tend to learn from each other and face common institutional challenges. It is in the best interest of Arab parliaments to invest adequate resources in developing a pool of qualified trainers who are sensitive to parliamentary technical assistance needs, and aware of parliamentary-specific working environments. There are many emerging regional and subregional associations which are said to be dedicated to Arab parliamentary development and show readiness to assist, e.g. the Islamic Development Bank, the Arab League, Arab Parliament, as well as UN regional bureaus (UNDP in particular) and regional chapters of donor organizations. Yet some donors are seen as spoiling MPs and sometimes staff with providing training and accommodation in luxurious facilities and offering travel in order to get a foot in the door to push for specific legislation and build political alliances. Therefore, it is vital for Arab parliaments to develop their own strategic plans for capacity building of members and staff.

Notes

1 Alphabetically: Algeria, Bahrain, Comoros Islands, Djibouti, Egypt, Iraq, Jordan, Kuwait, Lebanon, Libya, Mauritania, Morocco, Oman, Palestine, Qatar, Saudi Arabia, Somalia, Sudan, Syria, Tunisia, UAE, and Yemen. This list serves the purpose of the analysis and is based on membership of the League of Arab States. National constitutions recognize other spoken languages among regional or ethnic groups, as in Iraq, Morocco, Algeria, and Somalia.
2 The consultative legislative body of the League of Arab States, founded in 2005 as an Arab interim inter-parliamentary union, then became permanent in 2012, located in Cairo, Egypt, comprising delegates of all Arab parliaments, to study and propose legislative policies to summits of heads of Arab states.
3 It is not simple random sample; rather intentional sample from among experts and practitioners. Around 15 persons in each country were identified as possible participants, being MPs or recognized specialists in parliamentary research. The results reflect views of those who agreed to participate.

Committees in the Arab Parliaments 59

4 No responses were available from the following countries: Somalia, Libya, Yemen, Comoros Islands, Djibouti, and Mauritania
5 Egypt has altered parliament structure quite a few times since the inauguration of the first elected parliament in 1866, opting for a unicameral parliament for the first half of the 1990s, then creating a second chamber from the 1980s to 2011, then a unicameral from 2012 to 2019 when constitutional amendment brought back a second chamber, i.e. the Senate.
6 Globally, MPs of 190 of 193 countries account for over 46,000 national representatives. Source: SDC 2015.
7 First in the *consultative* council of the Emirates, then shortly in the *elected* house of Bahrain. Yet, there have been women deputy speakers much earlier in Morocco and Tunisia.
8 Iraq shows a political and constitutional challenge related to the status of the RoP of its parliament. As per article 51 of Iraq's constitution, 'The House of Representatives shall lay down its own bylaw to regulate its workflow'. When parliament initiated and passed 'Parliament law and its formations' in 2018, it tackled among others internal procedures of the house that have been subject of the RoP (e.g. holding ministers accountable for criminal offence if they fail to respond to requests for information submitted by individual MPs and not through parliament motion). The government objected that law and took it to the Federal Court, which in its ruling dated December 23, 2018 revoked and repealed parts of this law. So, some internal procedures are based on the law and others sustained in the RoP.
9 In small parliaments (consisting of 40 members as in Bahrain's both houses, UAE, or 50 as in Kuwait), the size of committees is about seven members, i.e. quorum of four is required for a meeting, and the absence of one or two members may lead to postponing or even cancelling it.
10 The speaker and deputies do not usually count as committee members, but the speaker chairs a committee meeting that he wishes to join.
11 This may even happen in larger parliaments if the size of committee is so dynamic that it goes down to seven or eight members (e.g. Women' Affairs Committee in Iraq).
12 That is called Government Statement (e.g. Egypt), Ministerial Approach (e.g. Iraq), and Cabinet Note (Tunisia).
13 In Bahrain, it is a two-year budget.
14 In many Arab parliaments, a bill refers to government's legislative initiative; a bill proposal refers to that submitted by members (Oman, Jordan, and Egypt) or committee (Iraq). A bill proposal differs from what is known in Western democracies as a private member's bill, since it does not deal with local or group interests. However, there are additional procedural steps for a bill proposal which make it more complicated to pass through (e.g. review and approval of Legislative Committee, and/or the House Bureau, and consent of the government (Iraq, Bahrain, Oman). There is constitutional and political debate over the nature of a bill proposal whether it has to be approved by the executive to make into a bill (Oman, Iraq, UAE, Saudi Arabia, Qatar) or can be directly submitted to the plenary for consideration (Kuwait, Lebanon, Egypt, Tunisia).
15 Complaints Diwan www.pal-plc.org/english.aspx (access: 26.10.2020).
16 For example, Committee for Displaced Persons and Refugees in Iraq, Anti-corruption Members Group in Kuwait, Committee on Gender Equality in Tunisia, Human Rights' Committee in Egypt.

17 Some parliaments have moved in this direction already, e.g. Bahrain embarks on parliamentary data bank, Iraq modernizes roster of experts and CSOs, and Egypt's parliament links with cabinet info centre.
18 Traditionally, some consider parliament staff as 'the un-elected legislators'.
19 See the first Global Parliamentary Report, UNDP & IPU, 2012, in particular chapter V.
20 Similar to explanatory note in Commonwealth parliaments.

Sources

Delcamp, A. (2018). How can parliamentary committees be made more effective? www.ua.undp.org/content/ukraine/en/home/library/democratic_governance/effectiveness-of-parliamentary-committees.html (access: 26.10.2020).

El-Mikawy, N. et al. (2000). Working paper institutional reform of economic legislation in Egypt. *ZEF Discussion Papers on Development Policy*, No. 30.

Germanos, L. (2019), The Parliamentary Support Structure. www.politicsweb.co.za/comment/the-parliamentary-support-structure

IPU, Common principles for support to parliaments. www.ipu.org/our-work/strong-parliaments (access: 26.10.2020).

Leston-Bandeira, C. & Norton, P. (2017). Parliamentary institutions – basic concepts. *UNDP.*

SDC (2015). Global mapping and analysis of parliamentary strengthening. *Democracy Reporting International*, Swiss Agency for Development and Cooperation.

De Vrieze, F. (2014). Baseline Assessment of the Committees in the Parliament of Trinidad and Tobago.

4 The role of parliamentary committees and legislative agreements in party bargaining during minority government in Denmark

Flemming Juul Christiansen and Henrik Jensen

Parliamentary committees in Denmark and policy bargaining

In his seminal work on minority governments, Strøm (1990) associated strong parliamentary committees with minority governments: committee powers to scrutinize legislation make it more attractive to remain in opposition and attempt to influence government from the parliament. Yet, Rommetvedt (1998; 2003) questions the power of parliamentary committees in Norway where minority governments are common. Also in Denmark, where minority governments are even more common, academic accounts of parliamentary committees (Jensen 1995, 2002, 2003, 2014) point out how parliamentary committees are not actors but arenas for party group activity and interaction. In addition, observers and a high number of former MPs point out that this interaction does not include policy negotiations, and some of them also criticize much of what goes on in committees as being 'without visions' and not meaningful for MPs seeking policy influence (Frandsen 2008; Berlingske Politiko 2015; Koch 2016).

The purpose of this chapter is to throw light on the Danish committee system. We analyse to what extent opposition parties during minority governments in Denmark use the powers of parliamentary committees to amend legislation via legislative agreements and control the government. We also ask whether committees form settings for negotiations and policy compromises. We find that bargaining and compromise are rare activities inside committees and that opposition party groups typically refrain from control activities via committees when they have a negotiated agreement with the government. To explain these patterns, the chapter draws on theories of bargaining and agenda-setting. We expect bargaining political parties to need space for evaluation of proto-deals without being subject to public scrutiny and attacks from other parties. When minority governments make deals with opposition parties, they not only offer policy influence in return for votes and passing of policy; they 'buy' *silence* on the political agenda (Christiansen & Seeberg 2016).

DOI: 10.4324/9781003106579-4

The chapter analyses several important aspects of relations between minority governments and parliamentary committees on the one hand and bargaining on the other, using both quantitative and qualitative sources, including statements from and interviews with Danish MPs, addressing topics of parliamentary committees, legislative agreements, and information acquisition. Not all the sources of data are ideal for our purposes, and to some extent, we had to rely on 'circumstantial evidence' for our judgements. Still, the chapter shows that actual legislative bargaining in Denmark takes place inside the ministries, supported by an informal yet highly institutionalized practice of legislative agreements (*politiske forlig*) between government and opposition parties, as explained in more detail below. The role of parliamentary committees in such bargaining is very limited; they are typically involved only after the legislative deals are settled, and the opposition parties involved in the deal do not use the parliamentary committees to keep a check on the government. Instead, they keep track of the government via informal channels of information. The opposition parties not involved in the agreement but represented in the parliamentary committees get less information than partners in legislative agreements do.

Minority governments, committees, and bargaining

Literature and theory

According to the 'decline of parliaments thesis' that dates back to Bagehot (1964 [1867]) and was coined by Bryce (1921), in Westminster parliamentary systems, the executive has the dominant policy-influence, something which is enhanced by strong party groups (Elgie & Stapleton 2006; Wheare 1963). In particular, committees in parliamentary systems are traditionally portrayed as less important than their counterparts in the US Congress, although the power of the latter may have been somewhat overestimated (see Chapter 18 on the US).

Contrary to this picture, which is in line with the decline of parliament-thesis, Longley and Davidson (1998: 1), in the introduction to a volume of the *Journal of Legislative Studies*, noted that many parliaments had reorganized and invigorated their parliamentary committees. They also stated: 'In contrast to the false impression of a "decline of parliaments" which gave birth to an extensive scholarly literature in the 1960s and 1970s, parliaments have, in the past three decades, become more influential bodies globally, and this has been due particularly to their newly created or revived committee system' (Longley & Davidson 1998: 5). They were thinking of permanent, issue-specific committees with amendment and scrutiny powers enabling information collection and specialization within a topic. The information is valuable not only for the individual MP but also for the party group that needs members holding such information (Krehbiel 1991; Cox & McCubbins 1993).

Strøm (1998: 47) argues that strong committees are at least a necessary condition for effective parliamentary influence in the policy-making process but questions whether they are also a sufficient condition, a point of view repeated by Martin (2014: 352). Somewhat in contrast, Rommetvedt (1998; 2003: 72–73; 88) argues that the Norwegian Storting got stronger due to weak minority governments while the committees at the same time weakened because they showed much more dissent in their recommendations. Hence, Rommetvedt raised the question whether we should dissociate the strength of parliament and the strength of parliamentary committees with a minority government as an intermediate variable (cf. Chapter 13 on Norway).

The literature associates minority government with strong parliaments since the government needs outside support to remain in office and pass bills into laws. It also associates strong parliaments and minority governments with powerful parliamentary committees. Elgie (2001) thinks of minority governments as a form of 'divided government' found in presidential systems when the party of the president does not control the legislature (Mayhew 1991). According to Strøm (1990), strong parliamentary committees – e.g. with strong formal capacity to amend or block passages of legislation – lowers the 'policy influence differential', the difference on the possibilities for an opposition party to influence policy by joining a government (Strøm 1990: 42–44). This reduces the incentive to join a government with the inherent and increased risk of losing votes at the next election, which in turn increases the likelihood of the formation of a minority government. Hence, parliamentary committees are expected, *ceteris paribus*, to be more active in the legislative process during minority governments. Committee members from opposition parties will use the committee to influence the legislative process.

More recent literature on coalition governance points out how coalition governments use several internal and extra-parliamentary governance institutions for coordination, control, and compromise such as coalition agreements, junior ministers, and internal committees. Martin and Vanberg (2011: 34–36) point at parliamentary committees as important for coalition governance, particularly for 'information acquisition' and 'amendment capability'. This means that members of government party groups will use the powers of parliamentary committees to control ministers, in particular from other parties in government. Martin and Vanberg (2011: 37) mention the Danish Folketing as an example.

Concerning minority governments, we should not mix up the 'capacity' and 'action' of parliamentary committees. Though their conditions are harder, minority governments share the ambition of majority governments in attempting to control the fate of the government's legislative initiatives. This could be in a more or less formal support arrangement from external parties for important parts of the government's programme. This was the case for the Danish Liberal–Conservative governments, from 2001 to 2011 (Christiansen & Pedersen 2012), and for the Danish Social Democratic government in office 2019. Another way for minority governments to find majorities is to negotiate policy deals with opposition parties before they present bills in parliaments, something also very common in Denmark (Christiansen 2008; Christiansen & Damgaard 2008).

According to the theory on bargaining (e.g. Raiffa 1982; Fisher et al. 2011), before a deal can be reached, negotiators often propose 'proto-deals' where they test 'zones of possible agreement'. They consider these proposals, amend them, or come up with other solutions. To reach a deal, partners should consider the result 'better than 'the best alternative to no agreement'.

In party politics, searching for such compromises is difficult to undertake with open doors since the political parties may be blamed, not just for the result reached but also for alternatives proposed and considered during the bargaining process. Hence, bargaining between political parties seems to require 'closed doors' (Warren & Mansbridge 2013). Are parliamentary committees suited as such a forum? On the one hand, closed committee meetings are very likely a necessary condition for parliamentary committees to function effectively to 'foster interparty compromise – because public meetings spur credit claiming, advertising, and position taking' (Strøm 1998; Mayhew 1974). On the other hand, committees are usually not useful settings because, having friend and foe alike as present members, it can be difficult for all members to possess the mutual confidence and overlapping interests that are required for policy bargaining. In closed meetings, parliamentary committees provide all of their members, including those of the opposition, with the same procedural powers when it comes to legislation and scrutiny. This gives committee members from opposition parties the opportunity to attack the government before the next election.

Attacks from the opposition are of course an essential part of a competitive democratic process. Yet it also means that governments have an incentive to avoid sharing more information than necessary with the committee members. They also have a strong incentive to avoid showing internal dissent with committees. Although a minority government needs external support, it does not need support from all of parliament, and often some opposition parties will remain opponents of government policy. In the setting of the committee, the government and its ministers generally have to treat committee members equally and cannot differentiate between opposition party members and government party members. Information from a minister to a committee goes to all committee members.

Agenda-setting theory contributes to our argument, too. Seeberg (2013) finds that in democracies with free and open media, the opposition holds an advantage when it comes to setting policy agendas because they can criticize the government for its conduct in office. Christiansen and Seeberg (2016) argue that policy compromises take place in the shadow of mediatization of politics and that one of its purposes is to reduce the impact of opposition criticism. Governments 'sell' policy influence, not only to receive support in legislative votes but also to buy silence and avoid certain policy agendas more beneficial to the opposition. For these reasons, we should not expect parliamentary committee meetings to be venues for actual policy negotiations.

To analyse the relations between minority governments, parliamentary committees, and policy bargaining, our case study of Denmark focuses on an informal decision-making system developed around the negotiated legislative agreements (*politiske forlig*). Here, policy preparation, deliberation, and information-sharing take place outside of the formal system before a bill is tabled and referred to a parliamentary committee. *Politiske forlig* result from minority governments seeking majorities, broad or narrow, behind their legislative initiatives. Legislative agreements are more than mere voting agreements or legislative coalitions because parties agree on a policy or a set of policies and bind each other for some time to come (Christiansen 2008). Hence, legislative agreements are durable: they bind across elections and shifts in government, and they bind the parties that enter them. Amendments to legislative agreements require consent from all parties involved, i.e. each party group, big or small, holds a veto power.[1] The legislative agreement also means that some bills at their introduction are already part of a legislative agreement. All parties from time to time take part in legislative agreements although opposition parties with ideological affinity to the government take part more often. Legislative agreements may be narrow, containing only parties from the government's own centre-left or centre-right block. When legislative agreements are broad, across the blocks, they are less vulnerable to shifts in power. A few legislative agreements are made by all parties.

The picture of parliamentary committees, legislative agreements in party group bargaining during minority government as described above, thus calls for answers to the following questions:

1. What is the role of parliamentary committees in party group bargaining of legislative agreements under minority government?
2. In what setting are legislative agreements negotiated?
3. How common are legislative agreements?
4. How does legislative bargaining affect the sharing of information among MPs?
5. How are we to understand the bargaining of legislative agreements in a party group perspective, and how does it affect the organization of the party group?

We shall try to answer these questions in a Danish context and to provide not only a snapshot of the current situation but, when possible, also try to assess the development over time. However, to do so, some short reflections on research design, data, and case selection are necessary as is the introduction of the relevant elements of the Danish political system.

Committees and legislative agreements under minority governments

With its high number of minority governments and its developed sets of norms for legislative agreements between government and opposition parties (Strøm 1990; Christiansen 2008), Denmark provides an interesting case for studying the relations between minority government, parliamentary committees, and bargaining. To shed light on this, we utilize previous studies made by the authors, including Frandsen (2006; 2008), a former MP and chair of a parliamentary party group (PPG), who has published two volumes on how the Danish parliament works in practice. We also use material from newspapers and websites in which former or present MPs speak out about how the parliament works. We draw from the minutes from a conference on the functioning of parliamentary committees held in the Danish parliament in February 2015 and in which Danish MPs, as well as academic and media observers, took part (Folketinget 2015).[2] Furthermore, we draw on MP interviews from previous studies on legislative behaviour (Hansen 2009, Riis 2012, Klöcker-Gatzwiller & Slabiak 2015; Nielsen & Kretchmar 2016).[3] Combined, they comprise around 30 MPs representing most parties, and with the MPs holding or having held various positions, such as party group leaders and spokespersons as well as former ministers. We have translated citations into English.

Under the current Constitution of 1953, the Danish Folketing is a unicameral parliament with 179 members. In the 2019 election, ten parties won seats, a high but normal level ever since the 'Earthquake Election' of 1973 that doubled the number of parties in parliament (Bille 1989). A low threshold of 2 percent in the electoral law makes it easy for new parties to enter parliament (Bischoff 2020).

Generally, the party groups are organized vertically with a party group leadership (chairman, deputy, secretary, and often a few more positions depending on the size of the group), and horizontally with one or more spokespersons for various policy areas. The horizontal division of labour reflects the division of labour of the committee system. It is rare for a spokesperson of a party group not to be a member of the committee in question. For smaller party groups, individual MPs take on more committee assignments and positions as spokespersons. For the major parties, some members may be committee members without a parcelled role of spokesperson and subordinated to the main spokesperson within the committee's policy area. Besides sharing the vertical and horizontal organizational principles, Danish party groups are highly cohesive, capable of showing a decision-making behaviour in policy matters as unitary actors (Jensen 2002); committee members, and ministers as well, are to be seen and conceived as party group representatives. In the literature on Danish parliamentary politics, the party groups are considered the most central actors in parliament and Danish politics as well (Worre 1970; Damgaard 1980; Jensen 1995; 2002; Bille 2000). They are the units that form governments and legislative coalitions.

Minority governments have been the rule since 1971, with only one exception (1993–1994). Since a major committee reform in 1972, the Danish parliamentary committee system has consisted of about 25 such permanent bodies with specialized policy areas or topics, most of them corresponding to a ministry dealing with the same topics. A few committees, such as finance, European affairs, and, since 2011, gender equality, address topics across policy areas. Almost all bills and proposals of motions for resolution are referred to a parliamentary committee after the first reading in parliament. Generally, proposals go to the floor if the proposers want it to, and, hence, committees do not function as veto points in the legislative process. The ad hoc committees before 1972 only dealt with one bill or a specific number of bills at a time and were then dissolved. Under the Constitution of 1953 MPs can put individual questions to ministers but the 'new' permanent committees also acquired powers for committee members to ask (written) questions, via the committees on matters not only related to bills, and request the presence of the responsible minister for a consultation in a closed meeting concerning matters within the sphere of competence of the committee. This change strengthened the oversight powers by giving committee members the possibility of putting questions to ministers in matters not related to bills under scrutiny by the committee and also allowed for specialization.

Ordinary committee meetings are not open to the public. In 2009, open consultations with ministers became an option and have since then become more frequent than the closed consultations (Christiansen & Skjæveland 2016). Members of the parliamentary committees can also access information through committee hearings where experts or interest groups are invited to discuss matters of interest. These are usually open to the public and media. Since 1973, it has been a common practice that opposition parties hold some of the committee chair positions; but it was not until after 2015 that the practice of the opposition parties having a share of the committee chairs became part of the standing orders of the Folketing.

According to Damgaard (1977), the argument for the 1972 reform was primarily to handle the increased workload of more proposals with a more complicated content, through increased specialization.[4] In a minor reform in 2011, the 'standard' number of committee members increased from 17 to 29, and committee members no longer had alternates, although there are committees with other numbers of members. The enlargement meant that even very small parties were more likely to have seats on all committees since committee memberships are distributed among parties proportionally[5] but it also meant that MPs became full members of more committees while at the same time no longer being alternate members.

Hansen (2013: 459) reports that, between 1994 and 2007, 23 percent of MPs with a committee assignment, left a committee during an electoral term, and usually got replaced by another member of the same party group, while Jensen (2002: 33), who calculated changes within five months, found a turnover about 12 percent. These numbers indicate that the majority of committee members stay on the committee for enough time to become specialized. Damgaard (1977) and Jensen (1995) observe 'sectorization' and 'segmentation' of the parliamentary committees, e.g. with an overrepresentation of teachers on the education committee. Yet, the educational background of

MPs may have changed since then, affecting this relationship. Committees are assigned to MPs by party group leadership who take individual wishes into account (Jensen 2002; Hansen 2019).

The higher number of parliamentary committee seats diverges very much from Norway, where each MP is member of exactly one committee, and a reduction of the number of members has been debated by parliamentarians (Folketinget 2015: 15). Danish MPs, who are members of many parliamentary committees, may instead focus their work on one or two committees. Jensen (1995; 2002; 2003; 2014; 2018) as well as Jensen and Damgaard (2006) consider the Danish parliamentary committees as arenas for party group interaction in policy matters and not actors in their own right; in contrary to parties and party groups, committees have no policy and are composed of representatives from different party groups. Parliamentary committee chairs are not leaders but rather *primus inter pares* whose influence should not be overestimated; they have almost no influence on the composition of the committees, hiring of staff, or the policy stands of committee members from other party groups. In policy matters, committees generally work as institutions or arenas in the sense that they have structural effects on party groups and can be used as instruments for committee members' political purposes (Jensen 1995).

The realities of legislative committees, policy-making and legislative agreements

Turning to the answers to the questions already stated, we shall try on a one-by-one-basis to throw some light on important aspects of the relations between parliamentary committees, legislative agreements, and party groups under minority government in a Danish context.

What is the role of parliamentary committees in party group bargaining of legislative agreements under minority government?

It is often assumed that parliamentary committees are venues for the negotiation of legislative agreements – but the reality is, they are not. It seems that only for a short period in the 1970s, after the general introduction of permanent committees, the parliamentary committees have been an instrument for bargaining among party group representatives. Thus, Frandsen (2006: 320), who was an MP for many years, including the early 1970s, mentions that back then actual policy negotiations did take place at committee meetings. He adds that this is not the case anymore and has not been so for a long time (Frandsen 2006: 320). This finding was backed up by a questionnaire among MPs at the beginning of the 1990s: 160 out of the 179 MPs – ministers were not included – were asked to participate in the survey, which 156 did (97.5 percent.). They were presented with the statement, 'The decisive political negotiations on bills and motions for resolutions far more often takes place outside the committee meetings than at the meetings'. No less than 97.4 percent (151) of the 155 MPs answering this question (one MP skipped the question) agreed completely or partly (Jensen 1995: 116; 170). Attendance of some 400 to 500 committee meetings in the late 1980s and the 1990s of one of the authors (H.J.) *qua* a position as committee secretary does in no way collide with this picture; on the contrary. A recent analysis of patterns of bargaining and deliberation in the Folketing, based on interviews with a group of former spokespersons reaches a similar conclusion. Committee meetings are not venues for bargaining of legislative agreements among party groups (Andersen 2019). Thus, actual policy negotiations on legislation are rare or absent in parliamentary committee meetings. Parliamentary committees do not fulfil a role as a venue for bargaining of legislative agreements. Even when all parties take part in a legislative agreement, the committees do not provide the setting for interparty negotiations.

The main argument explaining the absence of bargaining at committee meetings is just as short as it is strong. Jens Peter Christensen, a supreme court justice, professor of constitutional law and former academic secretary to a minister, has put it nicely: 'No reasonable politician would include participants in negotiations who are not likely to be part of an agreement. That would only make it more difficult or even in practice make it impossible if friends and foes alike are present at the table' (Folketinget 2015). For instance, Claus Hjort Frederiksen, MP (Liberals), an experienced former minister of finance, labour and defence, has stated that: 'The committees span from Liberal Alliance to the Red–Green Alliance. You do not expose yourself with all kind of matters when they are all present' (Klöcker-Gatzwiller & Slabiak 2015). Another argument pointing in the same direction is that parliamentary committees are usually staffed with only one or two academic secretaries. This means that they do not possess capacity to provide the necessary support for bargaining.

When bargaining of legislative agreements does not take place at committee meetings, it would be tempting to think that the parliamentary committees play no role in such bargaining at all. However, *ceteris paribus*, the parliamentary committees do play a role in legislative bargaining in two ways. Firstly, the parliamentary committees invisibly contribute to legislative bargaining because the division of labour inside party groups reflects the division of labour among the committees. Parliamentary committees thereby help to bring together representatives from the party groups, in particular the spokespersons who are active in the same policy areas and potentially involved in the bargaining process. Secondly, party groups that are not part of a legislative agreement are typically not part of the bargaining process. They therefore do not enjoy the privilege of accessing information directly from the minister and his civil servants as part of the bargaining process. They will depend on the committee as a slower and less efficient instrument for acquiring information on the policy matters in question by putting questions to the minister via the committee. Against that background, one may ask where, if any place, does the bargaining of legislative agreements take place?

In what settings are legislative agreements negotiated?

In principle, interparty bargaining between MPs can take place anywhere whenever representatives from two party groups are in contact with one another. For instance, a minister and a spokesperson may bargain on Danish legislation at a UN conference in New York City. However, in practice, policy negotiations on legislative agreements typically take place inside the ministries, which, in spite of the fact that most of them are more or less next door to the parliament, are far more suited as venues for negotiations than the committee rooms. Ministers, who usually host negotiations, have *qua* their position direct access to the legal and substantial expertise of their civil servants, who are necessary for drafting and finalizing legislative agreements. Drafting legislation, estimating effects of possible changes of legislation, judging whether possible political solutions and their likely effects are legally and economically defensible etc., are usually complicated matters. The knowledge of such matters, by and large, rests with the civil servants, and it is quite common that they are present at the meetings in the ministries and assist ministers in their negotiations with other party group representatives. It is also common to expect ministers, at least experienced ministers, to be able to lead the process of bargaining and make sure that a legislative agreement is reached. But how common are legislative agreements?

How common are legislative agreements?

Christiansen (2008) researched the development under the Constitution of 1953 up until 2005. He found that an average of 17 percent of all laws result from from such agreements, and that the share has increased over time, reaching about 30 percent of all laws in 2005.

Further projections show that the share has increased since then (Klöcker-Gatzwiller & Slabiak 2015; Nielsen & Kretchmar 2016). They concern the most important parts of the legislation which is in particular the case when these laws result from multi-issue agreements, which account for about 15 percent of all laws (Christiansen 2005).

How does legislative bargaining affect the sharing of information among MPs?

Thanks to their staff of civil servants, a government and its ministers have better access to information than parliament. Yet, party group representatives involved in a legislative agreement may have increased possibilities for access to information controlled by the government compared with MPs from opposition parties that are not part of such agreements. Thus, Riis (2012) concludes that parties as members of legislative agreement have increased access to information and that they hold meetings, regular or ad hoc, with the minister. Klöcker-Gatzwiller & Slabiak (2015) come to a similar conclusion.

When parties negotiate over legislative agreements, they show an increased interest in collecting information. Morten Østergaard, MP (Social Liberals), former deputy PM and minister of interior and economics, and former leader of the Social Liberals, states:

> When the same people who quarrel in a parliamentary committee meeting enter the meeting room of the minister, then they actually try to get factual information about the topics and to search for joint solutions. In the group of parties in a legislative agreement, you typically also follow the content of the agreement consecutively. Whenever you negotiate over something of real value, and you have a shared responsibility for the result, then it works. Both partners should have something at stake.
>
> (Folketinget 2015)

According to Mikkel Dencker, MP (Danish People's Party) between 2001 and 2019, as an MP, you are in a much better position when you are part of a legislative agreement. As his party's spokesperson on energy, he recalls to having met with a minister and his or her civil servants about once a month for one to two hours. Dencker states:

> You have the great advantage of getting access to information and also access to discuss in deep details how to implement the policy agreement. You have a discussion and negotiation about how to do it, and it is an advantage to have access to the civil servants. ... It is possible to get a point on the agenda for the meeting, and to get technical information. You cannot just ask for major analyses but you can get oral orientation and also shorter notes.
>
> (Folketinget 2015)

Unlike previously, civil servants are not allowed to appear in parliamentary committees without the presence of the ministers, neither for hearings where other experts, typically academics or from interest groups, are invited. In a letter from Christian Kettel Thomsen, the permanent secretary to the prime minister, to the permanent secretaries of the other ministries, he confirms this practice with the argument that it would blur accountability relations.[6] Hence, ministries tend to close down information to the parliamentary committees, except information that is supplied in questions and consultations. It implies that if the minister does not want to show up, the civil servants cannot provide the information to the parliamentary committee.

Meetings in a group of parties that have reached a legislative agreement also typically take place within the ministry in question. Jeppe Bruus, MP (Social Democrats) states:

> We meet at the ministry who sets the agenda. This is where the real work with and discussion about policy takes place. Some parties are not at

the table, and will not get there. The questions, we ask there, and the calculations, we ask for, they stay with the bargaining parties.
(Klöcker-Gatzwiller & Slabiak 2015)

Thus, information is of value in the bargaining process.

Parliamentary committees are entitled to ask questions. Could they then obtain information similar to that from parties in a legislative agreement? Some MPs point out that you need the knowledge necessary to seek knowledge and ask the right questions. Karsten Lauritzen, MP (Liberals), mentions that ministries are very reluctant to provide precise answers unless the questions are very specific and that it may require further questions, and hence further effort, to get to the bottom of matters. There are also several MPs among our sources, who mention that it requires strong analytical capacity to match the ministries, and the Folketing is not in any way evenly matched to do that (Klöcker-Gatzwiller & Slabiak 2015).

Frandsen (2006) notes that opposition parties usually do not ask parliamentary questions on issues where they have a legislative agreement with the government. This could be because they have better informal access to information through a legislative agreement system. Asking questions through the parliamentary committee is sometimes considered a conflictual activity, and it is part of the logic of a legislative agreement that the government has gained some freedom from criticism in return for policy influence (Christiansen & Seeberg 2016).

What is the role of parliamentary committees in parliamentary control with minority governments?

Since the reform of 1972, committee activities have grown in some regards both in numbers and scope, and have also changed partly in character. The number of parliamentary committee meetings has remained relatively stable, around 600 to 800 meetings each year (Folketinget 2020). However, the number of documents processed has risen from a level of around 5,000 annually in 1972 to a level between 35,000 and 45,000 over the most recent years. So, there has not been a decline in activity in parliamentary committees – on the contrary. Roughly speaking, more 'paper' has been spread electronically in the committees and increased the committee members' information load, indicating that large parts of the committee activity are not part of the committee meetings.

The number of bills has for years been at a steady level of 200 to 250. The number of (written) committee questions rose from about 4,500 on annual average (1972–1982) to 12,500 (2003–2015). The number of consultations with ministers increased from about 500 to a peak of 1,100 (2009–2010) – the first parliamentary year of open consultations – to 321 (2019–2020) of which 240 were open (Folketinget 2020).

Committees in the Danish Folketing 73

Thus, for the committees' role of parliamentary control with ministers and government, a general distinction is made between activities related to the committees' reading of bills and other types of committee activities called 'common part' ('*almindelig del*'). As activities related to the committees' reading of bills is part of the legislative activity, parliamentary control activities are to be found with 'common part' activities, in particular for putting questions to ministers. Most of these questions are generally not put at a committee meeting but are put by individual committee members via the committee's secretaries. From 1992 to 1993, less than 14 percent of the questions and 5 percent of the consultation questions were put in relation to committee meetings (Jensen 1995: 84). In other words, and well in line with the conception of committees as arenas and not actors per se, the committees as such generally do not question ministers, but rather are used as institutional instruments by individual members.

If one asks which party groups on a committee poses the questions, the short answer is the party groups outside government and in particular opposition party groups. In the parliamentary spring session of 1992, less than 4 percent of the questions were put by committee members of the government coalition parties (the Conservative Party and the Liberals), and about 75 percent were put by the two opposition party groups (Social Democrats and Socialist People's Party) (Jensen 1995: 89). A more recent picture of a single committee (the Committee on Environment and Food) around 2015 shows roughly the same pattern. Committee members of the government party group (the Liberals) did not put any questions at all while committee members of two opposition party groups (Red–Green Alliance and the Socialist People's Party) put two-thirds of the questions (Jensen 2018: 125). Looking at who inside the party groups put the questions, the party groups' spokespersons tended to be particularly active by putting 60 percent or more of the questions within their own party groups (Jensen 2018: 125). Thus, parliamentary control in the shape of questions is first and foremost carried out by the opposition party groups' committee members and, among these, primarily by their spokespersons.

As mentioned, questions and consultations may concern control ('*almindelig del*') or legislation (bills). From 2004–2005, almost 50 percent of the questions asked by the committee concerned legislation – but this number has dropped to about 20 percent around 2015 (Nielsen & Kretschmar 2016). Part of this change is most likely explained by procedural changes allowing some of the questions asked in the plenary, typically not about bills, to be put through the parliamentary committees. Nevertheless, the absolute number has fallen from around 5,500 to a little less than 3,000 concerning bills. These numbers indicate that committee activity related to the legislation process has reduced significantly.

When it comes to consultations related to control or *almindelig del*, an unknown part of this pattern is most likely to be seen as media-related 'advertising' and 'position taking' (Mayhew 1974). The relation between consultations and media is complicated and hard to analyse and depends in principle on the motives for demanding consultations with ministers. Nonetheless, at a time when consultations were closed to the public, no less than 92 percent of the MPs in a questionnaire pointed to the media as the most frequent source for committee questions (Jensen 1995: 80). Open doors and televised consultations at the committee meetings, along with the fact that the questioner – not the minister – chooses the subject of the consultation and, possibly, confrontation, are strong incentives for 'advertising' and 'position taking'.

Conclusion

The chapter has studied legislative bargaining in Danish parliamentary committees. The diverse evidence collected, both qualitatively and quantitatively, unequivocally points to the conclusion that parliamentary committees are not settings of actual policy negotiations. This stands contrary to expectations in much of the current literature but in line with other contributions in this volume. As a parliamentary democracy dominated by minority government, and having permanent parliamentary committees, Denmark is a setting where we should expect a strong legislative influence of opposition parties and their MPs *via committees*. Our chapter questions and qualifies these assumptions. Policy influence by party groups outside government is primarily reached through legislative bargaining that does not take place within parliamentary committees. It is generally played out in the ministries where ministers from the minority governments build up majorities and make legislative agreements with representatives from some, usually not all, opposition party groups by offering them policy influence and access to legislative information as part of the legislative agreements. Party groups participating in legislative agreements may also get the opportunity to monitor the implementation of policies of the legislative agreements. Party groups outside the legislative agreements do not have these advantages and are dependent on questioning of ministers, and hence on the committees as a formal and less efficient instrument for information-gathering. The control activities in the shape of questions are first and foremost carried out by non-cabinet parties (ct. Martin & Vanberg 2011); and when it comes to questions related to policy deals or legislative agreements, by the opposition parties that are not part of the policy deals.

Another relation between committees and legislative agreements is also to be noticed. The decreasing importance of legislative activity in parliamentary committees appears to be a possible effect of the increase in the legislative agreement as party groups behind the agreement are not dependent on the committees as an instrument for the gathering of information.

With legislative agreements, the opposition parties taking part in the agreements attain privileges compared to parties outside agreements who will be dependent on parliamentary committees. These have in turn increased in size, are not used as venues for policy deliberations, less often used for questioning ministers about legislation, but are still active and to a higher degree used as instruments for control and criticism of the government. A division of labour seems to exist between the two settings of parliamentary committees and legislative agreements but this division of labour is not politically neutral. It benefits the government – which is accountable to parliamentary scrutiny though – and the opposition parties that are invited to negotiate with the government.

Hence, it is not in the committee per se where opposition parties find a policy differential to make them stay in opposition (cf. Strøm 1990). Rather, it is found with legislative agreements that look like an informal yet highly institutionalized mechanism for minority governance. From this conclusion, we cannot rule out the potential power of parliamentary committees with regard to amendment and veto that impacts the government's willingness to negotiate with the opposition. Yet, in practice, parliamentary committees do not contest legislation against parties' wishes.

Notes

1 As an example, this norm was respected by five other and larger party groups forming a huge majority when the Conservatives in 2014, with only eight seats, vetoed a proposal about mandatory after-school workshops.
2 One of the authors of this chapter (H.J.) took part in this 2015 conference. In 2017, a follow-up conference took place, resulting in initiatives to put up a standard for 'good open consultation meetings (Folketinget, 2017). None of the authors participated.
3 These studies were BA and MA theses; one of the authors of this chapter (F.J.C.) was academic supervisor for Klöcker-Gatzwiller & Slabiak (2015).
4 Two former prime ministers, Anker Jørgensen (Social Democrat, PM 1971–1973 and 1975–1982) and Poul Schlüter (Conservative, PM 1982–1993), who were both elected since the election of 1964, agreed in a double interview that the new committee system had had the effect that every MP, even newly elected, took part in the party group's parliamentary work because they were elected to at least one committee (Jubilæumsbogen, 1989). Several MP memoirs about the time before 1972 records that back then freshmen rarely became spokesperson or received the ad hoc committee assignments.
5 Technically, the party groups form electoral alliance when this happens. Thereby, parties even too small to obtain a seat with their own votes, get seats nevertheless. The party Common Course, in parliament 1987–1988 with four seats, did not take part in such an electoral group and were only entitled to a minimum of seats guaranteed to a party group by the standing order of the Danish parliament.
6 Klöcker-Gatzwiller & Slabiak (2015) gained access to the letter on request from the prime minister's office. This clarification took place after the Ministry of Justice had opened somewhat again for letting civil servants provide relevant information at some thematic meetings with the members of parliamentary committee. However, it is not clear whether this triggered the letter.

References

Andersen, A.H.S. (2019). Deliberativt demokrati i Danmark? En analyse af beslutningsprocessen i Folketinget i et forhandlings- og deliberationsteoretisk perspektiv. Århus: University of Aarhus: Master's thesis.
Bagehot, W. (1964 [1867]). *The English Constitution*. London: Watts.
Berlingske Politiko (2015). Kritik: Politiske visioner er en kæmpe mangelvare på Christiansborg, December 15.
Bille, L. (1989). Denmark: The Oscillating Party System, *West European Politics*, 12(4): 42–58.
Bille, L. (2000). A Power Centre in Danish Politics. In Knut Heidar & Ruud Koole (eds.), *Parliamentary Party Groups in European Democracies: Political parties behind closed doors*. London: Routledge, 130–144.
Bischoff, C.S. (2020). New Parties: Game Changers or 'Much Ado About Nothing'?. *Scandinavian Political Studies*, 43(2), 80–89.
Bryce, J. (1921). *Modern Government*. New York: Macmillan.
Christiansen, F.J. (2005). Aftaler på tværs af sektorer i Folketinget. *Politica*, 37(4), 423–439.
Christiansen, F.J. (2008) *Politiske Forlig i Folketinget. Partikonkurrence og samarbejde*. Aarhus: Politica.
Christiansen, F.J. & Pedersen, R.B. (2012). The Impact of EU on the Coalition Formation in a Minority System: The Case of Denmark. *Scandinavian Political Studies*, 35(3), 179–197.
Christiansen, F.J. & Pedersen, H.H. (2014). Minority Coalition Governance in Denmark. *Party Politics*, 20(6): 940–949.
Christiansen, F.J. & Seeberg, H.B. (2016). Cooperation between counterparts in parliament from an agenda-setting perspective: Legislative coalitions as a trade of criticism and policy. *West European Politics*, 39(6), 1160–1180.
Christiansen, F.J. & Skjæveland, A. (2016). Folketinget. In J.C. Christensen, & J. Elklit, (eds.). *Det demokratiske system* (4. ed.). Copenhagen: Hans Reitzels Forlag), 94–129.
Cox, G.W., & McCubbins, M.D. (1993). *Legislative Leviathan: Party Government in the House*. Berkeley: University of California Press.
Damgaard, E. (1977). *Folketinget under forandring*. Copenhagen: Samfunds videnskabeligt Forlag.
Damgaard, E. (1994). 'The Strong Parliaments of Scandinavia: Continuity and Change of Scandinavian Parliaments'. In G.W. Copeland & S.C. Patterson (eds.) *Parliaments in the Modern World: Changing Institutions*. Ann Arbor: The University of Michigan Press.), 85–103.
Damgaard, E. (1980). The Function of Parliament in the Danish Political System: Results of Recent Research, *Legislative Studies Quarterly*, 5(1), 101–121.
DJØF-Bladet (2016) Farvel til Christiansborgs kadaverdisciplin, January 13.
Elgie, R. (ed.) (2001). *Divided Government in Comparative Perspective*. Oxford: Oxford University Press.
Elgie, R., & Stapleton, J. (2006). Testing the decline of parliament thesis: Ireland, 1923-2002. *Political Studies*, 54(3), 465–485.
Fisher, R., Ury, W.L., & Patton, B. (2011). *Getting to yes: Negotiating agreement without giving in*. Penguin.

Folketinget (2015). Referat fra plenumdelene af konferencen. Præsidiets konference om arbejdet i Folketingets udvalg i Landstingssalen den 4. februar 2015. Copenhagen: Folketinget.
Folketinget (2017). *Året der gik i Folketinget 2016–17.* Copenhagen: Folketinget.
Folketinget (2020). *Året der gik i Folketinget 2019–20.* Copenhagen: Folketinget.
Frandsen, A. (2006). *Politik i praksis.* Copenhagem: Jurist- og Økonomforbundets Forlag.
Frandsen, A. (2008). *Lovgivningsprocessen i praksis.* Copenhagen: Jurist- og Økonomforbundets Forlag.
Green-Pedersen, C. (2001). Minority Governments and Party Politics: The Political and Institutional Background to the 'Danish Miracle. *Journal of Public Policy,* 21(1), 53–70.
Hansen, M.E. (2013). Understanding change in committee assignments between elections: Evidence from the Danish case. *Journal of Legislative Studies,* 19(4), 450–466.
Hansen, M.E. (2019). Distributing Chairs and Seats in Committees: A Parliamentary Perspective. *Parliamentary Affairs,* 72(1), 202–222.
Hansen, T.K. (2009). Medier og topstyring i danske demokratier. En analyse af betydningen af interaktionen mellem medier og partier for graden af topstyring i partierne. Aarhus University: Master's thesis
Jensen, H. (1995). *Arenaer eller aktører? En analyse af Folketingets stående udvalg.* Frederiksberg: Samfundslitteratur.
Jensen, H. (2002). *Partigrupperne i Folketinget.* Copenhagen: Jurist- og Økonomfor bundets Forlag.
Jensen, H. (2003). *Europaudvalget – et udvalg i Folketinget.* Aarhus: Aarhus University Press.
Jensen, H. (2014). *Finansudvalget. Bag lukkede døre.* Copenhagen: Jurist- og Økonomforbundets Forlag.
Jensen, H. (2018). *Minister. Mellem ministerium og Folketing.* Copenhagen: DJØF Forlag.
Jensen, H. & Damgaard, E. (2006). Assessing strength and weakness in legislatures: The case of Denmark. *Journal of Legislative Studies,* 12(3–4), 426–442.
Klöcker-Gatzwiller, A. & Slabiak, M. (2015). Kampen om information mellem Folketinget og regeringen. Roskilde University: Project thesis.
Koch, P.B. (2016). Forliget fortrænger folketingsbehandlingen, *Altinget,* February 29.
Krehbiel, K. (1991). *Information and Legislative Organization.* Ann Arbor: The University of Michigan Press.
Larsen, C.A. & Andersen, J.G. (2004). *Magten på borgen. En analyse af beslutningsprocesser i større politiske reformer.* Århus: Aarhus Universitetsforlag.
Loftager, J. (2004). *Politisk offentlighed og demokrati i Danmark.* Århus: Aarhus Universitetsforlag/Magtudredningen.
Longley, L.D. & Davidson, R.H. (1998). Parliamentary Committees: Changing Perspectives on Changing Institutions. *Journal of Legislative Studies,* 4(1), 1–20.
Martin, S. (2014). 'Committees'. In Martin, S., Saalfeld, T., and Strøm, K.W. (eds.), *The Oxford Handbook of Legislative Studies.* Oxford: Oxford University Press, 352–368.
Martin, L.W. & Vanberg, G. (2011). *Parliaments and Coalitions. The Role of Legislative Institutions in Multiparty Governance.* Oxford: Oxford University Press.

Mayhew, D. (1974). *Congress: the electoral connection.* New Haven: Yale University Press
Mayhew, D. (1991). *Divided We Govern. Party Control, Lawmaking, and Investigations 1946–1990.* New Haven/London: Yale University Press.
Nielsen, M.M. & Kretschmar, L.K. (2016). Udviklingen i den danske lovgivningsproces. En analyse af lovgivningsprocessens demokratratiske legitimitet og kvalitet. Roskilde University: Master's thesis.
Pedersen, H.H. (2011). Etableringen af politiske forlig som parlamentarisk praksis. *Politica*, 43(1), 48–67.
Politiken (2015) Partierne styres som religiøse sekter, October 9.
Politiken (2016) Radikal: Mørklægning i kvælstofsag er magtfordrejning, July 14.
Raiffa, H. (1982). *The Art and Science of Negotiation.* Cambridge, MA: Harvard University Press.
Riis, M.S. (2012). Forligsindgåelsen i Folketinget. En analyse af perioden efter forligsindgåelsen. Aarhus University: Master's thesis.
Rommetvedt, H. (1998). Norwegian Parliamentary Committees: Performance, Structural Change and External Relations. *Journal of Legislative Studies*, 4(1), 60–84.
Rommetvedt, H (2003). *The Rise of the Norwegian Parliament.* London: Frank Cass.
Seeberg, H.B. (2013). The opposition's policy influence through issue politicisation". *Journal of Public Policy*, 33 (1), 89–107. Strøm, K. (1990). *Minority Government and Majority Rule.* Cambridge: Cambridge University Press.
Strøm, K. (1984). Minority governments in parliamentary democracies: The rationality of nonwinning cabinet solutions. *Comparative Political Studies*, 17(2), 199–227.
Strøm, K. (1990). *Minority Government and Majority Rule.* Cambridge: Cambridge University Press.
Strøm, K. (1998)." Parliamentary Committees in European Democracies". *Journal of Legislative Studies*, 4 (1), 21–50.
Strøm, K. (2003) 'Parliamentary Democracy and Delegation' in Strøm, K. & Müller, W. C. (eds.), *Delegation and Accountability in Parliamentary Democracies.* Oxford: Oxford University Press, 55–106.
Warren, M.E., Mansbridge, J., & Bächtiger, A. (2013). Deliberative negotiation. *Negotiating agreement in politics* 86.
Wheare, K.C. (1963) *Legislatures.* Oxford: Oxford University Press.
Worre, T. (1970). Partigrupperne i Folketinget. Et magtcentrum i dansk politik. *Økonomi og Politik*, 53, 143–188.

5 Committees in the Finnish Eduskunta

Cross-party cooperation and legislative scrutiny behind closed doors

Tapio Raunio

The Finnish political system is normally categorized as semi-presidential, with the executive functions divided between an elected president and a cabinet that is accountable to the Eduskunta, the unicameral national legislature. However, the new Constitution,[1] which entered into force in 2000, completed a period of far-reaching constitutional change that curtailed presidential powers and brought the Finnish political system closer to a normal parliamentary democracy. Cabinet formation is now based on partisan negotiations and the president is almost completely excluded from the policy process in domestic matters. European Union (EU) matters belong to the competence of the government, while foreign policy is co-led between the president and the government (Karvonen et al. 2016).

These constitutional changes mean that the Eduskunta is much more at the centre of things than before. However, Parliament's ability to influence policy and ensure government accountability is mitigated by EU membership and a tradition of strong coalition cabinets. This is where the committees come in. Like the other Nordic legislatures, the Eduskunta is more of a 'working parliament' and emphasis is on activities in its committees. According to Arter (1999: 211–217), the three criteria of a working parliament are a division of labour among parliamentary committees mirroring the jurisdictions of the respective ministries, standing orders that lift committee work above plenary sessions, and a work culture where MPs concentrate on legislative work instead of grand debates on the floor. Eduskunta decision-making is based on interaction between party groups and committees, with the latter also providing a key forum for deliberations and bargaining between political parties.

Drawing on interviews, parliamentary documents,[2] and existing research, this chapter provides an in-depth analysis of how the Eduskunta committees work and how influential they are within the Eduskunta and vis-à-vis the government. It starts by outlining the structure and formal competencies of the committees and then proceeds to examine the actual scrutiny performed by MPs in the committees. Behavioural indicators include legislative amendments, committee reports, number and types of experts heard by the committees, and votes and dissenting opinions expressed in the committees. Specific attention

DOI: 10.4324/9781003106579-5

is paid to the various outreach activities of the committees and to the roles of the Grand Committee, the Foreign Affairs Committee, and the Committee for the Future. This chapter argues that the Eduskunta committees wield more influence than previously estimated, but that this influence is difficult to capture through standard approaches used by parliamentary scholars.

Institutions, actors, and interactions

The committee system

The Eduskunta is undoubtedly an institutionalized legislature. Its internal structures have evolved gradually over the decades and party discipline is strong, with MPs expected to toe the party line in both the plenary and in the committees. Institutionalization also applies to committees, regarding both their jurisdictions and internal procedures (Forsten 2005; Helander et al. 2007).

The number of committees has remained quite stable, with an increase of only three after the Second World War. In 1991, two committees were abolished, and three new ones established. Committee jurisdictions were also reshuffled. As a result, the competencies of individual standing committees largely mirror the jurisdiction of the respective ministries. The number of ministries is currently 12, including the Prime Minister's Office. According to Section 35 of the constitution:

> For each electoral term, the Parliament appoints the Grand Committee, the Constitutional Law Committee, the Foreign Affairs Committee, the Finance Committee, the Audit Committee and the other standing Committees provided in the Parliament's Rules of Procedure. In addition, the Parliament appoints Committees ad hoc for the preparation of, or inquiry into, a given matter.

The Eduskunta currently has 17 permanent committees, including the Grand Committee which is the EU committee. The permanent committees are the Finance Committee (established in 1863), Legal Affairs Committee (1863), Commerce Committee (1863), Constitutional Law Committee (1907), Grand Committee (1907), Agriculture and Forestry Committee (1907), Social Affairs and Health Committee (1907), Education and Culture Committee (1908), Foreign Affairs Committee (1918), Transport and Communications Committee (1929), Defence Committee (1937), Administration Committee (1991), Employment and Equality Committee (1991), Environment Committee (1991), Committee for the Future (1993), Audit Committee (2007), and Intelligence Supervision Committee (2019). While the other committees are essentially appointed after each parliamentary election, the Intelligence Supervision Committee is established once the government has entered office after the parliamentary elections, unless the Eduskunta decides otherwise based on a proposal from the Speaker's Council. The Constitutional Law Committee is quite exceptional, as its principal function is to issue ex ante statements on the constitutionality of government bills and other matters. Therefore, it is supposed to be above 'party politics' and to base its opinions on legal evidence provided by expert witnesses (Lavapuro 2010).

According to the parliamentary rules of procedure, each permanent committee has 17 members and nine alternate members, apart from the Grand Committee (25 members and 13 alternate members), the Finance Committee (21 and 19), the Audit Committee (11 and six), and the Intelligence Supervision Committee (11 and two).[3] A committee has a quorum when at least two-thirds of its members are present, unless a higher quorum is specifically required for a given matter. The speaker of the Eduskunta or government ministers (who with certain exceptions serve simultaneously as MPs) do not sit on committees. Committees can establish sections or working groups for specific topics. The Finance Committee has eight permanent sections that prepare decisions for the whole committee. Each committee has a secretariat led by the committee secretary. Several committees have four clerks, whilst others, particularly those with broader jurisdictions, have more staff (six to ten). The secretariats draft the committee agendas, reports, and statements, compile the initial list of expert witnesses to be heard, and handle general matters related to committee organization and meetings.

Committees meet two to four times per week. The meetings are held behind closed doors unless specifically decided otherwise. This is regarded as a common feature of Nordic parliaments to emphasize the advantages of trust-based negotiation in closed settings in which opinion exchange and party-political bargaining can happen more easily among committee members. Normally only a condensed version of committee minutes, containing agenda items and related documents, participants, heard expert witnesses, and final decisions, is publicized after a meeting. The Eduskunta committees have increased the number of public meetings, but their number is still very small with notable variation between committees. Between 2008 and 2014, the committees held 44 public meetings, with 15 of these organized by the Committee for the Future. During the same time period, the total number of committee meetings was 10,246. In addition, committees held six public hearings related to citizens' initiatives (Seo 2017: 97–98).

Committee assignments

Each committee has a chair and a vice-chair, with the exception of the Grand Committee, which has a chair and two vice-chairs. Often, individual MPs act as the chair of the same committee for a long period, thereby leaving a strong imprint on its work. These positions are distributed between the party groups according to their respective seat shares (following the d'Hondt method). While the chair has some level of discretion when it comes to calling committee meetings, the committees essentially meet according to their established weekly schedules. Otherwise, the discretionary powers of committee chairs are limited. The committees decide, if needed, by majority and the goal is to arrive at unanimous decisions regarding matters of committee work and organization. The chair nonetheless performs an important function in building consensus, making sure that timetables are adhered to, and that committee operations proceed smoothly.

Eduskunta committees do not utilize rapporteurs. Party groups have their own coordinators or spokespersons in the committees that act as a link between the committee and the party group. Normally, the coordinators are more experienced MPs. The committee coordinators of governing parties, in particular, can be very influential in both the committees and in their party groups, making sure if needed that MPs are present and support the government proposals. Traditionally, female MPs have been under represented both among committee chairs and party group coordinators, but recent developments indicate a more even distribution between men and women (Forsten 2005; Holli 2014: 143–145). In the autumn of 2019, ten out of the 17 committees were chaired by female MPs, an all-time record (Siukola et al. 2020: 42).

Typically, an MP holds seats in two committees, or is a member in one or two committees and an alternate member in another committee. The committee assignments are for the four-year electoral period, but reassignments occur inside party groups during the electoral term. The composition of each committee reflects the relative strength of the parliamentary groups, although party groups can also be flexible and trade places between them. Within party groups, MPs are asked to indicate to the group leaders their preferred committees, and groups try as far as possible to accommodate such wishes. The procedures vary between parties. For example, after the 2003 elections, the Centre Party and the Social Democrats utilized a form in which MPs listed four preferred committees, National Coalition MPs submitted a list of five preferred committees via email, Left Alliance MPs expressed their preferences verbally to the group leaders, and assignments in the Swedish People's Party were based on discussions in the group (Forsten 2005: 108). Party groups' leaderships decide on the allocation of committee seats to their MPs, with formal votes as last resort.

Seniority, professional and educational background, policy expertise, and reputation or loyalty in the group explain both committee assignments and selection of committee chairs (Forsten 2005, Holli 2014: 136–140; Björk et al. 2018; Siukola et al. 2020). Constituency concerns also matter, with representatives seeking places on committees whose jurisdictions cover the interests of their geographical and/or sectoral constituencies (Raunio & Ruotsalainen 2018). Some committees, particularly those on Agriculture and Forestry, and Defence, have tended to attract mainly male MPs (Forsten 2005; Holli 2014; Siukola et al. 2020). Finance and Foreign Affairs have been regarded as the most prestigious committees, with Constitutional Law, Social and Health Affairs, and recently the Grand Committee counting among the more desired committees as well. The Legal Affairs and the Commerce committees have been seen as the least attractive and many first-time MPs were assigned to them (Wiberg & Mattila 1997; Forsten 2005, Holli 2014). MPs can develop considerable specialization through serving multiple electoral terms on the same committee, but obviously the length of service in the same committee depends on several factors, not least on the overall turnover of representatives and whether the MP had, upon entering the Eduskunta, received a place on her or his preferred committee. According to Forsten (2005: 134–135), only 11 percent of the MPs had served on the same committee for more than two electoral terms, while 3 percent had sat on the same committee for more than three electoral terms. Overall, more experienced MPs tend to navigate to more high-ranking committees.

Hearings

When processing the government's bills and other matters, the committees routinely hear experts that primarily represent the public sector and non-governmental organizations (NGOs). Normally, the selection of experts is fairly straightforward. The committees have their 'usual suspects' and the committee secretary draws up a list of who should be heard on any particular issue. Committee members can suggest additional names, and typically such additions are accepted. Often, only a few experts give evidence, although more complex matters may draw ten to 20 experts. In extreme cases (including the reform of social and health services during the 2015–2019 electoral term, see below), over 100 evidence-givers can be heard. Analysing the parliamentary data of committee consultations during 1997 to 2014, a total of 10,030 experts were heard by the committees in 2014 alone.[4] 60.5 percent were from the public sector (including the civil servants in the ministries responsible for the matters), 2.7 percent represented the private sector, whilst 27.4 percent came from the third sector, and 9.1 percent were academic experts (Seo 2017: 131).

Hearings are mostly held in closed committee rooms with tight time schedules and restricted modes of communication. The reliance on the 'usual suspects' limits the diversity of information received. For example, the Constitutional Law Committee relies on certain professors of law (Keinänen & Wiberg 2012), while Social Affairs and Health actively hears the views of the major labour market organizations. According to *Helsingin Sanomat*, the leading national daily newspaper, representatives from business and industry sectors were heard twice as often as trade union representatives between 1998 and 2013. That data also showed organized interest groups to be overall much more represented in parliamentary work than under-organized minorities or value-oriented NGOs.[5] In their survey of committee chairs and secretaries, Ahtonen and Keinänen (2012) found that civil servants from the ministry responsible for preparing the matter were seen to have the most influence on committee positions, followed by various independent experts such as academics. Least influential were representatives of NGOs and, perhaps surprisingly, business interests. Overall, actors with better resources tend to be more represented and, also, more influential. Holli and Saari (2009) and Siukola et al. (2020) in turn showed that women were heard less than men by the committees. Media and civil society activists have argued for the introduction of a transparent lobbyist registration system, but the Eduskunta has been reluctant to adopt such a lobby registry[6] (Seo 2017: 124–142; Seo & Raunio 2017: 626–627; Helander & Pekonen 2007: 81–98).

Apart from committee hearings, there are no processes allowing citizens or civil society actors to express their opinions on matters under committee deliberation. Nor have the Eduskunta committees commonly practised outbound trips for field investigation and public consultation. Committees do, however, travel abroad: between 1997 and 2004, committees made almost 300 trips abroad (Helander & Pekonen 2007: 99). The Citizens' Initiative, introduced in 2012, has somewhat increased parliamentary transparency since the committees have held open hearings when deliberating the initiatives that have reached the required threshold of 50,000 signatures. Overall, the Eduskunta committees' engagement with civil society is practised mainly through neo-corporatist channels of 'functional representation'; individual citizens beyond established organizations and professional experts can hardly influence the normal legislative process (for a more detailed analysis, see Seo 2017).

Decision-making and committee culture

The justification for committees meeting behind closed doors is to facilitate confidential exchange of views, both between parliamentary groups and between the legislature and the executive, which in turn should result in more informed and constructive decision-making. The 'Committee Manual' (see endnote 2) explicitly instructs MPs not to leak information about committee debates. Interview evidence indicates that MPs themselves appreciate the closed committee environment and there have been essentially no plans for changing to public committee meetings.

Committees are important fora for bargaining between parties of different ideological colours, including between the government and opposition. The fragmented party system, with no party winning more than 25 percent of the votes in recent elections, also facilitates consensual governance and ideological convergence between political parties. The debates are for the most part constructive and fact-based, but genuine party-political confrontations cannot be avoided. Yet, normally the government-opposition dynamic structures the debates and party discipline is strong (at least in law proposals or other matters contained in the government programme), with cabinet parties' MPs defending the government's proposals. MPs of cabinet parties seated on the committee can hold their own meetings if required. Particularly in more salient issues, the MPs of the party seated on the committee convene to discuss group positions, with the group coordinator on the committee in charge of such meetings. Inside whole party groups, members respect the autonomy of MPs seated on the committees and generally do not intervene in matters processed by the committees. Representatives have stated that there is not sufficient time for genuine debate (Pekonen 2011; Mykkänen 2010; Rinne 2020).

Committees reach decisions either by unanimity or by voting, but the goal is to arrive at unanimous decisions where possible. Votes must be held when MPs table dissenting opinions (officially 'objections' in the case of reports) to the committee reports and statements. Committee reports often contain a dissenting opinion, with the percentage of reports including one ranging from between approximately 30 percent in the early 1970s to 15 percent in 2001 (Helander & Pekonen 2007: 69–71). A more recent study that examined both reports and statements found that the number of dissenting opinions increased between the late 1990s and 2011, with over 20 percent of the reports and statements containing a dissenting view towards the end of the 2007–2011 electoral term (Mattila 2014: 128–130). The Defence Committee, Foreign Affairs Committee, and partially the Grand Committee have different decision-making cultures, as there the consensual approach prevails with hardly any formal votes taken. Interestingly, committee debates often find coalition partners questioning the government line – thus offering evidence for the Martin and Vanberg theorem (2011) about committees providing a forum for coalition parties to 'keep tabs' on one another.

Committees in the policy cycle

Strong formal rights in the shadow of majority governments

Procedurally, Eduskunta committees are vested with significant policy-influencing powers. Committee deliberations are a compulsory part of the legislative process, they precede the plenary stage, and committees must report to the plenary on all matters under consideration except private members' bills and motions. However, strong majority governments also enjoy majorities in the Eduskunta committees, with the consequence that committee influence is dependent on the cohesion of the governing parties' parliamentary groups. Should government bills encounter unexpected problems in the party groups or a committee of the Eduskunta, the government approaches their parliamentary groups about the matter. Often, this exchange occurs inside individual governing parties between the party leader or another minister and the chair of the parliamentary group. In other instances, the committee chair and party group spokespersons in the committee can be involved. Such exchanges are fairly routine, and the problems are more difficult to solve when the cabinet is not cohesive and/or the issue is not included in the government programme. If the issue at hand concerns the implementation of the cabinet programme, the PM or other ministers typically remind the MPs (on some occasions publicly) about their duty to respect the programme.

The parliamentary agenda has become busier over the decades and is essentially filled with the government's proposals and EU matters. In fact, committees must give priority to government bills and EU affairs in their meetings. Hence, committees have very limited possibilities to influence the agenda of the Eduskunta. Nonetheless, committees (and the whole Eduskunta) enjoy strong information rights. According to Section 47 of the constitution:

> The Parliament has the right to receive from the Government the information it needs in the consideration of matters. The appropriate Minister shall ensure that Committees and other parliamentary organs receive without delay the necessary documents and other information in the possession of the authorities. A Committee has the right to receive information from the Government or the appropriate Ministry on a matter within its competence. The Committee may issue a statement to the Government or the Ministry on the basis of the information.[7]

These constitutional provisions are very important in the sense that they prompt the government to providing the relevant information without any specific requests from the MPs. Moreover, the committees have on numerous occasions been alert when documents or information have not been delivered, reminding the government of its responsibilities. As in the case of crisis management and future reports (see below), the committees can also establish various ex ante and ex post reporting mechanisms.

The legislative process normally begins with a government proposal for a new law. Following a preliminary dispatch debate in the plenary, the law proposal is sent to one of the permanent committees that is designated as the committee responsible for producing a report on the matter, with other committee(s) submitting statements to the committee responsible for the issue. From 1980 to 1994, the committees wrote an average of 331 reports per year. Between 1995 and 2018 the corresponding number was 269. The Finance Committee and the Social Affairs and Health Committee produced the most reports. Regarding statements, until 1994, the committees wrote on average 69 per year. The corresponding figure for the period 1995–2018 was 306. In other words, after Finland joined the EU, the number of statements has quadrupled. In EU matters, the Grand Committee routinely bases its deliberations on statements from one or more permanent committees. Before EU membership, the Constitutional Law Committee delivered about 25 percent of the statements. After 1995, the distribution is much more even, but the Constitutional Law Committee nonetheless was still the most active committee in this regard.

Having heard experts, the committee conducts a general debate and tentatively decides on details. In the case of legislation, this includes going over a bill section by section. After a preliminary committee report has been produced, the final handling of the matter begins. As stated above, a vote must be held if the committee cannot reach unanimity and the minority can have its diverging views appended to the report. If the committee does not agree with the government's proposal, then it can rewrite bills, recommending to the plenary that the bill should be amended or even rejected. According to Helander and Pekonen (2007: 64–69), the committees have not hesitated to recommend amendments to the proposals: 34 percent of proposals were amended in 1951, in 1960 the share was 30 percent, and sank further to 20 (1972) and 17 percent (1983). In 1988, it grew to 28 percent and further to 44 percent (1993), and 48 percent (2001). Another study based on data from 2009 showed that committees recommended amendments to roughly half of the government proposals (Ahtonen et al. 2011).

As a general rule, the more complex the issue, the more likely the committees are to introduce changes to the bill proposals. Another factor that likely contributes to the increase in amended proposals is the deficient quality of the draft bills, with committees needing to correct various legal problems involved in the proposals. Overall, most of the amendments have been fairly minor or technical matters. Committee reports may also include a recommendation: if accepted by the plenary, the recommendation normally asks or requires the government to look into a particular question or monitor the implementation of a law. The number of such recommendations declined considerably between 1995 and 2011 (Mattila 2014: 128–129). Normally, committee scrutiny takes one or two months, but urgent matters can be dealt with in just a few days. However, the handling of major legislative reforms can easily take many months or even years (see below). Once the committee report has been published, it is sent to the plenary session, where it is subjected to two readings. During the first, the content of the bill is decided section by section. In the second, the bill is either approved or rejected with a simple majority, normally in line with the position of the committee responsible for the matter. At the end of the electoral period, bills are allowed to lapse, except for EU issues.

Finland has traditionally been categorized among countries in which opposition parties have a higher than average impact on government policy, not least through the committee system (Laver & Hunt 1992; Strøm 1990). More specifically, the now-defunct instrument of 'deferment rule' once empowered the opposition. According to this mechanism, one-third of MPs (67/200) could postpone the final adoption of an ordinary law until the next election, with the proposal adopted if a majority in the new parliament supported it. In 1987, the period of postponement was shortened to the next annual parliamentary session, with the whole mechanism abolished in 1992. The deferment rule partially explained the propensity to form oversized coalitions and contributed to the practice of inclusive, consensual decision-making that reduced the gap between the cabinet and opposition (Mattila 1997; Forestiere 2008).

Given the abolition of the deferment rule and broader constitutional changes, it is not surprising that, since the early 1990s, Finland has become a strongly executive-dominated polity (Raunio & Wiberg 2008). Nonetheless, as shown above, there is evidence that committees are not just rubber-stamping the government's proposals, but actually do alter the bill proposals. However, focusing only on legislative amendments may result in underestimating the policy influence of committees and parliaments (see Benton & Russell 2013; Russell & Cowley 2015). The remainder of this section thus uncovers further mechanisms through which committees exercise influence: the power of delay, ministerial hearings (EU affairs), refusal to be sidelined (foreign policy), and avoidance of myopia (the Committee for the Future).

Party disunity and the power to delay

According to the Parliament's rules of procedure, a 'Committee shall without delay deal with the matters referred thereto and, as the case may be, issue its report to the plenary session or its statement to another Committee'. But the meaning of 'without delay' is no simple matter; the more horizontal and salient the issue, the higher the number of experts giving testimony and the number of committees involved. Equally significant is party unity, as amending the government's proposals requires the backing of a committee majority, and opposition MPs need 'defectors' from cabinet parties to wield influence.

A recent illustration of this came during the 2015–2019 electoral term when Finland was governed by a centre-right coalition, led by Prime Minister Juha Sipilä, that brought together the Centre Party, the National Coalition, and the Finns Party (Blue Reform after the Finns split up in the summer of 2017). Previous cabinets had already failed to reorganize social and health services, and the issue became the clear top priority of the Sipilä government. The planned reform would have brought about a larger role for the private sector in delivering such services (a key objective for the National Coalition) and the introduction of directly elected regional councils (a key objective for the Centre, which wins most of its vote in the rural provinces). After considerable delay, the reform bill was finally introduced in the parliament in spring 2018, but by early 2019 the project had run into serious trouble in the Eduskunta, with some backbench MPs of the governing parties voicing strong criticism, indicating that they might not support the package. Finally, the project was buried in early March, with Sipilä immediately announcing the resignation of his government.

During the parliamentary processing of the bill, the governing parties were clearly agitated by the delays in the committees, with fingers pointing particularly at Krista Kiuru, the Social Democrat chair of the Social and Health Affairs Committee. Kiuru's committee continuously invited ever more evidence providers. The Constitutional Law Committee, chaired by Tuuli Lapintie from the Left Alliance, behaved in a similar fashion, seeking to hear more experts before producing its statement whilst expressing repeated concerns about the constitutionality of the reform bill. Kiuru and other opposition MPs may have been influential on the committees, but the delays would not have been possible without the (at least implicit) support of a sufficient number of MPs from the cabinet parties. A careful reading of the parliamentary standing orders and the 'Committee Manual' makes it clear that no committee chair can alone delay the processing of matters to the extent that was seen in connection with the social and health care reform package.

EU affairs and ministerial hearings

In the Eduskunta, the design of the EU scrutiny model was based on two features central to parliamentary culture: committees and strong information rights. In fact, the Eduskunta (2010: 14) itself has remarked that the scrutiny model was deliberately designed to resemble as much as possible the parliamentary procedures for processing domestic legislation. Regarding EU affairs, the only real difference is that the specialized committees report to the Grand Committee and not to the plenary. The goal was to guarantee the Eduskunta a position in EU decision-making that is as powerful as possible for any national legislature to maintain, with the parliament closely studying the work of existing scrutiny systems in national legislatures, particularly that of the Danish Folketing. When scholars have ranked the effectiveness of the various parliamentary EU scrutiny mechanisms, the Eduskunta has without exception been categorized as one of the strongest parliaments (e.g. Karlas 2012; Auel et al. 2015; Winzen 2017).

The emphasis of the EU scrutiny model is on giving directions to Brussels-bound ministers in the Grand Committee or the Foreign Affairs Committee. The former coordinates parliamentary work in EU affairs while the latter is responsible for EU foreign and security policy and treaty amendments. The Grand Committee is in a powerful position because it – and not the plenary – directs the government through specific mandates in EU affairs. The Grand Committee normally convenes on Wednesday and Friday afternoons. It has enjoyed high status in the Parliament since Finland joined the EU, and among its members are committee chairs and leaders of the party groups. The Eduskunta has explicitly and consistently stated that the main objective of the scrutiny system is the effective control of the government. The main procedural rules – relatively proactive engagement, delegation of scrutiny to specialized committees, strong information rights enshrined in the Constitution (primarily Sections 96 and 97), and confidential ministerial hearings in the Grand Committee – aim at facilitating government accountability. Inside the Eduskunta, European integration has further shifted the balance of power toward the committees that have a key role in scrutinizing EU matters. Roughly half of all matters handled by the committees are EU matters. European issues have therefore substantially increased the workload of most committees, which essentially means that MPs must be more selective in deciding which matters receive parliamentary attention.

The Grand Committee aims at unanimous decisions. The objective is to produce unanimous 'committee' opinions instead of decisions that pit the governing parties against the opposition.[8] However, the euro crisis at least temporarily changed the consensual mode of Grand Committee operations. Voting became more common, with the losing opposition minority adding its dissenting opinions to the committee statements. Much of this activity was explained by the strategies of the Finns Party.

The role of ministerial hearings deserves to be highlighted. When processing normal government bills, the other committees do not invite ministers to give evidence. The Grand Committee convenes, usually on Fridays, to hear ministers about Council or European Council meetings scheduled for the following week. In foreign and security policy matters, the ministerial hearings are in the Foreign Affairs Committee. The Grand Committee receives a report after the Council or the European Council meeting, and ministers must be also prepared to appear in the Grand Committee to explain any deviations from the given policy guidelines. In practice, the minister normally reports on the previous Brussels meeting when appearing in the Grand Committee. The PM has the obligation to inform the Grand Committee both beforehand and afterwards of European Council meetings, appearing before the committee the same way as other cabinet ministers do before Council meetings. If needed, the PM contacts the Grand Committee during the actual European Council meeting.

Ministerial hearings and active scrutiny of EU matters have arguably improved the overall dialogue between the government and the Eduskunta, thus strengthening parliamentary accountability also in domestic issues (Jääskinen 2000: 131–132). The hearings also force the ministers to study the issues more thoroughly than might otherwise be the case. Nonetheless, it must be stressed that the formulation of national EU policy is strongly government-driven, with the Eduskunta usually agreeing with the government's position. It is thus realistic to argue that instead of genuinely directing national EU policy, the Eduskunta sets constraints for government's European policy (Raunio 2015, 2016b).

Foreign and security policy: refusing to be sidelined

Foreign policy in turn offers an example of how a parliamentary committee can establish a strong position in a policy area often seen to be an almost exclusive domain of the executive (Raunio & Wagner 2017). The jurisdiction of the Foreign Affairs Committee covers general foreign and security policy, foreign trade, development cooperation, international treaties and organizations, peacekeeping operations and the EU's evolving common foreign and security policy. A real turning point was the 1987–1991 electoral term, when under the chairmanship of Markus Aaltonen, the committee began asserting its role in foreign affairs, demanding more reports from the government and issuing statements about them (until then the committee had merely discussed the reports), and hearing more experts. This proactive approach, which preceded the constitutional reforms that would a few years later give the government and the Eduskunta real powers in foreign policy, led to several conflicts between

President Mauno Koivisto and the Foreign Affairs Committee (Kallenautio 2007: 127–131; Meres-Wuori 2014: 135–150).

Under the new Constitution, the government is responsible for EU policy with foreign policy leadership shared between the president and the government (Section 93). The Foreign Affairs Committee considers EU issues pertaining to foreign and security policy, whilst according to Section 97, it 'shall receive from the Government, upon request and when otherwise necessary, reports of matters pertaining to foreign and security policy'. Constitutionally regulated access to information is of great importance for the Foreign Affairs Committee, which has not only insisted on the government fulfilling its reporting obligations but has also actively requested information from the cabinet. The formulation of the grand strategy document provides another important channel for ex ante parliamentary influence. Since 1995 it is titled the *Government Security and Defence Policy Report* and published roughly every four years. It provides an overall framework for subsequent foreign and security policy decision-making. The first reports were produced in the 1970s and 1980s by parliamentary defence committees where parties were represented based on their share of Eduskunta seats. Since 1995, the government has produced the reports, but the process is closely monitored by a parliamentary working group that brings together representatives from all Eduskunta parties. In the Eduskunta, the report is scrutinized carefully, with the Defence Committee submitting a statement to the Foreign Affairs Committee which produces a report on the issue for the plenary.

Committee involvement in crisis management operations is, in turn, based on a combination of ex ante and ex post instruments. The topic was particularly controversial in the 1990s, not least due to the changing security context and the associated move away from United Nations-authorized operations that had been a key dimension of national security policy. This period of politicization resulted in stronger participation rights for the Eduskunta and created a sense of 'ownership' among MPs toward crisis management. Not only does the government consult the Foreign Affairs Committee before each operation, the committee also receives information during the operations and ex post, for example, in the form of biannual crisis management overviews (Raunio 2018).

Overall, the agenda of the Foreign Affairs Committee is diverse and the Eduskunta essentially subjects the government to similar scrutiny in foreign policy as in other policy areas. In fact, it might be more appropriate to talk about regular cooperation between the government and the Eduskunta, with the cabinet seeking ex ante support from the Foreign Affairs Committee for its positions (Raunio 2016a).

Avoiding myopia

The final example of committee influence that is primarily indirect is the Committee for the Future. The decision to establish Government Reports on the Future and the Committee for the Future need to be understood in the context of the severe economic recession of the early 1990s following the collapse of the Soviet bloc. With the economic and political environment of Finland changing fast, there was broad support in the Eduskunta for the Committee for the Future. It was first appointed as a temporary committee in 1993 and became a permanent one in 2000, but many thought that it was simply unnecessary, believing existing standing committees could exercise long-term planning as part of their standard legislative scrutiny. Others rejected the idea of a permanent committee that had no legislative or budgetary duties (Arter 2000).

The Committee for the Future defines its mission as generating dialogue with the government on major future problems and opportunities. Its primary task is to prepare the response of the Eduskunta to the Government Report on the Future, which is presented once per electoral term. It also issues statements to the other committees about the national budget, the annual government report, and various 'future' matters when requested. Furthermore, it discusses future trends and related issues, analyses research and methodology focused on the future, and serves as the parliamentary body responsible for assessing technological development and its societal consequences. However, as the Committee for the Future proclaims on its website:

> the most important efforts are devoted to [the] Committee's own issues, its own projects. The power [to] decide its own agenda is one of the pillars of the strength of the Committee. 17 parliamentarians themselves stake out policy lines for the future. The time perspective is long and the scale of issues broad.[9]

Between 2000 and 2018, the committee produced 76 publications on a broad range of topics from gene- and nanotechnology to municipal democracy. The reports are usually extensive and thorough, exceeding 50, sometimes even 100 pages. The longer reports, often commissioned from external experts, are published as books, and are often praised for their quality.[10]

The Committee for the Future does not scrutinize legislative proposals and budgets, thus operating largely outside of the ordinary parliamentary process. Its working practices are also different.

It emphasises openness and inclusiveness: MPs can choose their projects, and depth is added to the preparation processes through open seminars, workshops, social media, and online discussions. Another distinct characteristic is a commitment to non-partisan, deliberative discussion. Moreover, its work is characterized by slowness and a liberal attitude toward schedules, as it does not need to follow the hectic pace of legislative processes. Hence, the Committee for the Future operates more like an academic seminar than a parliamentary committee. In addition to expert hearings, which are conducted in a more scientific style compared to standard committee hearings, the

Committee for the Future has made explicit use of future research methods like scenario-building.

The Committee for the Future can arguably be considered a moderate success. It has consolidated its position within the Eduskunta, and has also established a close and active relationship with the Prime Minister's Office, which is responsible for the national foresight system. The exact influence of the Committee for the Future is difficult to measure. On the one hand, it remains a 'harmless sideshow' quite detached from ordinary Eduskunta work, but, on the other hand, members can use their future-related knowledge in other committees and in their party groups. There is also evidence that the Committee for the Future has occasionally succeeded in influencing government programmes (Arter 2000, Boston 2017). Overall, the committee appears to be politically stronger vis-à-vis the government than inside the Eduskunta (Koskimaa & Raunio 2020).

Concluding discussion

This chapter has examined committees in the Finnish Eduskunta. The committee system has gradually evolved over the decades, and the working practices and 'committee cultures' have become firmly institutionalized. This makes it easier for MPs to switch between committees and, also, facilitates cooperation between individual committees. Finnish MPs seem largely satisfied with how committees function, and there have been essentially no demands for any major reforms.

Parliamentarians also appreciate the closed committee environment, which contributes to constructive bargaining between political parties, including between government and opposition parties. Traditionally, the Nordic countries have been noted for their inter-party cooperation across the ideological spectrum, and parliamentary committees provide an important forum for such cooperation. Finnish parliamentary culture does not appear conducive to embracing more transparency or participatory channels of influence. The Eduskunta focuses very much on controlling the government and specifically on scrutiny of government bills, not on 'reaching out' to citizens. There is a strong attachment to a traditional mode of representative democracy, and while the Citizens' Initiative might bring about a more participatory legislative culture in the long run, there persists a lukewarm attitude toward between-the-elections democratic innovations (Arter 2012; Seo 2017). This analysis has also shown that committee hearings are mainly dominated by 'usual suspects' at the expense of ordinary citizens and socially marginalized groups. Hence, committees could expand the scope of hearings by involving more diverse social sectors and enhancing engagement with the public (Seo 2017). Expert hearings could be opened to the public as a rule unless there is special reason for secrecy. Moreover, mechanisms like online consultation or 'E-Parliament' could be designed for citizens to submit their opinions to the committees.

Returning to the question found in the introductory chapter of this volume, are the Eduskunta committees the engine room or more like decoration? The Finnish polity is strongly government-driven. The cabinets are typically oversized coalitions that enjoy broad majorities in the Eduskunta. Unless party discipline breaks down, this essentially ensures that government bills are approved by committees with or without amendments. When government proposals encounter difficulties in the Eduskunta, the issues are normally solved inside or between party groups, seldom in actual committee meetings. Yet, this chapter has argued that focusing on amendments or other visible measures is not sufficient for capturing how committees or legislatures may influence government behaviour or national politics. Through ministerial hearings, the Grand Committee can impact the government's bargaining stances in EU institutions, while the Foreign Affairs Committee has through proactive measures managed to carve out an influential position for itself in Finland's external relations. Both EU affairs and foreign policy also illustrate the importance of ex ante and ex post reporting requirements. The Committee for the Future, in turn, has the potential to shape long-term developments in Finland. The exact influence of Eduskunta committees is difficult to estimate, but clearly any study of a legislature's policy influence must consider the variety of channels through which committees shape politics.

Notes

1 The Constitution of Finland, June 11, 1999 (731/1999, amendments up to 817/2018 included). An English translation is available at www.finlex.fi/en/laki/kaannokset/1999/en19990731.pdf (access: 26.10.2020).
2 Much of the information about committee and parliamentary procedures is from two sources: the Parliament's rules of procedure (Eduskunnan työjärjestys 17.12.1999/40 v. 2000); and the nearly 200-hundred page Committee Manual which contains detailed rules about committees (Valiokuntaopas 2015, Eduskunnan kanslian julkaisu 1/2015).
3 Section 35 of the Constitution specifies that the 'Grand Committee shall have twenty-five members. The Constitutional Law Committee, the Foreign Affairs Committee and the Finance Committee shall have at least seventeen members each. The other standing Committees shall have at least eleven members each. In addition, each Committee shall have the necessary number of alternate members'.
4 Data released by the Eduskunta. In the last parliamentary session of the electoral term (such as 2014), the number of governmental proposals is higher which increases the number of expert consultations.
5 Tuomas Peltomäki, 'HS-selvitys: Heitä eduskunta kuuntelee', Helsingin Sanomat, 28.4.2013.
6 Teija Sutinen, 'Eduskunta tuhoaa päivittäin tiedot talossa käyneistä vierailijoista – hävittäminen alkoi, kun oikeus määräsi tiedot julkisiksi', Helsingin Sanomat, 12.9.2017.
7 On the motion of a committee, the Speaker's Council may decide that information received by the committee is debated in the plenary. However, should that happen, the plenary will not make a formal decision on the matter.

8 These features caught the attention of a visiting delegation from the House of Commons. According to Matthew Kirk, the UK ambassador to Finland, the visitors were particularly struck by the strong consensus among Finnish politicians, the wide cooperation between the government and the opposition on EU affairs, and that in an otherwise transparent society such a large amount of parliamentary work was conducted behind closed doors. Annamari Sipilä, 'Suomen eduskunta antoi briteille mallia EU-asioiden käsittelyssä', Helsingin Sanomat 23.3.2005.
9 www.eduskunta.fi/EN/valiokunnat/tulevaisuusvaliokunta/Pages/default.aspx (access: 26.10.2020).
10 Personal interviews with MPs (Koskimaa & Raunio, 2020).

References

Ahtonen, R., & Keinänen, A. (2012). Sidosryhmien vaikuttaminen lainvalmisteluun — Empiirinen analyysi valiokuntakuulemisesta. *Edilex*, 2012(5).
Ahtonen, R., Keinänen, A., & Kilpeläinen, M. (2011). *Eduskunnan valiokuntien näkemys lainvalmistelutyön laadusta*. Helsinki: Oikeuspoliittisen tutkimuslaitoksen tutkimustiedonantoja 111.
Arter, D. (1999). *Scandinavian Politics Today*. Manchester: Manchester University Press.
Arter, D. (2000). The Model for Parliaments in the Future? The Case of the Finnish Committee for the Future. *Politiikka*, 42(3), 149–163.
Arter, D. (2012). The Finnish Eduskunta: Still the Nordic 'Vatican'? *Journal of Legislative Studies*, 18(3–4), 275–293.
Auel, K., Rozenberg, O., & Tacea, A. (2015). To Scrutinise or Not to Scrutinise? Explaining Variation in EU-Related Activities in National Parliaments. *West European Politics*, 38(2), 282–304.
Benton, M., & Russell, M. (2013). Assessing the Impact of Parliamentary Oversight Committees: The Select Committees in the British House of Commons. *Parliamentary Affairs*, 66(4), 772–797.
Björk, A., Paavola, J.M., & Vainio, A. (2018). *Sukupuolten tasa-arvon toteutuminen eduskuntatyössä ("Tasa-arvo eduskuntatyössä"). Kysely- ja haastattelututkimus 2018*. Helsinki: Eduskunnan kanslian julkaisu 1/2018.
Boston, J. (2017). *Governing for the Future: Designing Democratic Institutions for a Better Tomorrow*. Bingley: Emerald Publishing.
Eduskunta. (2010). *EU-asioiden käsittelyn kehittäminen Eduskunnassa: EU-asioiden käsittelyn kehittämistyöryhmän mietintö*. Helsinki: Eduskunnan kanslian julkaisu 1/2010.
Forestiere, C. (2008). New Institutionalism and Minority Protection in the National Legislatures of Finland and Denmark. *Scandinavian Political Studies*, 31(4), 448–468.
Forsten, T. (2005). *Valiokuntapeli eduskunnassa: Valiokuntajäsenyydet 1945–2002*. Turku: Turun yliopiston julkaisuja C:223.
Helander, V., & Pekonen, K. (2007). Eduskunnan vahvistuva valiokuntalaitos. In V. Helander, K. Pekonen, J. Vainio & T. Kunttu, *Valiokunnat lähikuvassa. Suomen eduskunta 100 vuotta, osa 7* (9–138). Helsinki: Edita.
Helander, V., Pekonen, K. Vainio, J., & Kunttu, T. (2007). Valiokunnat lähikuvassa. Suomen eduskunta 100 vuotta, osa 7 . Helsinki: Edita.
Holli, A.M. (2014). Sukupuoli, valta ja työnjako valiokunnissa. In T. Raunio & M. Wiberg (eds.), *Eduskunta: Kansanvaltaa puolueiden ja hallituksen ehdoilla* (132–149). Helsinki: Gaudeamus.

Holli, A.M., & Saari, M. (2009). *Sukupuoli eduskunnan asiantuntijakuulemisissa*. Helsinki: Sosiaali- ja terveysministeriö, tasa-arvoasiain neuvottelukunta, TANE-julkaisuja 11/2009.

Jääskinen, N. (2000). Eduskunta – Aktiivinen sopeutuja. In T. Raunio & M. Wiberg (eds.), *EU ja Suomi: Unionijäsenyyden vaikutukset suomalaiseen yhteiskuntaan* (114–134). Helsinki: Edita.

Kallenautio, J. (2007). Puolueettomuuspolitiikan linjalla kohti Euroopan unionia. In J. Kallenautio, T. Tiilikainen, T. Raunio, R. Paasilinna & I. Seppinen, *Kansainvälinen Eduskunta: Suomen eduskunta 100 vuotta, osa 11* (9–155). Helsinki: Edita.

Karlas, J. (2012). National Parliamentary Control of EU Affairs: Institutional Design after Enlargement. *West European Politics*, 35(5), 1095–1113.

Karvonen, L., Paloheimo, H., & Raunio, T. (eds.) (2016). *The Changing Balance of Political Power in Finland*. Santérus Academic Press, Stockholm.

Keinänen, A., & Wiberg, M. (2012). Perustuslakivaliokunta lausuntovaliokuntana ja asiantuntijoiden kuulijana. In *Oikeus*, 41(1), 86–106.

Koskimaa, V., & Raunio, T. (2020). Encouraging a longer time horizon: the Committee for the Future in the Finnish Eduskunta. *Journal of Legislative Studies*, 26(2), 159–179.

Lavapuro, J. (2010). Perustuslakivaliokunta perustuslain vartijana. In M. Wiberg (ed.), *Perustuslakihaasteet* (77–117). Helsinki: Edita.

Laver, M., & Hunt, W.B. (1992). *Policy and Party Competition*. New York: Routledge.

Martin, L.W., & Vanberg, G. (2011). *Parliaments and Coalitions: The Role of Legislative Institutions in Multiparty Governance*. Oxford: Oxford University Press.

Mattila, M. (1997). From Qualified Majority to Simple Majority: The Effects of the 1992 Change in the Finnish Constitution. *Scandinavian Political Studies*, 20(4), 331–345.

Mattila, M. (2014). Valiokuntalaitos. In T. Raunio & M. Wiberg (eds.), *Eduskunta: Kansanvaltaa puolueiden ja hallituksen ehdoilla* (pp. 119–131). Helsinki: Gaudeamus.

Meres-Wuori, O. (2014). *Valta ja valtiosääntö, Suomen ulko- ja turvallisuuspoliittinen valtajärjestelmä*. Helsinki: Unigrafia.

Mykkänen, J. (2010). Keskusteleva edustaminen ja luottamus eduskunnassa. *Politiikka*, 52(3), 219–233.

Pekonen, K. (2011). *Puhe eduskunnassa*. Tampere: Vastapaino.

Raunio, T. (2015). The Finnish Eduskunta and the European Union: The Strengths and Weaknesses of a Mandating System. In C. Hefftler, C. Neuhold, O. Rozenberg & J. Smith (eds.), *The Palgrave Handbook of National Parliaments and the European Union* (406–424). Basingstoke: Palgrave Macmillan.

Raunio, T. (2016a). Refusing to be Sidelined: The Engagement of the Finnish Eduskunta in Foreign Affairs. *Scandinavian Political Studies*, 39(4), 312–332.

Raunio, T. (2016b). The politicization of EU affairs in the Finnish Eduskunta: Conflicting logics of appropriateness, party strategy or sheer frustration? *Comparative European Politics*, 14(2), 232–252.

Raunio, T. (2018). Parliament as an arena for politicisation: The Finnish Eduskunta and crisis management operations. *The British Journal of Politics and International Relations*, 20(1), 158–174.

Raunio, T., & Ruotsalainen, T. (2018). Exploring the Most Likely Case for Constituency Service: Finnish MPs and the Change towards Personalised Representation. *Representation*, 54(1), 37–53.

Raunio, T., & Wagner, W. (eds.) (2017). Challenging Executive Dominance: Legislatures and Foreign Affairs. *West European Politics*, 40(1).

Raunio, T., & Wiberg, M. (2008). The Eduskunta and the Parliamentarisation of Finnish Politics: Formally Stronger, Politically Still Weak? *West European Politics*, 31(3), 581–599.

Rinne, J.M. (2020). *Deliberative Representation in Parliament*. Helsinki: University of Helsinki, Publications of the Faculty of Social Sciences 134 (2020).

Russell, M., & Cowley, P. (2015). The Policy Power of the Westminster Parliament: The "Parliamentary State" and the Empirical Evidence. *Governance: An International Journal of Policy, Administration, and Institutions*, 29(1), 121–137.

Seo, H.S. (2017). *Reaching Out to the People? Parliament and Citizen Participation in Finland*. Tampere: Tampere University Press, Acta Universitatis Tamperensis 2264.

Seo, H.S., & Raunio, T. (2017). Reaching out to the people? Assessing the relationship between parliament and citizens in Finland. *Journal of Legislative Studies*, 23(4), 614–634.

Siukola, R., Kuusipalo, J., & Haapea, K. (2020). *Sukupuolella väliä eduskunnassa? Sukupuolten tasa-arvo eduskuntaryhmien ja valiokuntien toiminnassa*. Helsinki: Terveyden ja hyvinvoinnin laitos, Raportti 5/2020.

Strøm, K. (1990). *Minority Government and Majority Rule*. Cambridge: Cambridge University Press.

Wiberg, M., & Mattila, M. (1997). Committee Assignments in the Finnish Parliament 1945–1994. In Guy-Erik Isaksson (ed.), *Inblickar i Nordisk parlamentarism* (221–244). Åbo: Åbo universitet, Meddelanden från ekonomiskstatsvetenskapliga fakulteten vid Åbo universitet, Ser A:470.

Winzen, T. (2017). *Constitutional preferences and parliamentary reform: Explaining national parliaments' adaptation to European integration*. Oxford: Oxford University Press.

6 Twenty years of attempts at reforming committees

A tale of reforms missing the mark in the French National Assembly

Claire Bloquet

A slow-moving process of constitutional empowerment characterizes the development of the committee system in the French National assembly.[1] When the current French Constitution was first drafted, one of its goals was to break from the former models of parliamentary hegemony, and a very weak committee system was installed in 1958. Subsequent reforms and revisions slowly tried to return small elements of power to the committees, without ever returning them to their former glory.

1958: the intentional reduction of committees' powers

Adopted in October 1958, the Constitution of the French Fifth Republic recently celebrated its 60th anniversary. Often described as the most stable system the French Republic has ever known, the Fifth Republic arose from a deeply agitated time. Following a Fourth Republic harshly criticized for its unprecedented governmental instability and apparent inability to contain the conflict that would eventually be known as the Algerian War (François 1996: 17–33), the new Constitution was drafted with the primary goal of making the institutions more efficient, capable of quicker response to a crisis, with fewer possibilities for blockage, a situation described as a more 'rational' institutional organization (François 1999: 31). This goal included reducing the powers of Parliament.

Symbolically speaking, the Parliament of the Fifth Republic is granted a lot less consideration by the Constitution than its Fourth Republic equivalent. For the first time, boundaries are placed on parliamentary intervention, and limits are drawn as to which topics can or cannot be managed through law. The MPs' amendment right, once limitless, was constricted by Article 40 of the Constitution, prohibiting any amendment which would increase state expenditures or decrease revenues, effectively preventing MPs from the most ambitious legislative changes.

The committee system, once extremely powerful, was domesticated at the same time. Article 15 of the Constitution of the Fourth Republic stated that: 'the National Assembly considers the bills that are submitted in the setting of committees, of which it decides the number, composition and jurisdiction',

DOI: 10.4324/9781003106579-6

therefore granting the National Assembly complete control over its own internal organization and allowing for an infinite number of committees to be created as needed, even though the actual number mostly oscillated between 18 and 19 (Rens 1961: 310). The Constitution of the Fifth Republic chose a radically different approach. Article 43 formally limited the number of standing committees in each chamber to a maximum of six, with each MP receiving exactly one standing committee assignment. It is decided by their parliamentary party group, according to the wishes MPs expressed, their professional and political background, but also their perceived political loyalty (Lecomte, Bouvard, Perez & Boelaert 2017: 188). With 482 to 579 MPs in the lower chamber throughout the period, and the National Assembly's rules of procedure stating that each committee should not have more members than a sixth of the total number of MPs, this resulted in gigantic committees generally amounting to between 80 and 96 members at all times,[2] a number that appears way too high for those committees to embody the ideal of specialized deliberation spaces described in the academic literature (for example Francis 1982: 834; Sartori 1987: 228).

Dividing all of the policy spectrum into six committees also means that the committee system did not mirror the ministerial bureaucracy in the slightest: in 1958, for example, the government had 21 ministers and six secretaries of state, each committee thus being in contact with several of them. As an example of their very wide jurisdiction, the Economic Affairs Committee is now responsible for any bill related to agriculture, fishing, industry, energy, applied research and innovation, consumption, foreign and domestic trade, post and electronic communication, tourism, urban planning and housing development. Before 2008, its jurisdiction also included environmental issues and civil engineering. Even though all standing committees have a primarily legislative function, one of them is usually, and somewhat misleadingly, called the 'Laws committee' – its official name being the 'Committee dedicated to Constitutional Laws, Legislation and General Administration of the Republic'. It deals with matters as diverse as constitutional law, criminal law, contract law, family law, election law, local and regional authorities, anything related to civil service and civil security, as well as petition or the chamber's rules of procedure. With that broad a field to cover, specialising and gathering expertise is made a lot harder for MPs, especially considering the Constitution does not allow for subcommittees to be created.

Article 43 of the Constitution of the Fifth Republic, however, did not actually plan for these standing committees to be the configuration in which most of the bills would be examined. On the contrary, it stated that 'the bills are, at the request of either the Government or the chamber, examined in an ad hoc committee specifically appointed to that end. Bills for which such a request is not made will be examined in one of the standing committees'. Nevertheless, the ad hoc committee process was neither handy nor usual enough for the legislative work to smoothly shift from one setting to another, and the ad hoc committees, though supposed to be the rule, never stopped being the exception.[3] If, as a consequence, stronger personal interactions and trust among MPs might have been achieved, it also led to increasingly overworked standing committees.

To solve the overloaded agenda problem, incentives were quite strong to decrease the thoroughness of the legislative work altogether: there was no time to do it, and it would most likely not be taken into account for the most part anyway. There is indeed no effective possibility for committees to delay the work on a bill; even though the committee chair is responsible for organizing their committee's agenda as they wish, Article 48 of the Constitution clearly delegated all control of the plenary's agenda (minus one day a month) to the government. Article 86 of the National Assembly's rules of procedure dictated the committee work on a bill be done early enough so that it would not interfere with the planned discussions in the plenary session. Contrary to the Fourth Republic, during which the discussion in the plenary could not begin if the committee stage had not been completed, the French constitutional court ruled in 1984[4] that an incomplete work on the committee's part during a bill's discussion does not constitute a procedural irregularity, securing the idea that a committee lacking time to do its work poses no threat to the functioning of the institutions (Cahoua 1985: 41–42), and confirming the idea that a committee cannot 'kill' a bill by refusing to analyse it. It is all the more understandable when taken into account that the committee stage did not, at the time, allow for modifications to the bill to be made: Article 42 of the Constitution stated that 'during the first reading in the plenary, bills are discussed according to the version of the text issued by the Government'. In other words, the committees could analyse the bill, draft amendments to be examined during the plenary, and make suggestions. But they did not have any amendment prerogative, their suggestions being allowed to be entirely ignored by the plenary if it came to it – though this rarely was the case since the strong party discipline ensured that committees' positions were not too different from the government's.

The Constitution's authors consciously limited the powers of the Parliament in almost every aspect of its existence, but the attack on committee structure had one of the most important and long-lasting impacts on the day-to-day organization of Parliament; and even though the governmental grasp slowly loosened over time, the committee system remains arguably weak.

The 2008 constitutional reform: a new dawn for committees?

This weakness in the institutional design of Parliament was soon framed as a democratic deficit, and several attempts were made over the years to rebalance the legislative process between the plenary and the committees. One of those endeavours was a revision of the National Assembly's rules of procedure in 1994: its goal was to 'extend the role played by [the committees] in the Assembly's functioning' (Assemblée nationale 1994: 10). However, those attempts remained limited in their effects. The 1994 revision allowed MPs to take part in meetings of committees which they were not a member of, without being able to speak or vote, and for the committees to publicize their work if they wished to do so. Requests by committees to audition a member of government would no longer have to be go through the president of the chamber and the Prime Minister – though in practice they had always granted their approval anyway.

With such small-touch changes, though, the committee system remained mostly unchanged for 50 years, up to a massive constitutional reform in 2008. This revision was the most important one of the Fifth Republic, as far as the number of amended articles is concerned. It officially aimed to make Parliament stronger. In its report, the expert group specifically appointed to suggest constitutional changes explicitly stated the goal of 'A Strengthened Parliament' in one of its three chapter titles and included a section named 'Turning committees into the linchpin of parliamentary work' (Comité de réflexion et de proposition sur la modernisation et le rééquilibrage des institutions de la Ve République 2007: 33, 45). To this end, a series of dramatic changes were made.

On a symbolic level, Parliament finally gained a constitutional definition of its functions, including voting legislation, overseeing government and evaluating policies, ideas that did not feature in the Constitution up to this date and had been insurmountable obstacles to attempts made by committees, through successive rules of procedure revisions, to oversee government, as the Constitutional Council did not recognize oversight as a parliamentary prerogative (François 2009: 86).

On a more pragmatic level, Parliament's organization was largely redefined, and as far as committees were concerned, it was a major change. The maximum number of standing committees, according to Article 43, went up from six to eight, allowing for committee jurisdiction to be redefined, and for their maximum number of members to drop to 73. As of 2020, the standing committees all have 71 to 73 members. An additional, overarching standing committee dedicated to European Affairs was created by Article 88–4. Members of it can also be members of a primary standing committee at the same time. The existence of ephemeral inquiry committees of 31 members, though allowed by law since 1958, is constitutionalized in Article 51–2, and the possibility for the standing committees to control and veto certain presidential nominations is introduced in Article 13. A minimum period of six weeks is stipulated before a bill can be brought to the plenary in Article 42, and even though this rule allows for numerous exceptions, it is meant to allow committees to have more time to properly study the bill. The chamber also legally won back part of the agenda control of the plenary from the government – two weeks out of every four – which was also intended to decrease committees' workloads and give them more autonomy in planning their work.

But the main change consisted in allowing committees to amend the bill before the plenary stage. Thus, the plenary discussion would be based on the amended version of the bill according to Article 42.[5] This modification of this quite specific Fifth Republic rule transformed the committees from expert groups with an opinion to actual legislative bodies. Since committees would now have the power to alter the government's wishes, attending said committee meetings turned more interesting for MPs. Closely monitoring them became more of a concern for the government. As a consequence, ministerial presence during the examination of a bill in a committee has become a lot more common. In 2009, commenting on the effect of the 2008 constitutional reform, the chair for the majority group in the National Assembly wrote:

> The executive branch will no longer be able to act on its own, only asking the MPs to blindly vote as fast as possible. It will need constant collaboration with the legislative branch, as it would in a ... presidential regime! It is my belief: France is shifting towards a presidential regime, with [...] a Parliament asserting itself as an actual power. Competent to take initiatives. Competent to oversee governmental action in depth. Competent to say no, if need be [...] It is no longer the Fifth Republic. But it is not the Sixth Republic either. It is the Fifth upgraded version.
> (Copé 2009)

Today's standing and ad hoc committees therefore have a few prerogatives. They examine the bills, produce a report about them to inform the plenary, and amend them. To that end, they can request data from the administration and conduct hearings, of scholars and activists or governmental officials and ministers alike, a prerogative they use quite regularly. Standing committees can also create inquiry committees on specific topics. Even though the committees may differ in terms of workload, rhythm of the work, reputation and desirability, and sociological composition or amount of oversight they do, MPs are still only allowed one membership in the standing committees. They can, however, combine as many ad hoc committee memberships as they want, as well as membership on the committee of European Affairs, inquiry committees, non-legislative committees dedicated to waiver of parliamentary immunity or the chamber's accounts, and even delegations, as long as their parliamentary party group allows.

Despite this series of ambitious changes, when asked in an interview about the most noticeable differences in the committees' functioning in 2019 compared to 2007, a socialist political advisor in charge of committees answered outright, 'the noise level'. He referred to the penalties MPs face for absence from committee meetings in order to boost attendance. In his opinion, it only marginally improved the MPs' involvement in those meetings, therefore favouring a continual background noise of whispered conversations while MPs wait out the meeting. And he does not appear to be the only one with mixed feelings. A conservative parliamentary assistant, interviewed in 2014, stated that these revisions, because they were not accommodated by other institutions and most importantly by the government, created a situation in which the workload got out of hand: committee work started taking more time and assuming greater importance, while at the same time, plenary work has not diminished proportionately, as MPs still use the more visible plenary debate as a platform to showcase their personal positions – defending amendments in the plenary already rejected at the committee stage, for example – and are reluctant to surrender their speaking right for the sake of timekeeping. Moreover, the amount of bills submitted by the government has remained similar, even though only half of the agenda is now dedicated to their review:

> The problem is, since the 2008 revision, our workload increased [...] We thought this revision would diminish the time we spend on each bill, but it really did not. A debate in committee will never be a worthy substitute to a debate in the plenary [...] And this 'sharing the agenda' thing is more of the same: we have some weeks to examine our own bills, great, [...] but then we get unbearable work conditions! On the same-sex marriage bill, we worked for two weeks, non-stop, Monday to Sunday, with debates lasting up to 4 a.m., I pulled all-nighters in here ... Because we share the agenda. Whereas we could have just granted a whole month to this government's bill, we would have read the project, sat in the plenary four days a week as we should.[6]

This observation seems to be corroborated by the numbers: since the 2008 revision, the number of amendments examined by committees has greatly increased, but the number of amendments examined in the plenary has not diminished proportionately. The number of hours of plenary debate even increased slightly over the same time (Godefroy 2018: 827).

Another tool introduced during the 2008 revision was supposed to decrease this pressure on MPs: the 'scheduled legislative time', the possibility to allow a set number of hours to each political party group to discuss a bill in the plenary. Once the hours are up, no member of the group is allowed to speak or defend amendments again. Aimed at keeping the length of plenary debates in check, this scheduled time allocation is not systematically used, but is accused of missing the point, with party groups allowing long, all-encompassing speeches at the beginning of the debate, and running out of time when it comes to discussing technical amendments.[7] In their 2012 evaluation of the 2008 revision, Costa, Schnatterer and Squarcioni found the same criticism in their interviews with MPs and listed both 'restriction of debate possibilities and lack of time' as the first and most recurring criticism of the revision (Costa, Schnatterer & Squarcioni 2012: 51).

Though reforms with arguably important effects were made over time to strengthen them, the committees still do not appear to be the supposed 'linchpin' of legislative work. This leads to an interesting conundrum: how can we explain that a string of reforms aimed at strengthening an extremely weak committee system apparently has not achieved its aim? This may have to do with two extra-legal obstacles to committee power: the growing transparency of committee work, and the institutional culture of party discipline, wrapped as an efficiency imperative.

The transparency imperative: a hurdle to political deliberation?

Committee powers are not the only aspect that went through a lot of changes over time: their working conditions were also transformed, as they received more and more attention from the public. In 1958, every committee meeting was conducted behind closed doors, and deliberation secrecy was the rule. A press release stating the most important decisions taken by the committee was issued after the meeting but did not chronicle the conflicts and arguments of the session. During the late 1980s and early 1990s, however, this amount of secret-keeping started to reflect badly on parliamentary work. In 1988, a revision of the National Assembly's rules of procedure allowed committees to open their hearings to the press if they wanted to. In 1994, a subsequent revision transformed the press release into minutes of meetings and Article 46 of the rules of procedure specified that committees are 'competent to organize the publicity of their work however they choose', secrecy remaining the premise that slowly became less and less admissible. The National Assembly's website was launched in 1995, and over the years, the National Assembly was slowly equipped with broadcasting technology which was sometimes used to record committee meetings and hearings, if the committee chairs allowed. From 2007 on, all meetings and hearings recorded were made available on the National Assembly's website. To this day, all of them can still be found online.

When he investigated the National Assembly committees in 2009 and 2010, Clément Viktorovitch noticed that fading imperative of secrecy, and stated that 'some doors are closed more tightly than others':

> [Committee] meetings and hearings are not public, except when the committee chair decides otherwise. And that's precisely the case for a majority of hearings in the committee I monitored in the National Assembly, which are open to the journalists. Up to twenty people can then assemble in front of the committee room – journalists, photographers, parliamentary assistants -, which starts to feel like a proper audience. Meetings to examine legislation were usually closed meetings though. Nonetheless, this closure felt quite porous: each time, the entry doors remained open, as numerous civil servants came and went. In addition, [...] a number of observers remain despite the secrecy: interns for this committee, civil servants from others, government collaborators.
>
> (Viktorovitch 2010: 102)

After a failed attempt to implement the idea in the 2009 rules of procedure revision, the secrecy principle was eventually overturned in the 2014 revision, when Article 46 was phrased to state: 'the work committees do is public', allowing for exceptions if it is publicly motivated, but effectively reversing a principle that had applied for decades. As a result, if we look at the meetings and hearings held by the standing committees of the 2018–2019 ordinary and extraordinary sessions, a large majority of them are recorded, and thoroughly transcribed for public examination – the only non-broadcasted meetings[8] mostly being when the bureau is elected, hearings with a state security component, or technical meetings to examine amendments filed after the committee has finished its work on a bill but before the plenary. Depending on how much the different committees are exposed to these exceptions, their work is more or less publicized, but a large majority of committee work has become entirely available (see Table 6.1).

Since 2018, accredited researchers are also allowed to attend public committee meetings, and each committee is issued an official Twitter account, providing daily content – pictures, video clips, links to different documents and information – for people to keep track of committee activity.

This spike in accessibility emanating from the institution itself has also been nurtured in outside projects, which have shed more light on parliamentary committees. The twin data-analysis websites, www.nosdeputes.fr and www.nossenateurs.fr,[9] are probably the most impactful and well known: collecting all available data from the National Assembly and Senate websites, they compile an ever-evolving ranking of MPs depending on different quantifiable aspects of their activity – be it committee attendance, number of times speaking, or number of amendments passed, for example. The relative reputation of these websites, as well as their simple methods of quantifying who is and is not a 'good' representative, puts extra pressure on MPs to adapt to the 'performance indicators' the websites monitor, which can prompt poor behaviour: for example, drafting amendments they know cannot be passed or are not legally sound, or interrupting a colleague talking so that it is counted as a speech. For backbenchers seeking to exist in often massive political groups, appearing in the top half of the ranking can often become a goal in itself.

The academic literature on deliberation has already stated that secrecy, or at least relative privacy, of the debates, is expected to allow deliberation to take place, while more public arenas tend to generate stiffer discussions (Elster 1994: 212; Stenelo 1972: 62–64, Viktorovitch 2010: 92). The hypothesis seems to hold in this context as well. When asked about the main changes she saw in committee organization during more than 30 years as an assistant in the National Assembly, an interviewee noted the growing mediatization the committees receive. She blames the phenomenon for making 'actual' deliberation near impossible in the committees, stating that she feels the effect has worsened considerably as the 2017 general election brought in a huge amount of newly elected backbencher MPs with no media attention. They might try to stand out by attracting attention however they can, including by a strong social media presence (a phenomenon already described by Chibois 2014: 8).

106 *Claire Bloquet*

Table 6.1 Percentage of non-broadcasted meetings per committee in France

	Laws	Finance	Culture and Education	Economic Affairs	Social Affairs	Sustainable Development	Foreign Affairs	National Defence	Total
Number of meetings	101	104	75	68	89	89	84	52	**662**
Number of non-broadcasted meetings	24	8	11	14	13	8	2	35	**115**
% of non-broadcasted meetings	24%	8%	15%	21%	15%	9%	2%	67%	**17%**

Source: Personally gathered numbers on the French National Assembly website, obtained by comparing the committees' agendas between October 2018 and September 2019, and the list of broadcasted committee meetings for the same period.

It's also their own fault you know, the MPs. Always tweeting everything, sometimes the meeting is not over yet that they all tweeted stuff... How do you want them to discuss after that? It's already on the record![10]

Another assistant, responsible for following committee activity for the past decade, sees it as a plus: mediatization, according to him, has motivated MPs to attend committee meetings and defend their ideas, stating that 'the National Assembly is a theatre stage', and that the debates need to have visible conflicts and dramatic statements for them to appeal to the viewers and convince people to take an interest in politics. When asked if he thinks that deliberation or bargaining is possible in the committees, his answer is an immediate 'no'. This analysis tends to confirm the description of committees not as deliberation spaces, but as 'rehearsal spaces, allowing the representatives to test out their arguments' (Viktorovitch 2010: 110). They also 'have a signalling role. They offer the MPs an opportunity to showcase their opinions and state how far they are willing to go to defend them' (ibid). As a consequence, very little legislative bargaining happens during committee meetings, even if it does happen between members of the same committee: if most of the legislative work seems to be decided by the government and MPs of the majority in other settings, interviewees also mention instant messaging, informal talks in the corridors, or in the Assembly's bar, as more suitable transpartisan bargaining spaces than the committees would be, far from the public eye.

Several interviewees – and it is a comparison that comes quite easily in any discussion on this topic – compare their work to the Senate committees' work, and perceive the Senate committees as more deliberative, less competitive, and more concerned about the betterment of bills. Viktorovitch found the same in his 2010 study, and partially explained this discrepancy by the relative secrecy – as well as lack of public interest – that surrounds the Senate (Viktorovitch 2010: 102–103). But for many reasons, both institutional and historical, the Senate is also much less sensitive to the pressures of party discipline, and the narrative of the efficiency imperative.

Efficiency as an imperative: marching the committees to partisan order?

Over the past decades, it appears the imperative for Parliament to pass bills faster – to be more 'efficient' by not acting as an obstacle to the executive will – only gained traction. The answers as to why this is so are all hypothetical at this point. Some constitutional scholars blame the 2000 constitutional reform. This revision reduced the presidential mandate from a seven to a five-year term, aligning it to the length of a parliamentary term and effectively turning the president from political mediator to majority chief, thus further differentiating the Fifth Republic from a traditional parliamentary system. This change is stated to have increased the weight of the policy results in presidential reelection, and therefore the pressure on the MPs to apply the president's promises at forced speed (for example Cohendet 2006: 313). Some interviewees blame it on a broader, less tangible change in the constituents' expectations of what a Parliament should stand for, and on a will to outpace the rise of anti-parliamentarism by showing off busy chambers (an intent that can also be found in Chibois 2016: 3–4). Whatever the reasons, the diagnosis remains: the National Assembly has to be as 'efficient' as can be, which, in practical terms, means that it should not stand in the way of what the elected President of the Republic is trying to achieve.

As a consequence, efficiency often tends to go hand in hand with the National Assembly forsaking part of its powers in order not to impede governmental action. For example, the 2008 constitutional revision, as has been said above, states that there must be a minimum of six weeks between the moment a bill is first introduced in committee, and the moment it is debated in the plenary. It was meant to make sure the committees had enough time to properly examine the bills. This principle has exceptions though, and the government can ignore this time limit if it chooses to have the bill examined through 'accelerated procedure', defined in Article 45 of the Constitution and formerly known as the 'urgency procedure'. No criteria must be met for this procedure to be chosen, and if the Parliament has a way to oppose this reduction of its agency, it is only if both chambers agree to refuse this procedure. Though it was attempted once in 2014, there are no instances of the Parliament ever successfully opposing the use of accelerated procedure (Lemaire 2017). Virtually unchecked, this procedure has become the norm in the French Parliament: between 2012 and 2017: about half the bills passed went through Parliament via the accelerated procedure. During the presidential campaign of 2017, Emmanuel Macron stated that he would, if elected, make 'urgency procedure [sic] the default procedure to examine the bills, to speed up parliamentary work'.[11] After his election in 2017, and even though no legal changes were made to make it the actual 'default' procedure, the accelerated procedure was heavily used: during the first two years of his term, 73 out of the 113 bills passed by the Parliament were adopted by the accelerated procedure. This process drastically limits the time committees can work on each bill, restricting the number of hearings they can hold, and the time they have to gather their own information on a topic, making them extremely dependant on the information the government provides. It also tends to lower the legal quality of the bills: laws passed through the accelerated procedure are far more likely than others to be partially annulled by the Constitutional Council for not upholding constitutional standards (Fuchs 2009: 761), a kind of work committees usually provide during the legislative back and forth between the chambers (Cahoua 1985: 43–45). Ultimately, these conditions accompany a wider phenomenon of legislative inflation that makes it even harder for committees to do their job: the number of MP and government amendments examined by the National Assembly jumped from 4,564 between 1958 and 1962 to 112,693 between 2012 and 2017, while the length of the bills nearly quadrupled (Hispalis 2005: 101–102, 110–111). Though the 2008 revision gives the committees some means to protect their agenda, the need to pass bills as quickly as possible does not allow for those protections to serve their purpose.

The same kind of logic also goes for the sharing of the parliamentary agenda: though the chambers are allowed to plan every two weeks out of four however they please, in practice the government has a lot to say about which bills are going to be examined during that time – choosing which parliamentary initiatives will be examined in those weeks as well, and sometimes going as far as to delegate bills written by a ministry to one or several MPs, as a trick to follow the rule in appearance, while also rewarding MPs' loyalty.

In this context, the apparent enhancement of parliamentary control over the agenda failed to translate into a rise of committee control over their own. The always-busy committee agenda was one of the issues addressed once again in the 2019 revision of the National Assembly rules of procedure but the chosen solutions were also double-edged: the motion of referral back to committee, which allows for a bill to be sent back to the committee if it appears it is not ready enough to be discussed in the plenary, was suppressed, and the possibilities given to other standing committees to give opinions on bills they are not primarily in charge of were limited. Both measures aim at alleviating the load of committees, but also tend to reduce their powers as well.

This efficiency argument is guaranteed by a strongly enforced party discipline that secures the government in its actions and ensures that in most situations, it will be able to obtain the bills it requires. Party discipline, especially in majority parties, has been a key component of the National Assembly's functioning since the 1960s, and generally implies an important delegation of the Assembly's prerogatives to the government. The task of the rapporteur on a bill, for example, should have been strengthened significantly by the 2008 revision and the decision to hold the plenary debate on the committee's version of the bill. Indeed, the rapporteur is the main correspondent of the minister in the chamber, and the best expert of the bill, a true centre point for the debate. Rapporteurs give their opinion on each amendment in the plenary before they are voted upon, are allowed to request debate suspensions, and can always demand to speak when the bill is discussed. The rapporteur's stand on an amendment or article is generally used, by the MPs who did not work on the bill, to determine where they should stand on each vote. Yet, as the rapporteur is always a member of the majority party when the bill is either introduced or supported by the government, in most cases, they work as a transmission belt for the minister's views.

In an interview, one political advisor summed it up, saying: 'the rapporteurs are chosen by the government anyway. Well, no, they aren't, the [parliamentary party] group chooses them. But they are'. He proceeded by giving the example of a bill on business confidentiality, to which a majority MP had dedicated a large portion of his career working on and was the greatest expert the committee had on the topic. Yet, a different, more compliant MP was appointed, because the government allegedly feared the first one would end up having 'too strong of an opinion' on the matter for the debate to go as planned, highlighting the need for the rapporteur to not only know the topic, but most importantly to agree to follow governmental directions. The same interviewee also recalls working on the legal definition of a new criminal offence with a rapporteur who was a law scholar and to whom he suggested a clearer legal phrasing. Appearing to agree, the rapporteur did not go with this version, because the government required a vaguer description.

> He glared at me and said: 'the government doesn't want that'. I'm an advisor, I advise and I'm not very impressed by what the government wants or does not want. But the look in his eyes, it was almost offended, as if to say: 'Of course I considered it, who do you take me for?' [...] That's the kind of moment when you can see how internalized, Jungian-level internalized, this discipline really is.[12]

This strong party discipline also helps explain why committees are not the main arena for positions to settle: political group meetings are. The main groups mostly determine their position in advance and defend it in committees as they would in the plenary. Whips for each party, and in each committee, take care of this aspect.

This exaggerated political rift can also, on occasion, appear to impede the investigation function the committees can have. One of the more recent examples was the 'Benalla affair', a national political scandal surrounding Alexandre Benalla, a security officer to President Emmanuel Macron, and his alleged involvement in illegal activities, which put into question both the safety and ethics of the President himself. When the affair was first discovered, a committee of inquiry was formally created in the National Assembly to investigate the issue, from July 20 to August 20, 2018. Two rapporteurs, one from the majority and one from the opposition, were appointed, but conflict quickly arose, as the opposition rapporteur accused the majority rapporteur of refusing most of his hearing requests, and actively trying to prevent him from conducting the investigation. On July 26, less than a week after the committee was created, the rapporteur from the opposition quit, stating that the inquiry committee was 'alas, a travesty'.[13] On the same day, the rest of the opposition MPs from all benches quit the committee as well. A couple of days later, the president of the National Assembly and former minister to the current government announced the committee would not meet again and would not make an official report of its work, rendering any form of systematic investigation impossible.[14]

Even more recently, in early March 2020, the Socialist Party's request to form a committee of inquiry to investigate the conditions in which the controversial impact study on a pension reform bill had been drafted, was denied, even though Article 141 of the National Assembly's rules of procedure states that 'each chair for an opposition or minority group is entitled, once per ordinary parliamentary session [...], to the creation of an inquiry committee'. The legal reasoning behind this refusal was questioned even by some MPs from the majority party, but without consequences.[15]

There are, of course, many counter-examples to this description of a completely tamed chamber. Discipline is less heavily enforced when a group stands on the opposition's, rather than the government's side. Some political configurations appear to be more prone to parliamentary rebellion (Lecomte et al. 2017: 193–196), or just parliamentary leeway, as are the rare cases when the majority is not absolute, or is composite, in the chamber. A parliamentary assistant also stated that some topics might be, by nature, more open than others. Similar statements were made by MPs interviewed about prostitution and gender equality.

> 'The group yields way less power [over the MPs] when they are questioned in their identity, almost ontologically. Topics like ... prostitution, migration, bioethics, filiation, social system ... The social norm is superior to the group's rules in some aspects'.

The rapporteurs, as docile as they often are, do hold some of the power and can co-construct the bills with the minister, and negotiate and obtain concessions on some aspects. In an interview, an assistant to the minister of parliamentary relations mentioned conflict between rapporteurs and ministers as a severe problem, requiring urgent intervention from the highest levels of the executive:

> It usually ensures we're set to lose, right? Because between the Minister's views and the rapporteur's, the group will usually favour the rapporteur [...]. So if an issue like that arises, it goes right to [the Prime Minister], and [the Ministry of Parliamentary Relations] is just flicked out of the way.[16]

Counter-examples of arguably efficient control against governmental interests can also be recalled. Between 2015 and 2017 for example, the Laws Committee constituted itself as an inquiry committee, to institute permanent monitoring of the implementation of the state of emergency put in place after the 2015 terror attacks in Paris. Regular reports were made, written by two rapporteurs from the majority and the opposition, publicizing statistics and data of the consequences of such regime, and forwarding the recommendations of human rights activists and organizations.

But the overall institutional trend does not appear to be moving towards a less strict party discipline. On the contrary, the 2019 revision of the National Assembly's rules of procedure decided to build on the idea that each political group expresses a single opinion: it limited the number of interventions per group at different stages of the plenary to one, as well as only allowing one author to defend their amendment if several similar ones were filed. If the organization of committee meetings is still entirely up to the committee chairs, it may be argued that these new rules do influence them as well, especially during the 2020 pandemic, which required parliamentary work – as everything else – adapted to social distancing. For example, on June 2, 2020, the Finance committee and the Social Affairs committee held a joint hearing of the Minister for Public Accounts about the consequences of the pandemic on the finances. During this hearing, only one speaker per group was allowed a short intervention, every other MP being granted the possibility to intervene only once after that, for a maximum of one minute. Similar organizations were reported – to the great frustration of some MPs – in the Laws committee or the Cultural Affairs committee at the same period.

In the nine months following this revision, the majority group LREM split, and two minority groups, one on the left of LREM, the other on the right, appeared. This episode, while being anecdotal and probably related to the way this specific party was formed in the first place, is still a first in the history of the Fifth Republic. The National Assembly counts ten parliamentary party groups in 2020, which is a record high by far in the last 60 years, and might indicate a difficulty, and general reluctance, in enforcing that high a level of discipline.

Conclusion

The committee system in the Fifth Republic National Assembly, though weak in the original design, is stronger than it used to be in many aspects – it has regained most of the traditional powers of committees in a parliamentary system, and continues to reform. The September 2019 revision of the rules of procedure allowed for legislation to be amended in committees only on the less complex bills, giving committee meetings the potential to be even more important.

Yet in practice, their powers have not increased as much as they do on paper. The ever-growing transparency of their meetings, though crucial to allow for democratic monitoring, appears to push deliberation further away from committees. The weight of internalized party discipline in a usually absolute majority system, and the pressure of implementing extremely ambitious presidential programmes in the short time of a term, do not help parliamentary autonomy.

It is not to say that the committees in the National Assembly are useless. They arguably do improve a bill's enforceability, in refining its legal phrasing and redressing details the government might have overlooked. They also are a space in which government officials, but also scholars or NGO activists, are regularly and publicly questioned about the main challenges they are facing on a particular topic. For MPs, they constitute an opportunity to access more specific information, and assert themselves as experts on a given issue, eventually leading to broader career opportunities for some of them.

But this brief history of failed attempts at reforming the committee system highlights the near impossibility to drastically change the functioning of an institution by the sheer modification of legal norms, without also changing the way other institutions relate to it, or the institutional routines and beliefs members of this institution hold (as demonstrated, notably, by Brunsson &

Olsen 1993). To draft a reform that goes further than the symbolic promise of change, an understanding of the institutional system as a whole, from a technical but also social perspective, is needed. Thus institutional reforms are interesting moments from a research perspective, as they 'offer a prime viewpoint on the core mechanisms in an institution, on the power relations inside of it, on the logics that promote its own reproduction, and on the conditions that allow for its change' (Le Lidec 2011: 110). Finally, this highlights the fact that, through time, legal, and political shifts, the tremendous influence of the President's figure as a political leader in the Fifth Republic never stopped obliterating other institutions, and remains at the core of understanding the functioning of the entire system.

Notes

1 All interviews without references were conducted in, and translated from, French by the author. I want to thank the National Assembly staff who carved time out of their busy schedules to help this paper be more accurate. Their contributions are priceless.
2 The Senate counting fewer members but with the same limits as to the number of committees, the standing committees are consistently smaller in the upper chamber, ranging from 45 to 55 members.
3 Out of the thousands of bills which went through Parliament since 1958, less than a hundred were examined in an ad hoc committee as of 2020.
4 Decision No. 84-181 DC, October 11, 1984, regarding the bill 'limiting concentration and assuring financial transparency of press companies'.
5 The new drafting of Article 42 also states that, if there is no official committee version of the bill, the debates in the plenary are based on the government's version, therefore confirming that a committee going through the bill is not required for the plenary debates to occur.
6 Interview with V., parliamentary assistant to a conservative MP, conducted at the National Assembly, on March 3, 2014.
7 See also 'Temps législatif programmé: l'heure du bilan', in *L'Hémicycle*, October 21, 2015.
8 The number of broadcasts is used here as a proxy to determine the number of meetings open to journalists: this second information is less readily available, and in most occasions press invitations and broadcasting go together.
9 Respectively meaning, roughly, 'ourMPs.fr' and 'oursenators.fr'.
10 Interview with A., staff member for the socialist party group in the National Assembly, phone interview, on September 25, 2019.
11 This quote can be found on page 27 of the 2017 'En Marche!' electoral programme, 'Emmanuel Macron Président'.
12 Interview with F., staff member for the socialist party group in the National Assembly, Paris, October 2, 2019.
13 See 'Affaire Benalla: l'opposition suspend sa participation à la commission d'enquête de l'Assemblée', in *Le Monde*, July 26, 2018.
14 To read a summary of the episode, see 'Affaire Benalla: la commission d'enquête de l'Assemblée ne publiera pas de rapport', in *Le Monde*, August 1, 2018.

15 To read a summary of the episode, see 'Réforme des retraites: LRM opposée à la commission d'enquête sur l'étude d'impact', published on March 5, 2020, in *Le Monde*, by B. Bissuel and R. Besse Desmoulières.
16 Interview with T., staff member for the Ministry of Parliamentary Relations, Paris, June 21, 2019.

References

Assemblée nationale. (1994). *La réforme du Règlement de l'Assemblée nationale II*. Paris: Assemblée nationale.
Brunsson, N. & Olsen J.P. (1993). *The Reforming Organization*, London: Routledge.
Cahoua, P. (1985). Les commissions, le lieu du travail législatif. *Pouvoirs*, 34, 37–45.
Chibois, J. (2014). Un 'appeau à journaliste' pour les députés, ou Twitter comme antichambre à la publicité parlementaire. Le Havre "Cultures et Identités (CECI)". IUT du Havre et UMR IDEES/CIRTAI: HAL Id: halshs-01087681.
Chibois, J. (2016). Combattre l'antiparlementarisme au début du XXIe siècle: Enjeux médiatiques à l'administration de l'Assemblée nationale. Paris: "Configurations populistes 2", EHESS. HAL Id: hal-01304751.
Cohendet, M.-A. (2006). *Droit Constitutionnel* Paris: Montchrestien
Comité de réflexion et de proposition sur la modernisation et le rééquilibrage des institutions de la Ve République. (2007). *Une Vème République plus démocratique*. Paris: La Documentation Publique.
Copé, J.-F. (2009). Hyperprésident et hyperparlement. *Slate.fr*. Retrieved from www.slate.fr/story/1873/hyperpresident-et-hyperparlement (access: 01.09.2020).
Costa, O., Schnatterer, T. & Squarcioni, L. (2012). *Peut-on revaloriser le Parlement français?*, Paris: Fondation Jean Jaurès.
Elster, J. (1994). Argumenter et négocier dans deux assemblées constituantes. *Revue Française de Science Politique*, 44, 187–256.
Francis, W.L. (1982). Legislative Committee Systems, Optimal Committee Size, and the Costs of Decision Making. *Journal of Politics*, 44, 822–837.
François, B. (1996). *Naissance d'une Constitution. La Cinquième République 1958–1962*. Paris: Presses de Sciences Po.
François, B. (1999). *Le Régime politique de la Vè République*. Paris: La Découverte
François, B. (2009). *La Constitution Sarkozy*. Paris: Odile Jacob.
Fuchs, O. (2009). La procédure législative d'urgence. *Revue de Droit Public et de Science Politique en France et à l'Etranger*, 27(3), 761–785.
Godefroy, F.E. (2018), Le temps parlementaire. *Revue française de droit constitutionnel*, 116(4), 821–836.
Hispalis, G. (2005). Pourquoi tant de loi(s)? *Pouvoirs*, 114, 101–115.
Lecomte, D., Bouvard, H., Perez, D. & Boelaert, J. (2017). 'Le respect de la boutique': L'étiolement de la discipline partisane dans le groupe parlementaire socialiste au cours de la 14e législature (2012–2017). *Politix*, 117(1), 171–199.
Le Lidec, P. (2011). Ce que les réformes font aux institutions. In J., Lagroye & M., Offerlé (eds.). *Sociologie de l'Institution* (75–104). Paris: Belin.
Lemaire, E. (2017). La procédure accélérée ou la regrettable normalisation d'une procédure dérogatoire. *Jus Politicum Blog*. Retrieved from http://blog.juspoliticum.com/2017/07/05/la-procedure-acceleree-ou-la-regrettable-normalisation-dune-procedure-derogatoire-par-elina-lemaire/ (access: 01.09.2020).

Rens, I. (1961). Les commissions parlementaires en droit comparé. *Revue Internationale de Droit Comparé*, 13(2), 309–326.
Sartori, G. (1987). *The Theory of Democracy Revisited. Part 1: The Contemporary Debate.* Chatham, New Jersey: Chatham House.
Stenelo, L.G. (1972). *Mediation in International Negotiations.* Lund, Sweden: Studentlitteratur.
Viktorovitch, C. (2010). Les commissions parlementaires à l'Assemblée nationale et au Sénat: un havre de paix? *Parlement[s], Revue d'histoire politique*, 14(2), 90–110.

7 No paradise of policy-making
The role of parliamentary committees in the German Bundestag

Sven T. Siefken

The empty plenary hall and work in committee

A recurring issue of public criticism about the German Federal Parliament is that MPs neglect their duties by not taking plenary sessions seriously.[1] Images of the almost empty plenary hall, where often only a handful of MPs debate the issues at hand, are used to illustrate this. In fact, many of the seats in the Bundestag do not even have their own desks – so are these mere spectator seats? In response to this old critique, politicians, political scientists, and political educators stress that the 'real' work in the Bundestag is not done by public deliberation in the plenary session. Modern parliamentary work, they say, is not a spontaneous 'battle of ideas', where representatives try to convince each other individually and across party lines with better arguments. Such an understanding of parliament is deemed naïve and not befitting of the role of this institution in a parliamentary democracy. It may have been applicable to the German Reich, where parliament had no role in electing the government and a limited one in policy-making. But the modern parliament is different. It elects the executive government, which depends on Parliament's support to remain in office. As Walter Bagehot famously formulated, in a parliamentary system the executive can be understood as a 'committee elected by the legislature' (Bagehot 1993 [1867]: 240). Consequently, the parliamentary committees are deemed the relevant places for substantial policy-making in the Bundestag. The numbers back this up for the German case; in the 18th electoral period (2013–2017) there were a total of 245 meetings in plenary session, but over 3,000 committee and subcommittee meetings (Feldkamp 2018: 214–216). The statistics for previous decades are similar.

According to this argument, it is in the committees where policy decisions are negotiated, where the arguments of constructive opposition parties may be heard and taken up, where deals are cut; and where the policy specialists develop a cozy relationship with each other, form 'departmental fraternities' and support each other. This differentiation of parliaments into subgroups is not only explained by deliberative reasons. Overall, MP specialization in a policy field eases coordination because with each decision, MPs do not need to start 'from zero' but can build upon acquired knowledge. As a party

DOI: 10.4324/9781003106579-7

whip in the Bundestag writes: 'The MPs in committee can get right into a topic, because everybody is already up to date. Long and time-consuming explanations are not necessary' (Grosse-Brömer 2014). Too much turnover in committee membership may disturb this. In other words, 'committees are the indispensable workhorses of the Bundestag, the machinery through which the greater part of its business must be processed' (Johnson 1979: 141).

This all sounds as if committees are the paradise of policy-making. But is it true? While many textbooks endorse this description, there is reason for doubt. Based on information from political practitioners and (a few) studies that employed observations and interviews, a different role of committees emerges. The 'mystical powers' that older literature ascribed to them is now considered outdated (Beyme 1997: 192), but in fact, committees in the Bundestag have neither been studied nor fully understood (Oertzen 2006: 191). One reason for this is simply that it is difficult to gain access to data about committee activities. According to the rules of proceedings, committee sessions in the Bundestag are closed to the public by default. That private sessions are the norm in the Bundestag follows from longstanding tradition and from the theoretical understanding of committees as deliberative bodies. Thus, a question with practical relevance follows: if that understanding is wrong, is there still a case to be made against more transparency of committee work? All in all, a paradox situation becomes apparent in Germany: even though committees are seen as the central organizational units of parliament, their academic investigation is rather limited (Siefken 2018b: 783). This chapter reviews the relevant findings about committees in the Bundestag, compares these with newer empirical data, and draws preliminary conclusions based on the research framework.

The institutional setting of committees in Germany

Committee types and portfolio allocation for the Bundestag committees

The differentiation of committee types suggested by Lees and Shaw (1979) applies to Germany; there are committees dealing with legislation, finance, investigation, administrative oversight, parliamentary housekeeping, and petitions. Only a handful of them are mentioned in the constitution: the Committee on the European Union, the Foreign Affairs Committee, the Defence Committee, and the Petitions Committee. Their role is not in legislation but 'rather accompanying administrative action' (Zeh 1989: 1093). Two other committees are set up by laws: the Budget Committee and the one for Election, Immunity, and the Rules of Procedure (Strasser & Sobolewski 2018: 34). All other Bundestag committees are at the disposal of each new Parliament and are decided upon as soon as government formation is concluded. In the early years of the Federal Republic, the Bundestag had a huge number of committees – a 'hypertrophy' breaking with older tradition in German parliamentarism (Dechamps 1954: 62, 76). Many were instituted ad hoc to deal with particular policy issues or with specific bills, often in the context of the reconstruction after the Second World War. In the first electoral period (1949–1953), 40 permanent committees held over 5,000 sessions; in the second period (1953–1957) there were 38 committees with still over 4,000 sessions (Schindler 1999: 2022). In the following years, the number has steadily declined and stagnated at around 20 committees. Nowadays, the typical format of the Bundestag's committee system is between 21 and 25 – in the 19th electoral period (2017–2021) it had 24.

This has to do with a de facto standard in the Bundestag since the late 1960s (Zeh 1989: 1091): committees strictly follow portfolio allocation of the ministerial bureaucracy, which is determined in the coalition agreement. When the ministerial structure changes, Parliament is quick to adjust committee structure accordingly. After the Bundestag election in 2017, the longest government formation in German history occurred. During the negotiations, building policy and homeland affairs ('*Heimat*') were added at the last minute to the portfolio of the Ministry of the Interior. While the parliamentary committee structure had already been set up according to previous plans, it was swiftly changed (Siefken 2018c: 420). But parliament also uses its committees to stress the relevance of certain topics, such as most recently digitalization which a dedicated committee has dealt with since 2014 (Schwanholz & Jakobi 2020).

Ad hoc committees for single bills or special topics are no longer used. Even during the COVID-19 pandemic, the committee structure has not changed. There are also no committees *exclusively* for oversight. Most committees are seen as primarily active in making laws, but studies show that today over 50 percent of committee time may be spent on other activities (Oertzen 2006: 237; Siefken 2018a: 293; Weng 1984: 34). In fact, 'effective legislation is inseparable from an extensive parliamentary control' (Heynckes 2008: 461). Current research suggests, for example, that the Committee of the Interior spends up to half of its time on oversight activities (Siefken 2018a: 293) – while older studies showed only a small proportion of non-legislative activities there (Johnson 1979: 120). Traditionally, committees had a clear focus on dealing with draft bills and preparing plenary debate (Zeh 1989: 1093). The same is true for parliamentary hearings – they deal with more non-legislative activities than is usually assumed (Hünermund 2021). The integrated committee activities in legislation and oversight are likely to increase the strength of committees because they lead to a deeper embedding of MPs in the respective policy networks – and potentially also to a different self-perception as principals of the executive along the chains of delegation (Strøm 2000: 269). Where exactly the focus of each committee is needs to be analysed. Two Bundestag committees deal with finances: the Budget Committee with spending, and the Finance Committee with income.

The Bundestag can install investigating committees with broader competencies – they can call witnesses under oath and acquire governmental documents. To set up an investigating committee does not require a majority decision – a qualified minority of 25 percent of MPs is sufficient. For this reason, investigating committees are an opposition right. Yet, as for all committees in the

Bundestag, their composition, leadership, and proceedings are governed by the share of seats for each parliamentary party group. Customarily, investigating committees deal with major political scandals. These committees are quite labour-intensive and the decision to establish them is always affected by considerations of the political consequences of their expected results (Radojevic 2016). Investigating committees have been studied quite well (Siefken 2018a, 191–198) but it is worth noting that they are the exception rather than the rule. The numbers show this clearly; while the first legislative period stands out, again, with an unusually high number of nine investigating committees, afterwards there have usually been two or three per electoral period (see Figure 7.1). Another type of committee, institutionalized in 1969, is the inquiry commission ('*Enquête-Kommission*'). They are a 'curious hybrid' (Johnson 1979: 112) composed of MPs and external advisors to discuss fundamental topics more generally and thoroughly, often over multiple years (Siefken & Schüttemeyer 2013: 166–168). In the 19th electoral period (2017–2021) two such commissions were set up: one dealing with artificial intelligence and one with digitalization in professional education.

Committee size

The theoretical argument for committee work holds that a small group is better at building trust among its members, at reaching solutions through argumentation, and that it is more efficient for bargaining. As of now, many committees in the Bundestag are much larger than the sizes that have been considered optimal from a decision-making perspective (Pfetsch 1987: 256; Sartori 1987: 228).

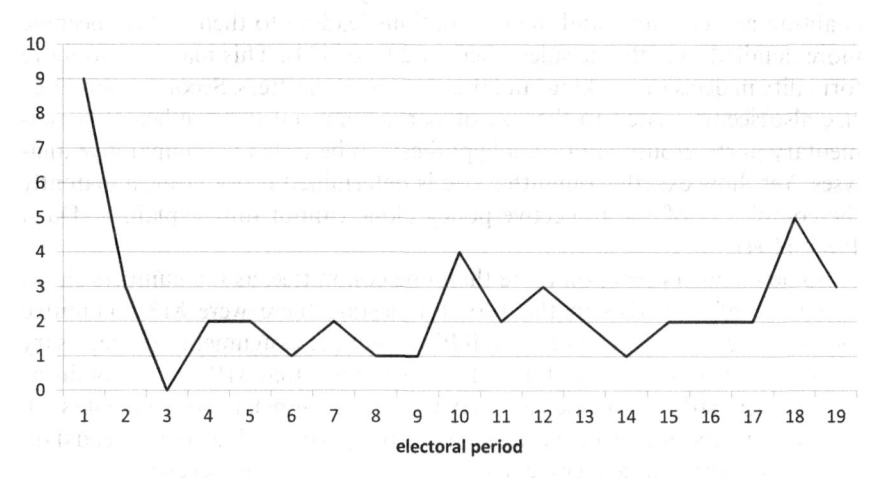

Figure 7.1 Number of investigating committees in the Bundestag (1949–2021).
Source: Data from Siefken (2018a: 194) and Deutscher Bundestag, 'Untersuchungsausschüsse'. www.bundestag.de/ausschuesse/untersuchungsauschuesse (access: 18.09.2020).

120 Sven T. Siefken

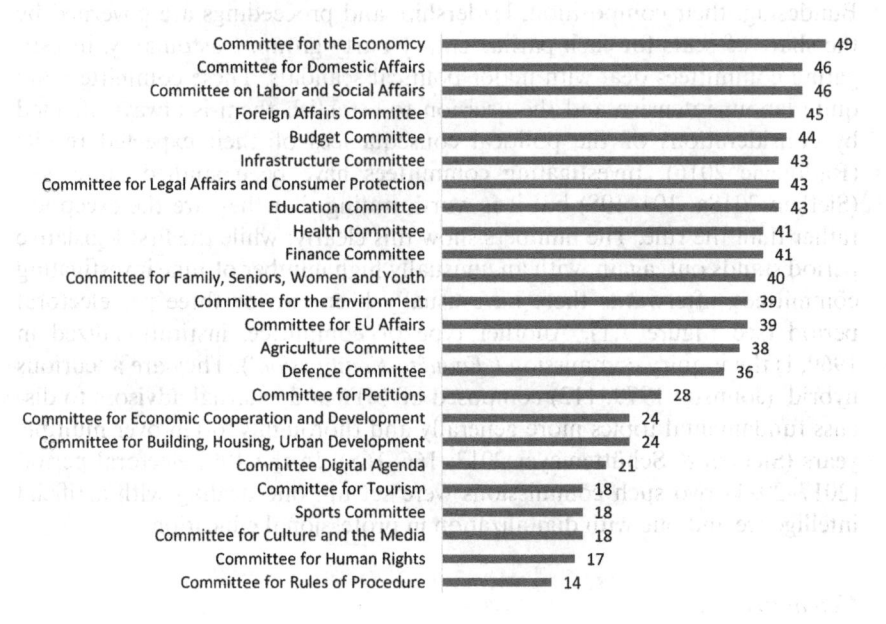

Committee	Members
Committee for the Economy	49
Committee for Domestic Affairs	46
Committee on Labor and Social Affairs	46
Foreign Affairs Committee	45
Budget Committee	44
Infrastructure Committee	43
Committee for Legal Affairs and Consumer Protection	43
Education Committee	43
Health Committee	41
Finance Committee	41
Committee for Family, Seniors, Women and Youth	40
Committee for the Environment	39
Committee for EU Affairs	39
Agriculture Committee	38
Defence Committee	36
Committee for Petitions	28
Committee for Economic Cooperation and Development	24
Committee for Building, Housing, Urban Development	24
Committee Digital Agenda	21
Committee for Tourism	18
Sports Committee	18
Committee for Culture and the Media	18
Committee for Human Rights	17
Committee for Rules of Procedure	14

Figure 7.2 Committees in the Bundestag (2018).
Source: Data from Feldkamp (2018: 216).

In the 19th Bundestag, 11 of the 24 committees had more than 40 members, setting a record (see Figure 7.2). This growth is mirrored in average committee size; it was at a record high of 34, which may result from two factors. First, coalition agreements – and the negotiations leading to them – have become more detailed over the decades (Siefken 2018c: 424). This may lead to more formality in decision-making, and thus bigger committees. Second, committee size also seems related to the size of parliament and the number of parliamentary party groups (PPGs), a hypothesis to be tested in comparative analyses. Yet, how exactly committee size is determined is not clear; apparently the complexity of the respective policy alone cannot fully explain it (Dach 1989: 1104).

Some members serve on more than one committee, as the numbers show; at a total of 709 MPs in the 19th Bundestag, there were 813 committee members (see Table 7.1). For a small PPG multiple assignments are necessary to adequately cover all portfolios. It is customary that MPs with prominent functions in parliament (such as party leaders or whips), in government (such as ministers and undersecretaries), and in the party (such as party heads) do not become committee members, so the actual difference is even higher.

It is necessary and possible to analyse committee membership from the MP perspective and to map changes and developments that may have repercussions on their policy expertise. Some authors have studied certain

Table 7.1 Committee size in the Bundestag (1990–2017)

Electoral period (starting year)	12 (1990)	13 (1994)	14 (1998)	15 (2002)	16 (2005)	17 (2009)	18 (2013)	19 (2017)
Number of committees	25	22	23	21	22	22	23	24
Average size committee	30.0	33.2	30.3	29.5	28.8	31.0	30.1	33.9
Committee memberships	751	730	698	620	634	683	693	813
MPs in parliament	662	672	669	603	618	622	631	709
Size parliament / average committee size	22.0	20.3	22.0	20.4	24.4	20.0	20.9	20.9

Source: Calculations by the author, data from Deutscher Bundestag (2018).

aspects, mostly regarding incentives for committee membership by mandate type (see below). Obviously, there is more potential in investigating career paths in and between committees and ongoing research projects may contribute to the understanding (Bailer, Manow & Hug 2019).

Closed by default – but more and more open in practice

By default, committee meetings of the Bundestag are not public, according to the rules and regulations of Parliament. Whether they *should be* public has been a perennial topic of political and academic debate (Oberreuter 1975).[2] Most recently, in 2017 and 2018, the two opposition parties in the Bundestag, the Green and the Left parties, have asked that all committee sessions be public by default. The classic thinking that private committee sessions help undisturbed and productive deliberation still prevails in Germany. As the parliamentary whip of the conservative CDU party wrote in an opinion piece: 'This constructive atmosphere can be realized far better without the public than under surveillance' (Grosse-Brömer 2014). But while this fundamental discussion is ongoing and not likely to lead to a quick resolution, parliamentary practice has begun to change. In 1995, the Bundestag adjusted its rules and regulations to allow for 'extended public committee sessions' (§69a GOBT). Meant to replace the final plenary debate, they did not take hold. But two other instruments did: committee sessions open to the public and public committee hearings.

While the default is non-public, committees have been able to hold public sessions since 1969. Twenty years ago, this option was rarely used (Dach 1989: 1121; Zeh 1989: 1098), but in the meantime that is different: There has been a strong increase in public committee meetings, especially in recent years; their number has more than doubled from the 16th to the 17th electoral

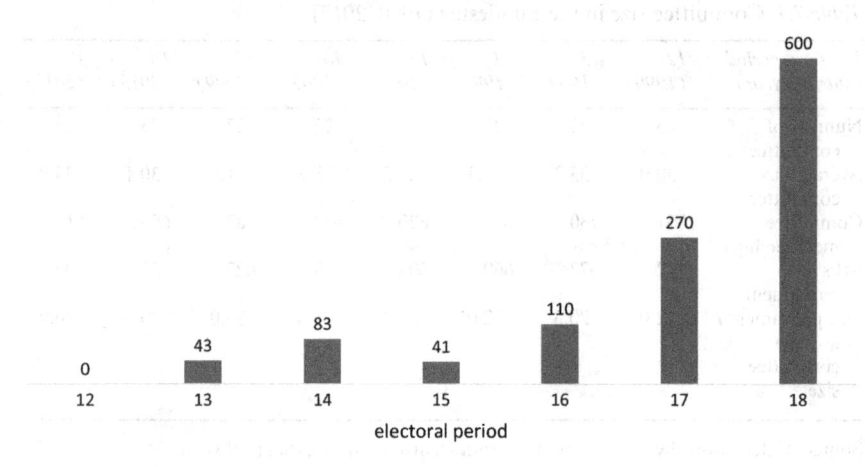

Figure 7.3 Committee meetings in the Bundestag open to the public.
Source: Data from Feldkamp (2010: 11, 2018: 216).

period, from the 17th to the 18th, and again from the 18th to the 19th (see Figure 7.3).

In the 13th period, 2 percent were held in public; in the 18th period (2013 to 2017) the share was 22 percent. This is worth closer investigation and provides the opportunity for a 'quasi-experimental' research approach, to see what effect publicness has on committee work and whether it is true that behaviour in public and non-public committee meetings is fundamentally different, as has been posited (Oertzen 2006: 239).

In fact, interviews with MPs show that from their perspective, committee meetings are already open. Some of them did not even know about the default rule (Siefken 2018a) and argued that the committee meeting halls are always full of spectators, anyway. They are right. According to the Constitution, members of the government and the Bundesrat have access to committee meetings and since 1990, PPG staff have also been permitted to attend (Ismayr 2012: 183). So, it is not correct to speak of private committee meetings, but rather of *partially* public ones (Zeh 1989: 1100). The argument that closed sessions reduce the opportunity for the party leadership to control MPs (Strøm 1998: 42) thus deserves doubt. This all leads to one question: if MPs perceive committee sessions to be public, can they still have the expected positive effects of non-publicness?

A second instrument has also gained strong traction: public hearings. They were introduced in 1951 based on examples from the United States (Loewenberg 2006) but only found widespread use a few decades later (see Figure 7.4). Nowadays, hearings are a standard tool in the legislative process; according to the parliamentary statistics, almost 40 percent of all bills that eventually pass undergo a committee hearing (Siefken 2018a: 175). Practitioners stress

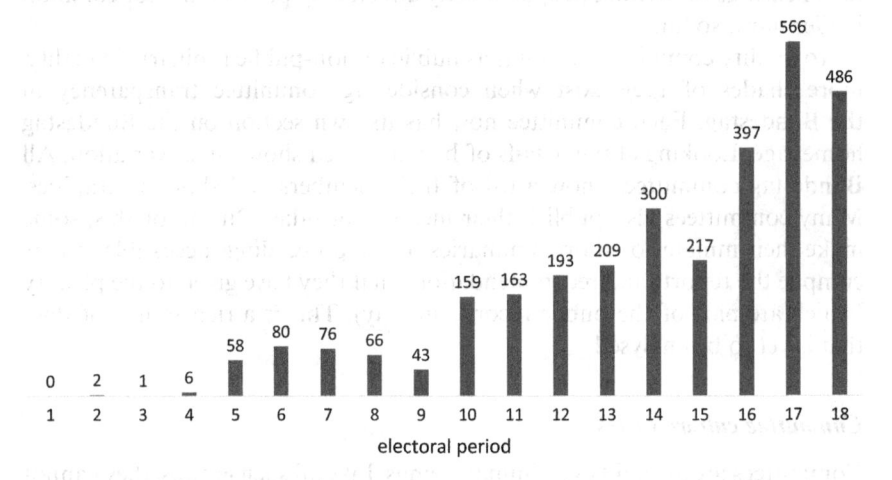

Figure 7.4 Public committee hearings in the Bundestag.
Source: Data from Feldkamp (2011: 944, 2018: 216; Schindler (1999: 2123).

that in some committees they are held for almost all bills. Usually, hearings take place relatively late in the process and have been characterized as 'largely ritualized and predictable events that are well-prepared by the parliamentary parties' (Oertzen 2006: 238). Their role is thus often more ceremonial in the communication of positions, thereby generating transparency, rather than bringing about new insights (Siefken & Schüttemeyer 2013: 170). This has been interpreted as a '(re-)production of legitimacy' by 'presenting decisions already taken as appropriate (Sack & Fuchs 2014: 163, 172). But hearings can also have major effects on legislation and may even result in stopping it, as was recently observed in the reform of real estate transfer tax, where a committee hearing halted the reform process.[3]

Participation in hearings varies from committee to committee; overall, they follow the logic of corporatism, but have become more pluralist, including numerous interests instead of just a prominent few (Dhungel & Linhart 2014: 762). Recent research has indicated that hearings can have an effect on policy and may provide an important venue for interest groups to exercise influence (Eising & Spohr 2017: 328) and that they are skewed towards business interests (Cross, Eising, Hermansson, & Spohr 2019: 19). However, causality is vague, and mechanisms of coordination and cooperation remain in the dark, i.e. there is not much light 'inside the black box', as only input and output of committees are compared. It is clear that committee hearings need to be understood better. This is particularly true in light of apparent changes in who is giving testimony there. While they are still dominated by organized interests, independent experts and public interest groups are on the rise – as is the total number of participants (Spohr 2018: 331). Conducting committee field hearings or inviting people directly affected by policies are not common in Germany, so far.

To qualify committee meetings as public or non-public is binary; in reality, more shades of grey exist when considering committee transparency in the Bundestag. Each committee now has its own section on the Bundestag homepage. Looking at the details of how it is used shows great variation. All Bundestag committees show a list of their members and short biographies. Many committees also publish their meeting agendas. On top of this, some make their minutes or short summaries of the proceedings accessible, others compile the reports and recommendations that they have given to the plenary (which are part of the public record, anyway). This is a rich source of data that is yet to be analysed.

Committee culture varies

Committees are assemblies of human beings. Like all such groups, they cannot be properly described as formal institutions alone. The concept of 'organizational culture' may help understand the informal aspects. Interviews have indicated a huge variation between different committees in Germany (Schäfer 2017: 171; Siefken 2018a: 414), as previously noted for the United States Congress (Fenno 1973: xiii). Some are more conflict-oriented, others more consensual. This is evident not only in the general atmosphere, but also in how speaking time is assigned, especially between majority and opposition parties. As with all human perception, there may be particular biases: 'Committee chairs generally judge the mood in their own committees as good and report a strong "we-feeling" ... They say that in "other" committees, the climate is worse' (Oertzen 2006: 211).

This variation may be a consequence not only of composition but also of the respective policy. Ideologically divisive issues can lead to a contentious committee culture. If policy content is classified according to the policy arena model, some mechanisms of how 'policies determine politics' (Lowi 1972: 299) may become apparent. One could expect a higher level of conflict for redistributive policy than for distributive policy, or more conflict for constituent policy than for regulative policy. For example, interviews have shown that in the agriculture committee, the level of conflict and formality in proceedings was high – which is similar to the US Congress (Evans 2013: 399). Yet, its reports have revealed significantly more consensus in that particular committee (Miller & Stecker 2008: 316). The interaction style of executive–parliamentary relations varies by ministerial department, too, which may have an overflow effect on interaction inside the committee. Finally, a microperspective can help to explain different committee cultures. The committee chair may have a strong influence on the interaction style because of their leadership position (Ismayr 2012: 176). But it has also been argued that the ranking members, the *Obleute*, are very important for this: 'The climate in committee results from their work style and their cooperation with the ranking members of the other parties. This is not to be underestimated for the efficiency of committee work' (Dach 1989: 1112).

Actors in the Bundestag committees: differentiation towards rapporteur governance

Influenced by scholarship on the US Congress, studies of the Bundestag committees have investigated formal arrangements and procedures with a rational-choice perspective. Accordingly, there is a focus on structure, process, and powers of committees, (Strøm 1998: 22) as well as committee assignment, where both 'constituency characteristics' and the regional balance within the parliamentary parties play a role (Mickler 2017a: 185). There have also been studies dealing with special topics such as committee selection (Edinger 1992). One influential comparative article developed the argument that directly elected MPs in Germany are more often members of committees that have the potential for constituency benefits (Stratmann & Baur 2002: 513). The validity of these findings has been contested for systematic reasons and could not be replicated based on larger data sets (Heinz 2010; Manow 2012). Another recent quantitative study also found no influence of the election mode on committee assignment, but showed that MPs with strong ties to their district were more likely to be assigned to the agriculture, transportation, and tourism committees – where 'pork' could potentially be delivered (Gschwend & Zittel 2018: 496). But various other factors play a role, such as seniority, previous expertise and interests of MPs (Mickler 2017c: 534) – and also relations to the PPG leadership (Schindler 2019: 368). Previous membership on a committee is relevant, too, but there has not yet been analysis on membership turnover. Assigning MPs to committees is a complicated leadership task usually fulfilled by the party whips – and it is a complex puzzle 'often full of conflict' (Ismayr 2012: 168).

For the German case, some helpful overview literature about committees exists in textbooks (Ismayr 2012) and book chapters (Dach 1989; Johnson 1979; Melzer 1989; Zeh 1989). A few articles have examined their institutional setting from a legal perspective (Vetter 1986; Winkelmann 2016). The Bundestag has one of the most comprehensive statistics departments about his own proceedings, which has for a long time reported committee activities in its data handbooks (Schindler 1999) and frequent updates (Feldkamp 2018). But many questions remain to be asked – and answered – regarding the political actors in the Bundestag committees.

For Germany, only a few studies have touched upon committee work in the Bundestag from the MP perspective, usually while investigating other issues such as the parliamentary parties (Schüttemeyer 1998), the roles of MPs in parliament (Oertzen 2006), and parliamentary culture (Schöne 2010). Others have investigated committees in the context of how central parliamentary functions are fulfilled, such as legislation (Beyme 1997), co-steering (Kewenig 1970; Schwarzmeier 2001), oversight (Siefken 2018a), and policy advice

(Eilfort 2019; Siefken & Schüttemeyer 2013). What is clear from the literature is that just as the old view of the plenary assembly was unrealistic, the same holds true for the perspective on committees at work; it is not the whole committee that is a relevant place for deliberation or negotiation, and these activities rarely seem to take place there. Instead, there is a strong internal differentiation inside the committees: policy speakers of the party groups, rapporteurs, committee chairs, and ranking members.

PPGs assign speakers for each policy area, leading to a 'sectorisation via the distribution of functional responsibilities' (Mickler 2017b: 188, 2019). Speakers have a strong 'monopoly' on the policy of their parliamentary party inside (and outside) parliament. This differentiation has been explained with a 'German commitment to professionalism and specialization in politics' (Johnson 1979: 109).

On top of that, for each bill and for each issue at hand, a number of rapporteurs ('*Berichterstatter*') are assigned. Formally – and that is where their name originates – their task is to report the committee results to the plenary (Weng 1984: 43). Thus, in the past, they were often nominated only after the committee was 'done' with its discussion – and usually the rapporteur relied very much on the support of the committee secretariat (Johnson 1979: 123). Nowadays, the responsibility as rapporteur is assigned early on and rapporteurs are the leading figures in the respective policy-making process (Dach 1989: 1121). One rapporteur is often assigned from each parliamentary party (Ismayr 2012: 178). Incidentally, this happens not just for legislation, but also for oversight of each administrative agency within the portfolio. One MP described her work as a rapporteur for the Federal Waterways and Shipping Administration in the following way: 'I do that as a "lone wolf": when it comes up in our party's working group, my dear colleagues ... "switch to standby". The working group agrees to what I suggest. Period' (Siefken 2018a: 260).

In other words, the assignment as rapporteur can develop a permanence and move the specialization further than to the committee level – and the role of rapporteur seems to have shifted over the last decades. While in the German case there is no foundation to talk of 'subcommittee governance' as in the US Congress (Evans 2013: 403), a case may be made for 'rapporteur governance' – at least in standard situations, i.e. non-contested policies. Together with the policy speakers, the rapporteurs are the main relevant actors and determine each PPG's policy position – so long as they do not stray too far from their party position. Rapporteurs and speakers are active in a context that is far beyond the committee itself: they build close ties to the parliamentary party and are members of its respective working group. They serve as a gateway to the party leadership on the policy issue at hand – and they are closely connected to the respective ministries and the broader issue networks. If they 'do their job well', they anticipate and include all intra-party concerns in their policy proposals; that is how an estimated '90 percent of topics are non-controversial' within the PPG (Mickler 2019: 456). This intense and detailed division of labour is particularly challenging for smaller parties struggling because of limited MP and staff capacities. The increasing parliamentary fragmentation in recent years makes this even more difficult.

The ranking PPG members in each committee (*Obleute*) are concerned with the process – rather than policy. Their task is to represent the interest of their own parties in committee work and in planning committee activities, as well as making sure members of their PPG are present and briefed when needed (Dach 1989: 1112). All in all, their role is more in procedural preparation of the committee sessions, much like the 'council of elders' is for the plenary (Oertzen 2006: 219).

The committee chair is more visible. Some authors see this as a powerful position with the potential to influence policy that may be stronger than that of a minister (Dach 1989: 1109). Thus, it has been argued that this position is used as a check between coalition partners (Kim & Loewenberg 2005: 1110). However, the factual competencies of committee chairs are rather limited and their focus is largely oriented 'to get the job done', i.e. move the committee's work plan forward (Oertzen 2006: 214). A recent comparative quantitative study has also found no support for hypotheses resulting from the 'checking the partner' arguments. According to this, the power of committee chairs in the Bundestag is rather weak and less than those in most other Western European countries (Sieberer & Höhmann 2017: 316). So, the committee chair is visible, but not strong in policy-making despite their institutional advantages such as agenda control.

Bundestag committees in policy-making

Legislation and control are two important functions of the Bundestag committees, but they perform other tasks that are more representational in character – for example receiving foreign delegations or conducting travels (Dach 1989: 1119). This relates to the communication function of parliaments (Oertzen 2006: 213) and public outreach. Combining them with the policy cycle shows how different functions come to the fore – the communication function during problem formulation and agenda-setting, the legislative function during policy formulation and the control function during implementation and evaluation (Siefken & Schüttemeyer 2013: 164).

Defining problems and setting the agenda

The role of German MPs in problem definition has not been studied systematically. But it is likely that both speakers and rapporteurs play important roles in their policy networks. However, they are limited by the norm of sectorization, i.e. they speak only on 'their own' issues. Yet through committee assignment, MPs become experts in their field and receive a prominent status, too. Consequently, they become active players in the policy network, in the working groups of their own party, and in dealings with the broader public.

Bundestag committees depend on input from elsewhere to start their legislative work, and they are therefore not fully able to control their own agenda. They do not have a right to legislative initiative and they have to report on everything that is submitted to them, so there is no right to 'kill a bill'. Since 1969, committees may take up topics within their portfolio and write reports on it (Dach 1989: 1116; Zeh 1989: 1091). So, to a certain degree, Bundestag committees can set and influence their own agenda, which may have implications for the broader parliamentary agenda and even the political agenda. But a systematic study of political agenda-setting in Germany and the role of MPs and committees in it does not exist. Political parties, PPGs and their leadership, and sometimes even individual MPs seem to be more relevant agenda-setters than parliamentary committees in Germany.

Formulating policy – inside and outside of committees

Committees in the Bundestag make neither first nor final decisions on the draft bills they deal with. Instead, they write up reports and make recommendations, which form the base for final decisions in the plenary assembly. Recommendations have to be formulated so that the plenary can vote 'yes' or 'no' (Dach 1989: 1128). Coming out of committees, these papers are published in the proceedings of parliament. Since 1949, a total of well over 30,000 committee reports have been published, available completely in digital format (see Figure 7.5). They deserve to be analysed in depth; new approaches of data mining may facilitate this.

As a general rule, 'the committee phase of the legislative process nearly always results in the revision of the government bill' (Kim & Loewenberg 2005: 1111). In political Berlin, this has been known as 'Struck's Law', named after the former head of the Social Democratic PPG in the Bundestag, Peter Struck: 'No bill ever leaves parliament as it entered'.[4] An analysis of legislative processes between 1976 and 2005 shows that 'every second bill that eventually became law' had been amended during the committee phase. The same analysis showed a clear variation by policy area regarding the length of the committee phase (Miller & Stecker 2008: 308–309), which is connected to the discussion of committee and policy variation above.

The validity of these results needs to be checked, as do certain variables taken from policy analysis that may help for a better understanding: is there a difference in influence between committees? and how far-reaching are the changes made? It will also be helpful to differentiate important from unimportant legislation, or to identify 'key decisions' (Beyme 1997: 239). As I argue elsewhere, according to the actual decision and its degree of politicization, interactions may vary in 'hot' and 'cool' situations of policy-making (Siefken 2020), based on the 'temperature of politics' (Sartori 2005

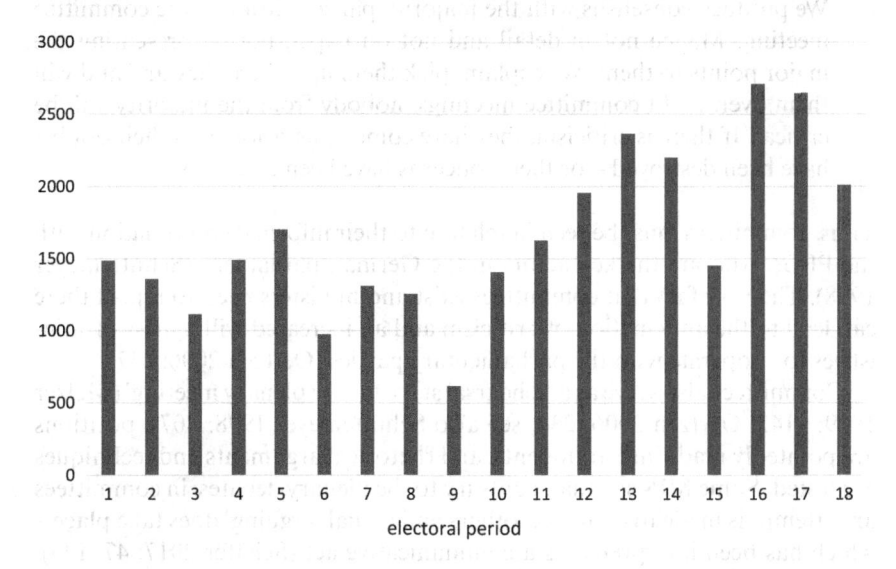

Figure 7.5 Committee reports and recommendations in the Bundestag.

Source: Data from Deutscher Bundestag, 'Drucksachen und Plenarprotokolle des Bundestages', Retrieved from http://pdok.bundestag.de/ (access: 02.09.2020); numbers include 736 reports and recommendations from investigating committees.

[1976]: 199). It may also be related to opportunities provided by majorities in the second chamber which influence visible conflict in the Bundestag committees: 'Opposition control of the Bundesrat significantly increases the likelihood of consensual decisions in committee' (Miller & Stecker 2008: 314). So, all in all, there is an opportunity to investigate committee output both in terms of available data and theoretical concepts. The report and recommendation data provide an entry point for analysis that – surprisingly – has not yet been widely used.

The process inside the committees is harder to grasp because of the lack of public access. Older models see committees as the key actors for making the most important policy decisions (for an overview: Oertzen 2006: 192–193). The current understanding, based on empirical research, however, stresses that while the style of interaction may be different than in the plenary, in terms of the content, they are rarely places for compromise. 'Inter-party cooperation, a policy-oriented and open discussion … does not occur in committee' (Oertzen 2006: 240).

Instead, Bundestag committees are better understood as a 'forum where the policies of the parliamentary parties can be checked' (Melzer 1989: 1143). The real decisions have usually been made elsewhere within the governing majority or the opposition. One ministerial department leader described this in an interview (Siefken 2018a: 228):

We produce consensus with the majority parties ahead of the committee meeting. Maybe not in detail and not on paper, but by presenting the major points to them. We explain, pick them up 'where they are' and win them over. ... In committee meetings, nobody from the majority will be critical. If there is criticism, they have come to us before and their doubts have been destroyed – or their concerns have been taken up.

Thus, committees must be seen in relation to their informal coordination with the PPGs, who are the key actors in the German parliament (Schüttemeyer 1998). The very fact that committees exist and ministers need to report there can lead to the anticipation of criticism and an increased willingness of ministries to cooperate with the parliamentary parties (Oertzen 2006: 237).

Committees also serve as a 'rehearsal stage for the plenary meeting' (Melzer 1989: 1142; Oertzen 2006: 234; see also Schüttemeyer 1998: 307): positions are pointedly made into arguments, and rhetorical arguments and techniques are tested. Some MPs say that, contrary to the plenary debates, in committees an 'attempt is made to convince' others and actual 'arguing' does take place – which has been interpreted as a communicative act (Schäfer 2017: 47–149). But in the end, the majority will push through its position by vote if needed – both in committee and in the plenary. The last round in committee is also used for a final 'cleaning' of the bill, a last check for errors (Oertzen 2006: 235). The communication style in committee deliberation is described by MPs as 'more policy-oriented', 'friendlier' and 'more reasonable' than in the plenary debate (Schäfer 2017: 150). In the end, the positions are clearly marked and written down – committees thus serving as 'parliamentary notary' (Oertzen 2006: 240). Yet, in Germany they have no right to make a final formal decision in place of the plenary.

Implementation oversight and evaluating – an overlooked task

The role of MPs and committees in monitoring policy implementation has not been studied for the German case. Formalized oversight strategies are not used, the control mode usually follows the model of 'fire alarm' rather than 'police patrol' (McCubbins & Schwartz 1984). Committees do sometimes ask the government for implementation reports, but there are no central statistics available. How often these reports are acted upon by committees and how often they are just filed away is unclear. More than one committee may be involved, as can be illustrated by the reform process of the waterways and shipping administration, where the budget committee took over the role of 'reform motor' while the 'transportation committee' reluctantly followed suit (Siefken 2018a: 249). Formal instruments for ongoing control by the Bundestag are the parliamentary questions and interpellations, but much information can also be received directly through personal contacts, letters to the minister, or local visits (Siefken 2018a: 422).

It is a modern development to formally evaluate policies; sometimes, an evaluation after a certain time is even mandated by the original legislation itself. From a functional perspective, parliamentary actors have long been active in policy evaluation when they check if a policy is working and bringing about the expected results (Bogumil & Jann 220: 235). Committees and their secretariats often do keep an eye on the topics within their jurisdiction, sometimes by official reporting requirements. Terminating a policy can be done through the so-called 'sunset legislation', i.e. laws with an expiration date (Veit & Jantz 2013). This is rare in Germany and hardly fits with its legal traditions. In other words, practically all termination of policy requires a parliamentary process to amend the original legislation. The role of committees in that does not vary from the ones sketched above in policy formulation.

Committees as crystallization points for policy-making

Parliamentary committees in the Bundestag are not the policy-making paradise they are often portrayed to be. In their actual work, neither arguing nor bargaining approaches to policy-making prevail. They serve more of a preparatory role for the plenary activities. However, this should not be confused with claiming that committees are irrelevant. The fact that parliament installs committees leads to the policy specialization of MPs – at least for a certain period of time. By nominating rapporteurs, committees – or rather the PPGs – assign them clear tasks and responsibilities. Those MPs then conduct their policy-making activities in many places – as members of their PPG working group, members of their PPG, in the network of the respective policy domain, and in contact with government and the executive. So committees are correctly classified as 'knots of influence within the parliamentary setting through which demands or reservations can be expressed' (Johnson 1979: 143). But they are certainly not actors nor mere arenas.

Much remains to be done: A closer study of committees in the Bundestag must focus first and foremost on their role in the policy-making process. But apart from this macro-level analysis, knowledge about the micro- and meso-levels must also be improved. It is of utmost importance to apply a broader view of institutions to include informal interactions. Approaches, models, and frameworks from public policy can aid this analysis. On the micro-level, a broad analysis of committee membership is required to study the practice and individual development of policy specialization in the Bundestag and the socialization effects of committee work.

Methodologically, a mix of approaches is helpful. Document analysis based on the available open-source data can help to analyse the readily available parliamentary instruments by new data-mining technologies. Information of biographical MP data can lead to better understanding of committee assignment and career paths. Participant observation – if possible – and expert interviews can help illuminate informal issues on the meso- and micro-levels. In this way, we can find out where the actual decisions are made and what role committees play in this process.

Such an analysis of German parliamentarism will also help devise steps to reform it – towards better accountability, higher transparency and increasing institutional support.

Notes

1 This chapter is partly based on Siefken (2018b) and papers presented at the IPSA World Congress 2018 in Brisbane, Australia, and the Valencia Workshop on Parliamentary Committees, 2019. I thank discussants and participants for their valuable comments.
2 See also: Bericht der Ad-hoc-Kommission Parlamentsreform, Deutscher Bundestag Drucksache 10/3600, p. 11.
3 Share Deals SPD will Steuerschlupfloch bei Grunderwerbsteuer schließen, in Handelsblatt, 17.07.2020, www.handelsblatt.com/politik/deutschland/share-deals-spd-will-steuerschlupfloch-bei-grunderwerbsteuer-schliessen/26014040.html?ticket=ST-4458537-QXNhwlKTQexcOcudN7TL-ap3 (access: 24.02.21).
4 Struck (2010: 46) writes in his autobiography that he did not coin this sentence but Chancellor Gerhard Schröder attributed it to him. Struck did not object, though.

References

Bagehot, W. (1993 [1867]). *The English Constitution*. London: Fontana.
Bailer, S., Manow, P., & Hug, S. (2019). *Parliamentary Careers in Comparison: Research Project*. Basel, Bremen, Geneva: Retrieved from http://parliamentarycareersincomparison.org/ (access: 02.09.2020).
Beyme, K. von (1997). *Der Gesetzgeber. Der Bundestag als Entscheidungszentrum*. Opladen: Westdeutscher Verlag.
Bogumil, J., & Jann, W. (2020). *Verwaltung und Verwaltungswissenschaft in Deutschland: Einführung in die Verwaltungswissenschaft*. Wiesbaden: VS Verlag.
Cross, J.P., Eising, R., Hermansson, H., & Spohr, F. (2019). Business interests, public interests, and experts in parliamentary committees: their impact on legislative amendments in the German Bundestag. *West European Politics*, 9(3), 1–24.
Dach, R.P. (1989). Das Ausschußverfahren nach der Geschäftsordnung und in der Praxis. In H.-P. Schneider & W. Zeh (eds.), *Parlamentsrecht und Parlamentspraxis* (1103–1130). Berlin: de Gruyter.
Dechamps, B. (1954). *Macht und Arbeit der Ausschüsse: Der Wandel der parlamentarischen Willensbildung*. Parteien, Fraktionen, Regierungen.
Deutscher Bundestag (2018). Das Datenhandbuch zur Geschichte des Deutschen Bundestages: Kapitel 8.4 Mitgliederzahl der Ausschüsse (version: 31.10.2018). Retrieved from www.bundestag.de/dokumente/parlamentsarchiv/datenhandbuch/08/kapitel-08-475944 (access: 02.09.2020).
Dhungel, A.-K., & Linhart, E. (2014). Interessenvermittlung in den Ausschüssen des Deutschen Bundestages. *Zeitschrift für Parlamentsfragen*, 45(4), 743–762.
Edinger, F. (1992). *Wahl und Besetzung parlamentarischer Gremien: Präsidium, Ältestenrat, Ausschüsse*. Berlin: Duncker & Humblot.

Eilfort, M. (2019). Fraktionen und Ausschüsse des Deutschen Bundestages. In S. Falk, M. Glaab, A. Römmele, H. Schober, & M. Thunert (eds.), *Handbuch Politikberatung* (187–197). Wiesbaden: Springer.
Eising, R., & Spohr, F. (2017). The More, the Merrier? Interest Groups and Legislative Change in the Public Hearings of the German Parliamentary Committees. *German Politics*, 26(2), 314–333.
Evans, C.L. (2013). Committees. In E. Schickler & F.E. Lee (eds.), *The Oxford Handbook of the American Congress* (396–425). Oxford: Oxford University Press.
Feldkamp, M.F. (2010). Deutscher Bundestag 1990 bis 2009: Parlaments- und Wahlstatistik für die 12. bis 17. Wahlperiode. *Zeitschrift für Parlamentsfragen*, 41(1), 3–17.
Feldkamp, M.F. (2011). *Datenhandbuch zur Geschichte des Deutschen Bundestages 1990 bis 2010*. Baden-Baden: Nomos.
Feldkamp, M.F. (2014). Deutscher Bundestag 1994 bis 2014: Parlaments- und Wahlstatistik für die 13. bis 18. Wahlperiode. *Zeitschrift für Parlamentsfragen*, 45(1), 3–16.
Feldkamp, M.F. (2018). Deutscher Bundestag 1998 bis 2017/18: Parlaments- und Wahlstatistik für die 14. bis beginnende 19. Wahlperiode. *Zeitschrift für Parlamentsfragen*, 49(2), 207–222.
Fenno, R.F. (1973). *Congressmen in Committees*. Boston: Little Brown and Company.
Grosse-Brömer, M. (2014). Sollen Bundestagsausschüsse öffentlich tagen? Retrieved from www.politik-kommunikation.de/ressorts/artikel/pro-kontra/sollen-bundestagsausschuesse-oeffentlich-tagen-15393 (access: 02.09.2020).
Gschwend, T., & Zittel, T. (2018). Who brings home the pork? Parties and the role of localness in committee assignments in mixed-member proportional systems. *Party Politics*, 24(5), 488–500.
Heinz, D. (2010). Mandatstypen und Ausschussmitgliedschaften der Mitglieder des Deutschen Bundestages – Eine empirische Untersuchung von 1949 bis 2005. *Zeitschrift für Parlamentsfragen*, 41(3), 518–527.
Heynckes, H.-W. (2008). Das Ausschussverfahren nach der Geschäftsordnung des Deutschen Bundestages. *Zeitschrift für Parlamentsfragen*, 39(3), 457–680.
Hünermund, S. (2021). Non-legislative hearings in the German Bundestag – A visible tool of parliamentary oversight? Paper for the IPSA World Congress 2021, Lisbon.
Ismayr, W. (2012). *Der Deutsche Bundestag*. Wiesbaden: VS Verlag.
Johnson, N. (1979). Committees in the West German Bundestag. In J.D. Lees & M. Shaw (eds.), *Committees in legislatures: A comparative analysis* (pp. 102–147). Oxford: Martin Robertson.
Kewenig, W.A. (1970). *Staatsrechtliche Probleme parlamentarischer Mitregierung am Beispiel der Arbeit der Bundestagsausschüsse*. Bad Homburg: Gehlen.
Kim, D.-H., & Loewenberg, G. (2005). The Role of Parliamentary Committees in Coalition Governments: Keeping Tabs on Coalition Partners in the German Bundestag. *Comparative Political Studies*, 38(9), 1104–1129.
Lees, J.D., & Shaw, M. (eds.) (1979). *Committees in legislatures: A comparative analysis*. Oxford: Martin Robertson.
Loewenberg, G. (2006). The Influence of U.S. Congressional Hearings on Committee Procedure in the German Bundestag: A Case Study of Institutional Diffusion. In T.J. Power & N.C. Rae (eds.), *Exporting Congress? The Influence of the U.S. Congress on World Legislatures* (102–118). Pittsburgh: University of Pittsburgh Press.

Lowi, T. J. (1972). Four Systems of Policy, Politics and Choice. *Public Administration Review*, 33(4), 298–310.

Manow, P. (2012). Wahlkreis- oder Listenabgeordneter, Typus oder Episode? Eine Sequenzanalyse der Wege in den Bundestag. *Politische Vierteljahresschrift*, 53(1), 53–78.

McCubbins, M.D., & Schwartz, T. (1984). Congressional Oversight Overlooked: Police Patrols versus Fire Alarms. *American Journal of Political Science*, 28(1), 165–179.

Melzer, M. (1989). Vorbereitung und Gestaltung der Ausschußarbeit durch die Fraktionen. In H.-P. Schneider & W. Zeh (eds.), *Parlamentsrecht und Parlamentspraxis* (1131–1143). Berlin: de Gruyter.

Mickler, T.A. (2017a). Committee autonomy in parliamentary systems – coalition logic or congressional rationales? *Journal of Legislative Studies*, 23(3), 367–391.

Mickler, T.A. (2017b). *Parliamentary Committees in a Party-Centred Context: Structure, Composition, Functioning*. University of Leiden: PhD thesis.

Mickler, T.A. (2017c). Who gets what and why? Committee assignments in the German Bundestag. *West European Politics*, 41(2), 517–539.

Mickler, T.A. (2019). What Happens after Assignments? The Room for Manoeuvre of Committee Members in the Bundestag and the Tweede Kamer. *Parliamentary Affairs*, 72(2), 445–463.

Miller, B., & Stecker, C. (2008). Consensus by Default? Interaction of Government and Opposition Parties in the Committees of the German Bundestag. *German Politics*, 17(3), 305–322.

Oberreuter, H. (1975) Scheinpublizität oder Transparenz? Zur Öffentlichkeit von Parlamentsausschüssen, *Zeitschrift für Parlamentsfragen*, 6(1), 77–92.

Oertzen, J. von (2006). *Das Expertenparlament. Abgeordnetenrollen in den Fachstrukturen bundesdeutscher Parlamente*. Baden-Baden: Nomos.

Pfetsch, F. (1987). Politische Theorie der Entscheidung in Gremien. *Journal für Sozialforschung*, 27(3/4), 253–275.

Radojevic, M. (2016). Die Einsetzung Parlamentarischer Untersuchungsausschüsse im Deutschen Bundestag: Welchen Einfluss hat die Auffälligkeit eines Themas? *Zeitschrift für Parlamentsfragen*, 47(1), 58–68.

Sack, D., & Fuchs, S. (2014). Wirtschaftskammern und Parlamente. In T. von Winter & Blumenthal, Julia von von (eds.), *Interessengruppen und Parlamente* (151–177). Wiesbaden: Springer VS.

Sartori, G. (1987). *The Theory of Democracy Revisited*. Chatham: Chatham House.

Sartori, G. (2005 [1976]). *Parties and Party Systems: A Framework for Analysis*. Colchester: Cambridge University Press.

Schäfer, A. (2017). *Zwischen Repräsentation und Diskurs*. Wiesbaden: Springer.

Schindler, D. (2019). *Politische Führung im Fraktionenparlament: Rolle und Steuerungsmöglichkeiten der Fraktionsvorsitzenden im Deutschen Bundestag*. Baden-Baden: Nomos.

Schindler, P. (1999). *Datenhandbuch zur Geschichte des Deutschen Bundestages 1949 bis 1999*. Baden-Baden: Nomos.

Schöne, H. (2010). *Alltag im Parlament: Parlamentskultur in Theorie und Empirie*. Baden-Baden: Nomos.

Schüttemeyer, S.S. (1998). *Fraktionen im Deutschen Bundestag 1949–1997. Empirische Befunde und theoretische Folgerungen*. Opladen: Westdeutscher Verlag.

Schwanholz, J., & Jakobi, T. (2020). There's a place for us? The Digital Agenda Committee and internet policy in the German Bundestag. *Internet Policy Review*, 9(4), 1–24.

Schwarzmeier, M. (2001). *Parlamentarische Mitsteuerung: Strukturen und Prozesse informalen Einflusses im Deutschen Bundestag*. Wiesbaden: Westdeutscher Verlag.

Sieberer, U., & Höhmann, D. (2017). Shadow Chairs as Monitoring Device? A Comparative Analysis of Committee Chair Powers in Western European Parliaments. *Journal of Legislative Studies*, 23(3), 301–325.

Siefken, S.T. (2018a). *Parlamentarische Kontrolle im Wandel: Theorie und Praxis des Deutschen Bundestages*. Baden-Baden: Nomos.

Siefken, S.T. (2018b). 'Plenum im Kleinen' oder Ort der Verhandlung? Verständnisse und Forschungsbedarf zu den Fachausschüssen des Deutschen Bundestages. *Zeitschrift für Parlamentsfragen*, 49(4), 777–792.

Siefken, S.T. (2018c). Regierungsbildung 'wider Willen' – der mühsame Weg zur Koalition nach der Bundestagswahl 2017. *Zeitschrift für Parlamentsfragen*, 49(2), 407–436.

Siefken, S.T. (2020). Parlamentarische Kontrolle und Opposition – realistische Grundlagen für ein dynamisches Verständnis. In S. Bröchler, M. Glaab, & H. Schöne (eds.), *Kritik, Kontrolle, Alternativen: Wie leistungsfähig ist die Opposition?* Wiesbaden: Springer VS.

Siefken, S.T., & Schüttemeyer, S.S. (2013). The German Bundestag and External Expertise: Policy-Orientation as Counterweight to Deparliamentarisation? In K. Schubert & S. Blum (eds.), *Policy Analysis in Germany* (161–180). Bristol: The Policy Press.

Spohr, F. (2018). Interessen und Informationen in den öffentlichen Anhörungen des Deutschen Bundestages. In J. Brichzin, D. Krichewsky, L. Ringel, & J. Schank (eds.), *Soziologie der Parlamente* (309–335). Wiesbaden: Springer Fachmedien Wiesbaden.

Strasser, S., & Sobolewski, F. (2018). *So arbeitet der Deutsche Bundestag: 19. Wahlperiode* (19. Wahlperiode). Berlin: NDV.

Stratmann, T., & Baur, M. (2002). Plurality Rule, Proportional Representation, and the German Bundestag: How Incentives to Pork-Barrel Differ across Electoral Systems. *American Journal of Political Science*, 46(3), 506–514.

Strøm, K. (1998). Parliamentary Committees in European Democracies. *Journal of Legislative Studies*, 4(1), 21–59.

Strøm, K. (2000). Delegation and Accountability in Parliamentary Democracies. *European Journal of Political Research*, 37(3), 261–289.

Struck, P. (2010). *So läuft das: Politik mit Ecken und Kanten*. Berlin: Propyläen-Verlag.

Veit, S., & Jantz, B. (2013). Sunset Legislation: Theoretical Reflections and International Experiences. In A. Alemanno, F. den Butter, A. Nijsen, & J. Torriti (eds.), *Better Business Regulation in a Risk Society* (267–282). Springer.

Vetter, J. (1986). *Die Parlamentsausschüsse im Verfassungssystem der Bundesrepublik Deutschland: Rechtsstellung, Funktion, Arbeitsweise*. Frankfurt am Main, New York: Lang.

Weng, R. (1984). Die Bedeutung des Berichterstatters im Parlament. *Zeitschrift für Parlamentsfragen*, 15(1), 31–43.

Winkelmann, H. (2016). Parlamentarische Ausschussarbeit. In M. Morlok, U. Schliesky, & D. Wiefelspütz (eds.), *Parlamentsrecht: Handbuch* (754–795). Baden-Baden: Nomos.

Zeh, W. (1989). Das Ausschußsystem im Bundestag. In H.-P. Schneider & W. Zeh (eds.), *Parlamentsrecht und Parlamentspraxis* (1087–1102). Berlin: de Gruyter.

8 From 'a rubber stamp' to influencing policy

A critical view of committees in the Parliament of Ghana

Ernest Darfour

Although parliamentary committees are often seen as the primary engines of policy-making in a parliament, their effectiveness has been downplayed. This is particularly true in Africa, where research on the performance of parliamentary committees remains underdeveloped. With the practices and operations of committees shrouded in secrecy and often not open to the public, speculation is rife as to what happens in committees during the policy-making process. This has led to situations where committees in the Ghanaian Parliament have been branded as inept, wasteful, and a mere 'rubber stamp' for the executive branch. While these descriptions remain the dominant view, they fail to recognize the intricacies of policy-making and the legislative process, as well as the stage at which committees can influence policy and legislative outcomes in Ghana. Using parliamentary data including Hansard, committee reports, interviews with MPs, and participant observation of committee affairs, this chapter presents evidence to show that on various counts, the committees of Parliament are far more influential in the policy-making process than is commonly assumed. It explores the stages of the policy-making and legislative processes and discusses the ways through which committees contribute and influence policy in Ghana.

The chapter is divided into three sections. The first presents a historical overview of the development of Ghana's committee system. The second discusses the formal and informal operational characteristics of committees under the current Fourth Republican Parliament, focusing on the composition, functions, interactions, and informal arrangements that have developed in committees over the years. The third details the committees' role and influence, concluding that the influence of committees in the policy-making process in the Ghanaian parliament has increased significantly – much more than was previously thought to be the case.

The evolution of the committee system in Ghana

The evolution of parliamentary committees in Ghana can be traced to the British colonial experience, where committees were first established to support the work of the legislative councils and assemblies that were in force at the time. Until the emergence of the Fourth Republic in 1993, Ghana had

DOI: 10.4324/9781003106579-8

seen three previous republics, that all featured parliaments with a more or less elaborate committee system. In the First Republican Parliament (1960–1966), there were five committees: the House Committee, the Committee of Privileges, the Public Accounts Committee, the Business Committee, and the Standing Order Committee (Ayensu & Darkwa 2018: xvii). These committees were seasonal and ad hoc in nature, their primary function being to facilitate the organization and conduct of parliamentary business rather than undertaking policy-making and oversight activities (Ayensu & Darkwa 2018). In the First Republican Parliament, committees were rarely used in the consideration of bills, which were mostly passed under a certificate of urgency by the whole House, chaired by the First Deputy Speaker (Ayensu & Darkwa 2018: 147). Michael Mezey may have been right when, in his 1979 classification of the policy-making powers of legislatures, he categorized the First Republican Parliament of Ghana as a 'minimal legislature' with 'little or no policy-making power' (Mezey 1979).

From the Second Republican Parliament onwards, the committee system developed gradually into a more elaborate system. The rationale for the introduction of committees in the Second Republican Parliament was the following recognition:

> Legislative work in modern states has tended to increase in volume and to cover very complex subjects. Owing to the vast volume of legislation that has to be dealt with and the complex nature of the subject matter involved, even the most assiduous of legislators have found themselves unable to understand most of the legislation which has to be churned out. If legislators are going to do a good job, they need more time and a certain amount of specialized knowledge in their work. A device to bring this about is the committee system. This is the system by which the House is divided up into a number of committees covering all major legislative fields. Members, depending on their field of interest or specialization, belong to at least one of such committees which meet regularly to study legislative proposals in a manner which cannot be achieved by the whole House.
>
> (Report of the Constitutional Commission, 1968: 121)

According to the (then) Clerk to Parliament, K.B. Ayensu,

> 'the Constitution reinforced the parliamentary committee system under which expert advice was sought and bills scrutinized before their presentation for debate. The committee system also helped to enhance debate and public participation in the legislative process that increased public awareness of the work of Parliament'
>
> (Ayensu & Darkwa 2018: 149)

Under the Third Republican Parliament, the powers of committees expanded and increased tremendously. Article 85 of the 1979 Constitution established and gave prominence to parliamentary committees that had not existed in any of the previous republican constitutions. It established seven constitutional parliamentary committees, including the Public Accounts Committee, the Business Committee, the Standing Orders Committee, the Committee of Privileges Committee, the Subsidiary Legislation Committee, the Finance Committee, and the Foreign Affairs Committee. Furthermore, it empowered the legislature to appoint such other committees of parliament as the rules of parliamentary procedure should provide. The duty imposed upon the newly established committees was to investigate and inquire into the activities and administration of the ministries or departments assigned to them. Such investigations and inquiries were permitted to be extended into proposals for legislation. The Constitution further empowered Parliament to, at any time, appoint another committee to investigate any matter of public importance. While it granted the right of members to belong to at least one of the committees appointed, it indicated that the appointment should, so far as possible, reflect the different shades of opinion in Parliament. To effectively perform its functions,

> each of the committees shall have all such powers, rights and privileges as are vested in the High Court of Justice or a Justice of the High Court at a trial in respect of- *(a)* enforcing the attendance of witnesses and examining them on oath, affirmation or otherwise; *(b)* compelling production of documents; and *(c)* the issue of a commission or request to examine witnesses abroad.
>
> (Article 85 (7), 1979 Constitution)

The 1979 Constitution deliberately established a system that would make committees an independent and autonomous institution of Parliament, with powers to investigate and conduct inquiries into matters of public importance. However, the legislature would not live long enough to experience what the Constitution envisaged.

The current Fourth Republican Parliament, which replaced the Third Republican Parliament after ten years in abeyance, inherited most of the committee structures that were established by the 1979 Constitution. The 1992 Constitution provided general provisions on the establishment of standing and other committees as Parliament deemed fit, instead of the detailed provisions in the 1979 Constitution. Nevertheless, parliamentary committees began to formalize their processes, engagements, and interactions through the codification of conventions that regulate their engagement and interactions with stakeholders in the policy-making space.

In their analysis of committees according to their level of autonomy and independence of the plenary, Norton and Armed (2003: 7) categorized committees into 'chamber-oriented legislatures' and 'committee-oriented legislatures'. Accordingly, a chamber-oriented legislature centralizes legislative power in the plenary, whereas a committee-oriented legislature devolves legislative power to its constituent units, particularly committees, and empowers them to be independent and autonomous. Based on the above description, the First Republican Parliament can be categorized as a 'chamber-oriented legislature', while the Second, Third and Fourth Republican Parliaments can all be classified as 'committee-oriented legislatures'.

Formal and informal characteristics of committees

Composition and types of committees

The committees of the Ghanaian parliament are categorized into standing, select, and special or ad hoc. The standing committees deal with matters relating to the conduct and organization of parliamentary business, privileges and rights of members, and other constitutional obligations. The select committees are responsible for conducting investigations and inquiries into the activities and administration of ministries and departments. Ad hoc committees are appointed under Order 191 of the standing orders to 'investigate any matter of public importance' as well as 'to consider any bill that does not come under the jurisdiction of any of the Standing or Select Committees' (Order 191). After completing their tasks, such committees are dissolved. Examples of ad hoc committees established are presented in Table 8.1.

The parliament of Ghana is currently composed of 31 committees, 14 standing committees, and 17 select committees (Tables 8.2 and 8.3). The size of committees in Ghana's Parliament ranges from 18 to 30 with an average committee membership of 20 MPs. The rationale for operating a larger committee size is to ensure that the composition of committees reflects as much as possible the different shades of opinion in Parliament. Furthermore, a large committee size provides an opportunity for political parties to allocate high-profile committee membership to loyal members.

Table 8.1 Examples of ad hoc committees in Ghana

Date of establishment	Subject matter	Size	Chairperson
February 15, 2017	Investigate the effects of sand winning in the country	5	Majority Member
July 4, 2013	Develop code of conduct for Members of Parliament of Ghana	7	Majority Member
February 11, 2014	Investigate the demolition exercise undertaken by the Tema Development Corporation (TDC) at Adjei-Kojo in Tema, Ghana		Majority Member
January 31, 2017	Investigate allegation of bribery against the Chairman and Members of the Appointment Committee of the Seventh Parliament	5	Majority Member

Table 8.2 Standing committees of the Parliament of Ghana

No.	Name of Committee	Size	Chairperson	Responsibility
1	Selection	20	Speaker (Majority)	Composition of membership of Committees
2	Standing Orders	20	Speaker (Majority)	Review of rules of procedure
3	Business	20	Majority Leader	Arrangement of the agenda and business of the House
4	Privileges	30	1st Deputy Speaker (Majority)	Conduct of members
5	Public Accounts	25	A member of Minority	Watchdog committee on the public accounts of Ghana
6	Subsidiary Legislation	25	A member of Minority	Secondary legislation
7	House	25	Majority Leader	The welfare of Members and Staff
8	Finance	25	A member of Majority	Financial matters
9	Appointments	25	1st Deputy Speaker (Majority)	Appointments
10	Members' Holding Office of Profit	25	2nd Deputy Speaker (Minority)	Permission to hold other offices
11	Government Assurance	25	A member of Majority	Monitor promises of Government
12	Gender and Children	25	A member of Majority	Gender and children matters
13.	Special Budget	20	Majority Leader	Independent constitutional bodies.
14.	Poverty Reduction Strategy	20	A member of Majority	Policy intervention to reduce poverty

Source: Parliament of Ghana, 2000.

Many observers have questioned the effectiveness of the large committee size in Ghana. First, the large size makes it extremely difficult to secure a quorum required for a committee to meet and conduct business. A quorum for the commencement of committee meetings is one-third of the members present. The high threshold required for a meeting to commence has placed many committee meetings in jeopardy due to a lack of a quorum. A convention that has emerged over the years is that the quorum should include the presence of both the majority and minority members of the committee. A quorum formed with only one side is considered inappropriate.

Table 8.3 Select committees of the Parliament of Ghana

No.	Name of Committee	Size	Chairperson	Responsibility
1	Food, Agricultural and Cocoa Affairs		A member of Majority	Food and Agriculture
2	Lands and Forestry	18	A member of Majority	Lands and Forestry
3	Health	20	A member of Majority	Health
4	Constitutional, Legal and Parliamentary Affairs	18	A member of Majority	
5	Works and Housing	18	A member of Majority	Water Resources, Works and Housing
6	Local Government and Rural Development	20	A member of Majority	Local Government and Rural Development
7	Communication	18	A member of Majority	Communication, Information
8	Foreign Affairs	20	A member of Majority	Foreign Affairs and Regional Integration
9	Employment, Social Welfare and State Enterprises	20	A member of Majority	Employment Labour Relations and State Enterprises
10	Defence and Interior	18	A member of Majority	Defence and Internal affairs
11	Trade, Industry and Tourism	20	A member of Majority	Trade, industry and tourism
12	Environment, Science and Technology	18	A member of Majority	Environment, science, technology and innovation
13	Education	20	A member of Majority	Education
14	Youth, Sports and Culture	18	A member of Majority	Youth, sports and cultural issues
15	Mines and Energy	18	A member of Majority	Mining, energy, power and petroleum
16	Roads and Transport	18	A member of Majority	Roads, highways and transportation
17	Judiciary	21	A member of Majority	Judiciary and the Judicial Service

Source: Parliament of Ghana, 2000.

Committees have distinct and autonomous jurisdiction. However, when issues overlap, involving matters that fall within the jurisdiction of more than one committee, joint committees are constituted to handle that specific issue, after which they are dissolved. Examples of joint committees include Finance and Trade, Industry and Tourism on the Customs (Amendment) Bill, 2020; Roads and Transport and Constitutional, Legal and Parliamentary Affairs on the Ghana Civil Aviation (Amendment) Bill, 2015; Committee on Communications and Finance on the Electronic Communications (Amendment) Bill, 2016, among many others.

Membership assignment

Given the prominent role of committees in policy-making, as will be shown later, it is important to look into who becomes members of these committees and how they are individually selected. Theories regarding the legislative organization and committee formation abound. Although the literature on committee assignment is focused on legislative institutions elsewhere, the theory it espouses is relevant and can be applied in the Ghanaian context.

The literature has identified three relevant approaches that may help us understand committee assignment and allocation in the Ghanaian context. The 'distributive approach' suggests that Members of Parliament (MPs) pursuing reelection will seek to serve on committees where they can derive some material benefit or specific interests for their constituents. The 'informational approach' postulates that MPs will seek to become members of committees where they can better exploit their policy expertise, acquired through their educational and occupational background. The 'party-centred approach' suggests that party leaders will use committee assignments to increase party unity and thereby control the legislature (Martin & Mickler 2019; Gilligan & Krehbiel 1990; Krehbiel 1991; Weingast & Marshall 1988).

Overall, the distributive, informative, and partisan explanations provide some predictive power in explaining patterns of committee assignment in legislatures, suggesting an interplay between MP aspirations and party control. In Ghana, the decisions about committee assignment are made by the Committee of Selection, chaired by the Speaker. Before the composition of the Committee of Selection, leadership of the House meets to agree on a formula for the composition of the committees, which is normally determined by the proportion of the parliamentary seats each party secured in the general elections.

After the allocation formula has been approved by Parliament, the parties are required to determine the list of members allotted to each committee in accordance with the proportion approved in the allocation formula. The allocation formula for the Seventh Parliament was a ratio of 3:2 for the New Patriotic Party (NPP) and the National Democratic Congress (NDC) respectively, the only two parties represented in the legislature. This was derived from the proportion of seats that each party received, which equalled 169 and 106 for the NPP and the NDC respectively. This means that on a committee of 20 members, the NPP has 12 members and the NDC eight.

The actual allocation of membership is arranged by the party whips through a rigorous process involving a series of consultation and negotiations with the parliamentary leadership and party leadership. What can be gleaned from the practice over the period shows that experience, seniority, expertise, continuity, competence, and educational background are major factors considered before assigning an MP to a committee. Added to this mix are the internal party dynamics, gender, ethnicity, regionalism, and geographical spread.

The seniority of members is a critical factor when it comes to assignment to Ghanaian parliamentary committees. While most senior and experienced members who have served for more than two terms may be assigned as members and chairs of high-profile committees, new members or backbenchers may be assigned to low-profile committees as members. However, with the requisite expertise, competencies, and academic qualifications, new members who may be inexperienced in parliamentary business may be members on high-profile committees, and even hold leadership positions. In composing parliamentary committees in the Sixth Parliament, the education and the expertise of members were critical in considering the membership for the committee assignments (Table 8.4).

Seventy-eight percent of the members of the Committee on Constitutional, Legal and Parliamentary Affairs were lawyers (Table 8.4). Similarly, 57 and 52 percent of the membership of the Education and Finance committees were experts in education and finance, respectively. This indicates that the assignment of committees largely corresponds with the informational approach, where committee assignment matches members' professional expertise.

The internal party dynamics is another critical factor in determining who should and should not be assigned to a particular committee. This corresponds to the party-centred approach, according to which political parties use committee assignment as a tool to enforce compliance from their members. Parties in government always reward individuals who are loyal to the party with placement on high-profile committees such as Finance, Mines and Energy, Education, Local Government and Rural Development, among others. The opposition party, on the other hand, believes that although party loyalty is a critical factor, a person who can effectively communicate the party's position on various sectoral issues is desirable, and may therefore be assigned membership to high-profile committees.

MPs who have expertise and interest in matters being addressed in committees other than those to which they are members, can participate in and contribute to the meetings of these committees, but they cannot vote,

Table 8.4 MPs' professions and committee membership in Ghana

Committee	Size	Concentration of professional background
Constitutional, Legal and Parliamentary Affairs	18	78% are lawyers
Education	20	57% are education workers and teachers
Finance	25	52% are accountants, economist, and financial experts
Health	20	48% are health workers and medical doctors

Source: Darfour 2016.

as set out in Order 197 (b). Such members are referred to as 'friends of the committee'.

Since the parties want to control their members and what they do on these committees, party interests often override everything else. Members are not free agents and those who do not follow the party line are sanctioned. In many instances, members do not have a say in the committee assigned to them. Their assignment is the sole prerogative of the whips and the Committee of Selection chaired by the Speaker. However, on a few occasions, the whips negotiate with senior and experienced members over their assignment before they are appointed to particular committees (interview with deputy majority whip, 2016).

Turnover in committee membership

The tenure of committee membership officially is for only one year. However, in reality, once a committee has been appointed it lasts the entire four-year parliamentary term. Turnover in committee membership occurs when a member of a committee is appointed as a minister or a deputy minister, resigns their membership, or is rescheduled to another committee. As a convention, ministers and deputy ministers are not allowed to serve on a committee which conducts oversight of the ministry they handle. J.H. Mensah, then-majority leader in 2001, argued that 'nobody holding ministerial office is proposed as the chairman of any select Committee; neither is anybody proposed as a member of the Select Committee dealing with a portfolio under his care' (Parliamentary Debates, 2001). This convention evolved from the Second Parliament of the Fourth Republic and consequently, when Johnson Asiedu Nketiah was appointed as deputy minister for Food and Agriculture under President Rawlings, he stepped down as the chairman of the Mines and Energy Committee. Similarly, Steve Akorli was removed as chairman of the Finance Committee because he was appointed a minister.

Since its inception, the Seventh Parliament has experienced a higher turnover in committee membership than any of the previous six parliaments. The high turnover recorded is mainly a result of the appointment of many committee chairpersons and members as ministers of state, deputy ministers of state, regional ministers as well as deputy regional ministers. According to the report of the Committee of Selection, these appointments hamper the work of the committees because of 'the frequent absence of such key members which adversely impacts the effectiveness of the Committees' (Parliament of Ghana 2019b).

Relevant roles in committees

Malcolm E. Jewel defined the concept of roles in a legislative system and referred to it as 'the pattern of expectations or norms of behaviour that are associated with a position in a social structure. The role of a legislator consists of the rights, duties, and obligations that are expected of anyone holding that position' (Kornberg & Musolf 1970: 462). The dominant roles in committees are the chairperson and the ranking member. The chairpersons of committees, except the Public Accounts Committee and the subsidiary legislation committees, are selected from the majority party, while the minority party has a recognized leader called the ranking member who protects the interests of the opposition on the committee.

Committee chairs play a key role in the work of the committees and the parliament as a whole. The chair presides over the meetings of the committee, speaks on its behalf when motions on its report are moved in plenary, and has an important function in the legislative process. The chair leads the committee during the consideration stage of bills and introduces all proposed amendments for and on behalf of the committee.

The ranking member, on the other hand, is the spokesperson of the opposition on the committees and they ensure that the minority position is canvassed in the policy-making process. For consensus-building, the views of the ranking members are heard on all matters before the committees and during the second reading stage and the consideration stage of the legislative process, as well as during debates on committees reports at plenary.

Committee meeting and decision-making

Meetings of committees are held in camera unless the committee decides otherwise. A committee would decide to sit in public when matters of urgent public interest or public interest legislation are referred to them for consideration and report. Despite the default position for committees to sit in camera, the Appointment Committee, the Public Accounts Committee and lately the Government Assurances Committee, have held all their meetings in public.

The model of decision-making in committees is either by consensus or by majoritarian decision. The pattern of interactions and deliberations in committees in Ghana's parliament has always been by consensus and a favourable report made to plenary. The committees rarely reject any government proposals but will adapt and modify them. However, rigorous policy bargaining and negotiations are undertaken, and compromises achieved, before issues are communicated to the plenary for approval. More than 90 percent of decisions that have been taken in committees have been by consensus. However, this legislative behaviour comes across to the public as a sign of weakness of the committees acting as a countervailing authority to the executive. In the mind of the public, the committees are rubber stamps, approving whatever policy the executive introduces.

Despite the high level of consensus in committees' decision-making, there are reported cases of disagreement and split decisions leading to boycotts, particularly by the opposition. The Appointments Committee's report on the president's nominee for ministerial and deputy ministerial appointments occasionally attracts disagreements, leading to majority decisions. In the Seventh

Parliament, the Appointments Committee's recommendation on Boakye Agyarko, minister designate for energy and Ms Otiko Afisah Djaba, minister designate for children and social protection were made by a majority decision, because the minority members of the committee disagreed with their nomination (Parliament of Ghana 2017).

Agenda-setting

The tasks of Parliament are many and varied, to the extent that committees are always overstretched for time to process all the referrals from the plenary. Considering the amount of time that committees have at their disposal, it would be very unlikely for them to process all the business referred to them. Döring stated that 'without agenda control, it would be difficult to pass the annual budget in time, to enact a government's legislative programme promised to the voters at the polls, or to make room for debate on urgent questions'(Döring 2001: 147). Agenda control, therefore, strives to achieve a delicate balance between 'the right of the majority to govern and the right of the minorities to be heard' (Huber 1994: 1).

The Ghanaian Parliament sets and controls its own agenda, with committees implementing the agenda that has been agreed to by plenary. The main vehicle for the processing and scheduling of the agenda for the plenary is the 25-member Business Committee, chaired by the majority leader, with a senior member of the minority party/parties as the ranking member. All parliamentary business except statements by MPs is programmed by the Business Committee. The committee meets every Thursday when Parliament is in session to determine the business for the ensuing week. The business statement of the week, including each day's activities, is presented to the House on Fridays by the majority leader for the information of and adoption by Parliament.

The prioritization of parliamentary business has led to a distinction between the businesses of government, legislative, and private members as shown in Table 8.5. Government business emanates from the executive in the form of policy proposals, legislation, the annual budget, legislative instruments, ministerial statements, financial and economic transactions, and loan agreements. Private members' business includes statements by MPs, parliamentary questions, private member's bills, private member's motions, and petitions. Legislative business entails all the activities of the Parliament, including reports of committee's initiatives, investigations, and inquiries. A study conducted by Darfour (2016) found that government business takes about 65 percent of all the floor time in Parliament, while private members' and legislative business occupy the rest as shown in Table 8.5. This shows the extent to which agenda-setting in the House is skewed towards the executive to the neglect of both private members' and legislative business.

Table 8.5 Types of parliamentary business in Ghana

Types of Business	Private Members	Public/Government	Legislative
Nature of Business	Statements, Parliamentary questions, Private Members' Motion (PMM), Private Members' Bills (PMBs).	Government Bills, Motions, Resoultions, Annual Budget, Supplementary budget, Loan Agreements, Request for waiver of taxes and duties, President state of the nation address and others.	Reports of committees' initiatives, investigations and inquiries; Auditor-General's reports on the public accounts of Ghana; Annual reports of state enterprises.
Percentage of business	15%	80%	5%
Floor time	25%	65%	10%
Comments	No PMBs yet; PMM often opposed and rejected; statements and questions are always included in the daily agenda of Parliament.	Constitutes a chunk of the business of Parliament, without which the legislature and committees become idle.	Committees initiated activities reports non-existent; occasional tabling of annual reports of MDAs; and very limited time for debate on Public Accounts Committee reports of the Auditor-General.

Source: Order Paper, Votes and Proceedings and Hansard.

Committees are normally allowed to determine their own agenda with respect to operational plans, internal organization, and work plans. The operational plans of the committees include scheduling of meetings times and what issues the committee may consider within its scope of authority. The plenary agenda is also of a major priority to committees who are supposed to support the legislature as a whole to deliver on its mandate. Apart from the committees' internal operations and organizational matters, referrals from the House are treated differently. These referrals, if they are bills, take precedent over the committees' own programmes of activities for the period.

The committees' agendas depend on the overall agenda of Parliament as the House has to wait for reports from committees before it can proceed on matters under consideration. As a result, committees are prohibited by the Constitution and the standing orders to unduly delay a bill introduced in Parliament by or on behalf of the president for more than three months (Article 106(14) of the Constitution). Apart from bills, a committee to which a matter has been referred is expected to report to the House before the end of each session of Parliament. If a committee is unable to complete consideration of the bill before the end of the session, it will report this to the House. All uncompleted business pending before the House or its committees lapses with the session (Standing Order 212). However, in some instances, committees have unduly delayed legislation, leading to its natural demise.

The policy-making process

The policy-making process involves four major stages: initiation, formulation, legislation, and implementation. Policy-making in Ghana is a shared responsibility between Parliament and the executive. Although both the executive and the legislature have the power to initiate policy according to the Constitution, the process has been dominated by the executive, with the legislature relegated to the background. Since the inception of the Fourth Republic, no legislation has emanated from Parliament through its members or committees. The following sections will explore the various stages of the policy-making process, highlighting the role of parliamentary committees and how they have influenced this process.

Initiation and formulation stage

A policy is first conceived and initiated as part of the formulation process through consultations with the actors in the policy-making space. The actors include policy-planning organizations, interest groups, government bureaucracies, Parliament, and the president. The policy initiatives and proposal are driven by inspirations from party manifestos, campaign promises of winning government, gaps in existing legislation, international obligations, agreements which the government and the state are a party to, and other societal actions that need to be regulated. Selecting a policy out of the numerous alternatives is a very complex and dynamic process involving ministries, departments, and agencies of the government. After a rigorous process of engagement, the policy is then drafted with the required policy instruments that would give legal and financial effect to the measure. If the proposed policy requires a legislative solution, a bill is drafted; however, if the policy requires a financial measure, a budget is drawn up and both are then presented to Parliament for approval.

A critical look at the policy cycle shows that in Ghana, the legislature does not play an active role in the initiation and formulation stage. While this is in accord with the principle of separation of powers of the Constitution, it is believed that the involvement of the legislature in the policy-making from the beginning would enhance the understanding of members on all the policy options available for the choice of a particular policy before they are introduced into Parliament. It will also save time, since members' concerns on the policy will be taken into consideration before it is finalized and introduced into the House.

In recent times, some efforts have been made to at least involve relevant parliamentary committees in initial stages of the policy-making process. The current situation is that government departments and agencies have developed a procedure for a pre-legislative discussion of policy proposals at the formulation stage, with relevant parliamentary committees responsible for the measure before the policy is formally introduced into Parliament. Civil society organizations that seek to influence a particular policy also lobby the relevant committees, party caucuses and individual members of Parliament to brief the members on that policy issue before its introduction into Parliament. This serves to build consensus among MPs as well as enable them to influence policy at the formulation stage before the policy is formally introduced.

Legislative stage

The legislative process in Parliament follows a cumbersome procedure that is set out in the 1992 Fourth Republican Constitution and the Standing Order of the Parliament of Ghana. Figure 8.1, shown below, depicts the legislative process in Ghana as consisting of seven stages with a defined timeline regulating the entire process.

The process begins with the formal introduction of a draft bill into Parliament. The bill is gazetted for 14 days, after which it is introduced and read for the first time in Parliament. When a committee determines that the bill is urgent, the requirement of the 14-day gazetting is waived. The bill is then referred to a single committee or joint committee for consideration, review, and report. At the second reading, the principles underpinning the bill are debated. The committee's report, together with the memorandum that accompanied the bill, are then debated and voted upon at the second reading stage. With a favourable vote, the bill is moved into the consideration stage, where the committee's amendments and any other amendments introduced

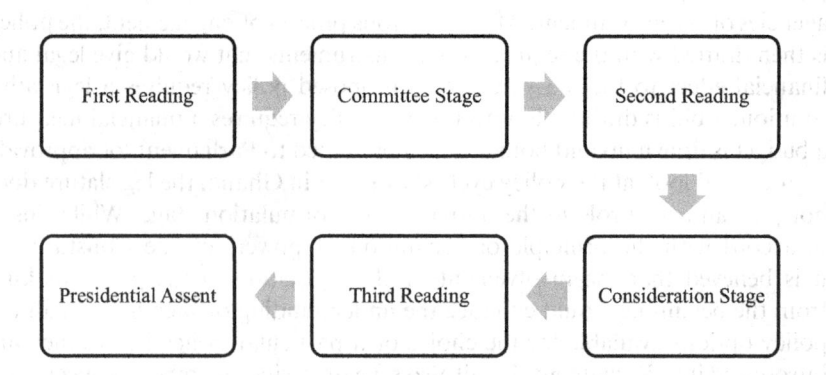

First Reading → Committee Stage → Second Reading → Consideration Stage → Third Reading → Presidential Assent

Figure 8.1 The legislative process in Ghana.
Source: Based on the Standing Orders of the Parliament of Ghana, 2000.

by MPs are debated and voted on in a clause-by-clause manner. During this examination, each clause of the bill is read out and thoroughly examined after which a vote is taken before that clause becomes part of the bill (Standing Order 129). Parliamentary officials interviewed confirmed the existence of an additional stage that has been introduced since 1999, with the increased number of amendments to legislation during the consideration phase. This new procedure is called the 'winnowing stage'. At that stage, all the different amendments to the legislation are synchronized, introduced, and voted upon. After the consideration phase, members have the final opportunity to make changes or amendments in a second consideration stage before the bill is ready for a third and final time and passed.

The powers and influence of committees in the legislative process

The approval stage is when the draft policy is introduced to Parliament. The legislative process for the approval of the policy is regulated by the 1992 Constitution and the standing orders of Parliament. Article 106 of the Constitution requires that, 'whenever a bill is read the first time in Parliament, it shall be referred to the appropriate committee appointed under article 103 of this Constitution which shall examine the bill in detail and make all such inquiries concerning it as the committee considers expedient or necessary'. It is further provided that 'where a bill has been deliberated upon by the appropriate committee, it shall be reported to Parliament' where 'The report of the Committee, together with the explanatory memorandum to the bill, shall form the basis for a full debate on the bill for its passage, with or without amendments, or its rejection, by Parliament'.

The role of committees in policy-making at the legislative stage gleaned from the Constitution and the standing orders are as follows: they examine the bills in detail, they make such inquiries the committee considers necessary and expedient, they present a report to the House with or without amendments, they build the basis for a full debate on the bill with their report and they recommend the adoption or rejection of the bill by Parliament.

All in all, committees in the Ghanaian Parliament have the power to adopt, reject, and amend legislation that is referred to them. While these formal powers are subject to approval by Parliament, the latter has always adopted the report and recommendation of committees – so the power of the former is final in the policy-making process.

Adoption and rejections of bills by committees

Table 8.6 shows that from 1993 to 2017, a total of 610 bills were introduced and referred to committees, out of which 479 were adopted. While 26 of the bills were withdrawn, 103 lapsed, with only two rejections. The data presented in Table 8.6 shows that the committees have the power to recommend to Parliament to either adopt or reject bills and proposals that are referred to

Table 8.6 Success rate of government bills introduced to the Parliament of Ghana (1993–2017)

	1993–1997	1997–2001	2001–2005	2005–2009	2009–2013	2013–2017	Total
Number of bills introduced	90	88	95	113	107	117	610
Number of bills passed	82	66	70	94	82	85	479
Number of urgent bills	8	3	6	6	7	-	30
Number of bills withdrawn	1	1	2	4	12	7	26
Number of bills that lapsed	7	21	23	15	13	24	103
Number of bills rejected	-	-	-	-	-	2	2
Number of bills that could not pass	8	22	25	19	25	33	131

Source: Parliament of Ghana, Table Office, 2019.

it. Although the executive, without parliamentary intervention, can withdraw bills introduced into Parliament, most of the bills withdrawn were occasioned by an intervention by a committee of the House, indicating the extent to which they can influence policy-making at the legislative stage. In Table 8.6, we observed an increased rate of withdrawal of bills from one in the First and Second Parliaments to 12 in the Fifth Parliament. The Sixth Parliament recorded withdrawals of seven bills.

This shows how the legislature can influence policy-making behind the scenes through committees. A number of reasons account for the withdrawal of bills by the committees, including a major deficit in the bill, the introduction of many committee amendments that if effected would greatly change the intent of the law, public opposition to the measure being introduced, and poor timing (Darfour 2016).

Although committees of Parliament can recommend in extreme cases to reject bills, rejection of bills is a rare occurrence because of the effect it may have on the confidence and image of the executive. However, for the first time, in 2013, the legislature rejected the National Fiscal Stabilisation Levy (Amendment) Bill, when the government refused to withdraw the legislation after it has been advised to do so by the Finance Committee. The Finance Committee's report stated that 'The Committee has thoroughly examined the Bill and considers the passage of the Bill to be premature and accordingly recommends to the House to adopt its report and not to approve the National Fiscal Stabilisation Levy (Amendment) Bill, 2013' (Parliament of Ghana 2013). Again, in 2016, the legislature by a majority decision (Ayes 125; Noes 95) rejected the Constitution (Amendment) Bill, 2016, that sought to change the date of the presidential election from December 7 to November 7 in each election year.

Committee amendments

Committees in Ghana's Parliament have strong formal powers. Through the instrumentality of amendments, committees can effect the desired changes and substantially transform legislation. The ability of committees to carry out legislative amendments to bills indicates how influential they are (Park 2002). For Blondel, 'strictly, legislatures are involved in decisions when they pass or amend bills of governmental origin' (Blondel 1973: 109). The bills passed by the legislature go through a rigorous process of amendment at both the committee and at the consideration stages in Parliament, as shown in Figure 8.1. Louise Thompson, in her study of the Public Bills Committees in the House of Commons, identified two categories of amendments: 'managerial and substantial' (Thompson 2015). The managerial amendment entails the deletions of redundant lines, clauses, and words as well as 'the correction of typographical and technical errors' to bring clarity to the subject matter of the bill (ibid). A substantial amendment, on the other hand, is the introduction or deletion of clauses, schedules, lines or words that may substantially 'change the aim, purpose or subject of the clause or schedule in question' (ibid).

To determine the extent to which the committees carry out amendments to government bills, four bills were selected for analysis. These were the Petroleum Revenue Management Bill, the Economic and Organised Crime Bill, University of Ghana Bill, and the Presidential Transition Bill. The four bills were among the 82 bills that were passed in the Fifth Parliament (2009–2013). These bills were selected based on the high public interest shown when they were first introduced on the floor, as well as the large number of amendments they received. Because of the high public interest that was shown, this study sought to establish the influence the committees have at the committee stage and the consideration stage of the legislative process. The analysis was based on the examination of the text of the selected bills and the Acts, as well as data gathered at the consideration stage of the bills in the Order Paper, which advertises the amendments, and the Votes and Proceedings, which reported on what was accepted, withdrawn, and rejected by the House.

The analysis shows that the committees that considered these legislation proposals made a significant impact on the legislative process by basically transforming the various legislative proposals of government into actionable policies.

Table 8.7 illustrates that amendments to government bills have become an avenue through which parliamentary committees can influence and shape government policy and contribute to legislation. In all, the four bills analysed show that the committees proposed a considerable number of amendments, with more than half of the proposed amendments approved. For instance, the Petroleum Management Revenue Bill attracted a total of 350 amendments, out of which 53 percent were approved by Parliament. The University of Ghana Bill received a total of 71 amendments of which 56 percent were accepted as part of the bill. The Presidential Transition Bill received a total of 54 amendments, of which 83 percent were accepted by the legislature. The Economic and Organised Crime Bill received a total 144 amendments, of which 91 percent were accepted.

Table 8.7 Amendments of selected legislation in Ghana

	Petroleum Revenue Management Bill (2010)	Economic and Organised Crime Bill (2009)	University of Ghana Bill (2010)	Presidential Transition Bill (2010)
Total amendments	350	144	71	54
Amendment accepted	185	131	40	45
Percentage accepted	53%	91%	56%	83%
First reading	July 20, 2010	July 7, 2009	July 2, 2010	Oct 28, 2010
Committee in charge	Finance	CLPA[a]	Education	CLPA[a]
Duration at committee stage	4 months	11 months	10 days	8 months
Second reading	3 days	1 day	1 day	1 day
Consideration stage	18 days	4 days	5 days	4 days
Third reading	March 2, 2011	August 2, 2010	July 29, 2010	March 16, 2012
Duration of passage	8 months	13 months	27 days	17 months
Presidential assent	April 11, 2011	Sept. 6, 2010	Oct 5, 2010	May 31, 2012
Act no.	815	804	806	845

Source: Parliament of Ghana, Table Office, 2019.
Note:
a. Constitutional, Legal and Parliamentary Affairs.

At both the committee and consideration stage of the legislative process, there is much bargaining and many trade-offs between government ministers, the chairperson of the committee, the majority leader, the leader of government business, and individual members, in order to get their amendments through. The success rate of the proposed amendment depends on the nature of the amendment, and whether it is of a substantial or managerial nature. While managerial amendments are easily approved, substantial amendments go through intense debate, negotiation, and compromise before they are either accepted or rejected by consensus. When the amendments are so substantial that, in the view of the committee, they may alter the original intent of the proposed legislation, the government is asked by the committee to redraw the measure, incorporate the changes, and reintroduce it.

The approval process, in theory, is controlled and dominated by the legislature and MPs. Parliament sets it own agenda, prioritizes its business, and controls the legislative process through the relevant parliamentary committees. However, in practice, the executive determines which business the legislature undertakes at any given time. Parliamentary committees lack independence and autonomy over the business that is referred to them, as the decisions and recommendations of committees are not absolute, but can be overturned by the House. For instance, the House varied the reccomendation of the Privileges Committee to suspend the member for Assin North constituency, Kennedy Agyapong, for a contemptuous remark that brought the institution of parliament into disrepute. Instead, the member was made to apologize for his action (Parliament of Ghana 2019a). Nevertheless, the legislature's influence in the process has been substantial in amending legislation.

Implementation stage receives little attention of committees

The implementation stage of the policy-making process is where governmental agencies responsible for the policy operationalize it after approval by the legislature. It also includes post-implementation activity conducted by the executive and Parliament to ensure that the policy is implemented successfully. Article103(3) of Ghana's Constitution states that 'Committees of Parliament shall be charged with such functions, including the investigation and inquiry into the activities and administration of ministries and departments as Parliament may determine; and such investigation and inquiries may extend to proposals for legislation'. Parliamentary committees are therefore responsible for conducting oversight of governmental activities.

Oversight, which constitutes a critical function of parliamentary committees, is relegated to the background in the Parliament of Ghana, since there is no obligation on committees to submit to the House or publish the reports and recommendations arising from investigations and inquiries that have been undertaken by committees. This means that many committees of Parliament that are expected to carry out investigations into the activities of government agencies have not done so. Since the inception of the Fourth Republic, no committee's report or recommendation has led to a proposal for legislation. A critical look at the mandate of the Committee on Employment, Social Welfare and State Enterprises indicates that the committee is responsible for the oversight of the operations of state enterprises in Ghana (Order 184). The committee is mandated 'to review and study on a continuing basis the operations of State Enterprises with a view to determining their economy and efficiency' (see Order 184). Additionally, the committee must 'examine the reports and accounts of public enterprises and in the context of their autonomy and efficiency, whether their operations are being managed in accordance with sound business principles and prudent commercial practices'. (ibid). Furthermore, the committee is to examine the income and expenditure of any public corporation and state enterprise, or other body or organization established by an act of Parliament. The accounts of these enterprises are audited by the auditor-general and form the basis of the investigations of the committee. The committee reports to the parliament and the recommendations contained in their reports are deemed to be directives to the respective corporations or statutory boards for due compliance.

Despite the enormous powers given to the Committee on State Enterprises, it has remained reluctant to engage in oversight activities.

Looking at the strong formal mandate of the committee, it was expected that the legislature, through the committee, would ensure accountability in the public enterprise sector. However, this sector has been a fraught with difficulties, causing the taxpayers enormous loss of revenue due to inefficiencies (Aryee 2019). While state enterprises, including the Electricity Company of Ghana, Volta River Authority, and the Ghana Water Company, for instance, have consistently proved inefficient, no efforts have been made by the committee to inquire into the practices of these entities.

The committee system has not yet taken firm root in the oversight and scrutiny function of Parliament. The intent of Article 103 of the Constitution, which empowers committees to act as high policy-making and oversight levers of the political system, has not so far been realized.

Conclusion: the strength of committees in policy-making

This chapter has examined the influence of parliamentary committees on policy-making in Ghana. The analysis has demonstrated that committees can be powerful at the legislative stage of the policy-making process, and that much of that power is exercised through amendments to the legislation, as well as the ability to recommend to the executive to withdraw policies or bills that have been introduced. Given the success rate of government bills, there is a strong temptation to simply conclude that Ghana's Parliament is a rubber stamp, as earlier literature has suggested. However, careful analysis suggests that the committees not only approve the government bills, but also make remarkable changes that transform proposed legislation.

It was noted the government remains a dominant actor in the policy-making process; it is the source of all policies and practically no legislation can be introduced other than by the government. Coupled with the fact that the government always has a majority who occupy all the levers of power and decision-making centres of the House, it is expected that their control of the legislative process would be absolute. However, as has been shown, the legislative process is firmly in the hands of the legislature, particularly its committees, and it has control over the process once a bill becomes the property of the House. The committees, more often than not, have contributed to the power of the legislature to influence executive proposals at this level. Recent evidence points to trends that have increased the effectiveness of parliamentary committees in the legislative process. The growing capacity and the increasing involvement of parliamentary committees in the various stages of the policy process have ensured that gradually committees in the Ghanaian Parliament have transformed from a rubber stamp to a policy influencer.

References

Aryee J. A. (2019) 'Six decades of the public sector in Ghana: issues and prospects', Institute of Democratic Governance Policy Brief, *LGR/001/19*. In Ayensu, K.B. & Darkwa, S.N. (2018). *The Evolution of Parliament of Ghana*. Sub-Saharan Publishers.

Blondel, J. (1973). *Comparative Legislatures*. Englewood Cliffs, NJ: Prentice-Hall, Inc.

Darfour, E. (August 9, 2014). The Parliament of Ghana: A countervailing force in the governance process? www.psa.ac.uk/sites/default/files/Ghana%20-%20Overview_EDarfour.pdf (access: 02.09.2020).

Darfour, E. (2016). Determinants of Legislative Trust in Ghana. University of Hull, UK: Unpublished PhD thesis.

Döring, H. (2001). Parliamentary Agenda Control and Legislative Outcomes in Western Europe. *Legislative Studies Quarterly*, 26(1), 145.

Gilligan, T.W. & Krehbiel, K. (1987). Collective Decision making and Standing Committees: An Informational Rationale for Restrictive Amendment Procedures. *Journal of Law, Economics, and Organization*, Volume 3(2), 287–335.

Gilligan, T. & Krehbiel, K. (1990). Organization of Informative Committees by a Rational Legislature. *American Journal of Political Science*, 34(2), 531–564

Huber, A. (1994). Reform of Parliament. Report for the New Delhi Conference of the Association of Secretaries-General of Parliaments, *Constitutional and Parliamentary Information*.

Kornberg, A. & Musolf. L.D. (ed.) (1970). *Legislatures in Developmental Perspective*. Durham, NC: Duke University Press.

Krehbiel, K. (1991). *Information and Legislative Organization*. Ann Arbor: University of Michigan Press.

Lasswell, H.D. (1951). The Policy Orientation. In D. Lerner & H.D. Lasswell, (eds.) *The Policy Sciences: Recent Developments in the Scope and Method*. Stanford: Stanford University Press, 3–15.

Martin, S. & Mickler, T.A. (2019). Committee Assignments: Theories, Causes and Consequences. *Parliamentary Affairs*, 72(1),77–98.

Mattson, I. & Strøm, K. (1995), Parliamentary Committees. In Herbert Döring (ed.). *Parliaments and Majority Rule in Western Europe*. St. Martin Press, 249–307.

Mezey, M.L. (1979). *Comparative Legislatures*, Duke University Press, Durham, N.C.

Ninsin, K.A. (2009). *How Parliament Decides: Decision Making in Ghana's Parliament*. The Advent Press.

Norton, P. (2005). *Parliament in British Politics*. Macmillan.

Norton, P. & Armed, N. (2003). *Parliament in Asia*. Frank Cass.

Ofori-Mensah, M. & Rutherford, L. (2011). Effective Parliamentary Oversight: Mission Impossible? *Institute of Economic Affairs*, 17(3), 1–9

Olson, D. M. & Mezey, M. (1991). *Legislatures in the Policy Process,* Cambridge University Press.

Park, C.W. (1999). "Change is short but continuity is long: policy influence of the National Assembly in Newly Democratised Korea" In P. Norton, & N. Ahmed (eds.). *Parliaments in Asia*, 66–82.

Park, C. W. (2002). Change Is Short but Continuity Is Long: Policy Influence of the National Assembly in Newly Democratized Korea. In P. Squire, G. Loewenberg & D. R. Kiewiet (eds.), *Legislatures: Comparative Perspectives on Representative Assemblies*, The University of Michigan Press.

Parliament of Ghana (2000). *Standing Orders of the Parliament of Ghana*.
Parliament of Ghana (2001), Parliamentary Debates, 01.02.2001.
Parliament of Ghana (2013), Parliamentary Debates, 12.12.2013.
Parliament of Ghana (2017), Parliamentary Debates, 03.02.2017.
Parliament of Ghana (2019a), Parliamentary Debates, 10.01.2019.
Parliament of Ghana (2019b), Report of the Committee of Selection on the Re-composition of Committees of the House, 28.06.2019.
Republic of Ghana. (1992). *Fourth Republican Constitution*, Assembly Press.
Russell, M. & Benton, M. (2009). Assessing the policy impact of parliament: Methodological Challenges and possible future approaches. *Paper for PSA Legislative Studies Specialist Group Conference.*
Thompson, L. (2015). *Making British Law: Committees in Action*. Palgrave Macmillan Ltd.
Warren, S. (2005). Legislative Performance in Ghana: An Assessment of the Third Parliament of the Fourth Republic, 2001–2005. *Critical Perspectives*, No.19.
Weingast, B. & Marshall, W.J. (1988). The Industrial Organization of Congress; or, Why Legislatures, Like Firms, Are Not Organized as Markets. *Journal of Political Economy*, 96, (1), 132–63.

9 Parliamentary committees in the Hungarian Parliament

Instruments of political parties and government agenda control

Csaba Nikolenyi

Similar to the legislatures of other post-communist democracies in East–Central Europe, the Parliament of Hungary also adopted a sophisticated and elaborate system of parliamentary committees (Khmelko, 2012).[1] This new committee system promised to provide important opportunities not only for the governing majorities to implement their legislative programme effectively but also for the parliamentary opposition to make a meaningful and significant contribution to the legislative process and to exercise oversight and scrutiny (Zubek 2015). However, the development of a strongly party-centred – and often party-controlled – political system left no room for the institutionalization of genuinely autonomous and meaningful committees. The subordination of parliamentary committees to political parties went hand in hand with the erosion of parliamentary autonomy since the 2010 election, which started the uninterrupted dominance of the conservative coalition of the Fidesz Party and the Christian Democratic Party ever since (Ilonszki 2007, 2019).

This chapter documents the evolution of the Hungarian parliamentary committee system over the past three decades (1990–2020). Its central argument is that the Hungarian case lends support to the conventional adage that the relationship between the power of legislative committees and political parties is inverse: committees can flourish and become autonomous legislative actors when parties are weak but, conversely, they will be marginalized where and when parties are strong. After providing an overview of the Hungarian political system, the chapter introduces the legal foundation of legislative committees. It proceeds to survey the key formal characteristics of the different committees in the Hungarian Parliament and their actual performance.

Committees, parties, and governments: a brief review of the literature

Legislative committees are embedded within a broader framework of political institutions that exert direct and indirect constraints on their effectiveness. According to Hazan (2001), the strength and function of parliamentary committees depend specifically on 1) the balance of executive–legislature

DOI: 10.4324/9781003106579-9

relations, 2) the party system, which shapes fragmentation of the legislatures as well as the size and composition of the governing coalition, and 3) the degree to which the electoral system encourages the emergence of strong and cohesive political parties in the legislature. A long tradition of legislative research claimed that the logic of separation of powers and checks and balances between the executive and legislature that characterized presidential systems of government led to stronger and more autonomous legislative committees there than in parliamentary systems (Lees & Shaw 1979: 400–1). Among the latter, however, there is considerable variation with regard to the type (coalition vs. one party) and size (majority vs. minority) of government, with important implication for committee strength and functioning (Zubek 2015).

A fragmented legislature should limit the power of political parties vis-à-vis parliamentary committees for a couple of reasons. First, large political parties can better afford to be present and advocate their positions in committee decision-making. Second, larger parties can also better afford to take advantage of the legislative specialization of their members than smaller political parties who have to send their members to multiple committees. Since by definition more fragmented legislatures tend to have fewer large parties, we should expect that committees in such assemblies will develop a greater degree of autonomy from parties.

The institutional mechanism by which the executive retains the confidence of parliament further affects the balance of power between the two branches of government. In most political systems, the legislature can censure the incumbent executive by passing a simple vote of no confidence; in a smaller number of polities the government can be terminated only by a *constructive* vote of no confidence. The latter leads to more stable and ideologically cohesive coalitions and it is reasonable to expect that the executive would prevail more easily over parliament (Piersig 2016; Rubabshi & Hasson forthcoming). In other words, the coalition agreement that the governing parties enter into will have much more of a bite and will be more enforceable when political institutions, such as the constructive vote of no confidence, make it more difficult for the legislature to overturn the executive.

Conventional wisdom about the effect of the electoral system on legislative committees is somewhat mixed. On the one hand, the strong candidate-centred nature of the US electoral system has been linked to lead to strong legislative committees. On the other hand, Martin (2011) notes that the logic of the US Congress case does not travel well to other cases and proposes that it is the mechanism by which a personal vote is cultivated – via fiscal particularism or non-fiscal means – that explains better the resultant strength of legislative committees.

Much research has focused on the relationship between political parties and committees. According to earlier work, there is an inverse relationship between the strength of committees and the strength of political parties (Khmelko 2012; Olson & Mezey 1991; Shaw 1990; Weingast & Marshall 1988), while more recently, scholars who build on the US 'partisan coordination school' (Cox & McCubbins 1993; Kiewet & McCubbins 1991) have claimed that strong parties could coexist with strong committees (Kim & Loewenberg 2005; Martin 2011). In the US Congress, the argument goes, the majority party maintains its control over the legislature by delegating power to strong committees that it will in turn closely monitor and scrutinize. In parliamentary systems, strong parties may need strong committees as a way to enforce their coalition agreements (Carroll & Cox 2012; Kim & Loewenberg 2005) or ensure strong government control over the legislative agenda (Döring 1995; Ilonszki & Jager; Zubek 2008, 2011).

Hungary's political institutions are marked by a party-centred electoral system and clear control over Parliament by the government of the day both in terms of legislation and oversight. At the transition to democracy, Hungary adopted a mixed-member system. It combined closed-list proportional representation with a modified two-round majority rule and a national compensatory tier that allocated seats among qualifying parties. In 2011, the electoral reform included the reduction of the total number of parliamentary seats from 386 to 199. Also, the two-round nominal tier was replaced by first-past-the-post districts, and the regional closed party lists were replaced by closed national lists. While the list tier of the reformed electoral system continued to provide mild compensation for smaller parties, it now also included a significant bonus for the party of the winning candidate from each district.

Largely as a result of the mechanical and strategic effects of the electoral system, Hungarian legislatures have been among the least fragmented ones in post-communist Europe. During the 1990–2010 period, the average effective number of parties in the National Assembly has been around three, which is indeed the smallest figure compared with the parliaments of the nine other post-communist EU member states (Nikolenyi 2014). Every post-election government was formed by a party that was either in control of a majority of the seats or at the very least it was in a mathematically dominant position.[2] As expected, governments tended to be very stable with Hungarian cabinets among the longest lasting in the post-communist region (Nikolenyi 2014). The stability of Hungarian governments was further buttressed by the constitutional provision for a constructive vote of no-confidence that made it very difficult for the parliamentary opposition to terminate the executvie.

The pattern of coalition governance in post-communist Hungary was characterized by regular alternation in power between the conservative and the social-liberal group of parties from the First (1990–1994) to the Fourth (2002–2006) Parliaments. In 2006, however, this pattern ended when the Socialist-Liberal coalition returned for another four-year term of majority government. The conservative coalition of the Fidesz and Christian Democratic parties won the 2010 general election and has remained in office ever since. During this period of conservative dominance, several institutional reforms were passed, all of which provided for the growing centralization of power in the executive branch and the gradual erosion of the autonomy and political relevance of parliament itself.

The legal foundations of the legislative committee system in Hungary

The organization of Hungarian parliamentary committees is anchored in three legal sources: The Constitution, the Law on Parliament, and the Parliamentary Standing Orders. The Constitution imposes a very general obligation on Parliament to establish standing committees that will be made up by elected Members of Parliament (MPs) (Art 5.1); it allows a parliamentary committee to oblige a member of the government to appear before it (Art. 8.1) and designates a parliamentary committee as one of the actors that can initiate legislation[3] (Art. 6.1) including on amendments to the Constitution (Art. S). Although the Constitution does not provide a taxonomy of parliamentary committees, it specifically mentions that at times of national emergency the Parliamentary Defence Committee can fulfil the function of the Parliament if the latter is unable to convene (Art. 50.4).

Committees in the Law on Parliament

The Law on Parliament identifies three types of parliamentary committees in addition to the House Committee that looks after the overall organization of Parliament's workflow: a) standing committees, including a special committee representing national minorities; b) investigative committees; and c) ad hoc committees. Although there is no restriction on Parliament's freedom to establish new standing committees and terminate or change existing ones, the law requires that there must be standing committees that deal with the following issues: members' immunity and mandate, the budget, the constitution, foreign affairs, EU affairs, defence, national security, and national solidarity. In addition to their right to initiate legislation, standing committees scrutinize and make recommendations about any legislative matter that the Speaker refers to them (Art. 15.3) and they can also issue an opinion and position statement on any matter that falls within their area of competence. The Law on Parliament explicitly states that 'the functions of standing committees shall be aligned with the governmental functions' (Art 16/1). In other words, while Parliament is free to establish its system of standing committees after any new election, their jurisdiction is fundamentally determined by those of government ministries. This helps committees fulfil their mandate of aiding Parliament to exercise executive oversight and control (Art. 15.1). The same law further allows standing committees to establish their own subcommittees as they see fit with the proviso that every standing committee must have one subcommittee that monitors the implementation of legislation in their area of competence as well as their social and economic impact (Art. 21.2)

The central principle in the Law on Parliament regarding the composition of standing committees is the proportional representation of parliamentary party groups (PPGs). Any deviation from the proportional representation of party groups requires the agreement of a very large four-fifths majority in the plenary. The 1994 standing orders stipulated that every party group, regardless of its size, must be given representation on every standing committee. Although this guarantee was no longer included in the new standing orders that took effect in 2014, every PPG was still given at least the right to send one of its members and participate in the meeting of a standing committee wherein the PPG was not otherwise represented (Dukan & Varga 2018: 140). The principle of proportionality does not extend to small parties that do not meet the minimum threshold for the official recognition of their PPG. Although independent MPs can also be nominated to serve as chair and members of standing committees, they do not enjoy the support and protection that a PPG can provide. Proportionality is also affected by changes in the composition of parliamentary party groups that occur as a result of splits, mergers, and individual party switching. Party control over standing committees is reinforced by the requirements that MPs' committee membership automatically ceases if their party affiliation changes and that the party group can always withdraw an MP's committee assignment (Art. 19.1). Committee members who are unable to attend a committee meeting can only be substituted by another MP.

Additional aspects of the work of standing committees that are regulated by the Law on Parliament include the principle that by default all committee meetings are open to the public with their minutes published on the website of Parliament (Art. 58). In matters of extreme personal sensitivity, data protection or national security, meetings can be held in camera but members can always request to hold a closed meeting. Finally, standing committees can also play an important role when a government minister's answer to an interpellation is rejected by Parliament.[4] In such an event, Parliament refers the interpellation to one of the standing committees which can provide the minister another opportunity to submit additional details and a supplemental answer. On the basis of this additional information, the standing committee reports back to the plenary which can take any one of the following three decisions: it can accept the minister's original answer retroactively; it can accept the minister's supplemental answer to the interpellation that was provided to the committee; or it can reject the answer once again in which case the standing committee is mandated to take further action on the matter (Art. 42.7).

The Parliamentary standing orders provide further detail about the composition, and operation of responsibilities of the different kinds of committees. The orders underwent a major reform in 2014 with two crucial but contradictory consequences for committees: a) standing committees appeared to have gained a more central role in the legislative process under the new orders, moving the detailed debate of bills from the plenary to the committee stage. However, b) standing committees have lost significant powers to the newly created committee on legislation, which became the final authority on all aspects of any piece of legislation, including any amendments that would be table for a vote in the plenary. Notwithstanding these changes, standing committees retained their gatekeeping authority over private members' bills (PMBs), which can only advance through the legislative process if the designated standing committee that reads it has consented to it. The party group of the MP who submits the PMB can request a plenary vote to override a negative committee decision; however, this privilege can only be exercised six times per parliamentary session. Bills that are submitted by the government, the president or another committee are not subject to committee gatekeeping.

In sum, the constitutional and legal foundations of the Hungarian parliamentary committee system clearly envision strong party control over committee structure and composition. Party groups are in charge of not only the initial committee assignments that MPs receive after the election but also any subsequent changes therein. Furthermore, since both the legislative and control functions of parliament are subordinated to the interests of the government of the day, committees have very little autonomy to make a substantive difference.

Key characteristics of committees in the Hungarian Parliament

The number of standing committees and subcommittees

Over the years, there has been a steady increase in the number of standing committees from the First to the Fourth Parliaments (1990–2006, see Table 9.1). The Socialist-Liberal coalition government that was reelected in 2006 promised in its government programme that it would work towards creating a more efficient and affordable state and system of public institutions and administration. As part of this agenda, the coalition partners sought to reduce the number of seats in Parliament and also introduce a more orderly system of legislative committees, which had nearly doubled between 1990 and 2006. Although the number of standing committees was slightly reduced, the committee system did not change significantly until the parliamentary reform of 2014, passed by the conservative Fidesz–Christian Democratic coalition, reduced the number of parliamentary seats by half. The conservative coalition government also reorganized the structure of the executive by cutting the number of government departments, which led to further reduction in the number of standing committees, since the latter fundamentally are aligned to the structure of the executive. The last column shows a surplus of legislative standing committees to government departments in the successive parliaments. The development of subcommittees reflected the same processes over time. Following a steady increase in the number of subcommittees, which allowed for greater specialization and scrutiny over the executive, their numbers also dropped after 2014.

Changes in the number of committees, as well as in the size of Parliament after 2014, had direct implications for how many opportunities MPs had to serve in committees. Between 1990 and 2010 there was a progressive increase in the number of committee positions, both in an absolute sense as well as in the percentage of MPs. However, with the start of the Fidesz–Christian Democratic coalition governments, these numbers started to drop. In the

Table 9.1 Legislative standing committees and subcommittees in the Hungarian Parliament (1990–2018)

	Number of standing committees	Number of standing committees chaired by an opposition MP (% of all standing committees)	Total number of subcommittees	Total number of committee positions (% of total number of MPs)	Total number of government departments (surplus of standing committees to government departments)
1990–1994	19	7 (37%)	24	300 (78%)	13 (6)
1994–1998	19	5 (26%)	9	334 (86%)	12 (7)
1998–2002	23	9 (39%)	97	478 (123%)	14 (9)
2002–2006	25	11 (44%)	74	492 (127%)	14 (11)
2006–2010	18	8 (44%)	44	496 (128%)	13 (5)
2010–2014	20	6 (30%)	66	438 (113%)	9 (11)
2014–2018	16	5 (31%)	28	196 (98%)	9 (7)
since 2018	16	5 (31%)	23	201 (101%)	9 (7)

Data from Szentgali-Toth, 2012:14; Parliament of Hungary, Ciklustörténet, www.parlament.hu/web/guest/bizottsagok-elozo-ciklusbeli-adatai (access: January 5, 2021).

four Parliaments between 1998 and 2014, the average MP had more than one committee assignment; since 2014 this is no longer the case. Of course, there are still MPs with multiple committee assignments since the Law on Parliament excludes members of government from committee service (Art 17.2). However, the norm has become for MPs not in executive office to serve on one standing committee only.

The composition of standing committees

The formation of the parliamentary standing committees takes place at the opening session of a newly elected parliament. Formally, the Speaker makes a motion to the House to recommend the adoption of the set of committees and their composition based on a prior inter-party agreement. Except for the opening session of the Sixth Parliament in 2010, the Speaker's motion was always accepted with broad consensus. That year, however, the two largest opposition parties (MSZP and Jobbik) did not agree on the allocation of committee chairs and their members did not support the motion, which, for the first time was passed only with a 70 percent support.[5] With the exception of the committees of National Security and the Budget, there are no restrictions about the allocation of committee chairs. These two committees must be chaired by a member of the opposition, the former according to a legal requirement and the latter per convention. The only other constraint for Parliament concerning the formation of standing committees is that the

166 *Csaba Nikolenyi*

Committee on Members' Immunity must have been established based on parity between government and opposition members.

The allocation of committee chair assignments to the opposition always exceeded the legal minimum mentioned above (Table 9.1). Between 1998 and 2010, when the parliamentary balance between the coalition and the opposition was narrower, the share of opposition committee chairs was noticeably higher than during other periods (1990 to 1998 and from 2010 onwards) when the parliamentary weight of the coalition was greater. In addition to the Budget and National Security committees, the standing committees that were chaired by an opposition MP most frequently were Human Rights, Foreign Affairs, Local Government, and Labour. Beyond this, there is no discernible pattern of which committee is chaired by an opposition MP.[6]

Political party groups take into account both professional and political factors when they decide about appointments to committee chair positions. Professional considerations frequently include MPs' actual expertise in the subject matter of the committee's area of jurisdiction as well as experience of past service on the committee. For example, chairs of the Constitution, Justice and Parliamentary Affairs committee included a number of notable Hungarian jurists and constitutional lawyers. In terms of political considerations, MPs' loyalty to the party line as well as the specific characteristics of their constituencies tend to be important.

Many committee chairs do not complete their term either because their party group gives them a different assignment on a different committee or in the party group, or, in case of coalition MPs, they receive an executive appointment. The number of committee chairs who served their full term kept increasing between the First and Third Parliaments but has been steadily declining ever since. In the Fourth (2002–2006) and Seventh (2014–2018) Parliaments the number of committee chairs who left their post before the end of the legislative cycle was higher than the number of chairs who stayed in their appointment for the full term.[7] More precisely, between 1990 and 2018, the average committee chair stayed in office for only 913 days, which represents only 62% of the entire four-year term of the legislature.

Between 1990 and 2018, there were 152 MPs who were assigned to chair at least one committee. Seventy-five percent of them (114) served only once, so there was hardly any opportunity to develop meaningful experience, specialization, and expertise in their role as committee member. Among these one-time chairs, two MPs were moved from the head of one committee to another during the term, three saw their term as chair interrupted but resumed on the same committee, and three of them stayed in their role during the term but representing different party groups due to changes in their affiliation. These few exceptions apart, the overwhelming majority of single-term chairs have served on one committee representing the party group that nominated them in the first place. It is of interest to note that among these single-term committee chairs we find two MPs who would later on become prime ministers (Gyula Horn and Viktor Orban) and also one MP (Peter Boross) who assumed the role of committee chair after he had completed his term as prime minister. To date, only 25 percent of MPs (38) who have served as committee chairs did so in more than one parliamentary term.[8] Although most of them (23) were reassigned to chairing the same committee that they had already chaired in the past at least once, a significant number received different committee assignments. In sum, these numbers show that there is considerable change in committee leadership that makes specialization extremely unlikely and thus limited only to a select few instances.

Similar observations apply to the volatility in committee membership as well: most standing committees experience fluctuation in their membership within a given parliamentary term and MPs' reassignment to the same committee from one parliament to the next, given that they are reelected of course, is never assumed. Over the past four parliamentary terms, the percentage of the committee members who left their committee assignments ranged between a high of 51 percent in the 2002–2006 term and a low 38 percent (2014–2018). In each of these terms, over two-thirds of these changes were carried out by MPs of the two largest parties, Fidesz and MSZP. There is discernible pattern as to which standing committees tend to see the most frequent changes in their membership. For example, the Standing Committee on Foreign Affairs witnessed the highest number of such changes in the 2002–2006 term (19 out of the 22 members leaving the committee at some point) while the same committee had no change at all in its membership during the 2014–2018 cycle.

The standing orders require an MP whose party group affiliation changes to sit as an Independent for six months before they can join another party group. There were three instances when the partisan affiliation of a committee chair changed in mid-term but the MP still carried on in his position as chair; there was only one instance when an Independent MP (Katalin Szili) was assigned as committee chair. The latter case, however, was exceptional given that this MP was previously a very senior member of the Socialist Party who had served as the Speaker of Parliament and was a runner up in the 2010 presidential election. The normal course of events is for the chair to lose their position when their party affiliation changes.

In addition to strengthening party control over committees, the principle of proportionality has also allowed governments to maintain their majority control over almost all standing committees (see Table 9.2). This is very important because committees make their decisions by the majority, which effectively means that the coalition partners can consistently maintain their control over the committees where they command a majority of the membership.

Investigative committees

An investigative committee can be established by a parliamentary resolution which specifies the committee's exact mandate, composition in terms of the number of MPs that party groups can nominate, and reporting obligation.

Table 9.2 The representation of the governing coalition on Hungary's standing committees

	Number of standing committees with coalition majority	Number of parity committees	Number of standing committees with coalition minority
1990–1994	17	1	1
1994–1998	16	2	1
1998–2002	14	6	3
2002–2006	24	1	0
2006–2010	17	1	0
2010–2014	19	1	0
2014–2018	14	1	0

Note: In the Third Parliament (1998–2002), the following were the parity committees: Economics, Immunity, Local Development, Health, Human Rights, and Employment. On the standing committees of Agriculture, Social Organizations, and Defence the opposition had a majority. Four of these nine committees were also chaired by an opposition MP.

Source: Author's compilation from data on the official website of the Hungarian Parliament. www.parlament.hu/hu/web/guest/bizottsagok-elozo-ciklusbeli-adatai(access: 01.09.2020).

The 2012 Law on Parliament makes it mandatory to establish an investigative committee when requested by a fifth of all MPs. As such, this type of committee is an important formal mechanism that is available for the parliamentary opposition to hold the government accountable for specific issues, crises, and scandals. The Law on Parliament further stipulates that the composition of such committees must be based on the principle of parity, i.e. equal number of members, between government and opposition MPs and that its chair must always be nominated by a party that belongs to the parliamentary opposition. If the inquiry investigates the political responsibility of several past governments or agencies and organizations under government control, the committee must be co-chaired by MPs who belonged to the opposition to those governments at the time of the events under investigation. For example, following the 1998 election, Fidesz MPs, who by then belonged to the governing coalition, requested the formation of an investigative committee about the surveillance of opposition politicians by the previous Socialist-Liberal coalition government. Since Fidesz was in the opposition at the time of the alleged surveillance, it had the right to nominate the committee chair even though the party was already the senior partner in the new coalition government.

Notwithstanding the formal opportunity that investigative committees present for the opposition to scrutinize the government, they rarely assume any significance (see Table 9.3). Of the 160 proposals that were submitted to Parliament since 1990 to set up such a committee, only 44 (27.5 percent) were granted, and only 31 (19.3 percent) of them were established. A little more than half of the committees 16 that were formed wrote and submitted

Table 9.3 Investigative Committees in the Hungarian Parliament (1990–2018)

	Proposed	Established	Formation	Report	Report adopted
1990–1994	24	1	1	1	0
1994–1998	27	7	6 (6)	3	3
1998–2002	24	6	4 (0)	3	1
2002–2006	29	15	13 (10)^2	3	1
2006–2010	17	8	1 (1)	1	0
2010–2014	22	7	6 (2)^1	5	5
2014–2018	17	0	0	0	0
Total	160	44	31	16	10

Note: The numbers in brackets in the fourth column indicate the number of committees chaired by an opposition MP. The numbers in superscript indicate how many of these committees also had a coalition MP as co-chair.

Source: Author's compilation from data on the official website of the Hungarian Parliament, www.parlament.hu/hu/web/guest/bizottsagok-elozo-ciklusbeli-adatai (access:01.09.2020).

a report to Parliament, which accepted a paltry sum of 10 over the past three decades. Further attesting to the gradual decline in the control function of Parliament under the conservative coalition, there has been an evident decline in the number of investigative committees established since 2010, making the Seventh Parliament (2014–2018) the first one without any such committee. An important reason for the absence of investigative committees is the numerical weakness and the bilateral division of the parliamentary opposition. On its own, no opposition party has had the required number of seats, a fifth, to request the formation of an investigative committee, which means that such committees would only be set up if the opposition parties were to coordinate. However, such coordination has proved elusive since the relative centrist positioning of Fidesz has led to a bilateral division of the opposition parties on its left and right.

Ad hoc committees

The third type of committee that Parliament can establish is the ad hoc committee which, similar to the committee of inquiry, is limited in its mandate to a specific period and a specific function. In this, ad hoc committees can play a variety of roles such as to help Parliament with 1) the nomination of a candidate to certain offices, e.g. the Constitutional Court or the Audit Office; 2) provide recommendations about concrete legislative proposals of major significance, e.g. preparation for the adoption of the new Constitution or the electoral reform; or 3) provide policy recommendations about a certain area in which the government wants to adopt new programmes or legislation; e.g. innovation and development. An ad hoc committee may be the seed for a new standing committee, which was the case of the ad hoc committee on Consumer Protection in 2007 paving the way for the formation of the new Standing Committee on Consumer Protection in 2010. Overall, ad hoc committees have played a marginal role in the Hungarian Parliament: only 34 such committees have been formed since 1990. They are always chaired by an MP from the coalition and made up of a majority of coalition deputies. Yet, ad hoc committees have at least the potential of becoming a bridge between Parliament and society in that the standing orders, as well as the 2012 Law on Parliament allow for up to half of their membership to be made up by non-parliamentarians, such as policy experts, without the right to vote. This potential, however, has remained unrealized; although experts are invited by ad hoc committees from time to time they do not become formal members.

Committees in action

Standing committees as legislators

Standing committees perform their most important function in the legislation area which includes the initiation, preparation, and vetting of bills. Their overall legislative workload, measured by the number of bills discussed, steadily increased from the Third to the Sixth Parliaments. However, following the introduction of the new standing orders in 2014, it showed a dramatic decrease. Notwithstanding these changes, the three most engaged of all standing committees have been consistently those on Constitution and Justice, Budget, and Economics (see Table 9.4). In every Parliament since 1998, the Constitution and Justice Committee accounted for the largest number of draft bills discussed, which ranged from 13.6 percent in the Fourth Parliament to 25.7 percent in the Seventh. The Budget Committee was the second most involved standing committee with the sole exception of the Seventh Parliament in which both the committees on Economics and Budget discussed a greater number of legislative proposals. The third most active committee has been the one dealing with Economics.

In addition to vetting and discussing the various draft bills, standing committees also have the right to initiate legislation. In this regard, committees have not played a particularly active role, which can be partly attributed to the fact that much of their time is taken up by reacting to the bills that are referred to them. Furthermore, since committees by definition are collective actors that bring together MPs from all party groups, much more coordination is required to act in a collective manner and to put forth legislation. Therefore, it is not surprising that committee-initiated legislation has accounted for a tiny share of Parliament's law-production, ranging between 2 and 6 percent. At the same time, it is important to note that the success rate of legislative proposals that were put forward by committees is consistently the second highest after that of the government: whereas over 90 percent of government bills have been successfully passed by Parliament since 1998, the same rate for committee bills is 70.7 percent (see Table 9.5; Dukan & Varga 2018: 438–9). It was only in

Table 9.4 Legislative activity of Hungarian standing committees (1998–2018)

	Total number of bills discussed by standing committees	Three most active standing committees by number of bills discussed
1998–2002	2,089	1. Constitution and Justice (15.5%) 2. Budget and Finance (9.5%) 3. Foreign Affairs (9.2%)
2002–2006	2,736	1. Constitution and Justice (13.6%) 2. Budget and Finance (11.1%) 3. Economics (10.9%)
2006–2010	2,262	1. Constitution, Justice and Parliamentary Affairs (17.6%) 2. Budget, Finance, and State Audit (14.2%) 3. Economics and Information Technology (12.5%)
2010–2014	2,730	1. Constitution, Justice and Parliamentary Affairs (24.7%) 2. State Audit and Budget (10.2%) 3. Economics and Information Technology (10.1%)
2014–2018	1,541	1. Justice (25.7%) 2. Economics (21.8%) 3. Culture (6.5%) / Budget (6.5%)

Source: Parliament of Hungary, Ciklustörténet, www.parlament.hu/web/guest/bizottsagok-elozo-ciklusbeli-adatai (access: January 5, 2021).

Table 9.5 Legislative initiative by standing committees in Hungary

	Total number of laws passed by Parliament	Number of bills proposed by standing committee (and percent of all bills proposed)	Number (and percent) of laws initiated by standing committee	Success rate of bills initiated by committees
1990–1994	432	56 (7.1%)	26 (6%)	46%
1994–1998	499	16 (2.0%)	11 (2.2%)	69%
1998–2002	460	34 (3.9%)	21 (4.6%)	62%
2002–2006	573	23 (2.4%)	17 (3.0%)	74%
2006–2010	539	37 (3.8%)	23 (4.3%)	62%
2010–2014	859	22 (1.4%)	20 (2.3%)	90%
2014–2018	730	24 (1.4%)	17 (2.3%)	71%

Source: Author's compilation from data on the official website of the Hungarian Parliament, www.parlament.hu/hu/web/guest/bizottsagok-elozo-ciklusbeli-adatai (access: 01.09.2020).

the Seventh Parliament (2014–2018) that PMBs submitted by coalition MPs had a higher rate of success than committee bills. In short, while committees may not be frequently relied upon to generate legislation, they perform very well when they do so. The success rate of committee-initiated legislation has ranged from 46.4 percent in the First Parliament to 90.9 percent in the Sixth Parliament. Success rate of committee-initiated bills is the percentage of such bills, reported in the third column, that became actual legislation, reported in the fourth column.

Standing committees vary tremendously in terms of their activity of legislative initiative. In every parliament, only a minority of the committees prepared and initiated legislation, the most active and successful of them being the Committee on the Budget. Except for the Third Parliament, every bill that was put forward by the Budget Committee was passed by Parliament and even in that cycle, there was only one such bill that was not eventually adopted. Other committees that played an active role in proposing legislation included those on Constitution and Justice, Local Government, and Economics. Most of those committee bills that do not become law are either withdrawn or they simply lapse before the plenary votes on them. In very few instances, however, committee bills were defeated on the floor.

In addition to initiating legislation, standing committees also play an important amending function during the legislative process. Although the bulk of amendments are proposed by MPs, committees are the second most frequent source of such changes to the draft bills. The revision of the legislative process in 2014 changed this reality by making the Committee of Legislation the final source of amending legislation. Standing committees continue to play this role as well, however, in a significantly reduced capacity. The revised standing orders also curbed MPs' ability to submit amendments; while previously they could do so at both the committee and the plenary stages of the legislative process, they can only do so now at the former.

The reduction in committees' legislative workload after 2014 is further reflected in the declining frequency of committee meetings. As a matter of routine, not every member attends committee meetings. Smaller party groups find it particularly difficult to ensure their MPs participation in all of their committee meetings since most of these take place within the same narrow timeframe tied to the schedule when Parliament is in session. In the Sixth (2010–2014) and Seventh (2014–2018) Parliaments, the average attendance rate of committee meetings by MPs was 67 percent and 69 percent respectively, with the opposition far-right Jobbik party registering the highest rates. Meetings of the committee on MPs' Immunity are among the best attended but the least frequently held; however, it is counterintuitive that the committee on the Budget, which is the most active in terms of legislative initiation, has consistently had lower-than-average attendance rates in the Sixth (2010–2014) and Seventh (2014–2018) Parliaments. Although committee members who are unable to attend a meeting can request to be substituted by another member, the relatively

Table 9.6 Submission and rejection of private members' bills by committees in Hungary

	2006–2010	2010–2014	2014–2018
PMBs submitted	425	902	777
by coalition MPs	170	356	169
by opposition MPs	255	546	608
PMBs rejected by SCs	151	475	570
submitted by coalition MPs	11	8	3
submitted by opposition MPs	140	467	567

Data from Dukan & Varga (2018: 439) and provided by the Parliamentary Directorate.

low participation rate hinders committees from developing a sense of collegiality among its members.

Standing committees as legislative gatekeepers

As mentioned earlier, standing committees play an important negative role in the legislative process by deciding whether to admit or reject PMB for further consideration. Given the entrenched control that the coalition parties enjoy over the committees, PMBs submitted by opposition MPs rarely pass the committee stage while those submitted by coalition MPs very often do (see Table 9.6).

This function of the standing committees has become especially important over the years as the overall number of PMBs has increased. It is worth noting that during the periods of conservative coalition governments (1998–2002, 2010–2014, 2014–2018) standing committees rejected PMBs at considerably higher rates (64.2 percent, 62.3 percent, and 79.7 percent respectively) than they did during the 2002–2006 and 2006–2010 terms of left-liberal coalitions (43.7 and 49.3 percent respectively). Although negative committee decisions can be appealed, such appeals rarely succeed. In other words, once a standing committee rules to reject a private member's bill from further consideration, that decision rarely ever gets overturned: therefore, it is safe to conclude that Hungarian standing committees are very powerful in terms of exercising negative agenda control and keeping bills away from the floor and the further legislative process.

Standing committees and parliamentary questions

As mentioned earlier, the standing orders allow standing committees to play a direct albeit limited role in Parliament's control function by preparing a detailed report in case the plenary rejects a minister's answer to an interpellation. Since 2014 there was not a single instance of a written question being rejected. Previously, the number of rejections was on the rise: in the Third Parliament (1998–2002), there were seven rejections, followed by 20 in the

Fourth Parliament (2002–2006) and 28 in the Fifth (2006–2010). The reports that committees prepared and submitted to the plenary were overwhelmingly accepted in the Third (1998–2002) and Fifth (2006–2010) Parliaments; only two were accepted in the Fourth (2002–2006) Parliament and the others were never voted on before the term of the legislature expired. The overwhelming majority of the questions that end up on the desk of the standing committees were submitted by opposition MPs.

Key findings and conclusions

The evidence presented supports the assessment that despite their formal institutional maturity and strength, Hungary's legislative committees' function at the disposal of political parties and specifically the governing majority. Although formal indicators of the number, types, and organization of committees suggest that the Hungarian committee system should be robust and have a high degree of institutional development, it is also evident that committees do not function autonomously from either the PPGs or the government. Parties maintain tight control over their MPs' legislative careers and move their committee assignment as they see fit, which, in turn, prevents committees from becoming a source of legislative specialization where MP can acquire and develop expertise. Committee meetings normally register party, government, and opposition positions that had been already negotiated and coordinated outside the formal committee setting.

An important consequence of a substantively weak committee system is that it cannot provide meaningful opportunities for opposition influence over the legislative process. Opposition parties chair few standing committees and overwhelmingly they remain in a minority on most of them. Whereas committees cannot prevent a government bill from reaching the floor of the assembly, they have been very successful and effective at filtering out private members' bills that are submitted by members of the opposition.

Notes

1 A preliminary version of this paper was presented at the IPSA RCLS workshop at the University of Valencia, Spain in October 2019. The author would like to thank Dr. Cabrera Alvaro and Dr. Edelman Annamaria, both at the Directorate of the Hungarian Parliament, for their helpful guidance and assistance with data collection. Any errors remain the author's responsibility.
2 For the mathematical concept of dominance in legislatures, see Roozendaal (1992).
3 Legislation can be also initiated by the President of the Republic, the government and any MP.
4 The plenary votes on a minister's answer only when the parliamentarian who asked the question in the first place rejects it (Art. 42 /6-7)
5 In other years, the establishment of standing committees was passed with the following percentage of MPs voting in favour: 1998: 87%, 2002: 98%, 2006: 89%, 2014: 93%, and 2018: 91%.

6 The Human Rights and the Foreign Affairs committees were chaired by opposition MPs in the First, Third, Fourth, and Fifth Parliaments; the standing committee on Local Government was chaired by the opposition in the First, Second, and Fourth Parliaments; and the committee on Labour was chaired by opposition MPs in the Second, Third, and Fourth Parliaments.
7 This difference was especially high in the Seventh Parliament (2014–2018): only five committee chairs served their full term while 11 chairs did not.
8 The overall rate of MPs' turnover, i.e. the rate at which MPs are reelected to parliament from one general election to the next, places an important upper limit on how many MPs can feasibll be reappointed as committee chairs.

References

Carroll, R., & Cox, G. (2012). Shadowing Ministers: Monitoring Partners in Coalition Government. *Comparative Political Studies*, 45(2), 220–36.

Cox, G., & McCubbins, M. (1993). *Legislative Leviathan*. Berkeley: University of California Press.

Döring, H. (1995). *Parliaments and Majority Rule in Western Europe*. Frankfurt: Campus Verlag.

Dukan, I., & Varga, A. (2018). *Parliaemntary Law: The Functioning, Responsibilities and Powers of the Hungarian Parliament and Its Associated Offices*. Budapest: Office of Parliament.

Hazan, R. (2001). *Reforming Parliamentary Committees: Israel in a Comparative Perspective*. Ohio State University Press.

Ilonszki, G. (2007). From Minimal to Subordinate: A Final Verdict? The Hungarian Parliament, 1990–2002. *Journal of Legislative Studies*, 13(1), 38–58.

Ilonszki, G. (2019). From Coaliton to One-Party Dominance. In T. &. Bergman, *Coalition Governance in Central Eastern Europe*, Oxford: Oxford University Press, 207–251.

Ilonszki, G., & Jager, K. (2011). Hungary: Changing Government Advantages - Challenging a Dominant Executive. In B.-E. Rasch, & G. Tsebelis, *Role of the Governments in Legislative Agenda Setting*, London: Routledge, 95–110.

Khmelko, I. (2012). Internal Organization of Post-Communist Parliaments Over Two Decades: Leadership, Parties, and Committees. In D.M. Olson G. Ilonszki, *Post-Communist Parliaments: Change and Stability in the Second Decade*, Abingdon: Routledge, 78–99.

Kiewet, R., & McCubbins, M. (1991). *The Logic of Delegation: Congressional Parties and the Appropriation Process*. Chicago: The University of Chicago Press.

Kim, D.-H., & Loewenberg, G. (2005). The Role of Parliamentary Committees in Coalition Governments. *Comparative Political Studies*, 38(9), 1104–29.

Lees, J., & Shaw, M. (1979). *Committees in Legislatures*. Durham: Duke University Press.

Martin, S. (2011). Electoral Institutions, the Personal Vote and Legislative Orgnization. *Legislative Studies Quarterly*, 36(3), 339–61.

Nikolenyi, C. (2014). *Institutional Design and Party Government in Post-Communist Europe*. Oxford: Oxford University Press.

Olson, D. M., & Mezey, M. (1991). *Legislatures in the Policy Process: The Dilemmas of Economic Policy*. Cambridge: Cambridge University Press.

Olson, D.M., & Ilonszki, G. (2012). *Post-Communist Parliaments: Change and Stability in the Second Decade*. Abingdon: Routledge.

Piersig, E. (2016). Reconsidering Constructive No-Confidence for Canada: Experiences from Six European Countries. *Canadian Parliamentary Review*, 39(3), 5–15.

Roozendaal van, P. (1992). The Effect of Dominant and Central Parties on Cabinet Composition and Durability. *Legislative Studies Quarterly*, 17(1), 5–36.

Rubabshi, A., & Hasson, S. (forthcoming). Government Termination and Government Stability. *West European Politics*.

Shaw, M. (1990). Committees in Legislatures. In P. Norton, *Legislatures*, New York: Oxford University Press, 237–71.

Szentgali-Toth, B. (2012). *The Committee System of the Hungarian Parliament (in Hungarian)*. Arsboni. Budapest: Studium.

Weingast, B., & Marshall, M. (1988). The Industrial Organization of Congress. *Journal of Political Economy*, 96(1), 132–63.

Zubek, R. (2008). Parties, Rules and Government Legislative Agenda Control in Central Europe: The Case of Poland. *Communist and Post-Communist Studies*, 41(2), 147–61.

Zubek, R. (2011). Negative Agenda Control and Executive-Legislative Relations in East Central Europe, 1997–2008. *Journal of Legislative Studies*, 17(2), 172–92.

Zubek, R. (2015). Coalition Governments and Committee Power. *West European Politics*, 38(5), 1020–41.

10 Strength and weakness

Legislative and oversight powers of the parliamentary committee system in Israel

Chen Friedberg

Parliamentary committees – where the real work takes place?

A parliamentary committee is defined as a body that operates within the legislature, and has tasks imposed upon it by the legislature. The committee structure is derived from the parliamentary rules of procedure and it works on behalf of the parliament and in accordance with the powers vested in it (Hazan 2001: 2). Lees and Shaw (1979) identified five main functions of parliamentary committees: 1. legislation, 2. oversight, 3. finance, 4. investigation, and 5. management of the parliament. They believed that the two most important functions of parliamentary committees are making decisions related to legislation and oversight of administrative activities. Another study, which investigated comparatively various key areas in 18 European parliaments, including parliamentary committees, found that in 16 countries parliamentary committees were involved mainly in legislation and oversight (Döring 1995).

Parliamentary committees evolved over the years in different ways and under different names. Some are quite universal (with certain variations), while others are unique to one parliament or another. It is common to classify them into two main types: permanent committees and ad hoc committees that disband when their task is completed or at the end of a legislature's term of office prior to an election (Olson 1994).

Committees, as Martin (2010) observed, are the key mechanism by which a parliament develops the ability to counter-balance the many advantages of the executive in terms of policy, development, and implementation. Evidently, there is tremendous cross-national variation in the degree to which parliamentary committees are capable of fulfilling this balancing mechanism. The prevalent approach to studying such variation has focused on the formal institutional and organizational characteristics of committee systems in democratically elected national parliaments (André, Depauw & Martin 2015; Martin 2014; Mickler 2017; Friedberg & Hazan 2009; Hazan 2001; Lees & Shaw 1979; Mattson & Strøm, 1995; McGee 2002; Mezey 1979; Ogul 1976; Pelizzo & Stapenhurst 2004a, 2004b, 2008; Strøm 1998). However, the literature overlooks the crucial distinction between committee strength on its two main functions: legislation

DOI: 10.4324/9781003106579-10

and oversight. This creates a major lacuna since committees may have very different degrees of strength in fulfilling these two principal functions as will be shown in this chapter by analysing the case of Israel.

Institutions, powers, and actors in the Israeli committee system

Institutional Setting of Committees

The Israeli committee system is composed of 12 permanent committees that are automatically reestablished after every election. The number of members in these committees is fixed; it shall not exceed 15, but in three committees (the Foreign Affairs and Defence Committee; the Constitution, Law, and Justice Committee; and the Finance Committee) the maximum is 17. Only the number of members in the House Committee is higher. It is determined by the Knesset, provided that the composition of the committee reflects, as much as possible, the composition of the Knesset.

Committee sessions and protocols are all open to the public unless the committee decides otherwise. Only in the Foreign Affairs and the Defence Committee are the sessions and most of the protocols classified in advance. The procedure of conducting formal hearings in the committees does not officially exist in the Knesset regulations, though on certain occasions committee chairs have conducted debates and called them 'hearings'. For example, in 2018 the chair of the Economic Affairs Committee organized such debates as 'hearings' about the issue of fatal traffic accidents. Eventually, the committee published a comprehensive report on the topic with recommendations to the Ministry of Transport and Road Safety and the Ministry of Internal Security. Another example is the Parliamentary Committee of Inquiry into the Financial System's Conduct in Credit Agreements with Large Business Borrowers. The committee chair conducted all of the debates like hearings with special seating arrangements, appointing committee members who asked the questions in each debate, and even hiring professional advisors who accompanied the committee members in the debates.

Actors in committees

Members of the Knesset (MKs) are appointed to serve in committees based on the decision of their parliamentary party group (PPG) and according to the relative size of each PPG. Usually, the coalition government controls the chairs in ten out of the 12 permanent committees and also holds a majority in all committees in order to pass its policy. It seems that, unlike many other parliamentary democracies, committee assignments in the Knesset are determined by three structural factors of the political system: multiparty oversized coalitions and high party fragmentation coupled with a small parliament. These factors involve considerations of coalition monitoring, as well as more functional constraints dictated by the small size of parties. Itzkovitch-Malka and Shugart

(2018) found in their research that both electoral considerations based on geographical interests and personal attributes such as prior occupational experience have a narrow effect on committee assignments in Israel. In other words, policy expertise does not necessarily lead to committee assignment. At best, committee assignment can sometimes lead to policy expertise, but only when the committee member serves on one or two committees at most, which – as will be shown later – is not the common case in Israel.

Turnover in committee membership is not very high in practice – except in situations when MKs resign from the Knesset and PPGs enter or leave the coalition government, an act that affects the composition of the committees as well. However, it is important to note that according to the Knesset rules of procedure, PPGs have the authority to replace (rebellious) committee members, so turnover has the potential to be higher.

Given the relatively small size of the Israeli parliament (120 seats), the high fragmentation of the party system, and the large size of Israeli governments, backbench MKs, especially those whose parties are in the coalition – typically serve on three committees on average. Since no limit on committee membership exists and most of the committee meetings are usually held at the same time, the attendance of MKs on each committee is often sparse.

The roles of the committees are anchored in three legal sources: the Knesset Basic Law (1958),[1] the Knesset Law (1994),[2] and the Knesset Rules of Procedure. They authorize committees to handle bills right after they have passed preliminary reading[3] (in the case of private members' bills) and first reading (in the case of governmental and committee bills) and to prepare them for the next stages of legislation. Once a private members' bill has been approved in the preliminary reading, the committee to which it was referred shall prepare it for the first reading or shall propose to the Knesset plenary to remove it from the agenda (Knesset Rules of Procedure, article 79(a)). Should a bill (governmental, committee, or private) be approved in the first reading, the committee to which it was referred shall prepare it for the second and third reading or, in the case of a private bill, shall propose to the Knesset to remove it from the agenda (Knesset Rules of Procedure, article 84(a)). At that significant phase, the committee is entitled to amend a bill or articles of a bill, as long as the amendments do not diverge from the subject of the bill (Knesset Rules of Procedure, article 85(a)). Once a committee has prepared a bill for the second and third reading, it shall submit it to the Speaker of the Knesset, in the wording decided, for voting.

Besides handling legislation, the committees are also entitled to exercise oversight over the executive branch through motions for the agenda that have been passed on to them by the plenary, and requests of citizens addressed to them. In these cases, the oversight role is imposed upon them by other actors. They can also exercise oversight by their own initiation (article 101(a) of the Knesset Rules of Procedure determines that the committee chairs and committee members can initiate discussions in matters that are relevant to their committee).

Committee chairs have great influence on committee functioning: they control the committee agenda which means that they are autonomous to decide which subjects will be included in the committee timetable, they can promote bills as they wish or push them aside, and they can invite witnesses and guests to discussions. They are also the only members of the committee who can grant permission to speak in debates.

Government officials regularly present in committees either by their own request or by committee request. In that case, committees are authorized to summon ministers, civil servants, and bodies that are connected to the state. However, the sanctions against those who are summoned but do not appear, or present false evidence are insignificant. Only the State Control Committee can fine those who were summoned but did not appear at its meetings. The committees can also invite NGOs or private citizens to their discussions but cannot impose any sanctions on them.

External actors such as professional lobbyists are entitled to act in the Knesset in order to influence MKs on matters relating to bills, secondary legislation, committee decisions, and so on, and must be recognized by the Knesset as such (Knesset Law 1994, chapter 12). Kremnitzer, Shapira and Sidur (2013: 7) argue that lobbying is legitimate, inevitable and, when it is done properly, even desirable in a liberal democracy. However, it can have potentially negative consequences: it could give powerful people and organizations excessive power, it can provide decision-makers with biased and even misleading information, it can impair transparency since it takes place in small forums, it can undermine the public's trust in decision-making processes, and it can interfere with decision-makers' work (Friedberg & Hazan 2009:4).

Since the 1990s, lobbying activities in the Knesset have been considerably expanded, particularly those of commercial lobbyists and in-house lobbyists. In recent years, lobbying activities have increased even further – with a concurrent rise in efforts to put pressure on MKs as well as to provide them with one-sided information – with the aim of affecting their considerations so that they will favour (in the committees and in the plenary) various interest groups, even at the cost of the public good (Cohen 2019).

Interactions in committees

Discussions take place in committee sessions and therefore it would be reasonable to assume that MKs change their mind, at least occasionally and most likely in nonpartisan issues, as a consequence of these discussions. Obviously, some bargaining and deal-making occur in committee sessions formally. However, when few members attend committee meetings, it would be also reasonable to assume that negotiation often takes place elsewhere, informally (such as in corridors, in the MKs' lunchroom, in the chairperson's office and the MKs' chambers, and through the MKs' assistants), but this has not yet been systematically investigated in the Israeli context.

Committees in the policy process

Apart from 12 permanent committees that are authorized to establish subcommittees (and often do so), the Israeli committee system is also composed of ad hoc committees, which are special committees that function in a similar manner to the permanent committees but have a limited term of office. Another type of committee is a parliamentary inquiry committee, appointed by the plenary to deal with particular issues viewed by the Knesset as having special national importance. Since 1949 and up until 2020, the Knesset has decided to establish 26 parliamentary commission of inquiry, four of them were established twice in two successive Knessets. A review of these commissions' work over the years shows that it needs improvement. Though some commissions of inquiry have investigated issues in depth, put them on the public agenda, dealt with them thoroughly, and made a real change in policy and in the public discourse, in many cases parliamentary commissions of inquiry have not been employed wisely and beneficially: some of them did not function at all or did not publish their findings. Failing to publish conclusions, writing general conclusions, drafting recommendations that cannot be implemented, or even not following up on implementation of the recommendations does not contribute to the effectiveness of the commissions as a significant oversight tool (Blander, Friedberg & Fridman 2019).

The Ethics Committee is a special committee that deals with Knesset members who have violated the Knesset's rules of ethics or who have been involved in illegal activity outside of the Knesset. The Knesset plenary or the House Committee may decide to set up joint committees made up of an equal number of members from two committees and having the status of a special committee for a particular matter. Also, committees themselves may set up subcommittees for handling certain issues.

There is no correspondence between the permanent committees' jurisdictions and government ministries, which means that the committees do not mirror the ministerial bureaucracy. In fact, the Knesset, controlled by the coalition majority, decided in the early days of the state that every permanent committee will be responsible for several ministries, and sometimes for all of them.

Problem definition

Influence in problem definition can be exercised in two ways. One is exercised by individual committee members in an informal way. The other is exercised by the entire committee in a formal way: through general statements in its reports, through committee reports, or draft legislation which may define problems that were previously not perceived. In this way it can help draw attention to relevant topics and, thereby, channel societal wants and demands as input into the political process (Easton 1965: 37).

Indeed, the 12 permanent committees published 40 reports during the decade between 2009 and 2019 (four Knesset terms) out of 48 reports possible in that period, that summarizes their activity in legislation, oversight, and other aspects during each Knesset term. In six cases committees did not published any report[4] and in two cases committees published reports that covered only part of the period.[5] However, it should be noted that writing such reports is not mandatory and each committee may decide whether to write them or not. These reports can help draw attention to relevant topics and guard public interest.

Agenda-setting

As a rule, the Knesset committees have tasks imposed upon them by others such as the plenary (handling bills, exercising oversight through motion for the agenda that have been passed on to them) and, rarely, also citizens (requests). Therefore, in that sense, they are not independent actors. However, they can initiate discussions in political and professional matters that are relevant to them and, moreover, three committees (the House Committee; the Constitution, Law and Justice Committee; and the State Control Committee) are entitled to initiate bills in the spheres of their competence on topics such as Basic Laws, the Knesset, Members of the Knesset (MKs), the elections to the Knesset, political parties, party financing, and the State Comptroller (Knesset Rules of Procedure, article 80(a)). Indeed, in the last decade (2009–2019) these committees initiated 36 laws (seven in the 17th and the 18th Knessets, two in the short-termed 19th Knesset and 20 in the 20th Knesset).

Most importantly, once a bill or a motion for the agenda is addressed to them, the committee chairs are autonomous to decide which subjects will be included in the agenda, which bills to promote, which to delay, or even 'bury'. For example, during the last decade (2009–2019) the permanent committees 'buried' hundreds of coalition and opposition private members' bills in preparation for the first reading: 360 in the 17th Knesset, 148 in the 18th Knesset, 153 in the 19th Knesset, and 195 in the 20th Knesset. The committees remained active in the next phase and continued to 'bury' private bills in preparation for the second reading, but the numbers at this stage were lower: 39 in the 17th Knesset, 37 in the 18th Knesset, nine in the 19th Knesset and 24 in the 20th Knesset (Nikoleney & Friedberg 2019).

Policy formulation and legislation

The Knesset Rules of Procedure determined that the permanent committees will be involved in the legislative process very early – after the preliminary reading and before the first reading in the case of a private bill, and after the first reading in the case of governmental bills. It also grants them the power to amend any bill when they work on it, for first, second, and third readings. In practice, the committees use this power extensively and exercise substantial influence by transforming draft bills. An innovative study that examined the influence of the Knesset committees on government legislation shows that there is a difference in the number of words between the government version of the bill and the final version of the bill, which is the committee version. There is also a difference in the number of words that were changed between the governmental version and the final version of the bill and a difference in the number of articles between the two versions (Makover 2017). In that respect, the committees are quite influential.

While all permanent committees operate in a quite similar manner, there is still a difference in the workload assigned to the committees in their legislative role. A recent study that examined the interface between the government and the Knesset with regard to government bills shows that the scope of government bills sent to the permanent committees from the first Knesset until mid-2018 is extremely uneven: two committees (the Constitution, Law and Justice Committee, and the Finance Committee) handled about half of all the government bills. Three additional committees (the Labour, Welfare and Health Committee, the Economic Affairs Committee, and the Internal Affairs and the Environment Committee) handled about one-third of these bills. In total, only five permanent committees handled almost all of the government bills in the Knesset, while the other seven remaining committees[6] handled only a handful of them (around 10 percent) (Kwartaz-Avraham 2020).

In summary, the Knesset committees demonstrate impressive strength in their legislative role. It is not only formal power, but actual power. As aforesaid, the committees enter the legislation process at a very early stage, and some of them have the power to initiate bills or amendments to bills in specific matters. In practice, they used this authority when needed and initiated dozens of bills during the decade examined. Moreover, the version of all bills that return to the plenary for a final vote, even the governmental ones, is the committee version which often includes substantial changes. Finally, the committees can recommend that the plenary remove bills that passed a preliminary and a first reading from the Knesset agenda by vote (of the majority in the plenary), and when preparing a bill for its first, second, and third readings, they are allowed to amend it. They can also postpone discussions on bills, or even bury them, since the chairperson controls the committee's agenda and decides what will be discussed and when. As shown, the committees have used this authority quite extensively, amending bills and burying hundreds of them throughout all of the committee legislation phases in the term examined. Such a record suggests that Israel's Knesset committees are relatively independent, and less subordinate to the government in their legislative role.

Implementation and oversight

Beside handling legislation, the permanent committees are also authorized to oversee the executive through motions for the agenda. Those can be passed on to them by the plenary, by requests of citizens addressed to them, and also result from their own initiation, usually not according to a predetermined plan, but when the need arises. However, in practice, committees have significant difficulty to fulfil this task effectively. Indeed, when there is no correspondence between committee jurisdictions and government ministries, the committees must oversee too many (and often different) fields of governmental activity. Moreover, since in order to oversee effectively, committee members are required to have knowledge, expertise, and time. However, when Knesset members serve on several committees at the same time – and need to jump from one discussion to another (most of them are held simultaneously) – they have neither the time nor the ability to study the issues thoroughly, prepare themselves for discussions, and become professional in the committee work, which is very complex and covers a wide range of issues. While committees do have the authority to compel witnesses to appear before them, they cannot impose significant sanctions against those who do not show up or present false testimony, and therefore this power is formal much more than it is practical. Finally, though committees form conclusions related to issues raised from the motions for the agenda and pass them to ministers for their response, this study clearly shows that the ministers do not take this task seriously enough. Out of the 85 conclusions that the permanent committees formed in the 19th Knesset (2013–2015) and the 509 conclusions that they formed in the 20th Knesset (2015–2019), ministers responded to only 19 conclusions (22 percent) in the first term and 149 conclusions (29 percent) in the second term (Friedberg 2019). No further actions were taken by the committees to get a response from the government. A lack of such activity means that the oversight process is incomplete.

Nevertheless, in two areas the picture is not that gloomy. First, in 2000 the Knesset established the Parliamentary Research Center that improved the committees' ability to gather reliable information and confront the government officials. Moreover, legal advisors are supplied to the committees by the Knesset. Second, the State Control Committee, which is the oversight committee of the House, has special powers. It discusses the annual reports and other reports of the State Comptroller and tables its conclusions regarding the annual reports in the plenary. After deliberation in the plenary those conclusions become a Knesset decision. The State Comptroller senior staff participate in part of the committee meetings as well as the officials of the supervised bodies, which have to report to the committee members what they had done to repair the faults that the State Comptroller detected in their organization. In 1990, the committee was granted the authority to require witnesses to appear before it and fine those who were invited but did not appear. Another unique authority granted to the committee by the State Comptroller's law (article 14b) is to establish, under special circumstances, a national commission of inquiry. No other committee in the Knesset was given such powers that helps strengthen the oversight role of the parliament (Friedberg 2013).

The strength and weakness of committees in the policy process

The Israeli committee system demonstrates strengths and weaknesses at the same time. Indeed, it is strong in the official sense due to optimal number and size of permanent committees that are authorized to establish subcommittees and their chairpersons control the committees' agendas, but this strength is diminished by control of the coalition government over almost all committee chairs, the majority that the coalition has in all committees, and the ability of parties to change or remove their committee members at will.

The Israeli committee system is also strong de jure and de facto in its legislative role. At the same time, it is weak and inefficient in its oversight role. A possible explanation to that diversity might be that parliamentary committees prioritize their roles according to various limitations that are imposed on them. As shown, they are more involved in legislation than in oversight activities mainly because the Knesset enables them, and even encourages them, to do so. Surprisingly, the Knesset has not placed limitations on the number, or the content of private members' bills that MKs can submit. Therefore, in the decade between 2009 and 2019, MKs submitted an amazing number of 13,532 private bills, 95 percent of which were halted in early phases of legislation; most of them did not make progress beyond the tabling stage and hundreds of them were stopped in the committees (Nikolenyi & Friedberg 2019) . Nevertheless, this leaves the MKs and the committees with very little time to do serious oversight work which demands expertise and is considered hard, prolonged, and unrewarding. Furthermore, the Knesset decided in the early days of the state, following the demand of the first prime minister of Israel, David Ben-Gurion, and his cabinet, that there would not be any correspondence between committees and ministries. That decision impaired the ability of the committees to oversee effectively the executive branch from the beginning.

It is also important to remember that the Knesset is a very small unicameral parliament (120 seats), while Israeli governments tend to be relatively large (around 30 members). Consequently, there are only about 90 MKs left to serve on the committees (ministers and deputy ministers can be members of the Knesset, but they are not allowed to serve as committee members or to submit questions and PMBs, due to the principle of separation of powers). Since the total number of committee nominations is more than double this, the average MK (who is not a minister, a deputy minister, the Speaker of the House, the opposition leader, etc.) needs to serve on approximately three committees. Furthermore, since the coalition majority must be maintained within each committee, MKs from the coalition parties could end up serving on as many as five or six committees. While this situation hardly affects the committee's legislative activity – since no quorum is required to pass bills and they can be promoted by any number of participants (even one) – it seriously impairs the oversight activity. When all committees meet at the same time (according to Knesset decision), the attendance of members in the discussions is meager[7] and they cannot obtain the knowledge and expertise they need to ask the proper questions in order to oversee the government effectively. Finally, the decision of committee chairpersons, who control the committee agendas, not to monitor the response of the government to their conclusions means that oversight activity is not at the top of their priorities. Perhaps MKs and committee chairpersons feel that oversight activity is a difficult, unrewarding, low-profile activity with almost no public recognition. Therefore, it would be wiser from their perspective to invest time and resources in a high-profile activity such as legislation, which does not require as much effort and specialization, can attract public and media attention, and can give them free publicity.

It seems that parliamentary committees are not necessarily either weak in both their legislation and oversight functions or strong in both of them. They can be strong in one function and weak in another. The reasons for this diversity may emanate from coalition control over committee members, a coalition majority in all committees, or from the fact that the committees themselves can prioritize their roles within the limitations of the formal framework they operate in. The study also shows that we must examine the strength of parliamentary committees in their legislative and oversight roles separately in order to build a profile of committee strength in both roles. Only then can the real strength of parliamentary committees be evaluated.

Notes

1 Since the Constituent Assembly was unable to put a constitution together, the first Knesset adopted the 'Harari proposal' in 1950, which determined that the Knesset would enact basic laws on various subjects, eventually constituting, with an appropriate introduction and several general rulings, the Constitution of the State of Israel. Following the adoption of this proposal, work began on the legislation of the basic laws, the first of which – Basic Law: the Knesset – was initiated by the Constitution, Law and Justice Committee and was adopted in 1958 by the Third Knesset. This work has not finished, and Israel does not yet have a formal constitution.
2 The Knesset Law (1994) regulates various aspects of the Knesset's activities that are too detailed to be included in the Basic Law: the Knesset, but too essential to appear only in the Knesset rules of procedures.
3 Private members' bill must pass four readings – preliminary reading and three more readings. Governmental and committee bills must pass only three readings.
4 The Finance Committee and the Committee on the Status of Women and Gender Equality in the 20th Knesset; the Foreign Affairs and Defence Committee in the 19th Knesset; the Internal Affairs and Environment Committee, and the Education, Culture and Sports Committee in the 18th Knesset; and the Education, Culture and Sports Committee in the 17th Knesset.
5 The State Control Committee in the 20th Knesset (only for the first half of the Knesset term) and the Internal Affairs and Environment Committee (only for the third year of the Knesset term).
6 The seven committees are the Education, Culture and Sports Committee; the Foreign Affairs and Defence Committee; the House Committee; the State Control

Committee; the Science and Technology Committee; the Immigration, Absorption and Diaspora Affairs Committee; and the Committee on the Status of Women and Gender Equality.
7 In an early study conducted by Hazan and Friedberg in 2009, it was found that the average attendance at committee meetings during the 16th Knesset (2003–2006) was low – between 25 and 30 percent at most.

References

André, A., Depauw, S. & Martin, S. (2015). Trust is good, control is better: Multiparty government and legislative organization. *Political Research Quarterly*, 69(1), 108–120.

Blander, D., Friedberg C. & Fridman A. (2019). *Parliamentary commissions of inquiry as a mechanism for oversight of the executive branch.* Jerusalem: Israel Democracy Institute (Hebrew).

Cohen, E. (2019). The activity of commercial lobbies in the Israeli Knesset during 2015–2018: Undermining or Realizing the Democratic Foundations? *Parliamentary Affairs 73*, 692–709.

Döring, H. (ed., 1995). *Parliaments and majority rule in Western Europe*. Frankfurt: Campus Verlag.

Itzkovitch-Malka, R. & Shugart, M.S. (2018). Party personnel practices and coalition management in a multiparty, fragmented setting: The case of Israel. Paper presented at the *34th Annual Meeting of the Association for Israel Studies*, Berkeley, CA, June 25–27, 2018.

Easton, D. (1965). A systems analysis of political life. New York: Wiley.

Friedberg, C. (2019). Dimensions of committee strength: Legislative and oversight powers of the parliamentary committee system in Israel. Paper presented in the RCLS-Workshop *on Parliamentary Committees*, Valencia, Spain, October 23–25, 2019.

Friedberg, C. (2013). The state control committee in the Israeli parliament – Form of accountability under stress. Israel Affairs 19*(2)*, 320–306.

Friedberg, C. & Hazan, R.Y. (2009). *Legislative oversight of the executive branch in Israel: Current status and proposed reform.* Jerusalem: Israel Democracy Institute (Hebrew).

Hazan, R.Y. (2001). *Reforming parliamentary committees: Israel in comparative perspective*. Columbus, OH: Ohio State University Press.

Kremnitzer, M., Shapira A & Sidur C. (2013). *Regulating lobbying in Israel*. Jerusalem: The Israel Democracy Institute (Hebrew).

Kwartaz-Avraham, N. (2020). *The interface between the government and the Knesset with regard to government bills.* Jerusalem: Israel Democracy Institute (Hebrew).

Lees, J.D. & Shaw M. eds. (1979). *Committees in legislatures: A comparative analysis*. Durham, NC: Duke University Press.

Makover, S. (2017). From in camera to on camera: The impact of the change on the strength of the Knesset committees in the legislative process. The Hebrew University Department of Political Science. Master's thesis (Hebrew).

Mattson, I., & Strøm, K.W. (1995). Parliamentary Committees. In H. Döring, ed. *Parliaments and Majority Rule in Western Europe*. Frankfurt: Campus Verlag, 247–309.

Martin, S. (2010). The committee system. In M. MacCarthaigh, M. Manning, eds. *The houses of the Oireachtas: Parliaments in Ireland*. Dublin: Institute of Public Administration, 285–302.

Martin, S. (2014). Committees. In M. Shane, T. Saalfeld & K.W. Strøm, eds. *The Oxford Handbook of legislative studies*. Oxford: Oxford University Press, 352–370.

McGee, D.G. (2002). *The overseers: Public account committees and public spending*. London: Pluto Press.

Mezey, M.L. (1979). *Comparative Legislatures*. Durham, NC: Duke University Press.

Mickler, T. (2017). Committee autonomy in parliamentary systems: Coalition logic or congressional rationales? *Journal of Legislative Studies* 23(3), 367–91.

Nikolenyi, C. & Friedberg, C. (2019). Vehicles of opposition influence or agents of the governing majority? Legislative committees and Private Members' Bills in the Hungarian Országgyűlés and the Israeli Knesset. *Journal of Legislative Studies* 25(3), 358–374.

Ogul, M.S. (1976). *Congress oversees the bureaucracy*. Pittsburgh, PA: Pittsburgh University Press.

Olson, D.M. (1994). *Democratic Legislative Institutions: A Comparative View*. Armonk, NY: M.E. Sharpe.

Pelizzo, R. & Stapenhurst R. (2004a). Legislatures and oversight: A note. *Quaderni di Scienza Politica* 4(1): 175–188.

Pelizzo, R. & Stapenhurst R. (2004b). Tools for legislative oversight: An empirical investigation. *World Bank Policy Research Working Paper* 3388. Washington, D.C.: WBI.

Pelizzo, R. & Stapenhurst R. (2008). Tools for legislative oversight: An empirical investigation. In R. Stapenhurst, F. Pelizzo, D. M. Olson, & L. Von Trapp, eds. *Legislative oversight and budgeting: A world perspective*. Washington, D.C.: World Bank Institute, 9–28.

Strøm, K. W. (1998). Parliamentary committees in European democracies. *Journal of Legislative Studies* 4(1), 21–59.

The Knesset. (2019) Knesset Rules of Procedure.

11 Japan's unusual but interesting parliamentary committees
An arena and transformative model?

Kuniaki Nemoto and Ellis S. Krauss

The Japanese Parliament, the bicameral National Diet, features simultaneously a standard and unusual example of a parliamentary committee system. At first glance, it presents a typical committee system with a structure organized along policies and the ministerial portfolio and functions fulfilled in deliberation, oversight, and accountability. In this regard, it is not different from its counterparts in European democracies. In its real role, however, the system has some unusual, but not necessarily totally unique, operations.

Three prominent factors have led Japan's parliamentary system to develop differently than many other democracies. Throughout this chapter, we will discern these three influences and how they affect the committee system. The first influence is the American occupation (1945–1952) that established its structure in the 1947 Constitution imposed on Japan. It was modelled after the British parliamentary system but included inspiration from the US Congress not found in the then-British model: two Houses of some influence in policy-making (although the lower House of Representatives has greater power over major legislation) and the extensive, specialized committee system itself in both elected Houses.

The second factor is the long-term dominance of one political party in the postwar period. The Liberal Democratic Party (LDP) was established in 1955 from the merger of two smaller conservative parties and then proceeded singlehandedly or in coalition to form the government from that time until 2009, with only one ten-month hiatus during which a coalition of parties that had mostly been in the opposition took power. From 2012 until the present, the LDP has remained in power in coalition with another smaller, former opposition party. This has had a formative influence on the actual operation of the committee system. As we will see, over time, the LDP developed the norm that deliberation should take place within the party before submission to the Diet, while deliberation in the Diet should be sidestepped. This norm made Diet committees more or less rubber-stamping organizations for government legislation, especially when the LDP had an 'effective majority' to control chairs and majorities in all committees.

A major electoral reform passed during the short hiatus of non-LDP parties in power in 1994 is the third relevant factor. This reform – combined with an

DOI: 10.4324/9781003106579-11

administrative reform in 2001 – helped bring about significant changes to the processes of Japanese politics, including some to the role of the committees. In 1994, the electoral system was changed from a very personalistic, single non-transferable vote system to a mixed-member majoritarian system with a first-past-the-post, single-member district component combined with a proportional representation component. The administrative reform of 2001 strengthened the role of the prime minister and the cabinet in policy-making. In conjunction, the electoral and administrative reforms helped increase the importance of programmatic policy competition in elections, increased the power of party leaders – and the prominence of two major political parties overall (Nemoto 2018). It is true that committees' direct impact on policy deliberation is still moderate at best, because the presence of the single-member district component makes it much more likely that a ruling coalition controls an 'effective majority' to bypass discussions in committees and promote swift government legislation. However, the Diet and its committees are gradually but steadily transforming themselves to an arena where the government and the opposition engage in policy competition. For instance, as described below, a new committee for the British-style question time was newly introduced, while bureaucrats are now banned from responding to the opposition's questions in committees on behalf of ministers.

In this chapter we will concentrate on the House of Representatives of the bicameral Japanese National Diet for a couple of reasons. First, although technically the lower house, it is in fact the more important of the chambers. The Constitution gives it priority over the upper house, the House of Councillors, in passing the most important legislation, budgets, and treaties, and in the selection of the prime minister. While the upper house cannot be dissolved, the prime minister can dissolve the lower house anytime. The public also considers the lower house more important, in part because it is the house to determine the prime minister and in part because its districts are smaller, and constituents feel closer to its representatives. Second, the structure, organization, and legislative procedures of the two houses' committees are very similar. Like committees in the lower house, committees in the upper house are divided along with the government bureaucracy's jurisdictions, and each member should belong to at least one of the committees. All bills are referred to one of the committees to undergo examination before plenary voting. Where necessary, we will indicate places where the upper house differs from the House of Representatives, but otherwise this article concerns the latter.

Institutions, actors, and interactions of committees in the Diet

Format and membership

As of 2020, there are 465 members of the House of Representatives. The committees are organized along functional lines corresponding in large part to the jurisdictions of the bureaucracy. There are 17 standing committees at present, in addition to nine special committees. The upper house, the House of Councillors, has 245 members at present, and its committee structure is almost identical with the lower house: 17 standing committees in addition to seven special committees.

All members of the Diet must serve on at least one committee, although the speakers and the vice-speakers of the houses, members of the cabinet (ministers, vice-ministers, and parliamentary secretaries), and special advisors to ministers are exempt from Diet committee duties (Diet Law, Article 42). Therefore, customarily, speakers and vice-speakers of the houses, and ministers and vice-ministers do not belong to committees, while parliamentary secretaries are assigned to committees as directors.

The size of committees in the House of Representatives varies between 20 (Discipline), 25 (Rules and Administration, i.e. steering), 30 (e.g., foreign affairs, environment, security), through 35 (judicial affairs) to 40 (most of the remainder) and 50 (budget). Special committee numbers vary from 25 to 45 (Table 11.1).

The structure of standing committees in the two houses is very similar, with a couple of minor differences: first, while the House of Representatives

Table 11.1 Standing committees in the Diet of Japan and their sizes

	House of Representatives	*House of Councillors*
Cabinet	40	20
Internal Affairs and Communications	40	25
Judicial Affairs	35	20
Foreign Affairs	30	-
Foreign Affairs and Defence	-	21
Financial Affairs	40	25
Education, Culture, Sports, Science and Technology	40	20
Health, Labour and Welfare	45	25
Agriculture, Forestry and Fisheries	40	20
Economy, Trade and Industry	40	21
Land, Infrastructure, Transport and Tourism	45	25
Environment	30	20
Security	30	-
Fundamental National Policies	30	20
Budget	50	45
Audit and Oversight of Administration	40	-
Audit	-	30
Oversight of Administration	-	35
Rules and Administration	25	25
Discipline	20	10

Source: The House of Representatives, Japan, www.shugiin.go.jp/internet/itdb_iinkai.nsf/html/iinkai/iinkai_jounin.htm (access: 23.09.2020).

has the standalone Security Committee, the House of Councillors integrates its functions to the Committee of Foreign Affairs and Defence; second, while the House of Representatives has the single Audit and Oversight of Administration Committee, the House of Councillors has two separate committees; and third, the size of committees tends to be smaller in the House of Councillors, as it is a smaller legislative body (242 members vs. 465 in the House of Representatives).

Publicity: officially closed but practically open meetings

The Diet Law stipulates that 'no persons other than members are admitted to a committee meeting as visitors' (Article 52 (1)). But in practice, what is discussed inside a committee is widely open to the public. Meetings may be open at the discretion of the chair and thousands of people attend committee meetings as public observers annually, as shown in Figure 11.1, suggesting that acquiring chairs' permissions to attend committee meetings should not be difficult.[1] Minutes of all the committee meetings are available online.[2] Generally, the major Budget Committee meetings are open and televised.

Committees are allowed by the Diet Law to hold public hearings: 'A Committee may hold open hearings on important matters of popular concern and for general purposes, and may hear views from the interested parties or people of learning and experience' (Article 51). The important Budget Committee is required to hold public hearings before committee voting for the budget: 'Open hearings ... must be held on the overall budget and

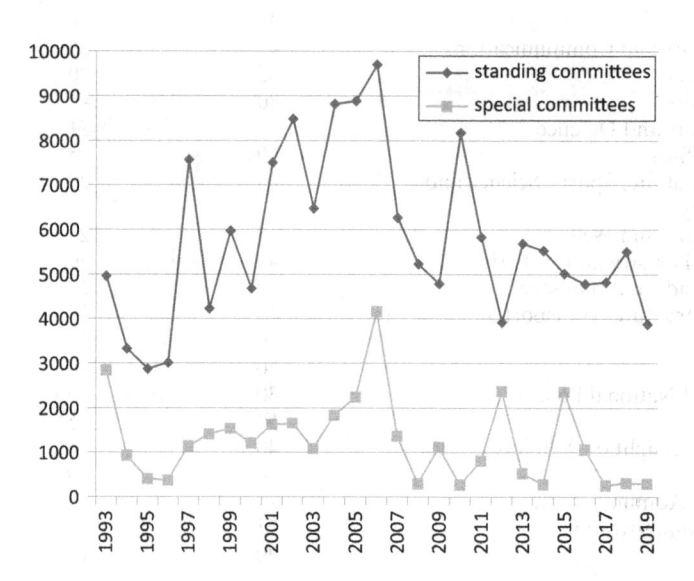

Figure 11.1 Public observers attending committees in Japan.
Source: Shūgiin Jimukyoku (1999–2019).

important bills concerning revenue' (Article 51). In practice, public hearings are rarely held – except by the Budget Committee, which is obliged to hold public hearings; the other committees held public hearings only 3.4 times on average per year during the period between 1999 and 2019. The Budget Committee tends to minimize the importance of public hearings too, since they are perceived as rituals before final voting (Mukoono 2018: 188–189).

Committee types

Most of the standing committees mirror the government bureaucracy's jurisdictions, except for some that are unique to the Diet. The Fundamental National Policies committees were newly launched in 2000 as an arena for the British-style question time. They are unique in that, unlike other standing committees, they do not discuss or deliberate legislation, but they are rather focused on holding 45-minute question-and-answer sessions between party leaders. The Budget committees discuss issues related to the budget and the government's general policy directions, while the Audit and Oversight of Administration Committee serves as a tool to check the executive's actions. The Rules and Administration, and Discipline committees deal with matters specific to the Diet. Almost all standing committees handle policy areas that pertain to only one ministry, although some cover jurisdictions over several agencies within the ministry that are also mirrored in the committee system. The one major exception is the Cabinet Committee, which deals with the policy issues pertaining to the Cabinet Office. After the government reorganization in 2000–2001, the Cabinet Office in Japan now encompasses 15 separate bureaucratic agencies, commissions, councils, and offices, and the Cabinet Committee has jurisdiction over these agencies.

Some committees are particularly important. The Budget Committees and the Fundamental National Policies committees, as they encompass most or all the nation's policy issues and ministerial jurisdictions, are particularly noteworthy and the object of greater media attention. The Cabinet Office Committee, as noted, has jurisdiction over many agencies. The Rules and Administration Committee sets the agenda for legislative priorities for the House and is the arena for particular bargaining between government and opposition parties over these priorities.

Meanwhile, special committees are created for 'particular matters which do not come under the jurisdiction of any standing committee' (Diet Law, Article 45). They tend to be created when important social events take place or when the government has urgent legislation to pass. For instance, after the 2011 Great East Japan Earthquake, a special committee for earthquake recovery was created. Another example is the special committee for post privatization created in 2005, when Prime Minister Koizumi wanted to push his pet policy, the privatization of the postal services (Nemoto et al. 2008).

Finally, the House of Councillors has three research committees. They were established in 1986 for the purpose of conducting long-term and comprehensive analyses on given policy issues, because the House of Councillors cannot be dissolved and members' terms are fixed at six years. Like regular committees, research committees may hold hearings from government officials and scholars, request reports from the government, and submit their own bills.

Legislative, control, and communication functions as a whole

The legislative function is performed when a bill is referred to one of the committees concerned, after it is presented to the Diet. In principle, all bills are first submitted to either chamber of the Diet and then the Speaker sends them to committees, so that they undergo committee examination before they are sent to the plenary session for final voting. Revisions may be added at the committee level. Committees can also submit their own bills under their jurisdiction, according to the Diet Law, Article 50-II: 'A committee may propose a bill concerning matters under its jurisdiction. The chairperson of the committee shall be the proposer of such a bill'. In 2019, for instance, 21 bills were submitted by committees, and all of them eventually became laws. The pass rate was so high because the norm in Japan is that bills are only submitted by committees when ruling and opposition parties already agree to pass them (Iwai 1988: 65). This means that committees submit only noncontroversial bills.

Despite these institutional prerogatives given to committees, in reality, their legislative functions may become minor when the plenary majority controls a majority in a committee, as described in detail below. This is because a majority in a committee is able to move for the immediate termination of examination and deliberation. Even 'consideration by the Committee may be omitted by a resolution of the House' (Diet Law, Article 56), although this power had been rarely used for a long time, perhaps because a plenary majority feared a backlash from the public. The House of Representatives never used this power to bypass committee deliberation between 1975 and 1999. After the late 1990s, however, the ruling coalition used it repeatedly when legislating the revised Basic Resident Registration Act in 1999, for instance.[3]

The control function may be performed through committees. Members, mostly from the opposition, exercise their right to conduct government investigations by calling for the testimony of witnesses, demanding reports and records, and asking questions of government officials, in particular ministers, in committees. Some committees, such as the Budget and Fundamental National Policies committees, are widely televised and are important arenas where the opposition attempts to keep the executive in check through oral questioning.

Although committees rarely reach out to the public through their own means, the communication function is carried out through NHK, Japan's national broadcasting organization. It provides live broadcasting of the Diet. The programme, which started in 1953, tends to focus on debate over important policy matters in the Budget Committee or the question time in the Fundamental National Policies committees. Live broadcasting and video archives are also available on the internet through a special website.[4]

Actors in committees

Committee assignment

The Diet Law provides that 'Members of Standing Committees shall be appointed by each House at the beginning of a session, and shall hold their membership until their term of office as Members of their House expires' (Article 42) and that 'membership of standing committees and of special committees shall be allocated to political groups in the House in proportion to their numerical strength, and then the committee members shall be appointed according to this allocation' (Article 46). In practice, however, the Rules and Administration Committee determines how many committee seats are allocated to each party. The presiding officer, i.e. the Speaker of the House, then appoints committee members according to the lists created by parties.

Generally, in determining committee assignments, the party accepts MPs' requests, but the party makes the decision based on seniority, constituency types, and MPs' backgrounds. For instance, MPs elected from rural areas tend to get assigned to committees dealing with agriculture and other distributive issues, while MPs from urban areas tend to assume positions in public policy-related committees, such as the Welfare Committee (Shugart et al. 2021). As described later, policy expertise may lead to placement on a certain committee, but constituency characteristics and electoral considerations have been more important for the LDP, particularly under the highly personalistic vote system before the electoral reform in 1994. Pekkanen et al. (2006) show that future leaders tend to assume positions in high-policy committees, such as security, diplomacy, and finance, while electorally vulnerable MPs are more likely to be assigned to committees that are useful for them to shore up votes through the provision of pork barrel benefits and constituency services. An MP's expertise might have have some impact on committee assignment, although it would be minor compared to seniority, constituency types, and MPs' backgrounds. Since the electoral reform of 1994 to a more party- and policy-oriented mixed-member majoritarian system, policy expertise should, in theory, have been taken somewhat more into account. This expectation is confirmed by an extensive comparative analysis of committee appointments under different types of electoral systems. It proves true of both the LDP and the main opposition parties, who have always taken expertise more into consideration than the LDP (Shugart et al. 2021, chs. 5 and 10).

As described above, all members of the Diet must serve on at least one committee, although some members, such as the presiding officers and cabinet ministers, are exempt from committee duties. MPs may serve on more than one committee. As of May 2020, MPs in the Diet are members of 2.2 committees on average. Yet there is remarkable variation: nearly 30 percent of the MPs (122 out of 424) are members of only one committee, while more than 10 percent of the MPs (44 out of 424) serve on four.

Despite the quoted legal provision that membership in the standing committees goes for the entire term, the factual norm in Japan is that all personnel, including committee membership, rotate annually. This is related to the practice that the cabinet is usually reshuffled annually. Since cabinet ministers are exempt from committee duties, newly appointed ministers leave committees and vacancies need to be filled. The result is the annual rotation of posts in the government, the Diet, and the party.

Meanwhile, the literature on the Japanese policy-making process suggests that MPs develop their policy expertise through their participation in committees (Schoppa 1991; Krauss & Pekkanen 2011). As explained later, before the electoral reform, some mid-career to senior MPs from the ruling LDP have exerted significant influence over the policy-making process as experts in given policy areas (*zoku giin* or 'policy tribes'). Becoming such experts requires the accumulation of knowledge and experience in the party's policy-making organ (the Policy Affairs Research Council), Diet committees, and cabinet posts (Schoppa 1991). How the Diet committees' training function has changed since the electoral reform should be an interesting research topic. One possibility is that such a function might have become stronger, since the reform to the party- and policy-oriented electoral system might have given the incentive for MPs to take advantage of Diet committees and their service on the party's Policy Affairs Research Council (see below) to develop policy-making skills. Another possibility is that Diet committees might be somewhat irrelevant in training MPs, since MPs usually do not stay in the same committee for more than one year and the centralization of powers into the cabinet and the prime minister would mean that MPs in committees are expected to serve as loyal agents for the party leadership, rather than independently developing their policy-making skills. Although no academic work has systematically tested these hypotheses yet, as long as policy expertise is taken into account in committee appointments (Shugart et al. 2021) MPs may want to make the most of their assignment to Diet committees to develop their policy-making skills.

Roles in committees with a clear differentiation and strong chairs

Within the committees there is a highly hierarchical structure and function of roles. The committee chair is the most important position, with a wide range of agenda-setting powers (Masuyama 2015: 26–27). Chairs maintain order inside the committee and determine the dates of committee meetings. They have the power to allow committee members to speak and limit the time for deliberation. While they usually do not participate in voting, when there is a tie, they can break it.

Therefore, controlling as many committee chair positions as possible is important for the party. In this way, the government can speed up legislation. Meanwhile, the opposition can use the agenda-setting powers of committee chairs to significantly delay government legislation. Since the chair in a committee of the House of Representatives is usually selected by a majority in a committee (Fukumoto 2007, 117–118) and committee seats are allocated proportionally to parties, parties want to win what is called an 'effective majority', as explained later. The norm as of 2020 is that two chairs are given to the opposition and the remaining 15 are given to the government. The upper house has a very different norm for the allocation of committee chairs: chairs are proportionally allocated to parties (Fukumoto 2007, 117–118).

Qualifications for the chair vary depending on the time periods, but seniority continues to be the top priority. The LDP institutionalized over time the seniority system, whereby each LDP politician must win a certain number of elections to climb to higher positions. By the 1980s, the norm held that becoming a committee chair would require five or more terms served in the House of Representatives (Kohno 1992: 374; Nemoto et al. 2008). This norm still seems to apply to the current era. For instance, in 2020, the average number of terms served by committee chairs is 6.6, compared to 4.1 by directors (below), and 3.8 by backbenchers.

The chair is aided by a number of *riji* (directors) who act as the more senior members of the committee from both ruling and opposition parties. The norm is that the procedural agenda is set by a consensus among the chair and the directors (Iwai 1988: 132), although a majority party can always resort to the institutional power to bypass committee deliberation as described above. Indeed, even though votes are taken within committees, the majority can always carry out its will through party discipline if it wants to.

Interactions in Diet committees

Deliberation and negotiation

As described above, all bills undergo committee examination before they are sent to the plenary session, but a majority in a committee may be able to move for the immediate termination of examination and deliberation. In addition, a committee chair, appointed by a majority in a committee, is given a wide range of agenda-setting powers. All of these institutional prerogatives given to committee majorities and committee chairs mean that when the opposition controls a majority in a committee, it can at least delay government legislation in the committee. Given the Diet Law provision that all bills on hold are shelved and not carried over to the next session (Article 68), delaying legislation may lead to significant modifications, or even the eventual killing of bills. According to Masuyama (2003), a committee chair from the opposition can significantly lengthen the time required for government legislation.

Thus, one significant factor affecting deliberation and discussion is whether the ruling coalition controls committee chairs and majorities in committees. It is important to note here that a plenary majority may not necessarily control majorities in committees.[5] In order to have what is called an 'effective majority' (*antei tasū*), or control over committee chairs and voting majorities in all committees, a party requires 244 out of 465 plenary seats (52.5 percent), not a simple majority of 233. When the ruling coalition has an 'effective majority', it tries to minimize time for deliberation, discussion, bargaining, and deal-making in the committee to promote smooth government legislation. Indeed, when the LDP had an 'effective majority' until the mid-1970s, committees' legislative functions were perceived as marginal: 'Members of the Diet denigrate the committee stage of deliberations. LDPers tend to perceive it to be a nuisance and a waste of time' (Baerwald 1974: 135). Similarly, committee chairs tended 'to be viewed as agents of the governing party rather than as guardians of a committee's prerogatives' (Baerwald 1974: 100).

This does not mean deliberation and negotiations did not take place at all, or just within the LDP instead of in Diet committees. Rather, deliberation and negotiations took place within the LDP's policy-making organ, the Policy Affairs Research Council (PARC), with subdivisions generally parallel to both the Diet committee structure and bureaucratic jurisdictions.[6] Since the early 1960s, the norm was that *all bills* must first be vetted and deliberated in the party before being introduced into the Diet (Krauss & Pekkanen 2011: 165–166). In practice this meant that the PARC was the major policy deliberator of legislation *before* a bill went to Diet committees, while the opposition's influence inside the committee was relatively minor, especially when the LDP had an 'effective majority'. All the opposition was able to do was threaten to resort to *dilettante tactics* and physical obstruction of final voting,[7] which might lead to minor adjustments. Even though a committee majority is institutionally able to ram through a bill by forcing a vote (*kyōkō saiketsu*, or 'forced' vote), the audience costs could be high and the opposition accusations of 'tyranny of the majority' could register with the public (Baerwald 1974: 112–120).

The flip side of these is that deliberation, discussion, bargaining, and deal-making between the government and the opposition can and does take place when the LDP loses its effective majority. The 1976–1980 'nearly equal power' (*hakuchū*) era was such a period, when the combined opposition parties came very close to a majority in the House as a whole. The LDP had to give up important powers to the opposition, depending on the committee, resulting in greater compromise between the LDP and opposition parties. One reason was the opposition parties had to be given either more committee chairships or had a majority on the committee. Thus, the LDP was forced to negotiate and compromise further. The percentage of government bills that found opposition party support, excluding the Communist Party, increased from 70 to 90 percent and the number of forced votes declined (Krauss 1984: 257–266).

While the institutional settings of committees explained above remain intact after the electoral reform, the reform might have had some indirect impact on how deliberation and negotiations take place. First, as explained in the introduction, the presence of the single-member district component in the new mixed-member majoritarian system makes it much more likely that a ruling coalition controls an 'effective majority'. In fact, since 2005, every government formed after the elections (2005, 2009, 2012, 2014, and 2017) won more than two-thirds of the seats in the lower house, controlling majorities in all committees and most of the chairs.[8] This should enable the ruling coalition to bypass discussions in committees and promote swift government legislation. As described above, the ruling coalition uses more often than ever the committee majority power to immediately terminate deliberation. This is probably because the opposition is very much fragmented and weak and the LDP does not fear being labelled as the 'tyranny' now.

The second change is that, now that the party's programmatic policy-making image and the performance of the prime minister matter much more under the new electoral system, the party leadership has much stronger powers to initiate policy and set the agenda. Under the previous system, the prime minister's policy-making powers were relatively minor, since any government legislation needed to get prior approval from the PARC, as described above. In contrast, with the centralized powers to endorse candidates and allocate campaign money, the party leadership sometimes bypasses inputs from the PARC,[9] which now seems to be more or less a 'rubber-stamping organization for the cabinet'.[10]

These factors combined suggest that committees as depicted by Baerwald (1974) nearly half a century ago may be reemerging. That is, with the LDP-led ruling coalition securing a two-third majority in the House of Representatives, the committee stage of deliberation may be perceived as a ritualistic waste of time and the government may be appointing loyal agents as committee chairs to speed up legislation. Unfortunately, to our knowledge, there is no academic work systematically investigating how the electoral reform changed – or not – the deliberative and bargaining functions of committees, but this is an interesting hypothesis to test.

Variation in committee culture

Which committees are conflictual or consensual should depend on which policy issues are important in the country in a given period. For instance, during the Cold War era, the major conflict between the government and the opposition was over foreign and security policy issues in Japan, with the government arguing for the stronger Japan–US Security Treaty and the opposition demanding its abolishment. Thus, when the government revised the treaty in 1960, security-related committees like the Foreign Affairs Committee tended to be conflictual and even chaotic, with violence and physical obstruction of voting fairly widely seen. Some legislative violence and disorder, such as physical obstruction of legislative deliberation, still takes place today, although more rarely as the basic defence and foreign policy cleavages continue to exist but have been less intense during the past few decades; for instance, in the 2016 Special Committee for the Trans-Pacific Partnership, where the opposition tried to physically stop the chair to force a committee vote, and in votes over the government's series of security-related bills between 2013 and 2017.[11]

Participants in committees

Government officials are normally not present in committees, but committees may request their participation. The significant exceptions are the Budget Committee and the National Strategy Committee. At the Budget Committee, normally the prime minister and the entire cabinet may appear since issues discussed span the entire gamut of national concerns. The National Strategy Committee hosts the British-style question time that is usually televised nationally. Up until 2001, it was common for top-level bureaucrats to attend and often respond to questions in place of the cabinet minister or another high-level elected official. However, since the administrative reform of 2001, ministers must respond to questions themselves, although bureaucrats may be present as observers or as witnesses. As explained in the introduction, this is one of the important reform measures made to transform the Diet and committees as an arena where the government and the opposition engage in policy competition.

Turning attention to interest groups, the Diet and committees play only minor roles in contacting interest groups. This is in part because, as described above, the party before the electoral reform and the cabinet after the electoral reform dominate the policy formulation process, while committees' legislative functions tend to be minimal. When the LDP firmly established its one-party dominance, it was rather the LDP and its PARC that to a large degree monopolized contacts with interest groups. Indeed, MPs who had served on the relevant PARC subdivisions, Diet committees, and cabinet posts in a specific policy area, became known as *zoku giin* or 'policy tribes' and were known to be not only experts in that policy area but the key contacts with interest groups and the relevant bureaucracy in that policy field. These *zoku giin* to a large extent dominated policy-making in that field until the electoral and administrative reforms of the 1990s. After the electoral and administrative reforms of the 1990s and the prime ministership of Koizumi Jun'ichirō, the PARC and therefore *zoku giin* have been increasingly sidestepped from the policy-making process, as seen above. The influence of the cabinet and the party leadership became greater (Krauss & Pekkanen, 2011: ch. 9), while committees still play only marginal roles in contacting interest groups.

In theory, a wide variety of people can participate in public hearings. A typical process to select attendants for public hearings is: (1) a committee decides to demand a public hearing; (2) the committee gets approval from the Rules and Administration Committee and the Speaker of the House; (3) the committee announces the holding of a public hearing through the government's official gazette (*kanpō*) and NHK to recruit attendants; and (4) the committee selects attendants. Usually, though, parties recommend scholars and influential opinion holders (Mukoono 2018, 189–190). A public hearing for the Budget Committee in 2019, for instance, was attended by business consulting firms, scholars, and NGOs.[12]

Committees in the policy cycle

Problem definition and agenda-setting

Although standing committees and special committees do not write any reports, research committees in the House of Councillors write three policy reports every three years.[13] Topics range widely, from fiscal policy and world trade to governance and energy. Reports may include policy recommendations to be dealt with by the government.

In addition, as described above, standing, special, and research committees can submit their own bills. One of the unique functions given to research committees in the House of Councillors is the power to recommend new legislation to other standing and special committees. Some major legislation recommended by research committees includes the 2001 law to prevent domestic violence and the 2018 gender parity law.

However, this is not the usual way that the agenda is set. Before electoral and administrative reform, it was usually the ministries and key members of the ruling LDP that set the agenda through the party's policy-making organ, PARC. The government ministries were more frequently the initiators of bills that were then sent to the PARC subdivision for review, alterations, or rejection before they ever came to the Diet committees. Only occasionally were PARC subdivision chairs or Diet committee chairs the initiators of legislative bills.

Now that the policy-making powers are more centralized into the hands of the prime minister, it is usually the cabinet that sets the agenda and initiates policy. The LDP's and its members' roles in initiating policy and setting the agenda were substantially cut. Note that out of the 94 bills that became laws in 2019, for instance, 71 (75.5 percent) were submitted by the cabinet.

All of these imply that, even though committees can in theory delay topics from moving to the plenary or even kill a bill, in practice, such powers are rarely used, especially when a ruling coalition holds an 'effective majority'.

Policy formulation

Despite the lack of a significant role in agenda-setting, committees play a role and have a function in policy formulation. Revisions are added at the committee level. If necessary, as described above, members in a committee can agree to propose a bill. Sometimes, the cabinet tries to legislate its bill in the original format without revisions, while in other occasions – for instance, when the ruling party does not hold a majority in the Diet – the opposition successfully incorporates its policy ideas through Diet committees, as in the cases of the Japanese financial reconstruction bills in the late 1990s.[14]

As we have seen in the description of the policy-making processes, however, when the LDP is in power singly or in coalition, only minor revisions will be usually made to bills, because LDP majority members will carry out the party's, its coalition partner's, PARC subdivisions', or government's prior decisions on legislation. The negotiations with the opposition parties in the committees nonetheless may be important because the extent to which accommodation between the parties in the committee is reached may influence the government's decisions about the agenda for the plenary session, and its strategic decisions concerning the priorities of bills to carry over (delay passing) or send to the plenary session for passage. Unlike in Spain and Italy, committees do not have any rights to make final decisions in place of the plenary. Most coordination for policy formulation is not done in the committees but externally. Avenues for policy coordination include the LDP's PARC subdivisions (especially before the electoral reform), a special joint committee between coalition partners in a coalition situation, or in the cabinet (especially after the electoral reform). The main policy coordination in the committees is between the government and the opposition parties, but again, these are usually minor adjustments after the core aspects of bills have already been formulated.

The Constitution (Article 59) and the Diet Law (Article 84) provide that when the two houses disagree on a bill, they can call for the meeting of a conference committee of both Houses. However, because of the control of both Houses of the Diet in many years of the postwar period by one party, this option has been exercised only rarely. For example, it was invoked in the passage of the electoral reform in 1994 by Prime Minister Hosokawa, but it was the first time this had been done in 43 years, and even then it was just used as a cover for decisions already taken by party leaders in the ruling coalition (Curtis 1999: 159).

Implementation and evaluation

Through committees, members, especially ones from the opposition, exercise their right to conduct government investigations, by calling the testimony of witnesses, demanding reports and records, and asking questions. During the period between 2009 and 2019, the government provided on average 134.8 reports to the Diet annually, suggesting that committees do regularly use their institutional right to ask reports from the government. As described above, some committees, especially the Budget and Fundamental National Policies committees, are widely televised and important arenas where the opposition attempts to keep the executive in check through oral questioning.

There is one committee dedicated to executive oversight functions: the Audit and Oversight of Administration Committee. However, this committee does not really have systematic control over the executive, as anyway, a parliamentary majority usually controls committees now.

Conclusion: the strength of committees in policy-making

As we have seen, committees in the Japanese Diet are neither completely irrelevant nor are they very influential, transformative agents within the policy agenda, formulation, and implementation-evaluation processes. Because of the long-term rule of the LDP in the postwar period and the subsequent integration of the party and parliamentary structures (i.e. PARC subdivisions and committees), parliamentary committees are, as in some other parliamentary democracies, to a large extent creatures of the ruling party and its relationship with the opposition parties of the time.

Nevertheless, as we have also seen, external political events can modify those committee relationships and therefore also, to some extent at least, the role and function of committees. The American Occupation's combining of a British parliamentary with a US Congressional-style, highly specialized, extensive committee system provided the opportunity for committees to exercise great leverage in agenda-setting, formulation, and implementation of policy. The establishment of a parallel and powerful division (committee) system in PARC within the LDP and the latter's long-term rule and strict party discipline over members, combined with the earlier postwar importance of the bureaucracy in agenda-setting and formulation, however, undermined the parliamentary committees' potential.

Even then, however, the extent to which it was undermined varied by subsequent external political developments. From the formation of the LDP in 1955 until 1976, it was, considered 'a waste of time' by LDP Diet members and even opposition party members considered it an 'ornament' (Baerwald 1974: 94). When the opposition parties came closer to power in the late 1970s and had more influence on committees, new norms of accommodation and conflict management evolved that gave the committees a greater role in these processes. With the return of the LDP to power in 1980 and for most of the 1980s, these new norms remained but the committees reverted back to a status of lesser importance.

The rise of *zoku giin*, or policy tribes and their influence over policy formulation within the LDP PARC – with its close integration with parliamentary committees – made the committees, at least as an adjunct of PARC subdivisions, somewhat more important. However, the even with the electoral and administrative reforms of 1994 and 2001, agenda-setting and formulation powers remain largely with the cabinet, party executives, and prime minister. The committees have never done much in the way of oversight or implementation.

The Japanese parliamentary committees are not unique in their subordination to the centralization of political party decision-making in the policy process, but they have been somewhat unusual in the way this has evolved and shifted over time.

Notes

1 Unfortunately, we have no idea what kinds of people attend committee meetings, since *Shūgiin no Ugoki* does not offer any additional information.
2 National Diet Library. *Kokkai Kaigiroku Kensaku Sisutemu*, available at https://kokkai.ndl.go.jp (access: 23.09.2020).
3 Nihon Keizai Shimbun, August 10, 1999, 2; other laws passed using this provision include the revised election law in 2000 (Nihon Keizai Shimbun February 3, 2000, 2), the special law to inject public funding to local financial institutions in 2004 (Nihon Keizai Shimbun June 15, 2004, 2), the National Civil Service Law in 2007 (Nihon Keizai Shimbun June 28, 2007, 2), and the law to punish organized crimes in 2017 (Nihon Keizai Shimbun June 15, 2017, 3).
4 House of Representatives Internet TV, www.shugiintv.go.jp (access: 23.09.2020).
5 This is because of the presence of even-numbered committees with 20, 30, 40, or 50 members. Controlling a voting majority in an odd-numbered committee, say, a 35-member committee, should be straightforward: the ruling coalition would require 18 seats. But controlling a voting majority in an even-numbered committee would require one additional seat in a committee and therefore more seats in the plenary, since committee seats are proportionally allocated to parties. See Krauss (1984: 259).
6 See Liberal Democratic Party of Japan: LDP organization chart, www.jimin.jp/english/profile/chart (access: 23.09.20); all LDP Diet members had to serve on at least two PARC divisions and their appointments were also rotated annually. Members of a committee are automatically also on a party PARC division.
7 One example of dilettante tactics is what is called *gyūho senjutsu*, literally a cow-walking tactic. Taking advantage of the fact that there is no time limit for roll-call voting, opposition members employing this tactic spend hours in walking to a ballot box at a snail's pace to cast their votes. As a last resort, opposition members may resort to physical violence to stop the speaker or the committee chair from declaring the passage of a bill, by obstructing entry to a meeting room. See Baerwald (1974: 108–112).
8 The norm since 2005 has been that chairs of the Audit and Oversight of Administration and Discipline committees are given to the opposition, while all the other chairs are controlled by the ruling coalition.
9 Asahi Shimbun, August 20, 2013, 4.
10 Yomiuri Shimbun, December 20, 2019, 4.
11 They include the 2013 State Secrecy Law; the 2015 Security-related laws; 2017 Subversive Activities Prevention Law. See the video of the 2017 bills' conflict in committee at: https://youtube/8uVxit75ie0 (access: 23.09.2020).
12 Shūgiin. The 198th Session, the Budget Committee Public Hearing, Volume 1. Available at www.shugiin.go.jp/internet/itdb_kaigiroku.nsf/html/kaigiroku/003019820190226001.htm (access: 23.09.2020).
13 They are available online at the House of Councillors website www.sangiin.go.jp/japanese/chousakai/houkoku.html (access: 23.09.2020).
14 Nihon Keizai Shimbun October 15, 1998, 7

References

Baerwald, H.H. (1974). *Japan's Parliament: An Introduction*. Cambridge: Cambridge University Press.

Curtis, G.L. (1999). *The Logic of Japanese Politics: Leaders*. In *Institutions and the Limits of Change*. New York: Columbia University Press.

Fukumoto, K. (2007). *Rippō no Seido to Katei*. [Legislative Institutions and Process] Tokyo: Bokutakusha.

Iwai, Y. (1988). *Rippō Katei*. [The Lawmaking Process] Tokyo: Tokyo Daigaku Shuppankai.

Kohno, M. (1992). Rational Foundations for the Organization of the Liberal Democratic Party in Japan. In World Politics 44(3): 369–397.

Krauss, E.S. Conflict in the Diet: Toward Conflict Management in Parliamentary Politics. In Krauss, E.S., Rohlen, T.P., & Steinhoff, P.G. (eds.), *Conflict in Japan*. 243–93.

Krauss, E.S., & Pekkanen, R.J. (2011). *The Rise and Fall of Japan's LDP*: Political Party *Organizations*. Ithaca: Cornell University Press.

Masuyama, M. (2003). *Gikai Seido to Nihon Seiji*. [Agenda Power in the Japanese Diet] Tokyo: Bokutakusha.

Masuyama, M. (2015). *Rippō to Kenryoku Bunritsu*. [Legislative Power and Democracy] Tokyo: Tokyo Daigaku Shuppankai.

Mukoono, S. (2018). Gikaigaku. [A Study of the Parliament] Tokyo: Yoshida Shoten.

Nemoto, K. (2018). Electoral systems in context: Japan. In Herron, E.S., Pekkanen, R.J., & Shugart, M.S. (eds.) *The Oxford Handbook of Electoral Systems*. Oxford: Oxford University Press. 825–849.

Nemoto, K., Krauss, E.S., & Pekkanen, R.J. (2008). Policy dissension and party discipline: the july 2005 vote on postal privatization in japan. *British Journal of Political Science* 38(3): 499–525.

Pekkanen, R. J., Nyblade, B. & Krauss, E.S. (2006). Electoral Incentives in Mixed member Systems: Party, Posts, and Zombie Politicians in Japan. *American Political Science Review* 100(2): 183–193.

Schoppa, L. J. (1991). Zoku Power and LDP Power: A Case Study of the Zoku Role in Education Policy. *Journal of Japanese Studies* 17(1): 79–106.

Shugart, M. S., Bergman, M.E., Struthers, C.L., Krauss, E.S., &. Pekkanen, R.J. (2021). *Party Personnel Strategies: Electoral Systems and Parliamentary Committee Assignments*. Oxford: Oxford University Press

Shūgiin Jimukyoku. Various Years. *Shūgiin no Ugoki*. [What Happened in the House of Representatives] Tokyo: Shūgiin Jimukyoku.

12 Exploring the gap between theory and practice in law-making and oversight by committees of the Nigerian National Assembly

Benjamin Ekeyi

Oversight and law-making are key functions of every parliament. Thus, by representing citizens, parliaments have the essential task of shaping policies through passage of laws as well as overseeing the executive arm of government to ensure that the policies (usually formulated after due consultation with the intended beneficiaries) are implemented effectively by scrutinizing the work of government and holding it to account. Despite the contested nature of the concept of oversight, it forms a critical aspect of legislatures in modern democracies and is documented by most constitutions (Oyewo 2007). Similarly, law-making, which involves translating policies into laws and giving legal framework to government policies, is a critical role of the legislature. In essence, parliaments play the pivotal roles of legislation and oversight and determine the extent to which these functions and activities contribute to government's policy-making process.

In Nigeria, legislation and oversight by the National Assembly has witnessed its highs and lows. While some scholars have posited that the Nigerian National Assembly has performed its legislation and oversight functions creditably well, a vast majority have criticized the legislature for having very little impact. The legislature's importance in the policy-making process through these two key parliamentary functions entails that legislators must be 'men and women of proven integrity and good character that eschew temptations of falling to such issues legislated against' (Ewuin et al. 2014: 140). Therefore, at the inception of the current democratic governance in 1999, there was a high public expectation from the legislature to deploy its powers in influencing the policy-making process in Nigeria through its committees. As in other parliaments across the globe, the committee system of the Nigerian National Assembly is the rallying point for legislative performance. This hope for effective performance and influence in policy-making has rather been dashed as committees in the National Assembly have continued to perform below expectation despite the presence of necessary structure and framework for the performance of their responsibilities.

Notwithstanding measures to insulate the legislature from corrupt practices and ensure effectiveness in policy-making on key national issues like the economy, education, housing, agriculture, or security, the National Assembly has not lived

DOI: 10.4324/9781003106579-12

up to expectations. Clientelism, faint political will, poor technical competence, and inadequate funding, among other factors, have posed a huge challenge to the effective policy-making powers of the National Assembly, leading to the negative public perception of the legislature's law-making and oversight capacities, and growing pessimism about the effectiveness of public policies in Nigeria. This chapter examines the role of the Nigerian National Assembly in policy making and concludes that the Nigerian legislature must wake up from its slumber and take its rightful place in the policy-making process through effective law-making and periodic or regular oversight to ensure that programmes and policies of government are implemented according to stipulated laws and on time, too. In this chapter, the terms 'parliament' and 'legislature' are used interchangeably, as are 'parliamentarian' and 'legislator'. The same goes for 'House' and 'Chamber'.

Committees as parliamentary engine room

Committees have been seen as the 'legislative backbone' of parliaments. Due to the impossibility of parliaments to carry out all their enormous tasks at plenary, sector-based or portfolio committees often known as select or standing committees are set up to serve as 'workshops' or 'workhorses' of legislatures. They are seen as the engine of parliamentary processes and procedures 'where the raw ingredients of good governance are processed and packaged for the consumption of the legislature' (Nwozor & Olanrewaju 2019: 166). As posited by Ogbonnaya et al. (2014: 31), 'legislative committees are units of organizations within a legislative chamber that allow groups of legislatures [sic] to review policy matters or propose bills more closely than would be possible by the entire chamber'. This position has been generally alluded to by several parliamentary experts like Olson (2015), Norton (2016), Aliyu et al. (2018) as well as Flegmann (1986), Erunke & Ndiribe (2013), Fasagba (2009a) and Ewuim et al. (2014). As La Palombara (1974: 123) argues, 'if the national legislature is to be a significant political factor, then it must have specialized committees of limited membership and considerable scope of power'. These powers include, among others, exercising control over the executive and encouraging deeper and more effective scrutiny of government proposals in the form of legislation.

In Nigeria, like other jurisdictions, these committees oversee sectors like education, health, solid minerals, works, defence, and tourism, and are expected to contribute to the policy processes in these sectors. Nigerian parliamentary committees, therefore, exist to boost the efficiency of the National Assembly in such a way that it can perform its numerous important duties more effectively. They also provide the 'informal collegial environment that facilitates interparty compromises on small matters and adds to technical improvements of legislation and creating platforms for public hearings which allow the general public to participate in law-making processes' (Nwozor & Olanrewaju 2019: 166). Apart from standing committees, the Nigerian legislature has instituted sub- and ad hoc committees to address emerging issues.

In European democracies and most contemporary parliaments across the globe, including Nigeria, parliamentary committees are 'by broad consensus, among the most significant organizational features of modern parliaments' (Strøm 1998:47). They have considerably developed their role in scrutinizing the work of government by holding inquiries into different aspects of executive decisions and policy-making (Asante & Debrah 2015; World Bank 2015). The development in countries such as Nigeria has, however, been very limited and has not fully served to strengthen the legislature as an entity for effective policy scrutiny. Nevertheless, in recent times, it has gained valuable resources of staff for administrative and research support.

Parliamentary work at the committee level is believed to be highly challenging for parliamentarians as 'it demands the power of reasoning and analysis rather than the display of rhetorical and debating skills, which are the most widely advertised aspects of parliamentary activity' (Boafo-Arthur 2005: 133). The latter is more oriented towards achieving broad national goals than parochial party interests. Consequently, parliamentary committees in Nigeria have attracted increasing public attention in the performance of their tasks which includes the scrutiny of legislations as policy-making instruments, supervision of ongoing projects, and inquiries referred by the House.

Committees are seen as the pivot around which some major legislative actions and activities take place. They serve as the vehicle for giving legitimacy and authority to government actors, authorities, and their policies. However, scholars have continued to debate the notion that strong committees equal strong parliaments and thus, effective policy-making, as posited by Strøm (1998: 47) who asserts that 'strong committees, it appears, are at least a necessary condition for effective parliamentary influence in the policy-making process'. This has been challenged by some scholars noting that in some parliaments like the Norwegian Storting, the parliament has continued to wax strong while committee influence has diminished (Rommetvedt 1998 and this volume). In the Nigerian context, the strength of the parliament is a reflection of how effective its committees perform.

Dynamics of parliamentary committees in the Nigerian legislature

Nigeria's formal experience of legislative politics dates back to the colonial era with the first formal legislature established by the British colonial government in 1862. It was referred to as the Lagos Legislative Council (Goitom 2017). The country adopted the bicameral legislative system in 1960 after establishing the Senate in 1959 in addition to the already existing House of Representatives. However, since independence in 1960, Nigeria has experienced a tortuous democratic journey truncated several times by military interventions, the first in 1966. Every time this occurs, the legislature was completely obliterated and forced to reengineer the wheel of legislative process afresh when democratic governance was restored. After several years of military intrusion in governance, a new democratic journey commenced in 1999 ushering in the current Fourth Republic. Fresh elections were held for the legislative arm with political novices winning positions in parliament. This was largely because not many persons trusted the military not to intervene again. The executive arm, which continued to exist even during military governments, became more developed in governance processes and dominated the legislature.

Currently, Nigeria's parliament comprises the Senate and House of Representatives which are collectively called the National Assembly, the highest elective law-making body of the nation. Parliamentary committees in Nigeria's national parliament have a firm legal framework for their existence. Thus, the committee system and their functions are underpinned by Sections 62, 88, and 89 of the 1999 Nigerian Constitution (as amended) as well as the Standing Orders of the two Chambers. The Constitution empowers both the Senate and House of Representatives to create committees, fill such committees with members and determine their mandates and modus operandi. It states that either Chamber may

> appoint a committee of its members for such special or general purpose as in its opinion would be better regulated and managed by means of such a committee, and may by resolution, regulation or otherwise, as it thinks fit, delegate any functions exercisable by it to any such committee.
> (Constitution of Nigeria, section 62)

The parliamentary committee system is the institutionalized mechanism of fragmenting the legislature into manageable units both for 'effectiveness and for appropriating the expertise of members in the examination of issues under the purview and competence of the legislatures' (Nwozor & Olanrewaju 2019: 172). They are now entrenched, inseparable parts of most modern legislatures. In Nigeria, legislative committees are seen as 'factories' where legislative expertise is developed in the process of thorough scrutiny of legislative instruments. They fundamentally act as

> 'a filtering device and a legislative stethoscope by which policy proposals and other related activities are not only scrutinized but also utilized to access [sic] the desirability, feasibility, sustainability, and healthiness of governmental policies'
> (Fashagba 2009a: 429–430)

Thus, parliamentary committee system in the Nigerian National Assembly has been referred to as a 'response of the legislature in meeting the twin challenges of effective representation and staying on top of issues in the face of increasing complexities of governance' (Nwozor & Olanrewaju 2019: 167).

At the dawn of Nigeria's current uninterrupted democratic voyage from 1999, the National Assembly was generally viewed as a rubber-stamp legislature that unquestioningly yielded to the needs of the executive. As Omotoso (2016: 8) asserts, the legislators sacrificed their expected autonomy 'on the altar of financial dependency, as it derives all its revenue from the executive arm of government'. This affected the functioning of legislative committees since the National Assembly depended on the executive for funding. With time, the committees' system has improved, leading to the creation of more and improvement in the quality of their work, albeit slowly.

The constitutional framework for the creation of legislative committees, and the need to improve their functions, informed the steady increase in their number since 1999. However, successive Presidents of the Senate and Speakers of the House of Representatives have continued to create additional committees for various reasons. From an already high number of 45 committees in the House of Representatives in 1999, the committees rose to 109 in 2019, while the Senate, which had an equally high number of 39 committees in 1999, rose to 64 in 2019. Some critics have variously attributed this increase to the clientelist nature of the Nigerian legislature and the use of the committee system to set up a 'complex web of patronage system' (Nwozor & Olanrewaju 2019: 173) to ensure regime survival because of the usually intense nature of the contest for leadership positions in both chambers of the National Assembly.

The steady increase in the number of committees has often been premised on certain justifications. First, is the heavy workload of some committees, hence the need to split them so that they can handle specific functions more effectively; for instance, the House Committee on Petroleum Resources was split into downstream and upstream. Similarly, the erstwhile single House Committee on Education has now been fragmented into House committees on Basic Education and Tertiary Education. According to Yakubu Dogara, Speaker of the House of Representatives between 2015 and 2019, in a speech at the inauguration of 96 committees of the House the extensive mandates of the committees has led to the conclusion that

> experience gained from the operation of Committees since 1999, shows that some Committees' functions and mandates are very wide indeed and cannot be effectively supervised and oversighted by a single committee.
> (House of Representatives 2015: 457)

Another justification offered for the continual increase in the number of parliamentary committees in the National Assembly is the need to meet the increasing intricacies of modern governance. The implication of this is often an equally enlarged scope of parliamentary duties and consequently, the constant demand for more committees and improved expertise in committee processes and procedures in the National Assembly. This, eventually 'necessitated creating specific committees to enable the National Assembly to develop the capacity to deal with all governance issues' (Nwozor & Olanrewaju 2019: 181). Furthermore, additional parliamentary committees were created in response to demands from development partners for more result-oriented law-making and oversight of some particular sectors by committees. Finally, there was a need to reduce frequent conflicts between committees due to their overlapping functions. It is however unclear if these conflicts have lessened with the creation of additional committees.

Table 12.1 Number of committees in the National Assembly of Nigeria

Assembly	Legislative Period	House Committees	Senate Committees
4th	1999–2003	45	39
5th	2003–2007	72	63
6th	2007–2011	85	54
7th	2011–2015	80	56
8th	2015–2019	95	68
9th	2019–2023	109	64

Source: Nwozor & Olanrewaju (2019: 180).

Both the Senate and House of Representatives have select or portfolio committees that oversees all government ministries, departments, and agencies (MDAs). In overseeing them, the committees are responsible for formulating relevant legal frameworks to back policies in that sector. At the same time, oversight requirements confer upon committees a legal ground to assess the operations of various governmental institutions in the implementation of policies passed by the National Assembly. Thus, oversight is seen as the actual exercise of parliamentary control powers through legislative committees to ensure that all government policies are executed as stipulated in the laws passed by parliament (Fashagba 2009b; Kazeem 2013). As stated earlier, both legislation and parliamentary oversight are backed by the Constitution of the country and supported by the various rules or Standing Orders of each chamber. Table 12.1 shows the number of National Assembly committees since 1999.

There are currently 64 committees in the Senate and 109 in the House of Representatives. Seven of the committees in both the Senate and House of Representatives are special committees while the others are standing committees. In the Senate (which has 109 seats), membership of committees ranges from six to 21, while in the House of Representatives (which has 360 seats), it is between 11 and 51 members. In allocating membership and leadership positions, considerations are paid to returning parliamentarians, professional background, loyalty to the leadership, political party lines, and geographic divides. In many instances, expertise and cognate experience are sacrificed on the altar of loyalty to the leadership or party affiliation. In a nutshell, committee membership is not primarily based on the parliamentarian's expertise, but on several other factors, thereby jettisoning the concept of 'round pegs in round holes' or 'square pegs in square holes'.

Another dynamic about committees in the Nigerian National Assembly is the classification of some as 'lucrative' or 'juicy' (Erunke & Ndiribe 2013). The 'luscious' committees are those that have very lucrative ministries, agencies, and parastatals under them and whose annual budget allocations are always very large. Committees who oversee government ministries, departments, and agencies that generate huge independent revenues are also regarded as lucrative and there is usually intense lobbying to either chair or at least gain membership of such committees. As chairs or members of such committees, many legislators grab opportunities to influence or corner contract awards in their favour, provide employment for their constituents, family and friends as well as benefitting from largesse such as sponsored travel, both local and foreign. The various cases of bribe-for-budget and other scandals where legislators are alleged to have demanded gratifications in the course of performing their duties are examples of how legislators have been involved in highly questionable behaviour that is clearly not in the public interest and which limits their legislation and oversight capacities. Furthermore, members of these committees exercise very high political influence and use such to score personal political advantages.

Nigerians have, however, decried the legislators' almost desperate quest for the 'juicy' committees for personal gain while performing their legislative duties. This is despite the fact that MPs' salaries and allowances are often seen as too high in relation to the level of abject poverty in the country. As Umaru (2017: 2) posited, legislators in the National Assembly 'have turned probes and public hearings [conducted by committees] into marketing assets'. Similarly, Ewuim et al. (2014), Otusanya et al. (2015), Nwagwu (2014) and Fasagba (2009) all agree that Nigerian legislators capitalize on their membership of legislative committees to amass personal wealth at the expense of their legislative duties. Indeed, this is seen as the major attraction for many aspirants to such positions. Thus, despite the National Assembly's occasional flashes of impressive performances, parliamentary scholars have argued that personal interests have continued to dwarf its oversight and legislative effectiveness which reflects on the effectiveness of its policy-making process.

Legislation, oversight, openness, and agenda-setting in the Nigerian legislature

The roles of legislation and oversight are usually assigned to the legislature in modern democracies. While legislation is generally referred to as the art of transforming policy proposals (often in the form of bills) into laws, the meaning of legislative oversight is widely contested by proponents of parliamentary studies. For instance, Olson (2008) argues that no consensus has been reached among scholars on a generally accepted definition of legislative oversight and, like the other broad concepts in legislative studies; legislative oversight is presently under-theorised. Despite this, recent studies have dealt extensively with the concept thereby expounding its meaning and practice. Wehner (2004), Pelizzo et al. (2012) and Fasagba (2009) describe it as a means for holding the executive accountable for its actions and ensuring that policies are implemented in accordance with existing laws. It entails monitoring the activities of the executive arm of government to ensure accountability. According to Pelizzo et al. (2006), the concept refers to the parliamentary supervision of the policies and programmes enacted by the government.

Legislative oversight can also be seen as parliament's responsibility of overseeing the executive arm in the implementation of policies and projects which Parliament has approved and funded in the appropriations process. It can therefore be deduced that three types of oversight exist: policy oversight which examines the policy direction of government; programme oversight which scrutinizes the various programmes that government puts in place to actualize the policy; and project oversight which looks at the physical projects that will aid the achievement of the policies. Policy oversight mainly has to do with legislative scrutiny of policy proposals before they are transformed into legal instruments through legislation. Thus, in broad terms, these can be carried out either by overseeing the preparation of a given policy (ex ante oversight) or supervising the execution and the implementation of given policies (ex post oversight).

Effective law-making and oversight are usually accomplished through several means. One of such and perhaps the most powerful technique parliament possesses is the power of the purse – the appropriations process, where parliament considers the budget proposal of the executive (which also contains government's policy proposals). Other oversight tools include ad hoc or special committees to conduct legislative investigations of specific issues, hearings, oversight inspections, bill referral, interpellation, and question time (Pelizzo et al. 2012; Stapenhurst et al. 2008; Hamalai 2015; Stapenhurst et al. 2016). The committees are expected to critically carry out these activities and present reports to the chamber at plenary.

The National Assembly of Nigeria is constitutionally authorized to perform its law-making and oversight functions. These powers are provided for in the 1999 Constitution (as amended) and in the Standing Orders and rules of the respective Houses. Both the processes of law-making and oversight began rather poorly in the early years of the Fourth Republic as the National Assembly was still evolving a viable legislative culture after long years of military rule. Scholars have argued on whether the oversight in the Nigerian Parliament has improved. According to Umaru (2017: 2), 'It has been observed by Nigerians that both Houses of parliament leverage on the oversight functions to enrich individual members instead of monitoring governance'. Similarly, Ewuin et al. (2014:150) conclude that with regard to oversight, Nigeria's National Assembly so far, 'has not lived to the expectation of Nigerians'. This indicates that legislative oversight in Nigeria has not met the yearnings of most Nigerians. However, Hamalai (2014: 21) opines that 'over the years, legislatures have become scrutinizing bodies, the principal role of which is to deliver responsible or accountable government'. Also, the President of the 8th Senate and Chairman of the National Assembly, Senator Abubakar Bukola Saraki, in his speech at the commencement of legislative activities in the 7th National Assembly, averred that 'the last four years have had far-reaching oversight investigations ... The legislative process is a marathon' (House of Representatives 2015). In a nutshell, law-making and oversight in the National Assembly of Nigeria have witnessed both their low and bright days. There is definitely a lot of room for improvement.

As stated above, it is believed that through legislation and oversight, committees provide the avenue for thorough scrutiny of policy proposals and their implementation by the government. To be effective, therefore, some scholars have argued for the need to make committee sessions more private than public to enable legislators to concentrate on the issues under discussion. Others argue that some issues before the committees, by their nature, do not require public interference. These issues include highly sensitive matters involving very senior government officials as well as security policy matters. While on the one hand, increased openness could add value to their work, as it allows for diverse (and sometimes, superior) views and ideas (Onwe et al. 2015), there is the risk that the wider disclosure of legislative committees' activities could undermine their ability to act as 'consensus-building' arenas, and thus affect their legislative capacity to effectively influence policy. This justification has been given for the predominantly private sessions by more than 60 of the 64 and about 100 of the 109 committees in the Senate and House of Representatives respectively. This is mainly because, committee sessions, by default, are closed, except where an exception is given by the leadership of the chamber. The Nigerian Parliament does not have an office for public interest monitoring or a parliamentary integrity officer who can objectively advise it on the merits or otherwise of closed and open hearings. This level of secrecy has drawn widespread criticism with several civil society organizations and the general public criticizing it as a ploy by the legislators to satisfy personal interests and consequently requesting for complete openness in the operations of parliamentary committees.

Committees in the National Assembly usually set their own agenda and, as part of their legislation and oversight functions, hold public hearings, to which government officials are invited when the need arises. This need ranges from the kind of investigation, the issues involved, and the need to respond to public demand for an open hearing. Also, in the last five years, the appropriations committees of both chambers have adopted the policy of conducting public hearings on the annual national budget proposals submitted by the executive for consideration by the National Assembly. Some committees, by the nature of their mandates, therefore, hold more closed or public sessions than others. For instance, the Public Accounts Committee holds public hearings all through the year to consider the report of the Auditor-General for the Federation. On the contrary, the committee on Pilgrims Affairs holds fewer meetings and public hearings due to the nature of its mandate. However, reports from the meetings, whether closed or open, and oversight exercises are expected to be submitted to the House at plenary for thorough debate. Yet in reality, this hardly happens. However, the reverse is the case with committee recommendations on legislation and policy proposals. These reports are always presented and deliberated upon at plenary and guide legislators in the passage of related bills into laws or reaching resolutions on the issues concerned.

As stated, other committee reports, especially on oversight exercises, seldom get to the plenary for consideration. When they do, they are rarely deliberated upon except where the issues are of 'urgent or serious national importance' and, in some cases, when the National Assembly responds to public pressure. It is also viewed that considering all committee reports at plenary will only amount to wasting useful legislative time. Other factors responsible for this include the absence of internal legislative framework and strong political will by the legislature to objectively discuss the reports at plenary. Perhaps, the most critical factor is the fact that the Nigerian legislature has no prosecutorial powers. It can only make recommendations to the executive for implementation. Records show that these recommendations are hardly ever implemented. As posited by Alao (2015: 37) therefore, 'the legislature finds itself incapacitated when it makes recommendations, and such are tossed in the dustbin of antiquity'.

Committee deliberations and decisions are largely taken at the committee sessions usually involving members of the committee, but the chair often wields huge influence on the final decision of the committee. It is, however, important to note that parliamentary committees in Nigeria are hugely influenced by public or external factors. These influences are largely noticed right from the appointment of the leadership and members of the committees to, in some cases, its internal workings and decisions. External influence comes from political parties, party stalwarts, professional bodies, civil society, citizens groups, and other interested parties. The aim is to advance the various interests of these groups through the committees. For instance, political parties can sway the decision of the leadership of the Chamber in the number and composition of the committees as well as the longevity of the leadership and membership of these committees. As Ogul (1990) observes, parties are among the crucial factors which can either promote or limit the potential for parliamentary oversight and legislation.

Indeed, apart from a professional background, party affiliation is a major consideration in allocating legislators into committees. This is because consideration is given to all political parties represented in the Chamber during their composition. The leadership of both Chambers therefore usually succumb to these external pressures to maintain the chairpersons and members of the committees, as well as carry out policy decisions promoted by these interest groups. Thus, typically, most committee chairs and memberships last until the end of the legislative assembly (four years). However, there have been cases of change as a result of fallout with the leadership, death, or exit from parliament as the result of a tribunal or court ruling nullifying the legislator's election, or just a need to reshuffle the committee leadership positions. While a few legislators have been relieved of their chairmanship positions as a result of corrupt practices, none has been recalled by their constituents on the account of criminal wrongdoing, ineptitude or corruption.

In Nigeria, legislators at committee stage wear different 'garments' (or 'hats'), depending on the interest they are pursuing at that time. These 'garments' include the legislature's interests, political party benefits, solicitors for external bodies, and personal goals. In many cases, the political party they represent may have a particular interest in a matter and would use the legislators to drive that interest. As observed by Mutisya et al. (2017: 385), 'parliamentary oversight over the executive organ takes place in a broad political context. Political parties constitute the chief actors in the exercise of parliamentary oversight'. Political party leanings often strongly sway individual and committee members' decisions, both in the performance of oversight and consideration and passage of legislations, in the Nigerian National Assembly. Attention is therefore given to party position on proposed policies during their consideration by the legislature.

The closed nature of committee sessions aids legislators, as representatives of their various parties, in the exercise of exclusive powers and influence over other parties during negotiations and deal-making. This aspect is also sometimes taken outside the formal confines of the legislature where party officials and interested societal groups may participate. Critics have, however, observed that many Nigerian legislators mainly pursue personal goals in their service both as committee chairs and as regular members (Kazeem 2013; Umeagbalasi 2013; Akhigbe 2015; Umaru 2017). Thus, getting elected into the National Assembly is seen as the first step in getting a piece of the 'national pie', that is access to extra resources from the national treasury as well as other offers from private organizations. Consequently, membership of parliamentary committees, especially the so-called 'juicy' ones (see above), is the next step in facilitating access to this pie through contract soliciting, tips during oversight visits, sponsored local and foreign trips etc., in spite of the alleged huge salaries and allowances already accruing to them as parliamentarians.

The Nigerian National Assembly in the policy cycle

Parliamentary scholars have tended to classify legislatures as either 'strong' or 'weak', 'active' or 'reactive', 'policy-making' or 'policy-influencing', and so on. For instance, Polsby (1975) categorizes parliaments into 'arena legislatures' or 'legitimizing assemblies', which simply debate and/or ratify to 'transformative legislatures' or 'policy-making legislatures' that enjoy the independent capacity to amend and transform executive policy proposals into law. To put these classifications in proper perspective, however, there is a need to take note of the peculiar circumstances of these legislatures. As Arter (2006: 247) puts it,

> Legislatures operate in countries with differing regime histories, differing constitutional rules and represent societies that differ, sometimes appreciably, in structure, wealth and wellbeing. They display differing levels of institutional development, work according to different rules of procedure and function in polities with differing degrees of executive stability.

For instance, vast scholarly works indicate that, apart from the use of conventional legislation and oversight tools, legislators in the United States of America can mobilize support for government policies by serving to interpret, justify, enlighten, as well as explain policy implications to their communities (Fenno, 1978; Beer 1990; Mezey 2008). This is similar in Nigeria. Like many other emerging democracies, it has a peculiar political culture which defines its legislative history, too. Its political culture is characterized by endemic clientelism concerning the electoral process and, many times, the legislative process as well. This has led to compromise by legislators which, in turn, dwarfs the legislature's contributions to national development through the policy-making process. In essence, legislators are unable to effectively serve as a check on the executive because actors within the legislature are beneficiaries of the patronage system of the executive. This notwithstanding, the National Assembly of Nigeria has strived to strengthen its influence on policy-making through its law-making and oversight functions, albeit with minimal success.

Researchers have posited that the strength of a parliament often determines its effect on the policy process. Consequently, a strong parliament, one which, through its legislation and oversight activities, has the power to constrain the executive, modify and reject executive proposals where necessary, is believed to have more impact on the policy process. This proposition is not without its critics. For instance, Norton (2013) argues that the power to reject, especially if only occasionally exercised, does not render a legislature a policy-'making' body.

Several factors determine the strength of the Nigerian National Assembly and, subsequently, its impact on the national policy process. These include legislative autonomy, resources, parliamentary–executive relations, legislative efficiency, parliamentary structure and political party influence. The National Assembly possesses (and often exercises) considerable autonomy. Though it is not well resourced with adequate and appropriate technical expertise and funding, formally, it has a well-laid out parliamentary structure, including its committee system. This is, however, ineffective in ensuring parliamentary influence in the policy-making process because of the absence of technical and financial resources to make the structure work effectively.

Generally, and in theory, the Nigerian National Assembly can be said to be both a policy-making and policy-influencing parliament. It has the constitutional powers to make policy decisions and take actions independently of the executive. It also has the right of legislative initiative, that is, 'the potential to influence government success or failure either as a policy-relevant institution with the capacity to affect authoritative decision making or, alternatively, as a political institution with the capacity to influence evaluations of policy enacted elsewhere' (Stark 2011: 115). Furthermore, in a few instances, its structure and resources are deployed to impact the policy process considerably. Some examples include cancellation of the controversial concession agreement between the Federal Government and a firm, Global Infrastructure Nigeria Limited (GINL), on the management of the Ajaokuta Steel Company (ASC) and National Iron Ore Mining Company (NIOMCO), in Itakpe, North Central Nigeria; reversal of the sale of defunct Nigeria Airways to an Indonesian company; and redefining the contracting process at the Sustainable Development Goals (SDGs) office to ensure accountability and prompt implementation of projects to achieve the goals, among others, Hamalai, (2014). Another outstanding example, according to Eniayejuni et al. (2015), was when in 2012, the National Assembly quickly intervened to avert a looming national crisis resulting from an executive policy to increase the pump price of petrol in the country. This policy was reversed following concerted efforts of Parliament and meetings between parliamentarians and various stakeholders, labour organizations, citizens groups, NGOs and government institutions.

Parliamentary policy impact is dependent on several factors. Arter (2006:248) posits that 'an active and specialist standing committee system is widely viewed as a necessary condition for a significant amount of legislative autonomy. Specialist committees have the means to collect information, cultivate policy expertise and reach decisions independently of other institutions'. However, while the Nigerian National Assembly committees can be said to be specialized and active, they cannot be said to possess adequate policy expertise and reach decisions independently. As stated, efforts are channelled more toward achieving personal and party interests than governance goals. Consequently, its efficiency in policy-making (determined by the political and technical competence of members and staff) and relations with the executive is seen as very low.

This apparent imbalance between the legislative powers of the National Assembly as well as its legislation and oversight activities on one hand and the poor outcomes from these activities on the other, explains the gap between the theory of legislative oversight and law-making in the policy process and its actual practice in Nigeria. While the theoretical framework exists, in practice the influence of legislation and oversight on policy-making is low largely because of capacity deficit both on the part of parliamentarians and staff, as well as adverse motivation for many legislators resulting from the described strong clientelist tendencies. The relationship between the National Assembly and the executive is also a key determinant of how effective the legislature can be in the policy-making process. The National Assembly tends to have more influence on the policy process when its relationship with the executive is 'cordial'. Parliamentary scholars like Aiyede (2005) , Omotoso & Oladeji (2019), and Okpe et al (2020) have posited that this can also reduce its ability to take independent decisions and not become stooges in the hands of the executive. Also, significant party influence on key decisions of the National Assembly tends to affect its performance in the area of policy-making or -influencing.

Bridging the gap: strengthening the National Assembly for effective policy-making role

The role of the National Assembly in enhancing development through its influence in policy-making is imperative. As representatives of the people, parliamentarians have the responsibility to 'collate the views, interests, demands and problems of their constituents, harmonise and translate them to policy proposal for legislature' (Nwogwugwu et al. 2019: 94). Furthermore, the legislature has the duty of overseeing the activities of the executive to ensure that they are in tune with existing laws. Both the job of legislative oversight and law-making are performed through the committees, thus the need for strong and well-resourced committees. Parliamentary committees in Nigeria are designed to provide both an alternative policy agenda to government and serve as avenue for debate and policy learning among a broad cross-section of organized interests and citizens. Since 1999, they have continued to develop in the performance of these tasks and other legislative activities but have also been plagued by potent challenges which have created obvious performance gaps in its use of oversight and legislation as a tool of influencing the policy-making process.

Clientelism and legislative corruption have remained a major impediment to effective oversight in the Nigerian National Assembly. As noted by Nwangwu (2014), corruption is at the heart of most oversight failures in Nigeria. Clientelism portends that 'delivery of a good or service on the part of both the patron and client is in direct response to a delivery of a reciprocal benefit by the other party, or the credible promise of such a benefit' (Hicken 2011: 291). Many legislators have turned the exercise of oversight and legislation into an avenue for amassing personal benefits to the detriment of serious policy issues and challenges. The implication is that despite the apparent benefits accruable from effective legislation and oversight as a tool for policy-making in a modern democracy, the legislature has continued to perform below expectations. As posited by Hicken, (2011:302), 'The consensus in the literature is that clientelism has profound negative implications for how democracy functions, citizen attitudes about the quality of their democracy, and the capacity of governments to produce needed public policies'.

Other challenges affecting the performance of legislation and oversight in Nigeria include the absence of an enabling working environment (technical capacity and funding), Parliament's divergent goals and interests, the weak collaboration between the legislature and other arms of government, lack of effective mechanisms to enforce parliamentary recommendations to influence the policy-making process, heavy external political and other influences, as well as the sheer lack of political will to conduct efficient and effective legislation and oversight that will positively influence the policy process. In essence, legislation and oversight effectiveness does not solely depend on the availability of relevant tools but also on other characteristics of the political and institutional environment in which parliamentarians operate.

The National Assembly can bridge the gap in the performance of its lawmaking and oversight functions and exercise its powers in effective policy-making when it undertakes deliberate and comprehensive reforms that will meticulously improve the legislature's ability to deliver on its constitutional mandate to serve the best interests of the Nigerian people in a manner that meets their expectations. These include strengthening its internal rules and ethics to fight clientelist tendencies, maintaining a robust and mutually beneficial relationship with other arms of government, demonstrating strong political will, reducing or eliminating deficiencies in its internal capacity and operating processes, as well as lessening the influence of party politics on the committee processes and procedures. In essence, though parliamentarians are elected on the basis of their various parties with the expected goal to pursue their party programmes, these programmes must align with national interests. Where there is a conflict, national interest must prevail.

References

Aiyede, R. (2005). Executive-legislature relations in Nigeria's emerging presidential democracy. *UNILAG Journal of Politics.* 2(1), 65–7.

Akhigbe, N. (2015, April 20). How audit indictees bribe lawmakers to cover findings. *Naija247news.* Retrieved from http://naija247news.com/2015/04/how-audit-indictees-bribe-lawmakers-to-cover-findings/ (access: 14.06.2015).

Alao, S.T. (2015). Performance of oversight functions by the national assembly: a critical assessment of Nigeria's 7th House of Representatives, 2011–2015. A dissertation submitted to the University of Benin in partial fulfilment of the requirements for the award of Master of Science in legislative studies.

Aliyu, M.K. & Bello, M.A. (2018). Analysis of the challenges of legislative oversight on good governance in Nigeria. *Developing Country Studies*, 8(8), 148–157.

Arter, D. (2006). Introduction: comparing the legislative performance of legislatures. *Journal of Legislative Studies*, 12 (3–4), 245–257.

Asante, R. & Debrah. E. (2015). The legislature and the executive in Ghana's fourth republic: a marriage of convenience. Paper delivered at the 14th General Assembly of Council for the Development of Social Science Research in Africa, June 8–12, 2015, Dakar, Senegal.

Beer, S.H. (1990). The British legislature and the problem of mobilizing consent. In P. Norton (ed.), *Legislatures.* Oxford: Oxford University Press, 59–62.

Boafo-Arthur, K. (2005). Longitudinal view on Ghana's parliamentary practices. In M.A.M. Salih (ed.) *African parliaments.* Palgrave Macmillan, New York, 120–141.

Boateng, E.A. (1996). *Government and the people: Outlook for democracy in Ghana.* Buck Press: Accra, Ghana.

Clark, T.D., Verseckaite, E. & Lukosaitis, A. (2006). The role of committee systems in post-communist legislatures: a case study of the Lithuanian Seimas. *Europe-Asia Studies*, 58(5), 731–750.

Eniayejuni, A. & Evcan, N.S. (2015). *Citizen's participation: Between continuity and change in Nigeria.* Retrieved from www.researchgate.net/publication/283828516_Citizen%27s_Participation_Between_Continuity_and_Change_in_Nigeria (access: 27.09.2020).

Erunke, J. & Ndiribe, O. (2013, July 4). National Assembly committees: The bony and the juicy. In *Vanguard Newspaper*, Retrieved from www.vanguardngr.com/2013/07/national-assembly-committees-the-bony-and-the-juicy/ (access: 27.09.2020).

Ewuim, N.C., Nnamani, D.O. & Eberinwa, O.M. (2014). Legislative oversight and good governance in Nigeria National Assembly: an analysis of Obasanjo and Jonathan's administration. *Review of Public Administration and Management*, 3(6), 140–153.

Fashagba, J.Y. (2009a). The roles of the committee system in enhancing legislative efficiency in Nigeria: The case of Kwara State House of Assembly. *Journal of Sustainable Development in Africa*, 10(4), 426–444.

Fashagba, J.Y. (2009b). Legislative oversight under the Nigerian presidential system. *Journal of Legislative Studies*, 15(4), 439–459.

Federal Republic of Nigeria (1999). *Constitution of the Federal Republic of Nigeria*. Lagos: Federal Government Press.

Fenno, R.F. (1978). *Home style: House members in their districts*. Boston: Little Brown and Company.

Flegmann, W. (1986). *Public expenditure and the select committees of the commons*. Aldershot, Gower Publishing Company.

Goitom, H. (2017). *National parliaments: Nigeria*. Retrieved from www.loc.gov/law/help/national-parliaments/Nigeria.php (access: 10.10.2020).

Hamalai, L. (ed.) (2014). *Committees in the Nigerian national assembly: A study of the performance of Legislative functions, 2003–2013*. Abuja: National Institute for Legislative Studies, National Assembly.

Hamalai, L. (2015). *Legislative oversight: a study of performance in Nigeria National Assembly*. Abuja: National Institute for Legislative Studies, National Assembly.

Hendriks, C. & Kay, A. (2019). From 'opening up' to democratic renewal: deepening public engagement in legislative committees. *Government and Opposition*, 54(1), 25–51.

Hicken, A. (2011). Clientelism. *Annual Review of Political Science*, 14, 289–310.

HoR (House of Representatives). (2015). Votes and Proceedings, 9 November. First Session, 8th National Assembly, No. 33. Retrieved from nass.gov.ng/document/download/7732, Abuja, Nigeria. (access: 10.10.2020).

Ijaiya, G. (2010). Legislative committees and oversight functions in Nigeria. *Nigerian Journal of Legislative Affairs*, 3(1+2),159–169.

Kazeem, A.O. (2013). Legislative oversight functions in Nigeria: odyssey of hunters becoming the hunted. *Acta Universitatis Danubius Juridica*, 9(2), 79–95.

La Palombara, J. (1974). *Politics within nations*. Englewood Cliffs, NJ: Prentice-Hall.

Manning, N. & Stapenhurst, R. (2002). Strengthening oversight by legislatures. *World Bank PREM Note 74*. Washington DC: World Bank,

Mezey, M.L. (2008). *Representative democracy: Legislators and their constituents*. Plymouth: Rowman and Littlefield.

Mutisya, S.M., Abonyo, J.O. & Senelwa, W. (2017). Influence of political parties' affiliations on county assemblies' exercise of oversight authority over county government in Kenya: A case study of Makueni County Assembly. *Saudi Journal of Humanities and Social Sciences*, 2(5), 385–392.

NDI (National Democratic Institute for International Affairs) (1996). Committees in legislatures: a division of labour. *Legislative Research Series* Paper #2. Retrieved from www.ndi.org/sites/default/ files/030_ww_committees.pdf (access: 10.10.2020).

Norton, P. (2016). *The British polity*. New York: Routledge

Norton, P. (2013). Introduction: the institution of parliaments. P. Norton (ed.), *Parliaments and governments in Western Europe*. New York: Routledge, 1–15.

Nwagwu, E.J. (2014). Legislative oversight in Nigeria: a watchdog or a hunting dog? *Journal of Law, Policy and Globalization*, 22, 16–24.

Nwogwugwu, N. & Ishola, A. (2019). Legislators and their oversight functions in policy implementation in Nigeria. *International Journal of Humanities Social Sciences and Education*, 6(3), 93–102.

Nwozor A. & Olanrewaju J.S. (2019). Oiling the legislature: an appraisal of the committee system in Nigeria's National Assembly. In J. Fashagba, O.R. Ajayi, & C. Nwankwor (eds.) *The Nigerian National Assembly. Advances in African economic, social and political development*. Springer, 165–187.

Ogbonnaya, U.M., Ogujiuba K, & Stiegler N. (2014). A comparative analysis of the interplay of administrative and political structures of the legislature in the legislative procedures of selected federal system. *Journal of Social Sciences*, 41(1), 27–35.

Ogul, M.S. & Rockman B.A. (1990). Overseeing oversight: New departures and old problems. *Legislative Studies Quarterly*, 15(1), 5–24.

Okpe V.V. & Othman M.F. (2020). Assessment of legislature-executive pattern of relations in Nigeria's democratic governance of the Fourth Republic: prospects and challenges. *Pertanika* 28(4), 2843–2860.

Olson, D.M. (2008). Legislatures and administration in oversight and budgets: Constraints, means, and executives. In R. Stapenhurst, F. Pelizzo, D.M. Olson & L. von Trapp (eds.) *Legislative oversight and budgeting: A world perspective*. Washington, D.C.: World Bank Institute, 323–331.

Olson, D.M. (2015). *Democratic legislative institutions: a comparative view*. London: Routledge.

Onwe, S., Ibeogu, A. & Nkwede, J. (2015). Imperatives of legislative oversight function in Nigerian democratic system. *Research on Humanities and Social Sciences*, 5(4), 1–9.

Omotoso, F. (2016). Democratic governance and political participation: introduction to the issues. In F. Omotoso & M. Kehinde (eds.), *Democratic governance and political participation in Nigeria 1999–2014*. Denver, Spears Media Press, 1–20.

Omotoso, F. and Oladeji, O. (2019). Legislative oversight in the Nigerian Fourth Republic. In J.Y. Fashagba, O.R. Ajayi, & C. Nwankwo, (eds.). *The Nigerian National Assembly.*, Switzerland: Springer, 57–72.

Otusanya, O.J., Lauwo, S., Ige, O J., & Adelaja, O.S. (2015). Sweeping it under the carpet: The role of legislators in corrupt practice in Nigeria. *Journal of Financial Crime*, 22(3), 354–377.

Oyewo O. (2007). Constitutionalism and the oversight functions of the legislature in Nigeria. A paper presented at the African Network of Constitutional Law Conference on Fostering Constitutionalism in Africa Nairobi, Kenya.

Pelizzo, R. & Stapenhurst, R. (2012). Democracy and oversight. In *Research Collection School of Social Sciences*. Paper 130. Retrieved from http://ink.library.smu.edu.sg/soss_research/130 (access: 27.05.2021)

Pelizzo, R. & Stapenhurst, R. (2012). *Parliamentary oversight tools: a comparative analysis*. New York: Routledge.

Pelizzo, R. & Stapenhurst R. (2014). Oversight Effectiveness and Political Will: Some Lessons from West Africa. *Journal of Legislative Studies*, 20(2), 255–261.

Polsby, N.W. (1975). Legislatures. In P. Norton (ed.). *Legislatures*. Oxford: Oxford University Press, 127–148.

Rommetvedt, H. (1998). Norwegian parliamentary committees: Performance, structural Change and external relations. *Journal of Legislative Studies,* 4(1), 60–84.
Stapenhurst, R., Pelizzo, R., Olson, D.M. & von Trapp, L. (eds.) (2008). *Legislative oversight and budgeting: A world perspective.* Washington, D.C.: World Bank Institute.
Stapenhurst R., Jacobs K., & Olaore O. (eds.) (2016). Legislative oversight in Nigeria: an empirical review and assessment. *Journal of Legislative Studies,* 22(1), 1–29.
Stapenhurst, R., Jacobs K., & Pelizzo R. (2014). Corruption and legislatures. *Public Integrity,* 16(3), 285–304.
Stapenhurst R. et al (eds)., (2008). Legislative oversight and budgeting: a world perspective. World Bank Publications.
Stark, A. (2011). Legislatures: help or hindrance in achieving successful crisis management? *Policy and Society,* 30(2), 115–127.
Strøm, K. (1998). Parliamentary committees in European democracies. *Journal of Legislative Studies,* 4(1), 21–59.
Umeagbalasi, E. (2013). Legislative oversight as a gold mine for Nigerian lawmakers. *News Express,* August 3, 2013. Abuja.
Umaru, U.D. (2017). Corruption and legislative functions in Nigeria. *IOSR Journal of Economics and Finance,* 8(1), 1–8.
Wehner, J. (2004). Back from the sidelines? Redefining the contribution of legislatures to the budget cycle. *World Bank Institute Working Papers Series on Contemporary Issues in Parliamentary.* Development, No. 28615.
World Bank, (2015). *Project document for a public financial management reform project.* Washington: The World Bank.

13 Norwegian parliamentary committees
Split and sidelined in the policy process

Hilmar Rommetvedt

For decades, various scholars have emphasized the importance of parliamentary committees. In a special issue of the *Journal of Legislative Studies*, Longley and Davidson (1998: 5) argued that 'due particularly to their newly created or revived committee systems', parliaments had become 'more influential bodies globally', while Strøm (1998: 47) claimed that 'strong committees, it appears, are at least a necessary condition for effective parliamentary influence in the policy-making process'. Well into the new millennium, Martin (2014: 352) found that 'the conventional notion is that a strong system of committees, however defined, is a necessary if not sufficient condition for the legislature to operate effectively, not least in terms of influencing the content of legislation and holding the executive accountable'.

Ever since its establishment in 1814, the Norwegian Parliament – the Storting – has used committees to prepare its work (Mo 1985: 22). However, in the special issue of *JLS*, I questioned the assumption that strong committees are a necessary condition for parliamentary influence. Based on a study of the Storting, I found it 'highly probable that the Norwegian Parliament's influence has increased simultaneously [...] with a poorer functioning of the standing committees' (Rommetvedt 1998: 81). In this chapter, I will revisit the Norwegian Parliament and make an inquiry into whether the Storting – contrary to the 'conventional notion' – still is a strong parliament, in spite of weak committees. The analysis is based on a variety of data from the Storting, personal interviews with four MPs carried out in 2018, and a survey among all MPs in 2019 to 2020.[1]

Strong parliament – strong committees?

Stronger parliament

For a long time, most Norwegian scholars and commentators adhered to the 'decline of parliaments' thesis. In the 1960s, Rokkan (1966: 107) claimed that 'the crucial decisions on economic policy are rarely taken in the parties or in parliament'. Kvavik (1976: 188) found that 'parliamentary institutions receive[d] an exceedingly weak evaluation' among interest

DOI: 10.4324/9781003106579-13

group representatives. And in the beginning of the 1980s, Hernes (1983: 300) included 'the weakening of the parliament' among the long-term trends in the Norwegian political system. However, at the same time, Olsen (1983: 72, 42) claimed that 'during the last part of the 1970s the Storting became a more rather than a less significant institution'. He suggested 'an ebb-and-flow perspective' on the importance of the Norwegian Parliament.

Since then, a variety of indicators clearly demonstrate that the Storting has gradually become much more active and influential. There are ups and downs (the latter particularly during majority governments), but the overall trends with regard to parliamentary questioning of government ministers, private members' bills and proposals, and approved requests to the government, show rather dramatic increases in the level of activity in Parliament (Rommetvedt 2003, 2005, 2017). The Norwegian Parliament has also engaged more actively in foreign policy, which traditionally is a prerogative of the executive (Rommetvedt et al. 2009).

Studies by Nordby (2010: 98) show that in the first postwar periods, most amendments in bills submitted by the government were mainly technical and approved unanimously. However, since the beginning of the 1970s, amendments have been increasingly approved after split votes in Parliament, thus indicating a more politicized process.

Since 1971, most Norwegian governments have been minority coalition governments. The exceptions are the Willoch government 1983–1985, the Stoltenberg government 2005–2013, and the Solberg government 2019–2020. Norwegian parties are highly disciplined, and MPs normally vote with their party (Heidar 2014: 404). In a parliament with cohesive party groups, majority governments can be expected to lose very few votes, while minority governments are expected to suffer more defeats. An analysis of the voting behaviour in the Norwegian Parliament from 1979 to 2009 confirms this expectation. In the beginning, even minority governments lost very few votes in Parliament, but since the 1980s, the trend among minority governments has been a substantial increase in the frequency of votes lost by the governing parties (Rommetvedt 2017: 99). Similar calculations are not available for the periods after 2009, but the minority governments headed by Solberg (2013–2019 and from January 2020) lost several votes in Parliament, particularly after the election in September 2017. Furthermore, in order to remain in office, minority governments have to negotiate compromises with one or more opposition parties. Opposition parties may thus influence policies even if this is not exposed in parliamentary voting (cf. Strøm 1990). Furthermore, both minority and majority governments frequently consult their own party groups in Parliament *before* they submit proposals.

When Norway celebrated its 200-year-old Constitution and the establishment of the Storting in 1814, a comprehensive study showed that the Storting was in a stronger position than 50 years earlier (Narud et al. 2014). Grønlie (2014) emphasized the strengthening of the Parliament with reference to legislation as well as oversight. He also accentuated a number of broad settlements regarding matters of great importance and a strong need for predictability that have been negotiated in Parliament among government and opposition parties.

The growing importance of the Norwegian Parliament is also acknowledged by external actors. Surveys among civil servants in government ministries show that in 1976 and 2016, 67 and 76 percent, respectively, answered that the Storting was fairly or very important when important decisions were made within their own dossier (Trondal 2019: supplementary data Table 13.3). Surveys among nationwide interest organizations show an increase from 13 percent in 1982 to 35 percent in 2005 in the proportion of groups who contacted the Parliament at least once a month. In 1982, 78 percent of the interest groups said that contacts with the Parliament were important, while 88 percent said the same in 2005. In 1982, the importance of contact with Parliament was ranked third after contacts with government ministries and agencies, but in 2005 it was ranked first (Rommetvedt 2017: 110f). Various international scholars agree that the Norwegian Parliament is comparatively influential. Damgaard (1994) included the Storting among the 'The Strong Parliaments of Scandinavia'. On their parliamentary powers index, Fish and Kroenig (2009: 756) ranked Norway 23rd among 158 countries. Finally, Garritzmann (2017: 12) calculated an opposition power index and ranked Norway second among 21 democracies, surpassed only by Sweden.

One may dispute some of the indicators used in these various studies, but it seems fairly clear that over time and compared to other countries, the Storting has become a relatively strong and influential parliament. The Storting has strengthened its position vis-à-vis the government, and based on the conventional notion that strong committees are a necessary condition for a strong parliament, we should expect Norwegian parliamentary committees to be strong.

Stronger committees?

Norwegian parliamentary committees are frequently portrayed as the political 'workshops' or 'workhorses' of the Storting. Based on interviews among MPs in the 1960s, Hernes gave the following description of the committees:

> They are, as a point of fact, the only stage at which issues can be scrutinized and worked over in detail; where new information can be brought to bear and where it can have an effect; where alternatives can be considered and their consequences evaluated; where outside groups can be heard and their opinions examined; and where changes in a bill or modifications in appropriations can be made. ... One could say that not only is the committee the first stage in decision-making in the Parliament: for most practical purposes it is also the last.
>
> (Hernes 1971: 68).

This description was given in a period when the Parliament was considered to be rather weak. Since then, the Storting has become stronger, but the 'official' description of the committees has not changed much. As this chapter is being written (October 2020), the latest edition of the 'main brochure' published by the Norwegian Parliament tells us that:

> Much of the work of the Members takes place in committees ... In fact, it is in the committees that the real decisions on most matters of business are made.[2]

Furthermore, the website of the Storting presents the following description of the standing committees:

> This is where the detailed case handling takes place. ... Committee meetings are held behind closed doors ... The reason for this is that one wants the committees to be 'political workshops' where the members can speak freely, let loose trial balloons and work out compromises based on trial and error without being quoted in the media.[3]

However, in 1989, upon retiring after 12 years in Parliament, Conservative MP Georg Apenes gave the following portrayal of the committees:

> It is my impression ... that the right of the committee factions [each party's representatives] to act freely and independently from detailed instructions, is reduced. ... Committee work is affected by the parties' significant and increasing influence. Less and less latitude is given to the MPs; more and more has to be cleared with and coordinated by party group leaders. ... Committee meetings are in the process of changing character: the long-lasting and intense discussions with a breakthrough and clarification during the meeting, occur less frequently.
>
> (Apenes 1989: 36)

The impression given by Apenes indicates that Norwegian parliamentary committees became weaker during the 1980s. In 2018, I interviewed four former and current MPs in order to reveal what goes on in parliamentary committees nowadays. Not only did the interviews support the trend described by Apenes, the weakening of the committees had become even more pronounced. One of the MPs said that 'there is very little political negotiation in the committee', while another voiced that 'there is no politics in the committee!'. Nowadays there are hardly any deliberations at all taking place in the full committee, they said. In other words, the Storting has strengthened its position, but at the same time the committees – contrary to what the conventional notion would imply – have become weaker, not stronger. As we shall see, the present-day description of the committees given by the Storting itself, is misleading. But first, we should take a closer look at the committee system.

Institutions, actors, and interactions

Committee structure and institutional setting

The committee system[4] of the Norwegian Parliament includes two internal committees, the Presidium which organizes the work of the Storting and the Election Committee, which formally assigns committee members, and two committees for consultations with the government: the Enlarged Committee on Foreign Affairs and Defence and the European Consultative Committee. In exceptional cases, Parliament may also set up a special committee or a commission of inquiry to deal with a particular matter.[5]

However, the most important committees, and the ones we will focus on here, are the 12 *standing committees*, which first handle almost all matters to be dealt with by the plenary. With the exception of the president, all MPs are members of one, and in almost all cases only one, of the 12 standing committees listed in Table 13.1. All party groups (nine in 2017–2021) shall be represented in the Standing Committee on Finance and Economic Affairs. For party groups that are not represented in all committees, the member of the Standing Committee on Finance and Economic Affairs or the member of the Standing Committee on Scrutiny and Constitutional Affairs may also be a member of another standing committee. At present, four of the 169 MPs are members of two standing committees.

The Standing Committee on Scrutiny and Constitutional Affairs is first and foremost responsible for ex post scrutiny and control of the activities of the executive, together with matters related to the Constitution. In this chapter, I focus primarily on the other standing committees. They all deal with policy-making, legislation, and state budget, including ex ante scrutiny of bills and proposals submitted by the government as well as private members' bills.

The number of committee members varies between ten and 20, and to the extent possible, all parties shall be proportionally represented in the committees. Thus, the size of the Norwegian standing committees seems to be fairly optimal (maximum 30, according to Sartori 1987:228).

Plenary debates and voting are normally based on recommendations from the respective standing committee or the Presidium. In 2018 to 2020, the standing committees submitted an average of 31 to 34 recommendations per year. Committee meetings are held in private, but the committees may also conduct public hearings with external actors such as government ministers, civil servants, and interest group representatives. The yearly averages in 2018 to 2020 amounted to between 31 and 32 meetings and eight or nine public hearings per committee.

Strøm (1998) argued that correspondence between committees and ministries strengthens specialization and the development of knowledge and expertise among MPs. Traditionally, the Norwegian Parliament's rules of procedure specified committee jurisdictions with reference to specific ministries. Correspondence was high, but due to a larger number of ministries,

Table 13.1 The standing committees of the Norwegian Parliament

The Standing Committee on	Chair's party 2017–2021	Members 2017–2021*	Meetings per year 2009–2013	Meetings per year 2013–2017	Hearings 2018–19	Hearings 2019–2020	Recommendations 2018–2019	Recommendations 2019–2020
Labour and Social Affairs	Progress Party	11/12/13	35	29	14	6	33	27
Energy and the Environment	Liberals	17	26	32	8	3	32	33
Family and Cultural Affairs	Conservatives	11/12	37	33	13	12	28	26
Finance and Economic Affairs	Conservatives	20	32	24	7	5	38	32
Health and Care Services	Christian People's Party	14/15	37	39	10	14	43	33
Justice	Labour	11/12	24	23	3	3	32	30
Local Government and Public Administration	Socialist Left	14/15	35	34	12	12	34	44
Scrutiny and Constitutional Affairs	Labour	9/10	32	35	5	6	42	39
Business and Industry	Centre Party	15	31	32	16	13	35	47
Committee on Transport and Communications	Conservatives	15	39	32	4	4	36	24
Education and Research	Progress Party	14/15	27	30	8	7	19	16
Foreign Affairs and Defence	Labour	16	28	32	6	9	31	22
Total	-	172**	383	375	106	94	403	373
Average per year	-	-	31.9	31.3	8.8	7.8	33.6	31.1

Source: Data from www.stortinget.no

* Changes in the numbers of committee members may occur during the election period.
** Total number of MPs is 169. A few MPs from small parties are members of two committees.

230 *Hilmar Rommetvedt*

some committees dealt with matters from more than one ministry. However, in 1993, the Storting implemented a reform of the committee structure (Rommetvedt 1998, 2017). In the new rule specifying the division of labour among the committees, all references to ministries were omitted. Matters to be dealt with by each committee were specified with reference to policy areas and specific issues only.

Figure 13.1 shows the standing committees that dealt with bills, reports, and budget chapters submitted to the Storting by each of the government ministries in the 2018–2019 session.[6] Thick lines show the most frequent connections between committees and ministries, while thin lines denote that

Standing committee	Ministry
1. Labour and Social Affairs	Labour and Social Affairs
2. Energy and the Environment	Petroleum and Energy
	Climate and Environment
3. Family and Cultural Affairs	Children and Equality
	Culture
4. Finance and Economic Affairs	Finance
5. Health and Care Services	Health and Care Services
6. Justice	Justice and Public Security
7. Local Government and Public Administration	Local Government and Modernisation
9. Business and Industry	Trade, Industry and Fisheries
	Agriculture and Food
10. Committee on Transport and Communications	Transport
11. Education and Research	Education and Research
12. Foreign Affairs and Defence	Foreign Affairs
	Defence

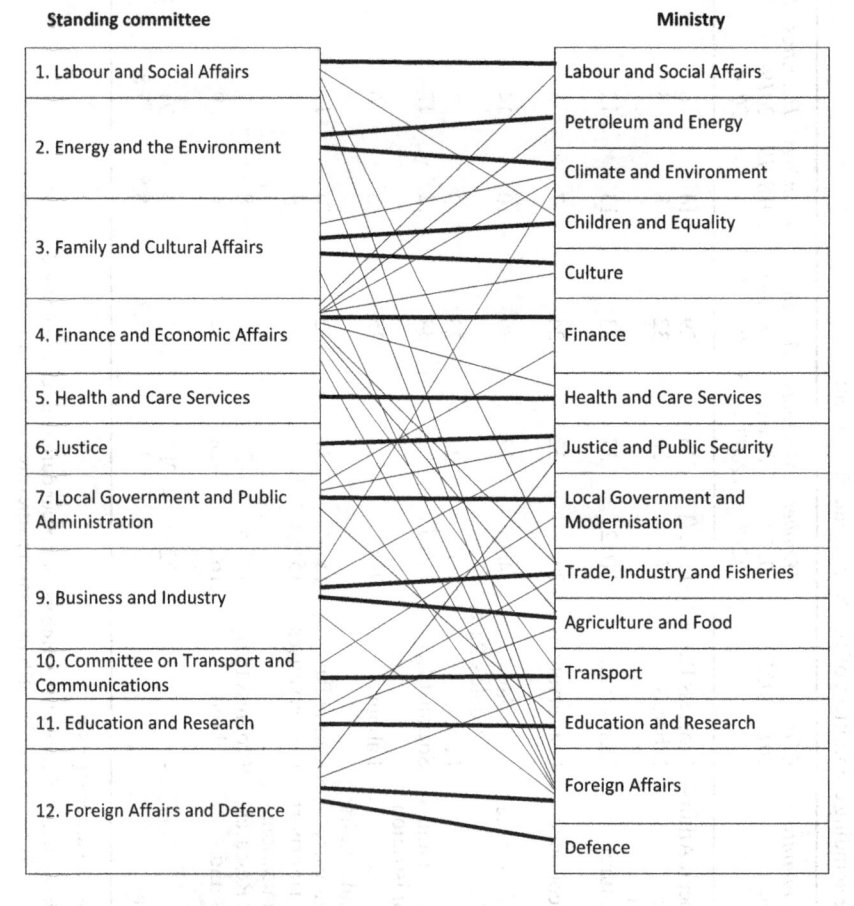

Figure 13.1 Parliamentary committees dealing with bills, reports and budget chapters from each of the ministries (2018–2019).

Scrutiny and Constitution excluded. Thick line: most frequent connections. Thin line: at least one budget chapter, bill or report from the ministry.

Source: Data from www.stortinget.no

the committee dealt with at least one budget chapter, bill, or report from the ministry. The committees still have their primary relationship with one or two 'main' ministries, but most of the committees deal with issues from different ministries. It should also be noted that the Standing Committees of Finance and Economic Affairs deals with the whole fiscal budget and budget limits for all policy areas, while the Standing Committee on Scrutiny and Constitutional Affairs (not included in Figure 13.1) scrutinizes all ministries. *Ceteris paribus*, the weakened correspondence between ministries and committees may have weakened the committees.

Actors in committees: proportional representation

Formally, committee assignments are made by the Parliament's Election Committee, but the real decisions are made by the parliamentary parties' leadership. When the Storting assembles after an election, the number of members of each committee and the allocation of chair positions are negotiated among the parties. MPs submit a wish-list to the board of their party, naming the three most desired committees. The board then decides who should become the party's member(s) and chair(s), based on the MPs' wishes, seniority, expertise, geographical background, gender, etc. Parties with more than one committee member may also appoint party spokespersons for more specific policy areas within the committee's jurisdiction.

For each bill or report to be dealt with, the committee appoints a committee spokesperson (rapporteur) who will formulate a draft version of the committee's recommendation. The committee spokesperson will also present the final recommendation when the plenary debates and votes on the issue. MPs from either government or opposition parties may be appointed committee spokespersons. Together with proportional representation and chairpersonships in committees, this may strengthen the influence of the opposition parties. Table 13.2 shows the party affiliation of all MPs and the chairs of the standing committees. As we can see, the correspondence between the shares of MPs and committee chairs is almost perfect.

Expert knowledge acquired through education and work is one of the elements taken into consideration during the committee assignment process. MPs who become members of the committee responsible for their field of expertise may further develop their expert knowledge. Long-lasting membership in the same committee has the same effect. We have no data on how long MPs serve in the same committee, but Table 13.3 shows the percentages of committee members who, after the election, were reelected to the same committee as after the previous election (Rommetvedt 2017: 134).[7] Here it should be mentioned that Norway has fixed elections every four years.

The table clearly demonstrates that the turnover in Norwegian parliamentary committees is high, and that it has increased since the 1970s and beginning of the 1980s. After a general election, most MPs move from one committee to another. Very few MPs get more than the four-year election

Table 13.2 MPs and committee chairs by party in Norway (2017–2021)

Party	MPs	Share of MPs	Committee chairs	Share of chairs
Labour	49	0.29	3	0.25
Progress Party	27	0.16	2	0.17
Conservatives	45	0.27	3	0.25
Christian People's Party	8	0.05	1	0.08
Centre Party	19	0.11	1	0.08
Socialist Left	11	0.07	1	0.08
Liberals	8	0.05	1	0.08
Greens	1	0.01	0	0.00
Reds	1	0.01	0	0.00
Total	169	1	12	1

Source: Data from www.stortinget.no

Table 13.3 Percentage of MPs that were reelected to the same committee as at the start of the previous election period (four years earlier) in Norway

Year	% reelected	Year	% reelected
1977	33.5	2001	24.2
1981	27.1	2005[a]	7.7/13.0
1985	29.9	2009	17.8
1989	13.9	2013	13.6
1993*	–	2017	18.6
1997	18.8		

* Not calculated due to the establishment of several new committees with cross-cutting jurisdictions compared to the period before.
a 7.7 percent exclude committees with changes in jurisdictions, while 13.0 percent include committees with fairly similar jurisdictions as previous committees.

Source: Data from www.stortinget.no

period to develop their expertise in the policy area of the committee. According to my interviewees, most MPs want to change from one committee to another because they were not assigned to their first-choice committee in their first period, or because they want to build broader political competence in different policy areas (or both).

Interactions in committees: formalities and realities

With the exception of public hearings, committee meetings are held behind closed doors. Members are not supposed to reveal what is said in the committee rooms; privacy is expected to improve the atmosphere for deliberation and negotiation among committee members. However, as we have seen, one may question what actually goes on in the 'black box'. The answer can be found in a survey among the MPs in 2019–2020.

Table 13.4 MPs' judgement about formal committee meetings in Norway

Formal committee meetings are about ...	Very often	Fairly often	Sometimes	Seldom	Never	Total (N=85)
Practical/administrative matters (e.g. work schedules, deadlines etc.)	68	25	6	1	0	100
Real political negotiations that may have an impact on the outcome of the issue	2	13	16	51	18	100
Meetings with the minister/other people from the ministry	2	8	18	54	18	100
General discussions on political matters	1	4	21	46	28	100

Source: Raknes & Rommetvedt survey among MPs (see endnote 1).

The MPs were asked, 'How often would you say that the formal meetings of the committee you are a member of, are about the following matters?' The answers presented in Table 13.4 show that policy is not negotiated in the committees. According to more than nine of ten MPs, formal committee meetings most often deal with practical and administrative matters. Seven of ten MPs said that real political negotiations with an impact on policy-making occur only seldomly or never. Sometimes, ministers and civil servants meet in the committee, but not often. This is also the case with regard to general discussion on political matters.

Building networks with interest groups may strengthen the committees, particularly if contacts with and the information presented by interest groups are 'monopolized' by the members of a specific committee. However, scholars have also argued that too-close contacts with specialized interests may lead to segmentation and iron triangles, thus reducing the ability to develop comprehensive policies across sectors (Egeberg et al. 1978; Hernes 1983). This problem was addressed by the President of the Storting, Jo Benkow (cons.), when the plenary discussed the committee reform in 1993. Referring to the proposed new Standing Committee on Business and Industry, a merger of three former committees on industry, agriculture, and fisheries, respectively, he argued that a 'pressure group society' had developed, and that different industries tried to gain support from the specialized committees. The committees were 'forced into the role of advocate of special interests of industrial and other sectors of society', but the new committee on business and industry represented 'a big step in the direction of a comprehensive industrial policy' (cited from Rommetvedt 1998: 71f). In other words, the president wanted to strengthen coordination across sectors and committees, and thus restrain the influence of pressure groups and specialized interests with 'advocates' among MPs in specialized parliamentary committees.

Table 13.5 shows how committee members' contacts with various interest groups and NGOs have developed. The figures are based on surveys among MPs in 1995, 2012, and 2019, and refer to contacts initiated by the interest groups (Rommetvedt 2017: 134).

To some extent, the patterns of contacts are in line with what one would expect. Business associations contact members of the business and industry committee, trade unions contact the work and social affairs committee, environmentalists the energy and environment committee, and so on. However, the pattern of contacts is not what one would expect, based on the thesis of iron triangles and a segmented state. Table 13.5 shows that all types of interest groups contacted members of a broad spectrum of committees on a weekly basis. If not weekly, most of the committee members were contacted at least monthly (not shown in the table). In other words, members of specific committees do not have privileged access to specific interest groups. In this respect, the degree of specialization is limited.

Previously, committee hearings were held in private. After a trial period, Parliament decided that public hearings should be a permanent arrangement starting in 2001 (Grønlie 2014: 142). In the 2018–2019 and 2019–2020 sessions, respectively, the committees organized 106 and 94 hearings with representatives from organizations and interest groups (cf. Table 13.1). The number of public hearings varied from three to 16 per committee per year. The total number of participating organizations and interest groups amounted to 1,953 in 2018–2019 and 1,673 in 2019–2020, but several of these were recurring appearances. In 2019, 18 percent of the MPs characterized the information value of committee hearings as very high. However, more than twice as many, 39 percent, said the same about personal conversations with representatives from interest groups. Thus, personal contacts with interest groups seem more important to MPs than committee hearings.

Committees in the policy process

Problem definition and agenda-setting

The agendas of the Norwegian Parliament and its committees are initiated primarily by the government or the MPs and their parliamentary parties. The agenda-setting function of the standing committees is limited. Virtually all matters to be decided by the Storting are first assigned to one of the standing committees. The Standing Committee on Scrutiny and Constitutional Affairs may inquire into scrutiny matters and constitutional responsibility on its own initiative, but the other standing committees may not deal with matters other than those submitted by Parliament. They cannot formally initiate legislation or write reports on their own initiative, but they may call for a debate in the plenary on matters within their sphere of responsibility. This may only be done twice within the same session, and proposals may not be put forward during the debate.

Committees in the Norwegian Storting 235

Table 13.5 Committee members' contact with interest groups and NGOs in Norway

Standing Committee on:	Business associations			Trade unions, professional organizations			Environmental organizations			Idealistic/other organizations		
	1995	2012	2019	1995	2012	2019	1995	2012	2019	1995	2012	2019
Work and Social Affairs	-	38	0	-	63	29	-	25	0	-	38	29
Health and Care	-	67	75	-	67	50	-	56	0	-	78	50
Social Affairs	30	-	-	40	-	-	20	-	-	50	-	-
Energy and Environment	70	40	63	40	40	25	60	70	63	40	40	50
Family, Culture[a]	67	33	50	33	44	33	11	13	33	44	67	100
Finance	93	77	75	67	31	63	60	23	25	40	46	38
Justice	50	56	0	50	44	25	13	22	0	38	44	50
Education, Research[b]	58	38	67	75	46	83	50	8	25	67	23	58
Municipal Affairs	91	-	-	73	-	-	46	-	-	55	-	-
Municipal Affairs and Govt. Admin.	-	43	33	-	14	33	-	29	20	-	43	17
Scrutiny and Constitution	40	71	0	40	29	0	20	43	20	0	57	20
Business and Industry	82	71	100	46	43	60	36	29	20	40	29	40
Communications	89	-	-	80	-	-	40	-	-	40	-	-
Transport and Communications	-	75	50	-	42	50	-	33	50	-	25	50
Defence	56	-	-	44	-	-	22	-	-	11	-	-
Foreign Affairs	67	-	-	44	-	-	44	-	-	22	-	-
Foreign Affairs and Defence	-	62	0	-	31	17	-	15	0	-	54	33
Total	68	57	46	54	42	43	38	28	33	40	46	46

Percentage of each committee's members who were contacted weekly by different types of interest groups and NGOs (total N=77).

a In 1995 and 2012, this committee included government administration.
b In 1995 and 2012, this committee included the state church.

Sources: Rommetvedt (2017:134), Raknes & Rommetvedt survey among MPs (see endnote 1).

The chair of the committee puts before the committee all matters that have been received from Parliament, and the committee sets a time limit for submission of its recommendation. A postponement of the time limit with consequences for the proceedings of the plenary requires the consent of the Presidium. Any decision to 'kill' a bill would need the approval of the plenary.

However, the Parliament and individual MPs have several opportunities to set the agenda and define political problems. The plenary may request the government to develop policy measures and to submit proposals to the Parliament, and the government has to deliver a yearly report on the follow-up of the requests. MPs may, either individually or on behalf of their parties, submit private members' bills and proposals, which are then referred to the relevant standing committee. MPs may also put interpellations and questions to a member of the government, who will then have to answer either orally or in writing. The number of requests to the government, private members' bills, and questions to government members, varies, but the long-term trend is a significant increase in these activities (Rommetvedt 2017).

Policy formulation: outside the committee

When a bill or proposal is submitted to one of the standing committees, the appointed committee spokesperson formulates a draft recommendation. The draft is posted on the committee portal of the computer system of Parliament, where the committee members and advisors have access. The committee members of each party may then post their comments and proposals on the portal, or – depending on the bargaining situation – wait until a later stage. When the full committee meets, it is normally just to report on the progress of work. Party representatives may inform that they have posted their comments, while members from other parties may indicate that they, too, can sign the comments if certain adjustments (normally minor) are made.

As we have seen (Table 13.4), the real discussions and negotiations do not take place in the formal meetings of the full committee. They take place outside the committee, among a limited number of committee members who represent the selection of parliamentary parties that are considered to be able to negotiate a compromise and muster a majority in the plenary. The committee members of the government parties normally try to negotiate compromises with one or more of the opposition parties, but compromises may also be negotiated among opposition parties. In periods with minority governments, compromises among opposition parties may be adopted by the majority of Parliament. According to one of the interviewed MPs, negotiations among the selected parties occur in face-to-face meetings outside the committee, and partly also via email. The final recommendations from the committees include a technical summary of the issue, comments from the whole committee, dissenting remarks from various party groups or single MPs. the committee majority's conclusive recommendation to Parliament, and alternative proposals from various minorities of the committee. In the 2018–2019 and 2019–2020 sessions, the standing committees submitted 403 and 373 recommendations respectively to the Parliament (cf. Table 13.1).

A united committee may be a strong actor, and Sartori (1987) argues that most of the time, committee decisions are unanimous. If 'the recourse to the majority principle is not an exception but becomes the rule ... we may say that a committee ceases to be a committee'. In his words, 'the majority principle represents the watershed between committees and non-committees or, if you wish, between functioning and malfunctioning committees' (Sartori 1987: 214, 230). Without following Sartori all the way, we may use the degree of unanimity or dissent in committee recommendations as an indicator of committee strength or weakness. Table 13.6 shows the proportion of recommendations with dissenting remarks from one or more parties (Rommetvedt 2017: 93).[8]

Until 1973, the standing committees seem to have functioned well most of the time. Approximately 85 percent of the recommendations were unanimous. However, the committees have gradually become more dissensual. From 2005 to 2013, only 28 percent of the recommendations were unanimous, while dissenting remarks occurred in 72 percent of the recommendations. In this respect the parliamentary committees weakened at the same time as the Storting became stronger.

In the 2019–2020 survey we asked the MPs where the real decisions are made when minority governments are in office. In Table 13.7 we see that according to 80 percent of the MPs, the real decisions are very or fairly often made in negotiations outside the formal committee meetings. Only 20 percent of MPs said the same about the committee meetings. The real decisions are seldom or never made during formal voting in the plenary, while in some cases the issue is in fact settled before it 'enters' the Parliament.

Table 13.6 Committee recommendations with dissenting remarks in Norway, percentage (budget recommendations excluded)

Election period	Recommendations with dissent	Election period	Recommendations with dissent
1945–1949	15%	1981–1985	35%
1950–1953	14%	1985–1989	35%
1954–1957	18%	1989–1993	58%
1958–1961	17%	1993–1997	67%
1961–1965	17%	1997–2001	60%
1965–1969	15%	2001–2005	68%
1969–1973	14%	2005–2009	72%
1973–1977	30%	2009–2113	72%
1977–1981	21%		

Sources: Rasch (2014: 395), Rommetvedt (2017: 93).

Table 13.7 Where are the real decisions made (in Norway during minority government)? Percentage of MPs

The real decisions are made ...	Very often	Fairly often	Sometimes	Seldom	Never	Sum (N=83)
Before the issue 'enters' the Parliament	17	28	37	12	6	100
In the formal meetings of the standing committees	4	17	22	25	32	100
In negotiations outside the formal committee meetings	33	47	14	5	1	100
Voting in the Storting plenary	2	4	13	49	31	100

Source: Raknes & Rommetvedt survey among MPs (see endnote 1).

Implementation and evaluation

Oversight and control of the executive is one of the main functions of the Parliament. From 1972 to 1981, the various standing committees of the Storting were responsible for the ex post control of the ministries within their jurisdictions (Mo 1985: 23). However, the MPs were more interested in policy-making, and the control function was neglected (Grønlie 2014: 143). In 1981, a separate control committee was set up, but it did not work very well. When the present Standing Committee on Scrutiny and the Constitution was established in 1993, more senior MPs were assigned, and the new committee became much more prestigious. The new committee became responsible for the ex post scrutiny of all government ministries.

In addition to matters related to the Constitution, the scrutiny committee makes recommendations to the Storting on matters concerning the performance of the government, the ministries, and public administration. Much of the work is based on regular reports from the government, including the records of proceedings of the Council of State, and from the Office of the Auditor-General. The latter is the audit agency of the Parliament and carries out audits of central government accounts and the implementation of parliamentary decisions, including productivity and goal achievement. While other standing committees only deal with issues submitted to them by the Storting, the Standing Committee on Scrutiny and Constitutional Affairs may act on its own initiative. One third of the members may require that the committee shall make inquiries into matters regarding the constitutional responsibility of ministers, or the work of the public administration.

No doubt, the oversight function of the Storting has been carried out much more actively since the establishment of the Standing Committee on Scrutiny and Constitutional Affairs (cf. Grønlie 2014). In some cases, the committee acts as a unitary actor vis-à-vis the executive, but committee members from government and opposition parties tend to respectively defend or criticize the government.

It should be added that important aspects of the oversight function (together with agenda-setting) are fulfilled by individual MPs through interpellations and questions to the ministers (Rasch 2014: 450). Such initiatives may be based on reports in the media or contacts with lobbyists. In the 2019–2020 survey, nearly 90 percent of the MPs agreed that inquiries from interest groups and other lobbyists improve Parliament's ability to check the government and the public administration's implementation and follow-up of parliamentary decisions and intentions.

Committees versus parties

No doubt, the parliamentary party groups play an important role in the Norwegian Parliament. Scholars disagree about the relationship between committees and parties, but Strøm (1998: 56) concluded that from a partisan perspective 'the strength of committees should co-vary positively with that of political parties'. However, as we have seen in the case of Norway there are hardly any negotiations at all during the meetings of the full committees. Committee recommendations are a combination of party dissents and compromises among two or more parties negotiated *outside* the full committee.

In my interviews, the MPs reported that there is far more discussion going on at the party group meetings than in committee meetings. The party's committee members will have a negotiating mandate clarified with the party leadership, the board of the party group, or the whole party group in one of its weekly meetings. One of the MPs said that in important matters, the mandate may be given in a confidential document of, for example, four to five pages specifying the party's aims and acceptable compromises, while a former MP from another party said that negotiating mandates were informal, stated orally only.

As we have seen, parliamentary committees have become more dissensual. The members of the parliamentary party groups, on the other hand, act very cohesively. MPs normally vote with their party (Heidar 2014a). Parliamentary parties operate as unified actors, the standing committees do not. Consequently, one may expect parties to be stronger than committees. In surveys carried out in 1996 and 2012, MPs were asked to assess the influence of various groups and institutions on the decisions made by the Storting. They were asked to use a scale from 1 to 10, and averages were then multiplied by 10 (Heidar 2014b: 382). The results in Table 13.8 show that the committee score dropped from 75 to 61 and the rank order from 3 to 6. On the other hand, the scores of the parliamentary party groups were quite stable, 83 and 85 respectively, but the rank order dropped from 1st to 2nd place. The latter was due to the increased score of the government and ministers, from 78 to

Table 13.8 MPs' assessments of various groups and institutions' decision-making influence in Norway

Groups and institutions	1996 Score	1996 Rank	2012 Score	2012 Rank
Committees	75	3	61	6
Committee chairs	47	7	50	8
Committee secretaries	20	10	26	10
Parliamentary party groups	83	1	85	2
Parliamentary party group leaders	74	4	78	4
Parliamentary party boards	70	6	74	5
Parliamentary party group secretariats	40	9	44	9
Party organization leaders	73	5	82	3
Government / ministers	78	2	95	1
Individual MPs	47	7	58	7

Source: Heidar (2014b: 382).

95. Here we should bear in mind that the Brundtland government in 1996 was a one-party minority government, while the Stoltenberg government in 2012 was a majority coalition. It is also interesting to see that while committee chairs are ranked 7 and 8, party group leaders are ranked 4, which reinforces that party groups are more important than committees.

The findings clearly indicate that committee and party strength is negatively related, and that the increased strength of the Norwegian Parliament is a reflection of an increased strength of parliamentary party groups, not the strength of committees as such. Staff resources is one of the factors that may explain changes in favour of the parties. The standing committees have one or two secretaries each, and a sparsely populated joint secretariat. There have been only minor changes in the staff resources of the committees, while the staffs of the parliamentary party groups (political advisors and office staff) have grown dramatically, from a total of 15 persons in 1964 to 186 in 2018 (Rommetvedt 2017: 91 and www.stortinget.no). The increased level of activity and influence of the Storting and the parties seems to be the effect of among other things a substantial increase in staff resources and thus their working capacity. In this respect, the standing committees are lagging behind.

Norwegian committees in the policy process: split and sidelined

As we have seen, several studies show that the Norwegian Parliament has strengthened its position vis-à-vis the executive. International scholars argue that strong committees are a necessary prerequisite of a strong Parliament, and the Storting itself claims that the detailed case handling takes place in the standing committees. However, this chapter has shown, these allegations are far from reality.

In spite of the strength of the Storting, Norwegian parliamentary committees are rather weak, they do not operate as unitary actors, and political compromises are negotiated among selected party factions outside the committees. Norwegian committees are *not* 'political workshops'. The full committees deal with practicalities, and they are more appropriately characterized as dispatch departments for party declamations. Thus, we may conclude that in the case of Norway, strong committees are neither a necessary nor a sufficient prerequisite for a strong Parliament.

The Norwegian Parliament has made use of committees ever since it was established more than 200 years ago, and today most of the parliaments and legislatures in the world have an organized committee system. In the case of Norway, most of the time, the parliamentary committees are sidelined in the 'real' policy process. Compromises are negotiated outside the committees, in smaller forums with a limited number of negotiators. But if parliamentary committees are not the 'workhorses' of Parliament, then why do most parliaments establish committees? What functions do the committee systems fulfil nowadays?

The amount of matters to be dealt with by a modern parliament is substantial and necessitates a relatively high degree of specialization. In this context, the crucial element seems to be the division of labour among the MPs of each of the parliamentary parties, not the parliamentary committees as such. Committee assignments are a simple and practical way to allocate parliamentary work and responsibilities among MPs, and thus make the workload manageable. In principle, specialization could be arranged without committees. Consequently, the strength of parliament could be facilitated without committees, but not without the division and specialization of work. In the case of Norway, the full committees are frequently sidelined in the policy process, but the committee members are not. The strength of the Norwegian Parliament depends on the capacity of MPs who act first and foremost as party representatives, not as committee members.

Notes

1. Various data have been collected from the website of the Norwegian Parliament, www.stortinget.no. The interviews were carried out by the author of this chapter and included MPs from three different parties. From 2009 onwards, they were members of two to four different standing committees each. All together the interviewees had experience in eight of the twelve standing committees. Two of the interviewees had been committee chairs. The survey was carried out September 2019 to March 2020 by Ketil Raknes and the author of this chapter. 91 of the 169 MPs (54 percent) answered at least some of the questions via email.
2. https://www.stortinget.no/globalassets/pdf/hovedbrosjyre-div-spraak/stortingetnorgesnasjonalforsamling_eng_web.pdf (access: 29.10.2020). Similar formulations are used in an updated version published in Norwegian. https://stortinget.no/globalassets/pdf/hovedbrosjyre-div-spraak/stortinget-og-demokratiet_2020_bokmal.pdf (access: 29.10.2020).

3 All translations from Norwegian to English by the author; https://the Storting.no/no/The_Storting-og-demokratiet/Arbeidet/Saksbehandlingen-i-komiteene/ (access: 29.10.2020).
4 For details, see rules of procedure, https://stortinget.no/globalassets/pdf/english/rules_of_procedure_october_2020.pdf
5 In March 2020, a special committee was established to deal with matters related to the COVID-19 crisis.
6 For a similar illustration of the 1994–1995 session, see Rommetvedt (2003: 83).
7 Most MPs serve in the same committee throughout the four-year period, but some changes occur during the election period. MPs who are appointed government minister have to leave their seat in Parliament, but if they leave their post in government, they return to Parliament. Such shifts are not taken into account in the table.
8 Source: Norwegian Centre for Research Data (NSD) and Grønlie (2014). Originally, data were collected by the author of this chapter, and later supplemented by NSD and Grønlie with the assistance of Torstein Monsen. See NSD: Fraksjonsmerknadsarkivet, www.nsd.uib.no/polsys/index.cfm?urlname=storting&lan=&institusjonsnr=1&arkivnr=7&MenuItem=N1_1&ChildItem=&State=collapse (access: 27.01.2021)

References

Apenes, G. (1989). *Løven gjesper.* Oslo: Universitetsforlaget.
Copeland, G.W. & Patterson, S.C. (eds.) (1994). *Parliaments in the Modern World.* Ann Arbor, MI: University of Michigan Press.
Damgaard, E. (1994). The strong parliaments of Scandinavia. In G.W. Copeland & S.C. Patterson (eds.), *Parliaments in the Modern World.* Ann Arbor, MI: University of Michigan Press.
Egeberg, M., Olsen, J.P., & Sætren, H. (1978). Organisasjonssamfunnet og den segmenterte stat. In J. P. Olsen, (ed.), *Politisk organisering.* Oslo: Universitetsforlaget.
Fish, M.S. & Kroenig, M. (2009). *The Handbook of National Legislatures.* Cambridge: Cambridge University Press.
Garritzmann, J.L. (2017). How much power do oppositions have? Comparing the opportunity structures of parliamentary oppositions in 21 democracies. *Journal of Legislative Studies,* 23 (1), 1–30.
Grønlie, T. (2014). Til forsvar for folkestyret. In H.M. Narud, K. Heidar, & T. Grønlie, (eds.), *Stortingets historie 1964–2014.* Bergen: Fagbokforlaget.
Heidar, K. (2014a). Partigruppene: Samordnings- og maktarena. In H.M. Narud, K. Heidar, & T. Grønlie, (eds.), *Stortingets historie 1964–2014.* Bergen: Fagbokforlaget.
Heidar, K. (2014b). Institusjon og arbeidsplass. In H.M. Narud, K. Heidar, & T. Grønlie, (eds.), *Stortings historie 1964–2014.* Bergen: Fagbokforlaget.
Heidar, K. & Rommetvedt, H. (2020). Er fagkomiteene eller partigruppene Stortingets 'politiske verksteder'? In J. Bergh, A. Haugsgjerd, & R. Karlsen, (eds.), *Valg og politikk siden 1945.* Oslo: Cappelen Damm Akademisk.
Hernes, G. (1983). *Det moderne Norge. Bind 5. Makt og demokrati.* Oslo: Gyldendal.
Hernes, G. (1971). Interest, Influence, and Cooperation: A Study of the Norwegian Parliament. PhD dissertation. Baltimore, Maryland: The Johns Hopkins University.
Kvavik, R.B. (1976). *Interest Groups in Norwegian Politics.* Oslo: Universitetsforlaget.
Longley, L.D. & Davidson, R.H. (1998a). *The New Roles of Parliamentary Committees.* London: Frank Cass.

Longley, L.D., & Davidson, R.H. (1998b). Parliamentary committees: Changing perspectives on changing institutions. *Journal of Legislative Studies*, 4(1), 1–20.
Martin, S. (2014). Committees. In S. Martin, T. Saalfeld, & K.W. Strøm (eds.), *The Oxford Handbook of Legislative Studies*. Oxford: Oxford University Press, 352–368.
Mo, E. (1985). Stortinget. In T. Nordby (ed.), *Storting og regjering 1945–1985. Institusjoner – Rekruttering*. Oslo: Kunnskapsforlaget.
Narud, H. M., Heidar, K. & Grønlie, T. (eds.) (2014). *Stortingets historie 1964–2014*. Bergen: Fagbokforlaget.
Nordby, T. (2010). *Grunnlov og styreform. Norge 1814–2010*. Oslo: Universitetsforlaget.
Olsen, J.P. (1983). *Organized Democracy. Political Institutions in a Welfare State – the Case of Norway*. Oslo: Universitetsforlaget.
Rasch, B.E. (2014). Opposisjonen. In H.M. Narud, K. Heidar, & T. Grønlie (eds.) *Stortingets historie 1964–2014*. Bergen: Fagbokforlaget.
Rokkan, S. (1966). Norway: numerical democracy and corporate pluralism. In R.A. Dahl (ed.), *Political Opposition in Western Democracies*. New Haven: Yale University Press.
Rommetvedt, H. (2017). *Politikkens allmenngjøring. Stortinget, regjeringen og de organiserte interessene i et nypluralistisk demokrati*. 3rd edition. Bergen: Fagbokforlaget.
Rommetvedt, H. (2005). Norway: resources count, but votes decide? From neo corporatist representation to neo-pluralist parliamentarism. *West European Politics*, 28 (4), 740–763.
Rommetvedt, H. (2003). *The Rise of the Norwegian Parliament*. London: Frank Cass.
Rommetvedt, H. (1998). Norwegian parliamentary committees: performance, structural change and external relations. *Journal of Legislative Studies*, 4(1), 60–84.
Rommetvedt, H., Zajc, D. & Langhelle, O. (2009). The internationalisation of national parliaments: the Norwegian Storting and the Slovene Drzavni zbor. *Politics in Central Europe*, 5(1), 55–85.
Sartori, G. (1987). *The Theory of Democracy Revisited*. Chatham, NJ: Chatham House Publishers.
Shaw, M. (1979). Conclusion. In J. D Lees & M. Shaw, (eds.), *Committees in Legislatures: A Comparative Analysis*. Oxford: Martin Robertson.
Strøm, K. (1998). Parliamentary committees in European democracies. *Journal of Legislative Studies*, 4(1), 21–50.
Strøm, K. (1990). *Minority Government and Majority Rule*. Cambridge: Cambridge University Press.
Trondal, J. (2019). Public administration sustainability and its organizational basis. *International Review of Administrative Sciences*, Online first October 31, 2019. https://doi.org/10.1177/0020852319869430

14 Committees in a party-dominated parliament
The Spanish Congreso de los Diputados

Pablo Oñate and Bernabé Aldeguer

Parliamentary committees were introduced in Spain in 1810 (Cortes Internal Governance Standing Orders), two years before the first Spanish liberal constitution was adopted, differentiating permanent or main and specific or ad hoc committees. As in many other parliaments, nowadays committees are – together with all-powerful and fully dominant parliamentary party groups – a key institutional element of the organization and functioning of the legislature (Strøm 1998; Cox 2006; Martin 2016; Gaines et al. 2019). Given modern complexity of politics, committees allow for specialization, labour division, and, therefore, efficiency in parliamentary activity.

After the Francoist authoritarian regime, the transition to democracy in 1977 and 1978 was a process conducted mainly 'from above'. 'New' and 'modern' (Oñate 2008) political parties led the process and developed an institutional system that expanded their cohesive, hierarchical, centralized, and disciplined organizations across the national, regional, and local levels of the country. Those political parties were reinforced, both financially and institutionally, by the rules and practices that they themselves designed. This included an electoral system with closed and blocked party lists and centralized hierarchical candidate selection processes in each party. A generous public electoral and institutional funding for parties made members' fees less relevant. Rigid and almost absolute control of party (or parliamentary party group) leadership over individual MPs and their activity was favoured by parliamentary party rules. High turnover of MPs in each electoral cycle (above 45 percent for three decades, and higher in the newly fragmented party system after 2015), as well as a high level of discontinuity of committee membership, has led to little policy specialization in many of them. Scarce resources for MPs both in staff (on average, there is not even one assistant for each backbencher MP, and the same goes in terms of secretariat personnel) and in terms of available expert advisors in the chamber's documentation department add to this. Consequently, the executive has a very prominent role in the initiation of the legislative process and influence over the rest of the process, too (Oñate 2000b; Oñate & Delgado 2006; Oñate & Camacho 2014; Oñate & Ortega 2019).

For more than three decades, the Spanish party system had two main parties (centre-left PSOE and centre-right PP) and one leftist party (IU),

DOI: 10.4324/9781003106579-14

together with several non-statewide parties in some of the regions (either ethno-nationalist or regionalist). The electoral outcomes created either a majority in Parliament (PSOE or PP) or a minority (PSOE or PP) which was able to form a government with the support of some of the non-state wide parties. This pattern changed with the emergence of new parties, raised as a consequence of the political malaise due to the economic, financial, and political crises that emerged in 2008. The severe deterioration of citizens' living conditions and corruption scandals affected most of the political parties. Two new parties broke through in 2014: left-wing populist Podemos and centre-liberal Ciudadanos. Together they captured more than one-third of the votes and 31 percent of the seats in the Congreso de los Diputados in the 2015 election, increasing both electoral and parliamentary fragmentation. They also were quite successful in the regional elections, gaining a good number of seats in many of the 17 regional parliaments. In the April and November 2019 national elections a new populist radical right party, Vox, won a relevant share of votes and seats for the first time in Spanish democracy: in the November national election, Vox got 15.1 percent of the vote and 52 seats (14.9 percent of the 350 seats), becoming the third biggest party group in a rather fragmented chamber. One of the outcomes of the new political landscape was that after the November election Spain had – for the first time – a minority coalition government (PSOE and Podemos). The new trends also impacted the working dynamics of the chamber and its committees. Now there are more actors and different agreement possibilities: 'Politics as usual' is no longer the way to operate in the committee system in the Spanish lower chamber.

Institutions and actors: MPs in committees

The Spanish committee system was designed and developed formally as a 'strong' one (Oñate 2000a; Martin 2011a): most of the committees have permanent tenure and fixed jurisdictions that usually mirror cabinet portfolios or are at least well delimitated (when the jurisdiction of the respective ministry is rather wide). Committees have remarkably strong legislative power: not only they do prepare and condition plenary legislation, but they discuss, vote on, and even pass large amounts of legislation on behalf of the plenary without further approval by the floor. Committees also have extensive and thorough oversight powers: MPs are entitled to request any information or document from the government and executive administration. They can also post written and oral questions to the executive and its members on specific matters within their portfolio, which are later answered in the committee, usually by junior ministers (whereas the ministers answer oral questions in the plenary).

The committee system evolved. The number and size of committees has increased, along with their specialization. But the committee system is largely conditioned in its everyday functioning by the all-powerful and dominant parliamentary party groups (PPGs): Their leaders are the main deciding actors, given that individual MPs are fully disciplined and subordinated in their directions. The PPGs' leaders will appoint the committee spokesperson, who organizes, controls, and decides on any matter in the committee in the interest of the PPGs. This includes what role each MP plays in the committee and what their party position for each policy decision is (Oñate 2000b; Jalali & Rodríguez 2019). The strong role played by PPGs is also a common feature in other European parliamentarian systems (Helms 2000; Whitaker 2001; McElroy 2006; Martin 2016; Martin & Mickler 2019), but PPGs' control over the individual MPs and the activity in the chamber is particularly strong in Spain.

The 1978 Constitution states that the two chambers (Congreso de los Diputados and Senado)[1] will work in plenary and in committees and that the plenary may delegate to the committees full authority and the power to discuss, vote, and pass legislation on its behalf, even if the plenary keeps the right to cancel this delegation anytime. It also enumerates some limitations for that delegation.[2] The Congreso Standing Orders (section 148) state this delegation shall be presumed for all bills not included in those exceptions set by the Constitution and as long as the plenary does not cancel the delegation by a floor vote. This outstanding delegation of power on committees is, though, controlled by the PPGs. Committees develop, anyway, intensive legislative powers (Table 14.1).

Table 14.1 Government and private members' bills and their success rates in Spain

	9th Congress (2008–2011)	10th Congress (2011–2016)	12th Congress (2016–2019)
Government bills	147	163	49
Passed	123 (83.7%)	160 (98.2%)	18 (36.7)
--- in plenary		84 (52.5%)	7 (38.9%)
--- in committee		76 (47.5%)	11 (61.1%)
Private bills	330	278	334
Passed	21 (6.4%)	9 (3.2%)	15 (4.5%)
--- in plenary		8 (88.9%)	9 (60.0%)
--- in committee		1 (11.1%)	6 (40.0%)

Source: Congreso de los Diputados, www.congreso.es (access: 29.09.2020).

Note: No legislative activity was developed in the 11th Congress since no agreement was reached to form a government, and new elections had to be called six months from the previous elections. There was a majority in the 10th Congress, whereas the more fragmented 12th Congress made the term much more unstable – it only lasted three years – there was a successful no-confidence vote on June 1, 2018. Due to the short length of the 12th Congress (only three years), 30 out of the 49 government bills didn not reach a final vote before the end of the term. Bills passed in committees with full-legislative delegated powers do not need a further approval in the plenary.

Standing legislative, standing non-legislative committees, non-standing committees, ad hoc committees, and inquiry committees

Most of the standing legislative committees 'mirror' one of the cabinet ministries and vary in accordance with the cabinet structure. Although there might be more committees than ministries, these are the committees that have that full legislative power delegation by the plenary. Among the 'standing non-legislative committees', there are the Rules, Members' Status, Petitions Appointments Consultation, Relations with Ombudsperson, European Union, Public TV, National Security Committees, or any other that may be created. The presidency board may create 'non-standing' or 'ad hoc committees' with a specific and temporary business, and 'inquiry committees' to conduct official research on a given specific topic. Additionally, there are the so-called 'joint committees' in which both MPs and senators will participate for those cases in which a joint decision is needed (usually when there is disagreement among the House and the Senate on legislation). There are very few committees, such as the Budget Committee, that cut across the jurisdiction of other committees, so the policy field of the committees – and the jurisdiction over it – do not usually overlap.

The committee presidency board appoints a formal ad hoc 'reporting subcommittee' for each bill, composed of a small group of committee members nominated by the respective PPGs' committee spokespersons[3] (usually one from each PPG). The members of the reporting subcommittee prepare a report on the draft bill and the tabled amendments to it – a report that, in most occasions, will not be substantially changed by the committee throughout the process (or, eventually, by the plenary). Those members of the reporting subcommittee are the ones who develop the most specialized work in the chamber. As opposed to committee sessions, the reporting subcommittee meetings are not held in public: this privacy allows PPGs to negotiate and reach agreements that are not that common in formal committee sessions, and do so in a more consensual fashion (Fernandes & Riera 2019). Negotiations for these reports may take place outside the reporting subcommittee or in the subcommittee. Other changes to the bill will take place when being discussed by the committee, but outside the committee, in private meetings.

The composition of the committees should proportionally mirror the size of each PPG in Parliament. Therefore, the size of the committees may vary with the number of PPGs in the plenary in each term, given that every PPG has the right to have at least one seat on every committee. In the current legislature (more fragmented than ever before), the size of the committees was enlarged, from 34 to 44, or even up to 50 members. The chamber presidency board decides on the size of the committees at the beginning of the term – after the board of PPG spokespersons has given its opinion about it.

Each PPG decides on the committee assignment for all its MPs (some of them may not be assigned to any committee due to their role in the PPG leadership or the cabinet). Usually, MPs are assigned to two or three committees, although there are some MPs – from smaller PPGs – that are members of many more. The PPGs may change the assignment whenever they think it is needed. They need to notify the Speaker before a given debate in the committee in which they want that MP to participate, and whether it is just for that occasion or permanently. The general pattern, though, is that MPs are assigned to a committee for the whole term. The usual – informal – procedure in all PPGs is that MPs are asked to name any committees they would like to be assigned to. When compiling that list, previous education or work experience are not always the main criteria, as opposed to the pattern in other countries (Whitaker 2011; Yardova 2009; Mickler 2019; Gianneti et al. 2019).

MPs generally 'get what they want' from the PPG leadership on most occasions, as is the case in other European parliaments and the European Parliament (Martin & Mickler, 2019; Whitaker 2019; Chiru 2019; Nikolenyi & Chen 2019). Nevertheless, party discipline also works on assignments, so leadership decisions will be accepted by MPs who will wait for changes, along with the term, if they want to 'move' to another committee. There are other incentives for MPs to accept their leadership's decision; for example, most if not all MPs are appointed either to a committee presidency board (chair, two vice-chairs, or two secretaries, all five of them being MPs) or as party spokesperson or deputy on the committee. Holding one of these positions entails an increase in the not-so-high MP salary that ranges from an additional 600 to 1,200 euros per month.[4] The respective PPG leadership makes these assignments of position without further discussion. Five MPs will fill the committee board positions which has an institutional character: The committee board sets the agenda of the committee and organizes its work and timing, being able, therefore, to speed up or slow down the process (or even to 'kill' a bill, recurrently extending the period to post amendments to the bill). Needless to say, the chair of the committee is the key role, although a majority on the board is needed to make most of the decisions (being, therefore, important to assure it, either because the required three MPs belong to the same PPG or because the chair successfully negotiates that support for their initiatives). On the other side, PPG committee spokespersons (and their alternates) have a political role: they meet weekly with other PPG committee spokespersons and PPG leaders to organize work schedules and make decisions as to which committee members participate on the committee with regards to each topic. They can even decide to establish a short-time assignment to the committee, so an MP who is not a member of the committee becomes so for the occasion; it only takes a letter from the PPG leader to the respective committee chair saying so.

Besides the committees they are assigned to, any MP may ask to be 'attached' to any additional committee they are interested in. This may be either because it is relevant for their constituency or because they have a personal interest in the jurisdiction of the committee. Being attached will entail that they receive (electronically) all the official documents produced and circulated in the committee, and that they may participate in the debates, although they cannot vote if they are not formally 'assigned' members. It is usual for most MPs to be assigned to three or four committees and attached, additionally, to a couple. Considering that available staff is quite scarce, it is reasonable to wonder how MPs manage. Certainly, division of labour also inside the committee facilitates achieving the collective tasks.

All committee sessions are held in public – actually, only the press has access – and are usually broadcast on the chamber TV. Very few sessions are held in private, exceptions being 'official secrets' or Secret Service activities. It is common to see reports on committees' activity on TV and in the press, especially regarding government oversight, where ministers, junior ministers, and MPs get into fierce debate.

As anticipated, there is a high turnover of MPs in each term: the average of chamber newcomers for the 1977–2011 legislatures was 45 percent (when in other parliaments the turnover rate used to be around 30 percent; Cotta & Best 2007). That figure has increased radically since 2015, as new parties (Podemos and Ciudadanos, and Vox in 2019) made it successfully to the chamber, with one of their key claims being to 'clean-up the Spanish political class'. Their candidates, therefore, had no previous parliamentary experience. In the Congress after the 2016 election, the turnover rate reached 65 percent. The breakthrough of Vox (winning 52 seats in the November 2019 election) contributed to keeping and increasing this high turnover rate: 236 (67.4 percent) out of the 350 members in the 14th Congress (elected in November 2019) were newcomers.

Therefore, before the new parties entered the chamber in 2015, the turnover in committee memberships was remarkably high: less than a third of the committee seats were occupied by MPs who had served on that same committee in the previous term (Oñate & Camacho 2014b).[5] But even when we only consider those MPs who remain in the chamber after a new election (disregarding, therefore, the newcomer MPs), the turnover in the Congreso de los Diputados committees is still remarkably high: less than 60% of the committee seats were occupied by an MP who was a member of that same committee in the previous Congress.

Given committees are 'places' for specialization (Mattson & Strøm 1995; Gilligan & Krehbiel 1990; Krehbiel 1999), where MPs become experts on the jurisdiction field after a term, following informational and partisan theories, continuity in committee membership should be of interest as a political asset, both for political parties and individual MPs (Cox & McCubbins 1993; Whitaker 2011, 2019; Martin 2016; Martin & Mickler 2019). Curiously enough, this does not seem to be the case in the Spanish Parliament, as explained elsewhere (Oñate & Camacho 2014b). And, what is more relevant, the same goes for the institutional frontbencher positions on the committee boards: less than 50 percent of the committee chairs had served on the same committee in the previous Congress. Less than 33 percent of the committee boards' members had served in the respective committee in the previous term. Regarding political frontbenchers on the committee (PPG committee spokesperson and their alternate, key actors who decide and coordinate all their party MPs' activity on the committee), less than 40 percent of them had served on the same committee in the previous term (Oñate & Camacho 2014b).[6] The figures of non-expert members in committees increased in the last Congresses with the arrival of the newcomer MPs from Podemos, Ciudadanos, and Vox. Therefore, in the Spanish Congreso de los Diputados there is a huge reshuffle after each election in the committee system and its leading positions. These frequent reshuffles weaken and diminish the quality of the committee system and its activities and results.[7] Perhaps reforms in the chamber standing orders (given PPGs do not seem to be keen to change their practices) might be necessary to ensure higher levels of continuity or tenure on the committees, at least in the key frontbencher positions.

It should also be taken into account, nevertheless, that regular MPs are members of several (two, three, or even more) committees, and therefore may remain in one of them, but leave the others in a new term, looking for new challenges on different committees. Interestingly, continuity rates increase remarkably when MPs (instead of committee seats) are considered: nearly 80 percent of reelected MPs are members of at least one of the committees they had served on during the previous Congress; and 33 percent of all reelected MPs remained members of all the committees they had been assigned to in the previous Congress, the committees thus profiting from their expertise in these particular, highly specialized political fields (Oñate & Camacho 2014)[8].

In terms of MPs' expertise in the jurisdiction fields of the committees they are assigned to, there is a wide variety of cases and big differences among committee members at the beginning of the term: some of them (10 percent) are highly specialized in the committee jurisdiction, whereas 33 percent have no previous experience in that field. More than half of the 748 analysed cases (10th Congress) did not even reach a 5 in the 0–10 specialization index value (Oñate & Ortega 2019).[9]

Of course, there are always some committee members who remain and keep track of the committee trajectory (or, at least, remain as members of the PPG), thus facilitating the socialization for the newcomers to the committee. But the expertise that is expected of MPs is not always reached. The Spanish Parliament is a legislature where PPGs play a key role in the development and implementation of the activity.

In the last Congresses, from the 2015 election in which new parties successfully entered the chamber, turnover figures in committee membership – and their leadership positions – have increased significantly. In the first three decades after the transition to democracy, committee chairs and the majority of the committee boards were occupied by MPs from the majoritarian PPG. Only two committees were traditionally chaired by MPs from the opposition PPG: the Budget Committee and the Foreign Affairs Committee. Nowadays, in a much more fragmented Congress. Many committees are chaired by an opposition party MP and the majoritarian party no longer necessarily holds the majority on committee boards. New compromises are needed for the regular functioning of committees and their work.

Taking into account the previous consideration, it is more likely that committee assignment leads to policy expertise than the other way around. As said, there are diverse incentives when looking for committees on which MPs wish to serve – and being experts in the respective field is not necessarily the prevalent one.

There has been a continuous increase in the number of female MPs, on a progressive path towards gender parity. Even though the numbers of female MPs are above 40 percent (in the current legislature, female MPs reach 43.7 percent of the members of the plenary), we still find some gender discrimination on committees: first, from the point of view of the vertical discrimination (gender discrimination in institutional or political positions), only slightly more than half of the committees have at least 40 percent of female members. And only one-third of the committees have a female chair, even though female MPs are half of the members of the committees' presidency boards (institutional positions). The number of female MPs has also increased among party committee spokespersons (the ones who lead the party activity in each committee); even so, there is still some room for improvement to reach gender parity in these political positions in order to avoid vertical discrimination.

Secondly, there still is some horizontal discrimination (Oñate 2014; Aldeguer & Oñate 2020), where there is a higher concentration of female MPs in 'traditionally feminine profile committees' when compared with 'traditionally masculine profile' ones. Again, the gap has been reduced in the last few years, but still remains large. And, considering the PPGs tend to pay attention to MPs' preferences when assigning them to the committees, we can think this horizontal discrimination has cultural roots shared by many of the female MPs. Perhaps legislatures should consider introducing, together with electoral quotas, regulation to make sure vertical and horizontal gender discrimination is diminished or eliminated.

Interaction in committees

As already mentioned, PPGs' leadership strongly control all the activity in the committees, mainly through the respective committee PPG spokespersons. The PPGs' leadership and committee spokespersons hold weekly meetings to prepare the agenda and set the PPG's political positions regarding all those matters that will be dealt with by the committees, as well as which MPs in the respective committees will take care of them. Even though the executive has a leading role in initiating legislation (government bills) and implementing policies, committees are still intensely involved regarding the policy cycle, especially in the early phases.

Committee sessions are not where political deliberation, bargaining, and deal-making take place. Given that the media have access to the sessions (and report frequently on their activity), it is more likely those activities take place in the corresponding reporting subcommittee (whose sessions are private), outside the formal sessions or away from committee, in bilateral or multilateral meetings (sometimes with the participation of the pertinent ministry officials). Formal committee sessions are used to a larger extent for debates, as shop windows, to publicly display any disagreement with the executive (and the majority parties), and to scrutinize their activity.

As stated, permanent legislative committees have extensive legislative powers that allow them to pass legislation that will not need further approval in the plenary (except in the abovementioned cases and topics, cf. endnote 2). Therefore, committees discuss the bills and the suggested amendments, making final decisions that usually have been negotiated and agreed upon outside and before the formal committee sessions. And this is the general pattern for all the committees, especially those with delegated full-legislative power. The strict control that PPGs exert over MPs and committee activity makes it difficult to find differences in the way committees work. There may be committees where personal relations do play a role in the procedures, but usually, this would happen in private and not in the public eye.

The Congreso Standing Orders permit government ministers and officials (not bureaucrats) to attend committee meetings anytime and participate in the debates, although they do not have voting rights unless they are MPs and formal members of the committee. Other than attending sessions due to committee oversight activity (when they are summoned), government officials may attend sessions on the occasion of a government bill being discussed. But given the close relationship and frequent contacts between ministers (junior ministers and high-ranking ministry officials) and the government PPG (leadership and committee party spokesperson), there is no need for the former to attend sessions: they will be immediately informed about the content and dynamics of each of them.

Committees develop extensive and intense oversight activities, as is the case in other European parliaments (Norton 2019): they may summon any public authority or private citizen – it is an offence not to answer this call. They can ask for any document or information from the executive, and post oral – and written – questions to ministers and junior ministers. On the other hand, government members may appear in front of the committee on their own initiative to explain whatever they consider necessary in the jurisdiction field of the committee.

When debating a bill, MPs frequently hold meetings with representatives of social organizations and interest groups involved in that policy area. All PPGs hold these kinds of meetings in or outside parliament, with both under their initiative or under the initiative of the social actors. Sometimes it is an individual MP who organizes the meeting (always letting the PPG leadership know about it beforehand), while in other occasions it is the PPG who does,

Committees in the Spanish Congreso 253

asking the individual MP (either front- or backbencher) to attend. When debating a bill, most of the policy field stakeholders (interest groups and NGOs) get in touch with the PPGs or the committee PPGs' spokespersons, and, usually, contact all PPGs – not only the majoritarian one – although they know very well who are the key actors in the process (Oñate & Camacho 2014a). Notwithstanding, social actors are fully aware it is the executive and its officials who play the key role in the legislative process: interest groups and NGOs will first contact the relevant ministry's public officials to influence a bill draft. Therefore, even if committees do hold meetings with social stakeholders of the respective policy field, they do not monopolize these contacts (Oñate & Camacho 2014a).

Besides holding meetings with NGOs and interest groups, when debating a bill, committees may also organize public hearings to ascertain different social points of view or expert knowledge. They may summon social actors, public officials, or academic experts, as suggested by the diverse PPGs. The participants will state their point of view and answer questions posed by the MPs. Nevertheless, on most occasions, these public hearings have a legitimizing and visibility-gaining objective: PPGs and MPs know beforehand about these diverse positions and have contacts with experts who may advise them on the bill draft at hand.

Committees and the policy cycle

Committees, as such, are not formally entitled to initiate legislation, but their members are (either one individual MP with the necessary support of another 14 – or one of the PPGs with the signature of its spokesperson).[10] Committees can produce many documents, non-legislative resolutions, or reports, either addressed to the government or to citizens at large, to influence the initiation of that process. These documents may include recommendations, guidelines, and objectives that the government should address. Nevertheless, it would be committees approving these documents, even if under the initiative of an individual MP or their PPG. Therefore, it is unlikely that the majority of governmental coalition parties would 'allow' these documents to be produced by a committee. This would only happen in a fragmented congress, where governmental parties do not have a clear majority. That was not the case until the Congress elected in 2016. As mentioned in the introduction, during four decades either PSOE or PP (supported by a non-statewide party in those terms when they did not hold a majority) would control the organization and activity in the chamber. With the increase in parliamentary fragmentation in the 2016 election, 'politics as usual' is no longer the rule. Nowadays, major parties face multilateral negotiations to form the government and to pass legislation: PP had to negotiate to retain government in 2016, and today the governing coalition (PSOE + Podemos) only totals 155 seats, far from the 176 needed for a majority. Negotiations and agreements are needed in the everyday life in Congress, and there have been occasions when government failed to pass a bill. One of the outcomes of this new situation is that in the 2016 and 2019 legislatures there are many committees whose chairs do not belong to any of the governing parties (as used to be the rule), and whose committee boards do not have a majority of MPs from the governing parties (see Table 14.2).

The committee calendar and agenda are approved by the committee board, led by its chair, in consultation with the house speaker and taking into account the order of business arranged by the presidency board of Congress. That is one of the most important roles of the committee chair, managing the agenda and calendar of the committee. And that is why it is important for the governing PPGs to have or to control a majority (three out of five votes) in the respective committee board. A skilled chair may speed up the process or delay any matter on the agenda and the calendar: the chair (with the support of the majority in the committee board) can manage to prioritize, delay, or 'kill' a bill (e.g., extending once and again the period to submit amendments to the bill). On the other hand, the government may request that priority be given to include a specific matter on the agenda.

Both when defining the problem (holding hearings if deemed necessary) and setting the agenda, as well as when debating and making a final decision on a bill, the committees – or to put it blankly, the PPGs in the committee – exert substantial power in the legislative process. And they do so both when the committee holds full legislative power and when it does not, and the plenary maintains the right to discuss and hold a final vote on the bill. The committee is the body where all the bills are to be discussed, amended, and voted on (even if it is to be sent later to the plenary for deliberation). Once the bill is sent to the committee, the committee board shall appoint the reporting subcommittee to prepare its report on the draft of the bill and the amendments tabled in the committee. In most cases, the subcommittee report will not be substantially altered during the process in the committee (or, afterwards, in the plenary in the case of final deliberation and vote). Usually, the committee does not substantially alter its subcommittee report, even though it could do so. Nevertheless, it is not the committee, as such, which exerts this power. It is the PPGs with their negotiating abilities, who host negotiations that usually do not take place in the formal committee sessions, but in private meetings. Even if the committees are 'strong' key actors, they do not act autonomously of the PPGs, but under their directions and coordination of their spokesperson on the committee. They will, eventually, introduce changes either in Congreso de los Diputados committees or in the Senate committees if negotiations are delayed and the process advances before reaching agreement on the bill.

The committees are also key actors regarding government oversight activity. Committees may summon members of the government or any public official and public servant, as well as produce reports or non-legislative resolutions or motions regarding these appearances (they can even produce a 'reprobation motion' to politically condemn a minister's activity). As already mentioned,

Table 14.2 Distribution (government-opposition) of committee chairs and committee board majority in legislative standing committees in Spain (1977–2020)

	1977	1979	1982	1986	1989	1993	1996	2000	2004	2008	2011	2016	2019
Governing party*	UCD	UCD	PSOE	PSOE	PSOE	PSOE	PP	PP	PSOE	PSOE	PP	PP	PSOE + Ps
Opposition chairs	8	2	2	1	1	6	5	3	5	4	2	10	6
Opposition board majority	8	2	0	0	0	6	14	0	6	5	0	21	5
(N)	21	19	11	11	11	14	15	14	16	22	17	21	21

* Governing party (in bold letters if they held a majority).

Source: Own elaboration with data from Congreso de los Diputados, www.congreso.es/portal/page/portal/Congreso/Organos/Comision (access: 01.09.2020).

Note: The legislatures elected in 2015 and April 2019 did not 'appoint' a government, so new elections were called within six months of the previous one. They have been excluded from the chart.

committee members can request any document or information from the government or any administration department, and they can also address questions – answers, which are compulsory, will be either oral or written – to the government members or any public official and public servant. On the other hand, ministers or junior ministers are entitled to appear in front of the plenary or the committee whenever they deem it necessary to inform the chamber or the committee about the development of any matter (junior ministers are usually the ones appearing in front of the committees). And, of course, committee members may address questions to them. There was a sustained increase in the numbers of initiatives regarding all these oversight instruments (and by duration of each Congress term). When the 'new' parties broke through, their MPs used these mechanisms to question the mainstream parties and their way of conducting politics 'as usual' both in government and in parliament.

The total number of requests for appearances (*comparecencias*) of government representatives (ministers or junior ministers) in front of committees in the 1977–2020 period amount 14,239, with a light growing pattern in numbers over time. The total number of requests for appearances of other authorities and public servants in front of committees for the same period is more than 19,000. Requests for appearances of other personalities in front of the committee in the same period reach 1,732. These initiatives entail those appearing in front of the committee to explain their point of view on the matter and answer the questions posed by members of the committee.

A different and more specific (in its object) instrument for oversight of government are the questions (oral and written) for the government members. Besides the regular oversight activity of the plenary (president of the government and ministers answer questions on Wednesday mornings), there is an intense oversight activity in the committees. The oral question debates (question, answer, follow-up, answer) in the committees may last longer than those posted in the plenary (up to 30 minutes, as opposed to five). It is usually the junior ministers or other high-ranking public officials who appear in front of the committee to provide the answers to those questions. The number of oral questions in the committees has increased over time (as shown in Figure 14.1 below),[11] as is the case in other countries (Yamamoto 2007; Martin 2011b; Sánchez de Dios & Wiberg, 2011; Maricut-Akbik 2020). Nevertheless, in order to reduce the large workload of the committees, in the last few terms the practice has been to change oral questions into written ones if they had not been answered in front of the committee by the time the respective session period (February–June or September–December) had come to an end (in that event, the MP who posted the question may still ask to hold it as an oral one to be answered in the following session period). It is worth noting that posting questions is the only activity individual MPs may develop without the previous authorization or knowledge of the respective PPG.

Even if the committee oversight initiatives increased over time (always considering the length of each congress term), many of these initiatives are

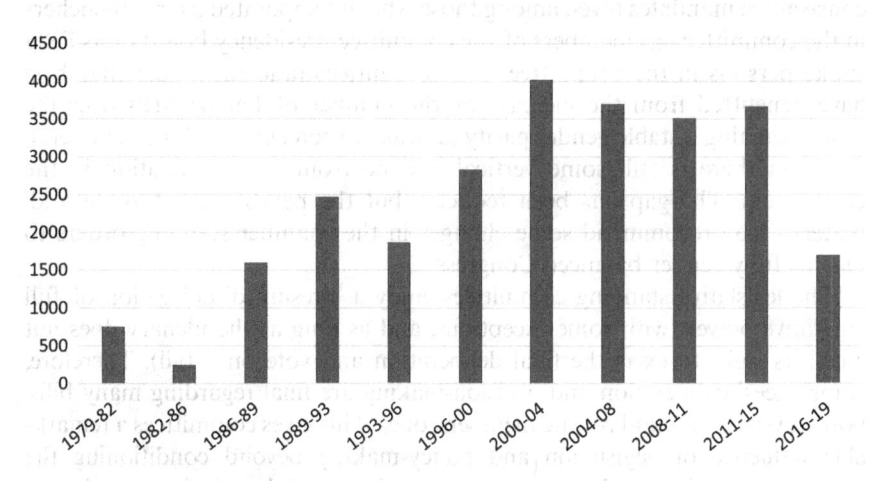

Figure 14.1 Development of oral questions to the government in committees of Congreso de los Diputados (1979–2019).
Source: Data from Congreso de los Diputados, www.congreso.es/web/guest/indice-de-iniciativas (access: 10.01.2021).

not used to control the implementation of policies in a structured way: as mentioned, MPs may request documents, reports, and information from the government and public servants on a given topic, but no implementation reports are regularly produced, nor are oversight strategies or plans developed. Nevertheless, committees' oversight over the government's policy development is intense and frequent.

Formally strong committees in a party-dominated legislature

This chapter analyses the main traits of committees and committee activities in the Congreso de los Diputados since democracy was restored in 1977. The system and its evolution over the years has produced 'strong committees' (dominated by political parties), with a clear and fixed jurisdiction (many of them 'mirroring' the cabinet ministries, to facilitate their oversight activity over government), a permanent mandate, remarkably influential legislative and oversight powers, and autonomy to set their agenda and exert some influence on the government's political one. Nevertheless, most MPs are members of several committees (three or four, or more in the small PPGs). And specialization does not seem to be incentivized by PPGs when deciding on the committee assignment of their MPs or when appointing committee frontbenchers, so there are many committee members with a low level of specialization in the substantive field of the committee they serve on. One of the key factors for this lack of specialization and expertise of many committee members is the remarkably high turnover in committee membership between consecutive mandates (even among those who are appointed as frontbenchers in the committee –as members of the committee presidency board or as PPG spokespersons in the committee. The committees (and the whole chamber) have benefitted from the increase of the number of female MPs over the years, reaching a stable gender parity (at least 40 percent of female members), although there is still some vertical and horizontal discrimination in the committees. The gap has been reduced, but the persistence of some 'old' patterns may recommend some changes in the chamber standing orders to reach a fully gender-balanced Congress

The legislative standing committees enjoy a 'presumed' delegation of full legislative power (with some exceptions, and as long as the plenary does not recall its right to exert the final deliberation and vote on a bill). Therefore, committees' deliberation and decision-making are final regarding many bills, both government's and private members' ones. This gives committees a remarkable influence on legislation and policy-making beyond conditioning the contents of the bills with their report on each one of them before the plenary deliberates and votes (when these functions are not delegated). Even though committees may summon experts or public servants and do hold meetings with social actors and interest groups when deliberating on a bill, the lack of resources – on average, there is nearly one assistant for every MP, as an average, and there are not many advisors in the documentation department in the House – may jeopardize the quality of their activity. Committees also develop an intense oversight activity over the government, developing numerous different initiatives to control the cabinet's everyday actions and outcomes.

Therefore, committees develop an intense and influential work in the policy cycle, in all of the different phases: defining the problems and setting the agenda, passing legislation and keeping contacts with policy networks and stakeholders, and conducting oversight activities on the government implementation of policies.

But these formally 'strong committees' are strictly controlled by hierarchical, centralized, and cohesive parliamentary party groups. The almighty PPGs' leadership organize nearly all the activities of their disciplined MPs through the committee PPG's spokesperson, who decides which MPs participate in the reporting subcommittees, sets the position of the PPG in each matter, and decides who participates in each specific debate or activity of the committee. PPGs, therefore, are the key actors in the Spanish committee system (in Congreso de los Diputados, the Senate, and the regional parliaments). The system, though, seems to work in an efficient and coordinated way. Parliament (and its committees play a key role in this regard) has enlarged and improved its specialized work. The arrival of new parties to Congreso de los Diputados in recent years (creating further fragmentation) introduced new challenges, which the chamber seems to be addressing quite well. Further negotiation and compromise are now necessary, and committees seem a good arena of practice and experience in this regard, even if much of this negotiation and compromise takes place outside the committees.

Notes

1 Given the committee system in the Senate is basically the same as in the Congreso de los Diputados, we will focus on the latter. The Spanish bicameral system is an 'asymmetrical' one, the lower chamber being the most important and powerful one.
2 Full legislative power delegated to the committees is not allowed for certain bills: constitutional reform, international issues, qualified bills (those which require a majority vote – *leyes orgánicas*), coordinating bills, and the annual budget bill or finance bill (Spanish Constitution, section 75). Committees cannot use full legislative power regarding bills previously vetoed or amended by the plenary of the Senate. Even if the full legislative delegation exists, the plenary always holds the initial debate and votes for the whole bill (if any amendment to the whole government's bill is tabled) and the initial 'taking into consideration' vote of the private members' bill, before sending it – if successful – to the relevant committee.
3 The committee also can appoint working groups to study and deal with a specific topic.
4 On the salaries of MPs in Spain, compared to some of their colleagues in other European countries, see Oñate (2013a and 2013b).
5 These and following figures are calculated using data from committee membership in the 8th and 9th Congresses (elected in 2004–2008 and 2008–2011), before the new parties made it to the chamber.
6 See previous endnote.
7 The strong, centralized, cohesive, and disciplined ('almighty') parties and PPGs (Oñate, 2000, 2008 & 2006), and the multi-level and multi-institutional political careers patterns (Oñate, 2018a & 2018b; Oñate & Viera, 2019) would explain most of these high turnover figures in committee membership in the Spanish Congreso de los Diputados.
8 See endnote 5.
9 For the calculation of the parliamentary specialization index (PSI), which ranges from 0 to 10, different elements are considered: previous education, professional experience, same committee previous membership, and previous experience as MP – not regarding the committee, but the knowhow of parliamentary life. The unit of analysis is not the MP but the 'MP member of a given committee', considering one MP may have several PSI values, in accordance with the number of committees they serve on.
10 The other legitimate actors to initiate legislation are the Senate, the government, the regional parliaments, and citizens gathering 500,000 supporting signatures.
11 The comparatively low amount of oral questions in the 2016–2019 term was probably due to its shorter length and the exceptionally successful no-confidence vote that put an end to the conservative PP government and opened the door to a socialist PSOE government in June 2018.

References

Aldeguer, B. & Oñate, P. (2020). Gender discrimination in the governance structure of Congreso Diputados in Spain. Paper presented at the 2020 *ECPR General Conference*.

Bailer. S. (2016). Interviews and surveys in legislative research. In S. Martin, T. Saalfeld, & K.W. Strøm (eds.) *Oxford Handbook of Legislative Studies*. Oxford: Oxford University Press, 167–193.

Chiru, M. (2019). Low-cost policy specialization, district characteristics and gender. Patterns of committee assignment in Romania. *Journal of Legislative Studies* 25(3), 375–393.

Cotta, M. & Best. H. (2007) (eds.). *Democratic representation in Europe. Diversity, change and convergence*. Oxford: Oxford University Press.

Cox, G. (2006). The organization of democratic legislatures. In B.R. Weingast & D.A. Wittman (eds.). *The Oxford Handbook of Political Economy*. Oxford: Oxford University Press, 141–161.

Cox, G.W. & McCubbins, M.D. (1993). *Legislative leviathan: Party government in the House*. Berkeley: University of California Press.

Fernandes, J.M. & Riera, P. (2019). Committee systems in Portugal and Spain. In J.M. Fernandes & C. Leston-Bandeira (eds.) *The Iberian Legislatures in Comparative Perspective*. London: Routledge, 71–88.

Fernades, J.M., Riera, P., & Cantú, F. (2019). The politics of committee chairs assignment in Ireland and Spain. *Parliamentary Affairs* 72, 182–201.

Gaines, B.J., Goodwin, M, Holden Bates, S., & Sin, G. (2019). The study of legislative committees. *Journal of Legislative Studies* 25(3), 331–339.

Giannetti, D., Pedrazzani, A. & Pinto, L. (2019). Personal ambitious, expertise and parties' control: Understanding committee assignment in the Italian Chamber of Deputies. *Parliamentary Affairs* 72, 119–140.

Gilligan, T.W. & Krehbiel, K. (1987). Collective decision-making and standing committees: An informational rationale for restrictive amendment procedures. *Journal of Law, Economics and the Organization* 3, 287–335.

Gilligan, T.W. & Krehbiel, K. (1990). Organization of informative committees by a rational legislature. *American Journal of Political Science* 34, 531–564.

Helms, L. (2000). Parliamentary party groups and their parties: A comparative assessment. *Journal of Legislative Studies* 6(2), 104–120.

Jalali, C. & Rodríguez, J. (2019). Parliamentary party groups in the Iberian Democracies. In J. M. Fernandes & C. Leston-Bandeira (eds.) *The Iberian Legislatures in Comparative Perspective*. London: Routledge, 49–70.

Krehbiel, K. (1999). Paradoxes of Parties in Congress. *Legislative Studies Quarterly*, 24, 31–64.

Krehbiel, K. (1990). Are congressional committees composed of preference outliers? *American Political Science Review* 84, 149–163.

Maricut-Akbik, A. (2020). Q&A in legislative oversight: A framework for analysis. *European Journal of Political Research*, DOI 10.1111/1475-6765.12411.

Martin, S. (2011a). Electoral institutions, the personal vote and legislative organization. *Legislative Studies Quarterly* 36, 339–361.

Martin, S. (2011b). Parliamentary questions, the behaviour of legislators and the functioning of legislatures: An introduction. *Journal of Legislative Studies* 17(3), 259–270.

Martin, S. (2016). Committees. In S. Martin, T Saafeld, & K.W Strøm (eds.) *Oxford Handbook of Legislative Studies*. Oxford: Oxford University Press, 352–368.

Martin, S. & Mickler, T.A. (2019). Committee assignments: Theories, causes and consequences. *Parliamentary Affairs* 72, 77–98.

Mattson, I. & Strøm, K. (1995). Parliamentary committees. In H. Döring (ed.). *Parliaments and Majority Rule in Western Europe*. Frankfurt: Campus Verlag, 249–307.

McElroy. G. (2006). Committee representation in the European Parliament. *European Union Politics*, 7, 5–29.
Mickler, T.A. (2019). Who goes where? Committee assignments in the Dutch Tweede Kamer. *Parliamentary Affairs* 72, 99–118.
Nikolenyi, C. & Friedberg, C. (2019). Vehicles of opposition influence or agents of the governing majority? Legislative committees and private members' bills in the Hungarian Országgyűlés and the Israeli Knesset. *Journal of Legislatives Studies*, 25(3), 358–374.
Norton, P.L. (2019). Post-legislative scrutiny in the UK Parliament: Adding value. *Journal of Legislative Studies* 25(3), 340–357.
Oñate, P. (2000a). La organización del Congreso de los Diputados. In A. Martínez (ed.), *El Congreso de los Diputados en España: Funciones y Rendimiento*. Madrid: Tecnos, 69–94.
Oñate, P. (2000b). Congreso, grupos parlamentarios y partidos. In A. Martínez (ed.), *El Congreso de los Diputados en España: Funciones y Rendimiento*. Madrid: Tecnos, 95–140.
Oñate, P. (2008). Los partidos políticos en la España democrática. In M. Jiménez & F. Vallespín (eds.). *La España del siglo XXI: La Política*. Madrid: Biblioteca Nueva Sistema, 617–643.
Oñate, P. (2013a). Committee assignment in Spanish Congreso de los Diputados: Do MPs "get what they want"? Paper presented in *10th Workshop on Parliamentary Scholars and Parliamentarians*. Wroxton College, Oxfordshire.
Oñate, P. (2013b). Los ¿excesivos? salarios de sus señorías. *ElDiario.es*. Retrieved from www.eldiario.es/agendapublica/nueva_politica/excesivos-salarios-senorias_1_5760984.html (access: 01.09.2020).
Oñate, P. (2013c). Italian members of parliament are paid substantially higher salaries than those in other West European countries. *LSE-Blogs*. Retrieved from https://blogs.lse.ac.uk/europpblog/2013/ (access: 01.09.2020).
Oñate, P. (2014). The effectiveness of electoral quotas on vertical and horizontal segregation in Spain. *Representation. Journal of Representative Democracy*. Special issue on electoral quotas, 50(3), 351–364.
Oñate, P. (2018a). Political elites and professional careers of MPs in multi-level Spain. In G. Lachapelle & P. Oñate (eds.). *Borders and margins: Federalism, devolution and multi-level governance*. London: Barbara Budrich Publishers, 245–258.
Oñate, P. (2018b). Cambio y continuidad en la elite parlamentaria. In F. Llera, M. Baras, & J. Montabes (eds.). Las elecciones generales de 2015 y 2016. Madrid: Centro de Investigaiciones Sociológicas, 415–436.
Oñate, P. & Delgado, I. (2006). Partidos, grupos parlamentarios y diputados en las asambleas autonómicas. In P. Oñate (ed.) *Organización y Funcionamiento de los Parlamentos Autonómicos*. Valencia: Tirant lo Blanch, 135–172.
Oñate, P. & Camacho, B. (2014a). They don't represent us! Contacts between MPs and citizens and social groups: The MPs' view. Paper presented an the 2014 ECPR General Conference. Glasgow.
Oñate, P. & Camacho, B. (2014b). Professionalization without specialization in Spanish Lower Chamber: An amateur political elite? Paper presented in the *11th Workshop on Parliamentary Scholars and Parliamentarians*. Oxfordshire: Wroxton College.
Oñate, P. & Belchior, M. (2019). The relationship between regional and national parliaments in Spain and Portugal. In J.M. Fernandes and C. Leston-Bandeira

(eds.) *The Iberian Legislatures in Comparative Perspective*. London: Routledge, 223–240.

Oñate, P. & Ortega, C. (2019). Committee parliamentary specialization index. Explaining MPs' specialization in the Spanish Congreso de los Diputados. *Journal of Legislative Studies*, 25(3), 394–408.

Oñate, P. & Viera, A. (2019). Perfiles de las elites parlamentarias tras las elecciones autonómicas de 2015 y 2016: nuevas caras, viejas tendencias. In N. Lagares, C. Ortega, & P. Oñate (eds.). *Las elecciones autonómicas de 2015 y 2016*. Madrid: Centro de Investigaciones Sociológicas, 389–408.

Saalfeld, T. (2000). Members of parliament and governments in Western Europe: Agency relations and problems of oversight. *European Journal of Political Research* 37(3), 353–376.

Sánchez de Dios, M. & Wilberg, M. (2011). Questioning in European parliaments. *Journal of Legislative Studies* 17(3), 354–367.

Strøm, K. (1998). Parliamentary committees in European democracies. *Journal of Legislative Studies* 4(1), 21–59.

Whitaker, R. (2001). Party control in a committee-based legislature? The case of the European Parliament, *Journal of Legislative Studies*, 7:4, 63–88

Whitaker, R. (2011). *The European Parliament's committees: National party influence and legislative Empowerment*. Abingdon: Routledge.

Whitaker, R. (2019). A case of 'You Can Always Get What You Want'? Committee assignments in the European Parliament. *Parliamentary Affairs* 72, 162–181.

Yamamoto, H. (2007). *Tools for parliamentary oversight: A comparative study of 88 national parliaments*. Geneva: Inter-parliamentary Union.

Yordanova, N. (2009). The rationale behind committee assignments in the European Parliament: Distributive, informational and partisan perspectives. *European Union Politics* 10, 253–280.

15 Parliamentary committees in the Grand National Assembly of Turkey (2002–2020)

Ömer Faruk Gençkaya

Committees have been a component of the parliamentary structure in Turkey since the first short-lived Ottoman parliament of 1876. Following the establishment of the Republic of Turkey in 1923, 20 parliamentary committees were created in 1927 under three categories: committees corresponding to the parliamentary duties, committees corresponding to all government services and committees corresponding to the ministries (İba 2009). The 1961 Constitution introduced a bicameral system, the National Assembly and the Senate; each had its own committees and joint committees such as Plan and Budget.[1] The original text of the current 1982 Constitution (1982c) is based on the empowerment of the executive and a unicameral parliament with 15 standing committees (Gençkaya 1990).

It is argued that 'strong committees are associated with a strong legislative policy-making role while strong political parties are associated with a more constrained legislative policy-making role' (Olson & Mezey 1991). Until recently, strong party discipline and majority-oriented rules weakened the autonomy of parliamentary committees and the Grand National Assembly of Turkey (GNAT). The constitutional amendments of 2017 introduced a *sui generis* presidential system which has been in effect since the early presidential and parliamentary elections of June 24, 2018. The president's decree authority and appointive powers have reduced the legislative process to a real 'rubber stamp' mechanism by directly or indirectly disabling and neutralizing checks-and-balances mechanisms, including the media and the constitutional court. The president is entitled to issue decrees in matters not regulated by law and to restrict fundamental rights and freedoms, even in the absence of a state of emergency. Moreover, oral questioning was eliminated, and a qualified majority became necessary for establishing a parliamentary investigation committee. All things considered, the recent constitutional amendments and editorial changes in the Rules of Procedure (RoP) further neutered Turkey's already weakened parliament.

The main objective of this chapter is to analyse the functions and roles of the parliamentary committees and their members in the policy cycle in Turkey. First, the changes in the formal institutional settings of the parliamentary committees in the period 2002 to 2020 (five legislative terms) will be

DOI: 10.4324/9781003106579-15

explained. Second, the committees' legislative activities will be evaluated in terms of their capacities in problem definition, agenda-setting, policy formulation, and oversight.

Organization of the committees

The legal framework of the legislative activities consists of the Constitution (Articles 87–98), the RoP, and the acts of parliament. Since 1992, new standing committees have been established, resulting in a current total of 19 functioning standing committees (see Table 15.1). The formal capabilities of these committees can be summarized as follows (Bektaş 2018: 143). Structurally, the number of committees is fixed and, apart from a few select committees, most have a standard size and permanent tenure for membership. Specialization of committees is essential, and subcommittees can be established. Procedurally, the distribution of seats and selection of chairs are proportional, committee meetings are usually open to the press, minority statements are attached to the committee report, and committees prepare the final document for the plenary debates. Finally, the committees have the right to amend bills, to control timetables, to call ministers and stakeholders (experts, NGOs etc.) and to request documents from all public institutions.

Committees are divided into two groups: standing (*specialized*) and temporary (*ad hoc*) committees. The standing committees are established by the Constitution, the RoP (Article 20 RoP) or the special law. The Plan and Budget Committee (PBC) and the parliamentary investigation committee are regulated by the Constitution (Articles 161 and 100 respectively). Until the recent amendments to the Constitution and the RoP, the PBC was the largest committee in size (45, out of which 25 seats were reserved for the government deputies), although it now has 30 seats.

There are two types of standing committees relating to the legislative function: first, there are committees corresponding to one or more ministries, such as the Justice Committee and the National Education, Culture, Youth, and Sports Committee, and second, there are committees that do not corresponding to a ministry, such as the Constitution Committee, Petition Committee, and the Security and Intelligence Committee. Most standing committees are legislative by definition, though some are non-legislative (oversight), such as Petition and Public Economic Enterprises. Others actually perform both functions, like the committee on Human Rights Investigation or The Plan and Budget Committee, which perform both legislative and oversight functions.

The first type of ad hoc committee is formed either by the Constitution (Article 100, parliamentary investigation committee and RoP, Articles 109–112 and 114) or the RoP (Articles 104 and 105, parliamentary inquiry committee) for the collection of information on a specific issue or to investigate criminal liability of the president and the ministers. The other type of ad hoc

Table 15.1 Relationships between standing committees and ministries in Turkey

Standing Committees (Number of members)	Relevant Ministries
Constitution (26)	
Justice (26)	Justice
Interior Affairs (26)	Interior Affairs
National Defence (25)	National Defence
Foreign Affairs (26)	Foreign Affairs
National Education, Culture Youth and Sport (26)	National Education/ Culture and Tourism/ Youth and Sport
Public Works, Construction, Transportation and Tourism (26)	Transportation and Infrastructure/ Culture and Tourism/ Environment and Urbanization
Environment (26)	Environment and Urbanization
Health, Family, Labour and Social Affairs (26)	Health / Family, Labour and Social Affairs
Industry, Commerce, Energy, Natural Resources, Information and Technology (25)	Energy and Natural Resources/Industry and Technology/Commerce
Agriculture, Forestry and Village Affairs (26)	Agriculture and Forestry
Auditing the Final Accounts of the GNAT*	none
Plan and Budget (30)	Treasury and Finance
Digital Platforms (17), 2020	All ministries
European Union Harmonization (26), 2003	All ministries
Security and Intelligence (17), 2014	All ministries
Women–Men Equality of Opportunity (26), 2009	All ministries
Public Economic Enterprises (35), 1987	All ministries
Human Rights Investigation (26), 1990	All ministries
Petition (12), 1962, 1984	All ministries

Source: Prepared by the author from various sources.

* This committee is de facto non-functional due to the Law No. 5018 on Public Financial Management and Control of 2003 which subjected the GNAT to internal and external auditing. Dates indicate the establishment dates of these committees by law.

committee is a joint committee, which temporarily merges for certain tasks assigned to them. For example, the joint committee of the Constitution and Justice Committees deals with the request for lifting parliamentary immunity and the loss of parliamentary membership in cases where an MP holds an office incompatible with membership, e.g. in public corporate bodies and their auxiliaries, public professional organizations, trade unions, (Constitution, Article 82 and RoP, Article 137), it also deals with non-attendance of deputies to the parliamentary work (RoP, Article 138).

Each committee has a secretariat composed of at least one legislative expert and one clerk. The committees may employ temporary staff from other units of the GNAT and may invite experts for consultation. The Office of the Speaker constitutes a board of review dealing with the unconstitutionality of the bills that provides the committees with advisory services. As of 2020, 111 legislative experts and deputy experts were employed in the standing committees, as well as the Directorate of Laws and Resolution, which offers major legislative services to MPs and committees (TBMM, 2020a). The number of legislative experts is insufficient, and the ratio of staff to the 600 MPs is 0.18.

Membership in the committees

The Office of the Speaker determines the number of committee members allocated to each political party group – 20 members at minimum – proportionally. Two elections are held for the committees in a legislative term (five years), during which committees' members are first elected for two years, and then three years (RoP Article 20). The average turnover in the committee membership for the last five legislative periods is 45.8 percent, which is below the average parliamentary turnover (56.17 percent) for these legislative periods (see Table 15.2).

The majority party controls the legislation by the assignment of MPs who will represent their aims and interests and act under the control of the political party groups. Therefore, deputies are not strong individually, but rather act as the 'foot soldiers' of the party group (Turan, 2000). An MP who ceases to be a member of a political party, or whose party loses its right to form a party group in the Assembly, loses their membership automatically (RoP, Article 22). The changes in the size of the party group are also reflected in committee assignments. The chairpersons, vice-chairpersons, spokespersons, and rapporteurs of all committees are elected through secret ballot by the majority of committee members (RoP, Article 24). Therefore, all committee chairpersons are elected from the majority party (see Table 15.3).

MPs without a party group affiliation and independent deputies are represented in a few committees such as Human Rights Investigation Committee (one member), European Union Harmonization Committee (one member), Public Economic Enterprise Committee (one member), and the Equality of Women and Men Committee (one member). Since the 2018 amendments to the RoP, membership in multiple committees is possible with the exception of the members of the Bureau of the Assembly of the GNAT, which is composed of the elected MPs (speaker, the deputy speaker, secretary members, and administrative members elected from among the parliamentary members) and deals with legislative activities and administrative matters.

Although the representation of women in the GNAT gradually increased from 24 (4.4 percent) in 2002 to 101 in 2018 (17.24 percent), the underrepresentation of women is obvious in the committees, as the legislature ranks 120th

Table 15.2 Average turnover in committees' membership by party origin in Turkey (2002–2020)

Committee/Party	Justice and Development Party	Republican People's Party	Democratic Society Party/ People's Democracy Party*	Nationalist Action Party**	Average
Constitution	53	48	50	39	47.50
Justice	42	50	56	42	47.50
Interior Affairs	52	55	56	50	53.25
National Defence	58	55	61	64	59.50
Foreign Affairs	54	47	53	53	51,75
National Education, Culture Youth and Sport	49	48	50	28	43.75
Public Works, Construction, Transportation and Tourism	57	52	50	22	44.75
Plan and Budget	48	46	44	33	42.75
Industry, Commerce, Energy, Natural Resources, Information and Technology	49	50	50	36	46.25
Agriculture, Forestry and Village Affairs	49	51	50	50	50.00
Health, Family, Labour and Social Affairs	58	46	39	50	48.25
Environment	65	64	61	47	59.25
European Union	50	38	33	39	40.00
Human Rights Investigation	53	56	50	53	53.00
Petition	69	81	50	17	54.25
Security and Intelligence	19	50	50	-*	29.75
State Economic Enterprises	57	58	50	44	52.25
Women–Men Equality of Opportunity	48	46	42	50	46.50
Total average (Committees' Membership)					45.80

* Since 2007. The Democratic Society Party was closed down in 2009 and the People's Democracy Party was established in 2012.
** Since 2007.
*** The Nationalist Action Party did not have a seat on this committee until the current legislative period. The recently established Digital Platforms Committee is not included in this table.

Table 15.3 Distribution of standing committee members by party groups in Turkey

Party Group/ Legislative Periods	Total Number of Members		Ratio in the GNAT		Number of Committee Members		Ratio in the Committees**		Difference	
	26	27	26	27	26*	27*	26	27	26	27
Justice and Development Party	316	291	58,9	50,7	15	13	50,2	54,4	8,7	3,7
Republican People's Party	131	138	24,4	24,0	6	6	20,1	25,1	4,3	0,7
People's Democracy Party	54	58	10,0	10,1	2+1	3	10.0	12,5	0	2,4
Nationalist Action Party	36	49	6,7	8,5	1+1	2	6,7	8,3	0	0,2
İYİ Party	-	37	-	6,5	-	2	-	8,3	-	1,8

Source: Data for the 26th period compiled from Yapıcı–Kaya (2019) and the 27th period collected by the author.

* Calculation is made by taking the number of committee members as constant (26). Until the 27th period, a total of 24 memberships, 15 + 6 + 2 + 1, could be distributed, while the remaining two memberships are given to the largest political party groups. According to the new system, it is distributed, 13 + 6 + 3 + 2 + 2 basically. However, the distribution of seats in certain committees vary: Public Economic Enterprises (17 + 8 + 4, 3 + 2), Plan and Budget (15 + 7 + 3 + 3 + 2), National Defence (13 + 6 + 2 + 2 + 2), Security and Intelligence (9 + 4 + 2 + 1 + 1) and Petition (6 + 3 + 1 + 1 + 1).

** This ratio is calculated = N. of Committee Members/Total N. of Members.

worldwide in terms of representation by women (IPU, 2019). As of November 2020, the number of female deputies varies across the standing committees, with the highest being in the Equality of Women and Men Committee (23), and the lowest in the Security and Intelligence (one), and National Defence (none) committees. The mode value is 4.5.

Committee meetings

The Quorum for convening committee meetings is one-third of the total number of members, and decisions require an absolute majority of the members present. Members are obliged to attend the committee meetings regularly unless there is a valid excuse.

Although the committees determine their agendas (RoP, Article 26) due to the disciplined party structure, the committee chairpersons act under the guidance of the political party groups to which they belong. The President of the Republic, as chairman of the party and contrary to the separation-of-powers principle, may become directly involved in parliamentary agenda-setting. For instance, ministries prepare the drafts and MPs from the majority submit these drafts as individual bills.

In practice, committees generally carry out their work on the days or during the hours when the plenary is not convened and cannot work during recess. Before the 24th legislative period, each committee had a separate meeting room, although currently all committees can use common meeting rooms by appointment.

The committees' ordinary meetings (deliberation on bills) are open to the members of the GNAT, the deputy president, ministers, deputy ministers, and senior civil servants. The committee members, the signature holder of a bill, the representatives of the executive, the relevant primary and secondary committees and the parliamentary party groups are invited to the committees' ordinary meetings. Members of the GNAT, the deputy president, ministers, and deputy ministers have priority in taking the floor, although only committee members are eligible to submit a motion of amendment and to vote.

For parliamentary hearings on a specific issue related to a bill under consideration (legislative hearing) or to a parliamentary inquiry (oversight hearing), the committee chairperson may invite experts from public institutions, civil society organizations, and scientific institutions. Representatives of civil society organizations have, in the past, been invited to committee meetings (especially from the 22nd period as a consequence of the EU candidacy), but this is no longer practised. Until recently, the participation of NGOs in the law-making process took place after the bill was submitted (at the committee stage) and before the referral of the GNAT committee's final report to the plenary. MPs can now initiate bills, meaning that the practice of posting government drafts on the relevant ministries' websites and receiving opinion from the relevant stakeholders has ceased. Individual MPs may consult stakeholders when they prepare a bill, but this is an informal practice.

Non-governmental organizations can contribute to the examination of a bill at the committee stage in different ways. The relevant committees, including the parliamentary inquiry committees, may receive written opinions or call NGO representatives to meet in person, at the request of NGOs. A list of participants, including public organizations and their contact information, is kept (Yapıcı-Kaya 2019: 473). Unless the committee holds a closed session, meetings and hearings are open to the press. The GNAT's television channel rarely broadcasts the committee meetings. The meeting minutes of some committees have been published online since 2012. However, NGO participation does not provide a technical contribution in the final formulation of the bill and is limited to providing an opinion. The average number of invited and attended NGOs to the Plan and Budget Committee during the 26th and the 27th periods (as of May 2020) were 6.62/9.38 and 9.14/11.86 respectively (Akkuş 2020).

On rare occasions, a closed session in the committee may be requested by one-third of committee members. For example, the Internal Affairs

Committee held a closed session on January 14, 2004 to discuss the Draft Fundamental Law on Public Administration (İba 2004). The committee members, the deputy president, and ministers can attend closed meetings without the approval of the chairperson. The minutes are kept confidential (RoP, Article 32).

Committee meeting duration varies from committee to committee according to substance and procedure. For example, in 2012, the subcommittee on the draft bill on the 12-year compulsory education system worked for two days and then the National Education Committee examined the subcommittee's report for ten days (Yapıcı-Kaya 2019: 474). On the other hand, the Foreign Affairs Committee completed about a dozen international treaties within a few hours. For example, in 2017 the committee discussed ten draft international agreement laws within two hours, and another five draft laws in 30 minutes (Yapıcı-Kaya 2019: 474).

The Foreign Affairs, Plan and Budget, Justice, Health, Industry, and National Education committees come first in submitting the committee reports (Table 15.4). The Human Rights Investigation and Women and Men Equality of Opportunity committees convene frequently, while the Agriculture, Forestry and Village Affairs committees convene very rarely.

Policy influence

The flow of the law-making process in the committees passes through defined stages (RoP, Articles 35–44 and 74–89, Figure 1). Currently, the President of the Republic – who is entitled to issue executive decrees, orders and regulations in ordinary times, and emergency decrees (Constitution Articles 106 and 119) can only submit the next year's draft budget law (Constitution, Article 161), and all other bills must be initiated by one or several MPs. According to the content of the bill, the Office of the Speaker refers the draft bills to the relevant primary committee(s), and when a bill covers multiple matters, the secondary committee. The secondary committee must submit its report to the primary committee within ten days following the referral. For example, as of July 2020, a total of 106 individual bills were referred to the Human Rights Investigation Committee as the secondary committee. Yet neither the primary nor the secondary committees have submitted their reports on these bills as yet.[2]

The committee first considers the constitutionality of the bill as a whole, and if a bill is found unconstitutional, it is rejected without deliberation. If it is deemed constitutional, then the committee starts examining the bill article by article. Sometimes the committee may decide to set up a subcommittee to prepare a detailed report on the bill, and then deliberate on the bill. Although it is not mandated by the RoP, subcommittees may be established occasionally within the primary committees. For instance, in the 24th period a total of 23 subcommittees were established: Agriculture (one), Health (three), Human Rights (ten), Industry (three), Interior (three),

Table 15.4 Meetings and law-making activities of the standing committees in Turkey*

Committees/Legislative Periods	Committee Meetings					Government Drafts/Individual Bills Arrived					Committee Reports Submitted					Bills Enacted				
	22	23	24	26	27	22	23	24	26	27	22	23	24	26	27	22	23	24	26	27
Constitution	na	na	17	31	2	168	65	99	121	99	27	30	11	10	2	21	24	10	5	1
Justice	na	na	70	17	14	349	163	455	375	444	150	52	80	9	7	82	42	78	9	19
European Union**	na	na	21	9	1	na	0	0	0	0	na	0	0	0	0	na	0	0	0	0
Public Works	na	na	21	2	5	86	34	52	50	64	37	19	7	0	4	23	15	8	2	4
Environment	na	na	21	4	4	10	2	15	33	40	6	1	0	0	1	3	0	0	10	2
Foreign Affairs	na	na	93	43	20	587	509	541	564	198	427	403	495	436	440	188	345	282	397	55
Interior Affairs	na	na	25	5	6	285	123	391	406	441	105	24	15	12	5	56	20	24	12	3
HR Investigation*	34	47	38	15	10	0	0	3	3	0	0	0	9	1	0	0	0	0	1	0
Women–Men**	na	21	33	10	9	na	24	2	3	3	na	0	21	3	0	na	0	0	1	0
National Education	na	na	31	12	8	134	110	167	189	195	63	39	25	18	5	36	28	36	15	5
National Defence	na	na	14	11	4	115	127	53	49	72	45	36	10	25	3	25	36	15	22	4
Plan Budget	na	na	154	113	70	1461	833	1187	1169	1434	379	227	200	39	21	221	70	0	39	24
Health	na	na	26	8	5	105	39	150	136	142	41	9	25	3	1	35	8	43	2	2
Industry	na	na	38	20	6	108	83	73	76	77	38	30	20	27	5	34	27	29	23	7
Agriculture	na	na	14	8	4	55	26	60	60	73	35	12	16	5	3	25	8	17	4	3
Digital Platforms	-	-	-	-	na	-	-	-	-	na	-	-	-	-	na	-	-	-	-	-
Total	-	-	706	248	158	3,463	2138	3574	3234	3882	1,353	882	1229	602	210	749	623	542	544	209

Sources: Compiled by the author from www.tbmm.gov.tr/develop/owa/komisyonlar_sd.liste (access: 01.09.2020), TBMM Komisyonlar Bültenleri I–VIII, 22. Dönem, Türkiye Büyük Millet Meclisi 23. Dönem Yasama, Denetim ve Yönetim Faaliyetleri, 22 Temmuz 2007 7 Nisan 2011, Türkiye Büyük Millet Meclisi 24. Dönem 4. Yasama Yılı Faaliyet Raporu, 1 Ekim 2013–10 Eylül 2014 and Yapıcı-Kaya, 2019, Figures 18, 20, 22, and 24.

* 22nd (2002–2007), 23rd (2007–2011), 24th (2011–2015), 26th (2015–2018), and 27th periods (2018–July 31, 2020). The 25th period (June–November 2015) was a short-lived parliament therefore excluded from the analysis.
** These committees basically serve as secondary committees.
*** Note: Workload inclusive only of primary committees.

National Education (one), and Petition (two); in the 26th period a total of 16: Constitution (one), Health (one), Human Rights (three), Industry (one), Interior (one), National Education (one), and Petition (eight); while in the 27th period only six: Foreign Affairs (one), Human Rights (two), and Petition (three). Committees may examine separate bills together if they are relevant. However, committees cannot initiate a new bill or divide and examine a bill in separate texts. Eventually the primary committee may accept the bill in its original form, partially amending it, or rejecting it. The committees submit their reports to the Office of the Speaker with a general and article-by-article reason of statement including dissenting opinions (minority reports). During the plenary debates the committees may withdraw an article when the plenary approves an amendment with which the committee disagrees. Before the final voting on a bill in the plenary, the primary committee may withdraw the bill as a whole or part only once (see Figure 15.1).

Until the 23rd legislative period (2011–2015), the Office of the Speaker referred all bills which had a financial component to the Plan and Budget Committee as the primary committee, and other committees as secondary ones with their specialization. Therefore, the PBC dominated the legislative process, playing the role of a 'shadow ministry' in scrutinizing the governmental drafts. Currently, the bills are referred to the committees by considering their substance only (see Table 15.4).

Committees may start debating the matters referred to them only 48 hours after the date of referral and complete their reports within 45 days (RoP, Articles 36 and 37). This timeframe should enable committee members to comprehend, debate, and prepare a detailed report on the draft bill. Theoretically, committees have the potential to prepare their final reports on individual bills independent of the executive power. However, the president, as the leader of the majority party in the GNAT, can influence the committees' chairpersons in setting the agenda and drafting the committees' final reports. Since the beginning of the current 27th period, the standing committees completed 57 reports on individual bills, excluding the draft budgets, international treaties, inquiry reports, immunity reports, amendments to the RoP, and a five-year development plan. All of them were submitted by majority-party MPs, except for one, which was a joint bill of all party groups on the 'State Cemetery'.

Recently, the majority party frequently requests that the GNAT's consultative council, composed of the deputy-chairs of party groups under the Speaker, which basically set the plenary agenda (order of the things), may decide to take the committee report onto the agenda without the 48-hour waiting requirement (RoP, Article 52), which undermines the effective deliberation in the committees and quality of the legislation. If there is no unanimity among the members of the council, the plenary decides on this matter. This is not formalized but considered to be a de facto amendment to the RoP. The constitutional court did not annul this practice (Bakırcı et al. 2020: 323). For example, the draft bill amending Military Service Law was adopted by the GNAT without regard to this requirement in July 2018.

Turkey's Grand National Assembly 273

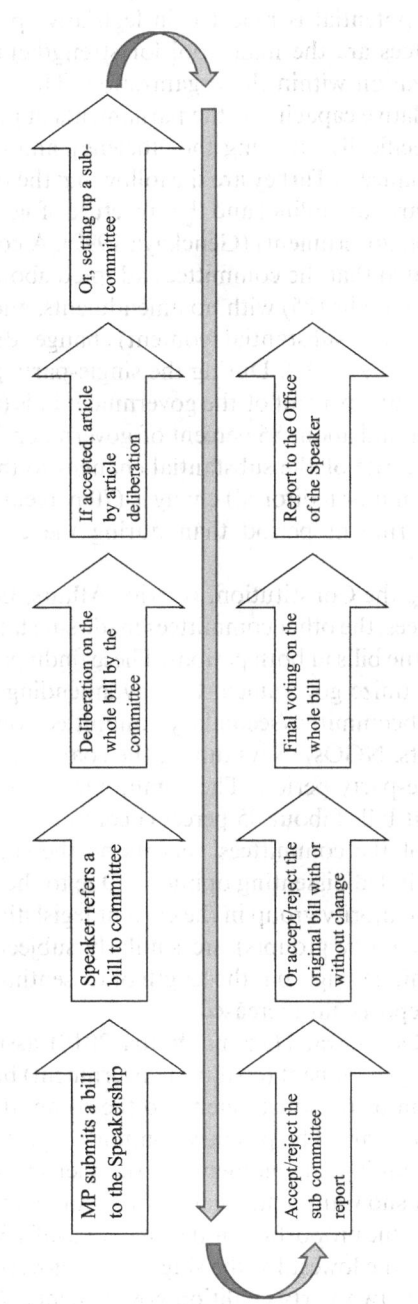

Figure 15.1 Flow of law-making in the committees in Turkey (since July 2018).

As committees have the means of collecting information, they can enhance legislative capacity by developing policy expertise. However, they cannot guarantee that this potential is reflected in legislative performance (Yüksel 2019). The committees are the main tool for strengthening the division of labour and specialization within the organization. There are several factors influencing the legislative capacity of the parliaments in general (Arter 2006). The two factors specifically affecting the efficiency and effectiveness of the committees' performance in Turkey are the following: the party group (leadership structure and party discipline) and the structure of government (majority government/coalition government) (Gençkaya 1999). A comparative analysis (Bektaş 2018) indicated that the committees adopted about 30 percent of the government-sponsored bills (25) with no amendments, and 60 percent of the government bills (51) with substantial (content) changes during the coalition-government period (1999–2002). During the single-party government period (2011–2015) only about 7 percent of the government bills (four) were adopted with no amendments and about 86 percent of government bills (54) with substantial changes. The rate of the substantial changes to the government bills were generally more minor (editorial) changes (70 percent) during the single-party majority government period than during the coalition-government period (36.5 percent).

Overall, excluding the Constitution, Interior Affairs, Education, Defence, and Health committees, the other committees made substantial amendments – over 70 percent – to the bills in both periods. These findings may prove that the committees can scrutinize government bills by amending them substantially and included the subcommittee/secondary committee contributions and the stakeholders' (experts, NGOs) views during the coalition-government period more than the single-party period. The committees' reports on single-party majority government bills (about 85 percent) contained dissenting opinions, yet only one-third of the committees' reports on the coalition government bills (33 percent) included dissenting opinions. Due to the increasing irreconcilable stance of the majority group in the current legislative 27th period, bills supported by the majority group(s) are similarly subject to more editorial changes in the committee stage, but the length of dissenting opinions attached to the committees' reports has increased.

Another study (Gençkaya, Hazama & İba 2018) assumed that not the number of parties in government (coalition government) but the majority size affects the proportion of the amendments to the committee's final report on the draft bill in the plenary. The primary committee, party groups, and individual deputies can initiate amendments in the plenary stage. The findings of this study did not show any statistical relationship between the number of governing parties and the proportion of the amended bills. While the mean rate of amended bills was the lowest for the single-party governments, the highest rate was found for the two-party coalition governments. While the ratio of a minor and substantial amendment to the selected bills in the committee stage was about 70 percent during the coalition period (1999–2002), the ratio of amendments adopted by the plenary was 26 percent for the same period. In other words, it can be said that committee autonomy is more likely under a coalition government when and if the coalition parties are committed to a reliable coalition protocol especially.

Since 2007 (23rd period), the majority and opposition parties have not sought reconciliation in the committees. Especially in recent years, bills have not been discussed by the committee(s) at length. The recent case of the Bill on Amendments to the Attorneys' Act and Some Laws was submitted to the Office of the Speaker on June 30, 2020 has been a typical example of this (Bianet, 2020). The committee debated the bill over 52 hours. A total of 296 deputies expressed their concerns and 1,255 pages with the dissenting opinions to the draft bill were recorded.

Reconsideration of a bill by the primary committee or the plenary

The primary committee may reconsider any part of the bill only once before submitting its final report. The distribution of the printed committee report to the MPs shows that the report is tabled on the plenary agenda and ready for plenary debate.

The deliberation of a bill in the plenary follows an order similar to the committee stage. The committees are seated to the right of the Bureau of the Assembly and are represented by their chairperson, deputy chairperson, or spokesperson(s) who have been particularly assigned for that duty in the plenary. The absolute majority of the plenary may decide to vote on the committee's text upon the primary committee's request without debating the motions of amendments on a specific article raised in the plenary. If the committee's text is adopted, it is deemed that the motions are rejected. During the plenary stage, the primary committee can propose unlimited motions of amendments on each article, party groups can propose one amendment for each article, and all individual MPs can raise only seven motions of amendment for each article. Subsequently, the motions are voted separately by show of hands.

Reconsideration of a bill by the primary committee as a whole or by article can be possible under certain circumstances. First, the primary committee may withdraw the whole of the bill or a few articles together with the motions of amendments submitted during the plenary before the motions are voted upon, and then either revises the bill accordingly or insists on its previous text. Second, the primary committee is obliged to withdraw and reconsider the whole text if the plenary rejects the committee's rejection report. Third, when the plenary accepts a motion of amendment on the article with which the committee disagrees, the primary committee may withdraw an article and either revises it or insists on its original text. Finally, before the final vote on the whole of a bill, the primary committee may request the reconsideration of a specific article – excluding debates on constitutional amendments – in the plenary. From the 22th legislative period until the end of 26th period, a total of 44 reconsiderations were initiated, more than half (23) took place during the 22nd period where 80 percent of deputies were newly elected and sought a more 'democratic and consensus-oriented culture' (Bakırcı et al. 2020: 480). Nevertheless, in a plenary-oriented parliament, the final decision rest with the majority in the plenary.

Considering the decrease in the number of committee meetings and the number of committee reports (see Table 15.4 above) especially since 24th period, it can be concluded that 'the [majority of] the GNAT has carried out only the procedural work at the committee stage for the agenda it envisages becoming law' (Bakırcı 2018) without deliberating the bill in depth. In other words, the GNAT sets the agenda with the requirement of the executive, and therefore, Parliament's ability to make public policy independently and spontaneously on social needs stays in the background.

The committee member who has signed the committee report cannot ask any questions to the spokesperson or make a statement contrary to the committee's report in other committees or in the plenary, except about the points in the committee report they have objected to or abstained from in writing (Çeliker 2006: 160). During the 21st period, the Committee on Industry, Commerce, Natural Resources, Information, and Technology added few financial provisions to the bill in favour of the public servants concerned. When the speaker did not take any action against this favour, the chairperson of the PBC, as the secondary committee, took the floor in the plenary and warned that such practices would harm Parliament. Therefore, issuing minority reports allows committee members to inform the plenary and the public of their dissenting opinions and thus increases the level of saliency of the government's proposal.

Committees are obliged to keep a synopsis of the meeting minutes. However, a committee may decide to record verbatim minutes. The committee members who are present can attach their dissenting statements to the minutes. The Plan and Budget Committee keeps full minutes, which are publicly available. The Office of the Speaker publishes committee bulletins twice a year. The current stages of the matters referred to the committees, withdrawn by the committees from the plenary, or given back to the committees by the plenary, are stated in the bulletin. The bulletin is attached to the plenary minutes (Article 47).

Committees cannot deal with works other than those referred to them. There is some evidence that parliamentary inquiry committees and even subcommittees sometimes go outside Ankara – domestic or international – for on-site inspections (Meclis Haber 2005).

Expedited legislative process: guillotine motion (*temel kanun*) and omnibus law (*torba kanun*) methods

The method of 'guillotine motion' (basic law, *temel kanun*) was first introduced by the amendment to the RoP in 1996. The constitutional court annulled it several times and then the current provision was adopted by the GNAT in 2005. The RoP (Article 91) describes 'basic law' as aiming at shortening the duration of plenary debates and keeping the coherence of the laws when an amendment is needed in those laws. Thus, with the proposal of the government, the essential committee or party group(s), and the advice of the consultative council of the GNAT, the plenary of the GNAT decides on this special procedure. In theory, this method should encourage the committees' initiative in deliberating the bills and increase efficiency in the plenary debates. This method was first used for the mandatory amendments to be made in major laws in 1990 and then by the majority of governments in order to shorten the legislative processes. Parliament was turned into a 'law factory', yet the actual performance of laws is open to question (Bakırcı 2016) (see Table 15.5).

Laws that are not related to each other and amend a large number of other laws can be called 'omnibus laws' (bag law, *torba kanun*). The number of

Table 15.5 Practices of guillotine and omnibus law methods in Turkey

Legislative Periods	Special Law-making Methods			
	Guillotine Motion	*Omnibus Law*	*Guillotine Motion + Omnibus Law*	*GM+OL/ Total Number of Adopted Bills*
24th Period (November 28, 2011–April 4, 2015)				
1st Legislative Year	-	-	-	118/542
2nd Legislative Year	25	15	40	21.8%
3rd Legislative Year	25	10	35	
4th Legislative Year	15	10	25	
5th Legislative Year	12	6	18	
26th Period (November 17, 2015–May 16, 2018)				
1st Legislative Year	18	10	28	67/544
2nd Legislative Year	12	10	22	12.3%
3rd Legislative Year	3	14	17	
27th Period (July 7, 2018– July 31, 2020)				
1st Legislative Year	-	2	2	52/209
2nd Legislative Year	6	15	21	24.8%
3rd Legislative Year	4	19	23	
4th Legislative Year	2	4	6	
Average of 3 Periods (%)				19.63

Source: Data for the 24th and 26th periods were compiled by the author from Yüksel, 2018, Table 1 and Figure 1, pp. 199–218; for 27th period (as of December 31, 2020) date were compiled by the author from www.tbmm.gov.tr/develop/owa/kanunlar_sd.sorgu_baslangic (access: 01.09.2020).

Explanation: The 25th period (June–November 2015) was a short-lived parliament therefore excluded from the analysis. However, a total of 323 government drafts including remaining drafts from the previous periods, and 535 individual bills were initiated, yet none was examined.

laws which are amended by an omnibus law varies between two and 76, and averages more than ten. This method disables the conventional committee deliberation. Moreover, the number of articles increases exponentially in the committee process (İba 2011). During the last three legislative periods (24th, 26th, and 27th), an average of 20 percent of total bills were adopted using either omnibus law or guillotine motion.

The party group's extraordinary status in the Constitution (especially Article 95) and the RoP, strong party discipline, closed-list proportional representation, and leadership domination hinder the effectiveness of legislative performance of individual MPs with insufficient legislative experience (Kim et al. 1984; Kalaycıoğlu 1995; Hazama 2005). The structural (fixed number of members, permanent tenure, specialization, and subcommittees) and procedural (a proportional distribution of seats, proportional chair selection, public meetings, minority reports, and preceding plenary stage) powers assigned to them (rewriting bills, control of its agenda, summon ministers, summon stakeholders, and demand documents) hinder Parliament's autonomy vis-à-vis the executive (Bektaş 2018). Majority parties use parliamentary committees strategically; at the outset they give the impression that they are looking for a consensus in a structure where the majority can decide ultimately yet they adopt their own text without any change.

Communication, cooperation, and coordination between standing committees

As underlined earlier, committees may directly correspond with any ministry and request necessary information from ministries to conclude the matters referred to them. However, relations between the primary committees and the secondary committees are not always effective. If the primary committee submits its report, in many cases, the secondary committee does not prepare any report at all. This situation can be interpreted in the way that intercommittee cooperation, coordination, and communication are not effective, and the primary committees dominate. In fact, the speaker is entitled 'to oversee the committees of the GNAT; to warn the chairpersons and members of the committees and inform the plenary in case of a backlog in the committees' (RoP, Article 14/6). Neither the administrative strategic plan of the GNAT (TBMM 2018) nor the annual press statements of the speaker refer to such issues.

Oversight committees

Petition Committee

The right to petition was introduced by the 1961 Constitution and extended to resident foreigners in Turkey, with the condition of observing the principle of reciprocity in international law by the 2001 constitutional amendments

(Constitution Article 74). Individuals, including public officials, can submit their requests and complaints to the GNAT, independent of judicial and administrative remedies.

The Petition Committee has existed in the parliamentary system since the 1876 Constitution and was established by a special law. The scope of its activities includes examining complaints and notifying the relevant public authorities for the necessary actions. The processing of the petitions takes three stages. These are the initial review phase (review of the chairperson's board composed of the chairperson, secretary member, and spokesperson of the committee), the committee's review phase, and the plenary review phase. The committee's decisions are not binding, but it can inspect the operations of the public administrations in terms of legality as well as propriety. Starting from 2016, the committee has kept full minutes of the meetings and processes, receiving and responding to the petitions electronically. The distribution of responded-to and received petitions for the 22nd through to the 26th periods is 11,679 of 12,447 (22nd period), 9,015 of 9,123 (23rd), 4,597 of 9,908 (24th), and 15,906 of 16,030 (25th).

Public Economic Enterprises Committee

In accordance with Article 165 of the Constitution and Law No. 3346, the Public Economic Enterprises Committee, which is responsible for auditing the public economic enterprises, performs its oversight function through the audit reports prepared by the court of accounts. The main committee evaluates the reports by the subcommittees and makes decisions about the public institutions. During the February 24, 2019–July 27, 2020 period, three main and 34 subcommittees were set up, and the audit reports of 74 public economic enterprises for 2018–2019 periods were examined by the Public Economic Enterprises Committee in 37 meetings.

Ad hoc committees for supervision

The GNAT is entitled to obtain information from and conduct supervision of the executive by means of a parliamentary inquiry, general debate, parliamentary investigation, and written questioning (Constitution, Article 98, 105; RoP, Articles 96–114). Written questions are parliamentary questions that are put to the Speaker of the GNAT, the deputy president, and ministers in writing by MPs. Two other mechanisms enable an in-depth investigation of a particular issue. First, a parliamentary *inquiry* is an examination conducted to obtain information on a specific subject. Second, a parliamentary *investigation* is an investigation concerning the president, the deputy president, and the ministers. The constitutional amendment of 2017 introduced the criminal liability of the president, the deputy president, and the ministers, yet it is subject to qualified majorities which are practically impossible (Constitution, Article 105 and RoP, Article 114). The GNAT's control of the executive

Table 15.6 Motions of parliamentary supervision in Turkey

Legislative Periods	22nd	23rd	24th	26th	27th
Parliamentary Inquiry Received	434	1,100	3,309	2,828	3,365
Accepted	65	134	115	66	50
Committee Report Debated	20	12	4	5	0
Parliamentary Investigation Received	13	3	13	2	0
Accepted	7	0	1	0	0
Committee Report Debated	7	0	0	0	0

Source: Compiled by the author from www.tbmm.gov.tr/develop/owa/meclis_sorusturma_onergeleri.sorgu_donem?d

Explanation: The 25th period (June–November 2015) was a short-lived parliament therefore excluded from the analysis. However, a total of 104 motions of parliamentary inquiry were initiated yet none was examined.

has been declining (see Table 15.6). Unless the majority parties support the motions of supervision, these mechanisms seem to be obsolete.

Parliamentary inquiry committees

Committees of inquiry were first established during the 1867 constitutional period of the Ottoman state and became a part of the parliamentary system of the republican period since the 1924 Constitution. The political party groups, or at least 20 deputies, may request the opening of an inquiry and the plenary decides to set up an inquiry committee, which consists of MPs proportionally to the strength of parties. The number of members of the committee is proposed by the speaker and the plenary decides on it. The committee completes its report in three months and an additional one-month term.

The parliamentary inquiry committee has the authority to request information from, carry out inquiries and obtain information by, inviting the relevant personnel of ministries and other public institutions, including professional organizations having the characteristics of public institutions and associations working in favour of public interest. State secrets and commercial secrets are excluded from the scope of a parliamentary inquiry.

Starting from the 22nd period through the 26th period in which the Justice and Development Party controlled the majority in the parliament, the number of accepted motions of parliamentary inquiry and the deliberation of the inquiry committees' reports dropped sharply (see Table 15.6). About 70 percent of 41 reports of parliamentary inquiry committees which were deliberated by the plenary, dealt with violations of state governed by the rule of law, such as legal security, prevention of arbitrary administration, and protection of fundamental rights (Güzel 2019). As of July 2020, none of the 46 parliamentary inquiry committees completed their reports during the current

27th period. In other words, the majority explicitly hinder the effectiveness of parliamentary inquiry.

Parliamentary investigation committees

The motion of parliamentary investigation against the president and deputy president and ministers, former prime ministers, and ministers shall be tabled by the absolute majority of members of the GNAT. Although the deputy president and ministers are responsible to the president, they are at the same time subject to parliamentary investigation 'on allegations of perpetration of a crime regarding their duties'. As mentioned, initiating a parliamentary investigation, setting up an investigation committee and approving the committee's report to send the relevant person to the supreme court for trial, are subject to qualified majorities. Only the president can address the plenary before voting on setting up an investigation committee.

A parliamentary investigation committee consists of 15 MPs who are selected by drawing lots among the candidates of each of the political parties in the parliament. The parties nominate three times the number of members they are allocated to the committee in proportion to their size. The quorum for convening and decision is the absolute majority of members.

The activities of the committee are confidential. Political party groups cannot make binding decisions regarding a parliamentary investigation. The duration of the investigation committee is limited to two months from its establishment and can be extended for another two months.

In addition to the powers of the inquiry committee, an investigation committee can organize hearings on the president, deputy president and ministers, other people concerned, witnesses and experts, and may also seek assistance from judicial authorities. The president and other individuals concerned can defend themselves before the committee. If necessary, the committee may decide to establish subcommittees.

The deliberation on the report is put into the plenary agenda within ten days after its distribution to the MPs. During the debate, the floor is given to the committee, six deputies on behalf of themselves and the president, deputy president or minister concerned. They have the right to address to the plenary without any time limitation. The plenary decides on the committee report through secret ballot with a two-thirds majority.

During the 22nd period, the motions of parliamentary investigations about a former prime minister and seven former ministers were accepted, and they were referred to the supreme court by the plenary, yet one motion of investigation about corruption affairs of four ministers during the 24th period was rejected by the majority in plenary pursuant to the investigation committee's report (Turan 2018). Due to the qualified majorities set by the constitutional amendments and the RoP after 2018, no motion of parliamentary investigation was submitted, and this oversight mechanism is null in practice.

Joint committees

Joint committees were typical during the 1961 Constitutional period (1961–1980), during which the GNAT was a bicameral parliament: National Assembly and Senate.

Two standing committees dealing with oversight function, namely the Human Rights Investigation Committee and the Petition Committee, established eight joint committees since 2011 – three in the 24th period, three in the 26th period, and two in the 27th period. The joint Petition and Human Rights Investigation Committee nominates candidates from among the applicants for seven memberships of the council of judges and prosecutors who shall be elected by the plenary. Furthermore, the joint committee nominates three candidates for the chief ombudsman to be elected by the plenary, and selects ombudsmen directly from among the applicants.

The joint committee of the Constitution and Justice Committees commonly examines the matters related to the Constitution and the RoP. During the 26th period, two joint committees of these committees were established. Requests for lifting the immunity of an MP (Constitution Article 83) shall be examined by the Joint Committee of the Constitution and Justice Committees. To examine the immunity files, the chairperson of the joint committee elects a preparatory committee by lot, consisting of five members. The chairperson and a secretary who shall also act as a spokesperson, are elected by secret ballot. This committee examines all documents and, if necessary, hears the MP concerned, but cannot hear a witness. The committee submits its report within one month at the latest. The joint committee recommends whether to lift the immunity or defer the prosecution until the end of legislative term. The MP concerned has the right to defend him/herself, at the preparatory committee, the joint committee and the plenary. As of July 2020, the number of MPs concerned in lifting the immunities for the last six legislative periods is as follows: 152 in 22nd, 160 in 23rd, 197 in 24th, 87 in 25, 187 in 26th, and 184 in 27th (TBMM, 2020b).

If an MP holds an office incompatible with membership contrary to the Constitution (Articles 82 and 84), the Bureau of the Assembly first examines the case and then sends the file to the joint committee comprised of the members of the Constitution and Justice committees. The joint committee examines the situation in line with the procedures on lifting legislative immunities and draws up a report which shall be debated and voted by the plenary.

Other ad hoc committees

Inter-party reconciliation committees have become a common practice since 2000. Three committees of this kind were established to amend the Constitution in 2001, 2009, and 2016 (Meclis Haber, 2001, TBMM, nd.;

Meclis Haber 2016). The last two did not bring a productive outcome. Another reconciliation committee for RoP was formed by the vice-chairmen of the party groups in October 2008 and submitted its preliminary report in February 2009 (TBMM 2009), yet no comprehensive reform has been completed since then.

A special ad hoc democracy committee was established to promote more effective and participatory work of the GNAT and to get the opinions of NGOs, various segments of society, and citizens in 2005 (Meclis Haber 2005).

Concluding remarks

There are important issues regarding the performance and quality of the committees' work (Bektaş 2018; Yüksel 2018). First of all, immature bills are submitted to Parliament in the form of individual proposals. Second, the committees' deliberations are concluded without sufficient and qualified debates. However, the legislative drafts are being improved by several motions of amendments in the plenary.

From the perspective of the individual MPs, several factors affect members' behaviour and attitudes in the committees and plenary. Until the current 27th period the inclusion of third parties such as subcommittees, non-committee members, and government representatives increased the likelihood of substantial amendments to government drafts and individual bills. Similarly, the presence of the relevant minister in the committee meeting enabled the MPs to become more informed and able to make necessary changes by relying not only on written information.

It is obvious that until recently some actors of the committees – the chairman and the senior members – play a critical role in 'maturing' the bills at the committee stage. Although there is no formal post-legislative scrutiny or regulatory impact-assessment mechanisms (SGI 2019), committees scrutinize government bills retrospectively. Thus, for example, the Plan and Budget Committee examines the performance of the previous year's public financial accounts, at least procedurally. Promoting the oversight function of the existing committee and/or establishing a separate Public Accounts Committee is a vital need.

Majoritarian rule in the committees as well as in the plenary encourages members of the majority party to maintain their party's discipline and demonstrate it to the public. In this respect, the ratio of 'killing' bills submitted by opposition MPs at the committee stage gradually increased, indicating the dominance of parliamentary majority. Therefore, rewriting or amending the RoP and making them compatible with the new presidential system may include a qualified majority for all procedures. The principle of equal representation and assigning opposition MPs to chair positions especially in the oversight committees may enhance the committees' autonomy in terms of oversight function.

Notes

1 Inspired from the French system the term 'yasama komisyonu' (parliamentary commission) is used since the 1961 Constitutional Period.
2 For the list of unreported bills see, www.tbmm.gov.tr/develop/owa/komisyonlar_sd.calismalar?p_kom_kod=14&p_islem=1 (access: 23.09.2020).

References

Akkuş, C. (2020). Türkiye'de Sivil Toplum Kuruluşlarının Yasama Sürecine Katılımı. Basılmamış Yüksek Lisans Tezi. Sosyal Bilimler Enstitüsü, İstanbul: Marmara Üniversitesi.
Arter, D. (2006). Introduction: Comparing the legislative performance of legislatures. *Journal of Legislative Studies*, 12 (3–4), 245–257.
Bakırcı, F. (2016). Yasama Sürecinin Hızlandırılması ve Sakıncaları, In Y. Üner (Yay. Haz.), *Kanun Yapma Tekniği* (21–61). TBB Yayınları.
Bakırcı, F. (2018). The committees in the Turkish Parliament: Existing problems and solutions after 2017 constitutional reform. *The Eurasia Proceedings of Educational & Social Sciences*. 11, 198–227.
Bakırcı, F., Gençkaya, Ö.F., Ergül, O., Kılıç, A., Aslan, G.A., Işık, S. & Yüksel, İ. (2020). *Parlamento Hukukuna Giriş*. Lykeion.
Bektaş, Ü.E. (2018). The role of legislative committees in parliamentary governments' accountability: A comparative analysis of the United Kingdom and Turkey. Unpublished Ph.D. dissertation. Ankara: İhsan Doğramacı Bilkent University.
Bianet (2020, July 8). Government wants to profile the entire legal system with the bill on multiple bars. *Bianet*. Retrieved from http://bianet.org/english/politics/226994-government-wants-to-profile-the-entire-legal-system-with-the-bill-on-multiple-bars?bia_source=rss (access: 29.10.2020).
Çeliker, E. (2006). Türkiye'de Yasa Yapma Süreci. Yayımlanmamış Yüksek Lisans Tezi. Ankara: Türkiye ve Orta Doğu Amme İdaresi Enstitüsü.
Devereux, R. (1963). *The first Ottoman constitutional period*. Baltimore, MD: The John Hopkins University Press.
Gençkaya, Ö.F. (2020). The Grand National Assembly of Turkey: Decline in legislative capacity. In I. Khmelko, R. Stapenhurst & M. L. Mezey (eds.) *Legislative decline in the 21st Century a comparative perspective* (82–93). Routledge.
Gençkaya, Ö.F. (1999). Reforming parliamentary procedure in Turkey. In Ö.F. Gençkaya, R. Keleş & Y. Hazama, *Aspects of democratization in Turkey* (2–21). Institute of Developing Economies.
Gençkaya, Ö.F. (1990). The impact of organizational attributes on legislative performance. Unpublished Ph.D. dissertation. Istanbul: Bogaziçi University.
Gençkaya, Ö.F., Hazama, Y. & İba, Ş. (2018). *Parties, seats and legislative outcomes in Turkey, 1991–2004*. Unpublished manuscript.
Güzel, M.N. (2019). Meclis Araştırması ve Görüşülen Meclis Araştırma Komisyonu Raporlarının Hukuk Devleti İlkesi Bakımından Değerlendirilmesi. Yayımlanmamış Doktora Tezi. Diyarbakır: Dicle Üniversitesi.
Hazama, Y. (2005). Constituency service in Turkey: a survey on MPs. *European Journal of Turkish Studies*, 3.

İba, Ş. (2004). TBMM'nin Toplantı Düzeni Yönünden Kapalı[Gizli] Oturum Kavramı ve Türk Perlomento Tarihinde Kapalı Oturumlar. AÜSBFD, 59(3), 105–129.

İba, Ş. (2009). *Parlamento İçtüzük Metinleri Osmanlıdan Günümüze*. Türkiye İş Bankası Yayınları.

İba, Ş. (2011). Ülkemizde 'Torba Kanun ve "Temel Kanun" Uygulamaları. *Ankara Barosu Dergisi*, 1, 197–202.

Inter-Parliamentary Union (IPU), Women in Politics: 2019, Infographics, Retrieved from www.ipu.org/resources/publications/infographics/2019-03/women-in-politics-2019 (access: 27.05.2021).

Kalaycıoğlu, E. (1995). The Turkish Grand National Assembly: A brief inquiry into the politics of representation in Turkey. In Ç. Balım et al. (eds.), *Turkey: Political, social and economic challenges in the 1990s* (42–60). E.J. Brill.

Kim, C.L., Barkan, J.D., Turan, I & Jewell, M. E. (1984). *The legislative connection: The politics of representation in Kenya, Korea, and Turkey.* Durham, NC: Duke University Press.

Meclis Haber. (2016). *Anayasa Mutabakat Komisyonu*. Retrieved from https://meclishaber.tbmm.gov.tr/develop/owa/haber_portal.aciklama?p1=135640 (access: 29.10.2020).

Meclis Haber. (2005). *TBMM Demokrasi Komitesi Kuruldu*. www.tbmm.gov.tr/develop/owa/meclis_bulteni.bulten_sayfa?psayi=116&psayfa=43 (access: 29.10.2020).

Meclis Haber. (2001). *Anayasa değişikliği teklifi hazır*. Retrieved from www.tbmm.gov.tr/develop/owa/meclis_bulteni.sayfa?psayi=84&psayfa=7 (access: 29.10.2020).

Olson, D.M. and Mezey, M.L. (1991). Parliaments and public policy. In D.M Olson & M.L. Mezey (eds.), *Legislatures in the Policy Process the Dilemmas of Economic Policy* (1–24). Cambiridge: Cambridge University Press.

SGI. (2019). Turkey, key findings. *SGI*. Retrieved from www.sgi-network.org/2019/Turkey/Key_Findings (access: 29.10.2020).

TBMM. (2020a). İstanbul Miilletvekili Sezgin Tanrıkulu'nun yazılı sorusuna verilen yanıt. Retrieved from www2.tbmm.gov.tr/d27/7/7-28460c.pdf (access: 29.10.2020).

TBMM. (2020b). Mersin Milletvekili Alpay Antmen'in yazılı sorusuna verilen yanıt. Retrieved from www2.tbmm.gov.tr/d27/7/7-31167c.pdf (access: 29.10.2020).

TBMM. (2018). TBMM Başkanlığı İdari Teşkilatı 2018-2020 Stratejik Planı. Retrieved from www.sp.gov.tr/upload/xSPStratejikPlan/files/R4ADY+TBMM_SP_18-22.pdf (access: 29.10.2020).

TBMM. (2009). *TBMM İçtüzük Uzlaşma Komisyonu Tarafından Hazırlanan Tbmm İçtüzük Taslağı İle İlgili Açıklamalar*. www.tbmm.gov.tr/ictuzuk/taslak_2009/3_uzlasma_komisyonu_raporu.pdf (access: 29.10.2020).

TBMM. (nd.). *Anayasa ve İçtüzük*. https://anayasa.tbmm.gov.tr/tutanak.aspx (access: 29.10.2020).

Turan, H.C. (2018). Türk Parlamento Tarihinde Meclis Soruşturması ve Uygulamadaki Etkinliği (1982-2017). Yayımlanmamış Doktora Tezi, İstanbul: Galatasaray Üniversitesi.

Turan, İ. (2000). Parlamentoların Etkinliği ve Türkiye Büyük Millet Meclisi, In İ. Turan (Koor.), *TBMM'nin Etkinliği* (15–30). TESEV Yayınları.

Yapıcı-Kaya, H. (2019). Yasama komisyonları karşılaştırmalı bir inceleme. Basılmamış Doktora Tezi. Ankara: Ankara Üniversitesi.

Yüksel, İ. (2018). 1982 Anayasası'na Göre Türkiye Büyük Millet Meclisi'nin Kanun Yapma Yetkisi. Basılmamış Doktora Tezi. Ankara: İhsan Doğramacı Bilkent Üniversitesi.

Yüksel, N. (2019). Türkiye'de Yasama (Kanun Yapımı) Performancı Tartışmaları. *Yasama Dergisi*, 39, 131–197.

16 The role of legislative committees in the policy process
The case of the Ukrainian Parliament

Irina Khmelko, Oleksii Bruslyk and Liudmyla Vasylieva

The Ukrainian Parliament – Verkhovna Rada (Rada hereafter) – is one of the 15 post-Soviet legislatures that took on a path of democratic institutional reforms during the last decade of the 20th century. Rada was able to develop institutionally from a Soviet 'rubber stamp'-type institution into a legislative institution with vital policy roles (Khmelko 2010; Khmelko 2011; Paul, Kravchuk & Kuzio 1999; Pigenko, Wise & Brown 2002; Wise & Pigenko 1999). The development of committees capable of operating in a multiparty environment has been an important part of Rada's institutional evolution. Rada has succeeded in building an effective system of legislative committees where key deliberations could take place (Whitmore 2006; Khmelko & Pigenko 2010; Khmelko, Wise, & Brown 2010). However, the last decade brought significant changes to the policy-making power of parliaments around the world, and many legislatures have been losing influence to more powerful executives (Khmelko 2019; Khmelko, Stapenhurst & Mezey 2020). The research points to a connection between the overall strength of a legislature and the committee strength. Legislatures with effective committees usually assume active policy roles (Olson & Mezey 1991: 208). Therefore, it is important to discuss committee roles in the modern policy process in Ukraine. This chapter focuses on the Ukrainian legislative committees and analyses factors that influence a committee's decision-making process.

Institutional setting of committees

The policy process in Ukraine is a result of the interactions and influences of multiple policy actors, such as the legislature, the president, and governmental ministries. Rada is a unicameral legislature composed of 450 members serving four-year terms. Each four-year term is called a convocation. Rada began its present, the 9th, convocation in 2019. All legislators are usually members of different parliamentary party groups that are called factions.[1] Factions can be formed by members of multiple parties elected to parliament during that convocation. Factions then form a majority coalition. A legislator can join only one faction. In addition, each legislator serves on a committee. Finally, Rada has administrative support. Thus, the secretariat of Rada is an administrative

DOI: 10.4324/9781003106579-16

body where administrative staff perform organizational, legal, scientific, documentary, informational, expert and analytical, technical, and financial functions. In addition, each committee has its own secretariat that provides administrative support to a committee. The number of administrative staff for each committee usually ranges between ten and fifteen.

Rada factions are active in pursuing their policy objectives on the floor of the parliament and in its committees. As in most world parliaments, committees are internal working bodies of this legislature and are organizational units of this legislature where multiple policy actors are pursuing their agendas. As in many other parliaments, Ukrainian legislative committees work with draft laws before the floor, prepare those for plenary discussions, provide time and space for substantive policy discussions, and allow coordination of positions and finding consensus among different political groups.

In addition, Ukrainian committees are active in conducting legislative oversight of the executive branch. Committee oversight hearings can be televised, which allows people outside of Rada to follow committee work live. Committees have the power to oversee the work of ministries, and no government official wants to be on the list of those that a committee is investigating or questioning.

Multiple legal acts regulate the work of Rada's legislative committees. The Constitution of Ukraine has provisions on legislative committees and determines their functions. Specifically, Article 89 points to committee roles in legislative and oversight processes and stipulates that Rada forms committees from its members and then elects a committee leadership. In addition, Article 1 of the Law 'On Committees of the Verkhovna Rada of Ukraine' (hereafter Committee Law) names committees as organizational units entrusted with carrying out work on draft laws and preparation and preliminary consideration of issues related to the powers of the Verkhovna Rada of Ukraine.

The number of committees usually ranges between 23 and 29 (Table 16.1). During the first session of each convocation, the Ukrainian Parliament

Table 16.1 Number of legislative committees in Rada of Ukraine

Convocation (Electoral Period)	Dates	Number of Committees – at the beginning and the end of the convocation
1.	1990–1994	24/25
2.	1994–1998	23/23
3.	1998–2002	22/23
4.	2002–2006	24/24
5.	2006–2007	26/26
6.	2007–2012	28/28
7.	2012–2014	29/29
8.	2014–2019	27/27
9.	2019–present	23/present

establishes a system of its legislative committees, defines the subject area of their competence, approves staff, and determines the leadership of committees. The leadership of committees consists of chairpersons, first deputies, deputy chairperson, and secretaries.

Both the Rules of Procedure of Rada (hereafter RoP) and the Committee Law identify the quota principle in forming committees and selecting committee leadership. For example, if the number of factions is equal or larger than the number of parliament committees, each faction sends at least one representative to each committee. However, Rada exercises a lot of flexibility as to how to implement the quota principle in practice, and committee membership is not exactly proportional to the size of each party.

Committee assignment is of high value to legislators, which is evident by how contested committee assignments can become in Rada and conflicts and tensions that this process generates among factions at the beginning of each new convocation. It should be noted that the conflicts develop both inside the majority coalition among parties that form this majority as well as between the majority and the opposition[2] groups in Rada. Therefore, the process of determining the number, membership, and committee leadership is highly politicized in Rada and often becomes the subject of political bargaining.

Legislators have multiple demands on their time. Therefore, the priority that they give to committee assignments tells us about the importance of committees as influential organizational units in Rada. In other words, legislators would not fight over committee assignments and spend their time and political capital on getting assigned on committees in their areas of policy interests if committees were inconsequential, 'rubber stampers', and in general powerless organizational units.

Rada votes on the committee members on the plenary and uses an open roll-call vote. This list is usually approved by the Reconciliation Council of Factions.[3] At the same time, existing rules provide for certain safeguards that prevent the concentration of control over the activities of a committee in the hands of a particular political force. Thus, the existing rules require that the committee leadership may not all be members of the same faction (Article 82 of the Rada RoP and Article 6 of the Committee Law). The law also prohibits the election of the Speaker of Rada, his first deputy and deputy chairperson to parliamentary committees. It also prohibits leaders of factions from holding committee leadership positions.

Rada has made multiple changes in the rules that regulate committee work over the course of its post-communist history. For example, there are differences between rules regulating committee work during the 7th and 8th convocations. Thus, Rada committees of the 7th convocation could include no less than nine and no more than 30 legislators (Rada Resolution on Committees of the 7th Convocation). However, Rada committees of the 8th convocation could include no less than six and not more than 35 legislators. In addition, Rada of the 7th and 8th convocations differed in how the list of committees was approved. For example, Rada of the 7th convocation approved the list of parliamentary committees, their number, jurisdictions and management composition by a single resolution.[4] However, Rada of the 8th convocation had voted on multiple resolutions. One resolution approved the list of committees and committee sizes, and another resolution approved committee leadership.[5] In all convocations, the parliamentary majority has broad discretion in making decisions on committee membership and their leadership.

Committees are usually formed along policy lines. Some of these committees are directly related to the policy area of a ministry. For example, there are ministries and legislative committees that deal with environmental, economic, education, and many other policies. There are also complex committees that deal with multiple policy areas, and their policy expertise will correspond to multiple ministries. For example, Rada of the 9th convocation has established the Committee on Human Rights, Deoccupation and Reintegration of Temporarily Occupied Territories in Donetsk, Luhansk Regions and the Autonomous Republic of Crimea, National Minorities and Interethnic Relations that deals with policy issues that multiple ministries deal with. Table 16.2 provides details on policy connections between legislative committees and governmental ministries.

In addition, some committees are formed based on the functions that they perform, for example, such as the Committee on Rules of Procedure and Organization of Work of the Verkhovna Rada of Ukraine. This allows the Ukrainian committee system to address both policy issues as well as issues related to regulating the processes and procedures of committees and overall Rada work. In addition, forming a legislative committee along policy lines allows for specialization and professionalization of committee works. While serving on committees, committee members develop professional expertise in a particular policy area. This gives a legislative assembly the benefit of professional and policy expertise, which contributes to the overall strength of a legislative assembly. Some committees address industry-specific issues, and some are intersectoral committees. Table 16.2 summarizes the list of committees during the 9th convocation of Rada and provides information on the party affiliation of a chairperson of each committee as well as the corresponding ministry.

As Table 16.2 demonstrates, both members of the majority and opposition (minority) have committee leadership positions. Given that a majority has a significant number of seats in Rada, it is not surprising that the majority chairs most committees. However, the majority coalition does not have absolute control of committee work. This is because the majority coalition consists of multiple factions that differ in their views on many important policy issues and the leadership of each committee consists of members of different party groups.

Rada has the option of making changes to its committee system in response to new circumstances or tasks that may appear on its agenda during each convocation. Changes may include terminating its committee. Rules specify two main reasons for committee termination: if their size goes below the

Table 16.2 Committees of the Verkhovna Rada of Ukraine of the 9th convocation

Committee	Number of Committee Members	Committee Chairperson	Ministry
Committee on Agrarian and Land Policy	30	Sluga Narodu (Servant of People) majority[a]	Ministry of Economic Development, Trade and Agriculture of Ukraine
Committee on Anti-Corruption Policy	18	Sluga Narodu majority	Ministry of Finance of Ukraine Ministry of Justice of Ukraine Ministry of Internal Affairs
Committee on Budget	34	Sluga Narodu majority	Ministry of Finance of Ukraine
Committee on Humanitarian and Information Policy	17	Sluga Narodu majority	Ministry of Culture and Information Policy of Ukraine
Committee on Environmental Policy and Nature Management	18	Sluga Narodu majority	Ministry of Environmental Protection and Natural Resources of Ukraine
Committee on Economic Development	16	Sluga Narodu majority	Ministry of Economic Development, Trade and Agriculture of Ukraine
Committee on Energy, Housing and Utilities Services	24	Sluga Narodu majority	Ministry of Energy of Ukraine
Committee on Public Health, Medical Assistance and Medical Insurance	15	Sluga Narodu majority	Ministry of Health of Ukraine
Committee on Foreign Policy and Inter-Parliamentary Cooperation	14	Sluga Narodu majority	Ministry of Foreign Affairs of Ukraine
Committee on Ukraine's Integration into the European Union	9	European Solidarity, opposition	Ministry of Foreign Affairs of Ukraine
Committee on Youth and Sports	7	Batkivschina (Motherland), opposition	Ministry of Youth and Sports of Ukraine
Committee on National Security, Defence and Intelligence	18	Sluga Narodu majority	Ministry of Defence Ukraine

(*continued*)

Table 16.2 Cont.

Committee	Number of Committee Members	Committee Chairperson	Ministry
Committee on State Building, Local Governance, Regional and Urban Development	27	Sluga Narodu majority	Ministry of Development of Communities and Territories of Ukraine
Committee on Education, Science and Innovations	12	Sluga Narodu majority	Ministry of Education and Science of Ukraine
Committee on Human Rights, Deoccupation and Reintegration of Temporarily Occupied Territories in Donetsk, Luhansk Regions and the Autonomous Republic of Crimea, National Minorities and Interethnic Relations	16	Za maybutne (For the Future), opposition	Ministry of Reintegration of the Temporarily Occupied Territories, Ministry of Defence Ukraine
Committee on Legal Policy	22	Sluga Narodu majority	Ministry of Justice of Ukraine
Committee on Law Enforcement	25	Sluga Narodu majority	Ministry of Internal Affairs of Ukraine
Committee on Rules of Procedure, Parliamentary Ethics and Administration of Verkhovna Rada's Work	11	Sluga Narodu majority	
Committee on Freedom of Speech	5	Opoziciyna platforma Za zhyttia (Opposition Platform for Life), opposition.	Ministry of Justice
Committee on Social Policy and Protection of Veterans' Rights	9	Sluga Narodu majority	Ministry of Social Policy of Ukraine, Ministry of Veterans Affairs of Ukraine
Committee on Transport and Infrastructure	23	Sluga Narodu majority	Ministry of Infrastructure of Ukraine
Committee on Finance, Taxation and Customs Policy	34	Sluga Narodu majority	Ministry of Finance of Ukraine
Committee on Digital Transformation	10	Sluga Narodu majority	Ministry of Digital Transformation of Ukraine

a Sluga Narodu ('Servant of the People') a Ukrainian umbrella political party which was officially registered at the Ministry of Justice on March 31, 2018. In the 2019 Ukrainian parliamentary election the party won 254 seats out of 450.

limit for committee membership determined at the beginning of each convocation (Article 8 of the Committee Law), and if a committee fails to conduct three scheduled meetings (Article 43 of the Committee Law). Finally, Rada may form special commissions for the purpose of addressing new tasks that may appear on its agenda during each convocation (Constitution of Ukraine, Article 89).

Rada also uses a system of subcommittees. Usually, each committee has anywhere between four to nine subcommittees. Committee members are divided among subcommittees and work on assigned tasks with the subcommittee before the committee as a whole will start working on the issue. Each committee can decide on what and how many subcommittees they will form. Committees use an open voting system to approve a system of subcommittees by a majority vote and elect their chairpersons. Subcommittees are usually established with the explicit purpose of an in-depth and thorough analysis of some policy issues. This allows for more effective committee operations. Committees determine the policy area of its subcommittees. Each subcommittee has at least three members from the general committee members.

Actors in committees

Committee leadership plays an important role in the functioning of committees. As we discussed in the previous section, the appointment of committee leadership is regulated by existing laws and rules. However, Rada has certain discretion in the process of implementation of these rules. For example, Article 34 of the Committee Law stipulates that 'a committee consisting of not more than ten people should have one deputy chairperson, and a committee consisting of eleven to twenty persons should have the first deputy and deputy chairperson', and a committee with more than twenty members should have an extra deputy chairperson. However, nine committees had different compositions of leadership than outlined by law regarding the number of deputy chairperson of the committee. For example, in the 8th Rada, the Committee on Veterans, Combatants, Anti-Terrorist Operations, and People with Disabilities had only seven members, including a chairperson, a first deputy, and three deputy chairs when the law stipulates only a chair, deputy chair, and secretary.

There are additional challenges in forming committee leadership when legislators in committee leadership positions resign their Rada membership. This usually happens when they accept cabinet positions in government. When they resign, their committee leadership positions become vacant. For example, in six out of 27 Rada committees of the 8th convocation, as well as in the Special Control Commission on Privatization, positions remained vacant for more than three years. Their functions were performed by first deputies or regular committee members. This happened because of unresolved political conflicts among factions, which were unable to agree on the appointment of new chairs. This effectively left some committees without stable leadership and led to disorganization and an overall lack of planning in some committees.

The position of the chairperson is highly coveted by legislators because it brings them prestige and authority; it also has high value for parliamentary factions. This is because of the political influence that this position brings. A chairperson of a committee has significant powers in terms of organizing the work of the committee. Specifically, they may simply not put a draft law on the agenda for committee meetings, thereby putting it on what is called a 'pause'. The draft law may remain on this pause indefinitely. A chair can also prioritize some draft laws and move those ahead of the others. Furthermore, a chair carries out the general management of the secretariat of the committee, and, therefore, has significant control over administrative resources. For example, they instruct staffers on which draft law to work on. Moreover, a chair has significant control as to not only which draft law a committee will be working on, but also when. They also exercise influence in running the committee meetings. Additionally, committee chairs manage interactions with external policy actors and Rada leadership. Finally, committees are places where draft laws are discussed, debated, and the wording is finalized. Committees usually go line by line and article by article while working on a draft law. The power of committees to approve, edit, amend, or reject the wording of the draft law coupled with the powers of the committee chairperson, makes committees influential units in Rada.

Rada has the authority to remove any committee leader from a position of power based on their own demand or if they fail to perform their duties (Part 3 of Article 7 of the Committee Law). The practice of parliamentary work shows that factions have broad discretion in deciding who will be removed from the position of leadership, and this can be a politically or ideologically driven decision, but it can also be a result of a scandal or some other extraordinary situation. For example, on October 30, 2019, media outlets published correspondence between Bohdan Yaremenko, chairman of the Committee on Foreign Policy and Interparliamentary Cooperation, with a prostitute. The legislator was communicating with her during a plenary meeting. A scandal erupted, and Yaremenko was replaced by Oleksandr Merezhko as chairman. It should be noted that although factions are in a position to initiate the process of replacing a chairperson of a committee, they do not have full control over the decision-making process on this issue because their influence is limited by a general vote on the plenary that is required to replace a chair. The voting process on a plenary gives all factions an opportunity to influence the outcome of any attempt to remove a member from a leadership position. Therefore, although removing a chairperson from their position is possible, it is not an easy process because the replacement requires that Rada votes on the plenary and amends the original resolution on the approval of the personnel of the Rada. Committee chairpersons are influential actors in Rada.

Therefore, getting a majority vote on the plenary to replace a committee chairperson is not an easy task, even if a faction that originally wanted this person in this position of leadership and is now highly motivated to replace a chair. Therefore, this faction may fail in this process.

Rada rules also allow for changes in the personal composition of a committee. These changes can be a result of multiple factors, such as the election of a new member of the committee, recall of a member of the committee, or early termination of powers of a legislator. Article 84 or the Rada RoP stipulates that a legislator may request transfer to another committee by first getting the approval of the head of their faction and then writing to a speaker of Rada, who will then review the request and forward it for further consideration to the committee of interest to the legislator. The committee considers the petition and prepares a draft of a resolution that Rada will vote on in the plenary session. The principle of proportional and quota representation of parliamentary factions in committees is frequently at the centre of discussions in assigning members to committees. However, political considerations of different factions are important in this process as well.

Committee influence: an empirical analysis

The Ukrainian Parliament has been named as one of the largest European 'law spammers'[6] in Europe. For example, during the 8th convocation, 821 new draft laws were submitted to Rada, with 111 adopted by the end of the convocation. However, if we count all laws, amendments, and procedural acts that were submitted during this convocation, then the number comes to over 7,000 drafts filed in Rada. This creates an appearance of legislative activities to allow legislators to report to their electorate that they work tirelessly on their behalf. These draft laws are usually submitted by all three subjects of legislative initiative in Ukraine – legislators, the president, and the ministries. Legislators can be members of a parliamentary majority or opposition. All subjects of the legislative initiative have been actively exercising the right of legislative initiative in all convocations of post-communist Rada. These draft laws are submitted to the Rada secretariat, which is an administrative body of the Parliament. Then, the secretariat forwards it to the Speaker or Vice-Speaker, who then decide which draft law goes to which committee. They may send it to more than one committee, but they will appoint the main or what is called a 'profile' committee. This committee will take the lead but will also consult with other committees which may provide expertise on an issue that is in the policy area of their committee. For example, a draft law may predominantly concern industry but can also have an impact on the environment. Therefore, more than one committee needs to participate in preparing the draft law for the plenary discussion. On a plenary, the main committee will report the decision of the main committee, but they may have another person, a co-rapporteur from the other committee. The committee decision is usually an important predictor of the success or failure of a draft law on the plenary. The majority of draft laws supported by the profile committee are usually adopted on the plenary. However, a committee can give a negative evaluation of a draft law and come up with justification as to why Rada should vote against it. This usually has a very negative impact on a draft law's fate, and Rada is likely to 'kill' the draft law on the plenary. This is in addition to a committee putting a draft law on 'pause' and not bringing it to a plenary vote at all for an indefinite period of time. The average rate of a draft law becoming law in Rada is approximately 12 percent.

To further investigate the influence of committees on Rada's decision-making process and to gain additional insight into the decision-making process inside the committee, we collected data for this study from the official parliamentary database.[7] Specifically, the dataset is constructed by reviewing 1,002 amendments to six different draft laws. These six laws were selected to make sure we had two draft laws submitted by each of the subjects of legislative initiative in Ukraine. All of these draft laws were proposed and reviewed by committees during the 8th convocation of the Ukrainian parliament. A committee may adopt an amendment in full, partially, or as an edited version. The list below provides information on each of the six draft laws included in our dataset, including a subject of the legislative initiative and the number of amendments for each:

1 The draft law 5491 from 12.06.2016, adopted 03.23.2017 as the Law of Ukraine 'On Ukrainian Cultural Fund' (legislators) – 97 amendments.
2 The draft law 0915 from 11.27.2014, adopted 02.05.2015 as the Law of Ukraine 'On Voluntary Amalgamation of Territorial Communities' (ministries) – 82 amendments.
3 The draft law 7117 from 09.18.2017, adopted 11.14.2017 as the Law of Ukraine 'Draft Law on the Promotion of the Availability and Quality of Medical Service in Rural Areas' (president) – 125 amendments.
4 The draft law 8152 from 03.19.2018, adopted 06.21.2018 as the Law of Ukraine 'Draft Law on Currency' (president) – 291 amendments.
5 The draft law 5598, from 12.26.2016, adopted 06.08.2017 as the Law of Ukraine 'Draft Law on the Energy Efficiency Fund' (ministries) – 315 amendments.
6 The draft law 6010 from 02.01.2017, adopted 03.23.2017 as the Law of Ukraine 'Draft Law on Simplification of Procedures for Capitalization and Reorganization of Banks' (legislators) – 92 amendments.

Our analysis confirms that the success of a draft law in a committee is a strong predictor of the success of the draft law on the plenary. Thus, there is almost a perfect correlation of .910 between committee support of a draft law and a success of a draft law on the plenary. In other words, if a profile committee supports a draft law, then there is a very high probability of the success of a draft law on the plenary.

Given that committee decision is a strong predictor of the success of a draft law on the plenary, it is important to look at what factors predict successes or failures of a draft law inside of a committee. Therefore, we use this data to analyse the success of draft laws proposed by each of the three subjects of the legislative initiative. The premise here is that if draft laws proposed by one of the subjects of legislative initiative succeed at a higher rate on committees, then it could be a strong indicator that a committee is 'captured' or dominated by one subject of legislative initiative.

In addition, we control for extraneous factors that may influence the outcome. Thus, we include a few control variables that we believe may impact the rate of success of amendments in the committee. Each amendment was carefully reviewed regarding its impact on the bill in terms of whether it was a substantive or procedural amendment. Substantive amendments are those that have influence over the policy process. Procedural amendments are usually minor and include changes that make no policy difference but are of a more technical nature. For example, inserting a comma or making minor editorial changes to language are all examples of procedural amendments. The substantive significance of each amendment requires reviewing the initial proposal, changes presented in the amendment, and the final version incorporated in the bill. As in many cases, it is hard to assess the wording or technical subjects addressed in amendments. Therefore, each one of the 1,002 amendments was reviewed and deemed either substantive or procedural by three different experts (each holds a reputable degree in law in Ukraine) to minimize bias and avoid uncertainty.

Of the total of 1,002 amendments in our dataset, 440 (43.9 percent) were substantial. Each subject of the legislative initiative proposed both substantive and procedural amendments, with legislators proposing 17.5 percent of substantive amendments, the president proposing 51.8 percent of substantive amendments, and ministries were in between the president and legislators proposing 30.7 percent substantive amendments out of 440 total substantive amendments.

In addition, we control for majority coalition influence. Thus, we look at the rate of success of draft laws supported by the majority coalition. The expectation can be that the support of a majority coalition would allow for the success of a draft law on a plenary. Therefore, we look at what percentage of draft laws supported by the majority coalition have actually succeeded in the plenary.

Table 16.3 provides descriptive statistics for the total number of amendments proposed by each initiator and the number not voted on committees. Given the power of committees to 'kill' amendments by not voting on a draft, it is important to analyse what percentage of drafts proposed are not voted on.

Table 16.4 provides percentages for each category of committee decisions out of total proposed by each subject of legislative initiative (legislators, president, and ministries) as well as providing percentages of draft laws proposed by independent legislators, substantive draft laws, and those supported by the majority coalition.

Table 16.3 Draft laws submitted and not voted on in Ukraine by initiator

The subject of legislative initiative (Initiator of an amendment)	Total number proposed by each initiator (percentage)	Not voted on committees (percentage out of total by each initiator)
Government (ministries)	416 (41.5%)	99 (24.9%)
President	397 (39.6%)	176 (42.3%)
Legislators	189 (18.9%)	77 (40.7%)
Total	1002 (100%)	352 (35.1%)

Table 16.4 Committee decisions on substantive amendments in Ukraine by initiator

Committee Decision	Draft laws proposed by President	Draft laws proposed by ministries (Government)	Draft laws proposed by legislators
1) Not voted on committee	40.4%	26.1%	42%
a) Amendments adopted with some editorial changes	3.3%	18.1%	5.3%
b) Amendments adopted partially	9.8%	7.2%	3.2%
c) Amendments adopted in full	46.5%	48.5%	49.5%
2) Total adopted a+b+c (with some changes, partially or in full)	59.6%	74.2%	58%
N of substantive amendments by each draft initiator	228	135	77

The analysis demonstrates that more than 50 percent of substantive draft laws proposed by each of the three subjects of legislative initiative succeeded on committees either in full or partially, or with some amendments. All subjects of the legislative initiative have been active in proposing draft laws. Ministries seem to enjoy the larger percentage of overall adopted draft laws and the lowest percentage of laws not voted by a committee. However, this can be explained that ministries are entrusted with the implementation of laws. They frequently propose amendments that do not involve any highly polarizing and ideologically charged political issues that are a subject of a heated political debate in Ukraine. Instead, these address necessities of administrative work. These administrative issues are usually accepted by all as necessary for governing the country.

Finally, our analysis confirms that the majority coalition does not enjoy full control of committee work. Table 16.5 shows that 31 percent of draft laws supported by the majority coalition were not voted on committees. Committees adopted in full 53 percent of draft laws supported by the majority coalition, and the rest were adopted either with some editorial changes or partially.

Table 16.5 Support of majority coalition and committee decision in Ukraine

Committee decision	Percentage	Total number
Not voted	31.5%	352
Adopted with edits	9.3%	87
Adopted partially	6.2%	69
Adopted in full	53.0%	494
Total	100.0%	1,002

The majority coalition enjoyed a 69 percent total success rate of their drafts on committees (either in full or partially or with edits), which is slightly lower than the government but somewhat higher than for a president or legislators. However, the percentages are not far apart among all actors and support the conclusion that the Ukrainian policy process is a result of interactions and influences of multiple policy actors inside and outside of the Ukrainian Parliament.

Given that all subjects of legislative initiative enjoyed considerable successes on committees, it does not appear that committees serve as a 'rubber stamp' to any particular subject of legislative initiative or a majority coalition. They appear to be working bodies of this legislature that review draft laws and render decisions on some, but not necessarily all, draft laws. This corresponds to the qualitative part of our research and is in line with a theoretical argument on a 'gatekeeping' power a committee that can stop the draft law by not reviewing it or influence the policy process by working on it line by line and changing the wording, amending it or adopted it partially.

Conclusion

The purpose of the chapter was to discuss the system of legislative committees in the Ukrainian Parliament – Verkhovna Rada – to discuss their policy roles, and to investigate the role of different policy actors and their influence over the committee decision-making process. We have evaluated the Rada's committee system as it has been designed and discussed how institutional design and the modern institutional arrangements, laws, and rules manifest themselves in the observed legislative outcomes in terms of successes and failures of draft laws in passing the committee stage.

This study allows us to conclude that Rada's legislative committees are influential organizational units in the Ukrainian legislative process. The support of a profile committee is a strong predictor of the success of a draft law on the plenary. Heated debates over committee leadership selection and committee assignments are further evidence of the importance of committees in the decision-making process in Rada. In addition, committees have a gatekeeping power and can 'kill' a legislation. Committees also provide space for different parliamentary and external groups to negotiate policy details.

Committees can also exercise power by making changes in the wordings of draft laws. Finally, committees have an oversight power, which allows them an additional mechanism of influencing the policy process in Ukraine.

Our study concludes that the policy process in Ukraine is a result of the interactions of multiple policy actors. Thus, the Ukrainian government is an influential actor, and its drafts enjoy a somewhat higher rate of success on committees than those proposed by the other subjects of legislative initiative, but all policy actors have relatively high levels of success on committees, and no policy actor has a clear advantage there, and all policy actors have comparable rates of draft laws and amendments that the committees do not vote on. This study concludes that the influence of the majority coalition on the committee decision-making process is comparable to the other policy actors.

To conclude, committees are an essential part of the legislative process in Rada. Rada committees monitor ongoing governmental operations, identify issues suitable for legislative review, gather and evaluate information, and recommend courses of action to the plenary. Committee decisions are strong predictors of successes and failures of draft laws and amendments on the plenary. In general, legislative committees of the Ukrainian parliament are working bodies of this legislature that not only developed but also use multiple tools actively that allow them a significant influence in the policy-making process.

Notes

1 Faction is a group of members of a party and is a term used in literature on Post-Soviet parliaments and is similar to Parliamentary Part Groups (PPGs) in Western parliaments. In general, a parliamentary faction is an association of parliamentarians based on a common party interest.
2 Ukraine does not have a law on opposition, and therefore, Ukrainians use the term 'parliamentary minority' instead. However, for clarity and consistency of the volume we will use the term 'opposition' here.
3 Council of Factions is an advisory body consisting of representatives of all factions in Rada that is entrusted with preparation and consideration of organizational issues in Rada.
4 Rada Resolution on Committees of the 7th and 8th Convocations.
5 Resolution of the Verkhovna Rada of Ukraine on the Election of Committee Chairs, Deputy Chairs, First Deputy Chair, Committee Secretaries, and Members of Special Oversight Commission of the Verkhovna Rada on Questions of Privatization.
6 Ukrainian Parliament remains Europe's 'largest law spammer' – Voters Committee of Ukraine, 112 Ukraine, January 15, 2018, https://112.international/politics/ukrainian-parliament-remains-europes-largest-law-spammer-voters-committee-of-ukraine-24606.html (access: 05.01.2021).
7 Each draft law has a page on the official Rada website, which includes the first version of the draft law as it was registered in the parliament with supporting documents (explanatory note, comparative table, submission claim, etc.).

References

D'Anieri, P., Kravchuk, R., & Kuzio, T. (1999). *Politics and Society in Ukraine*. Westview Press.

Kitschelt, H. (1992). The formation of party systems in East-Central Europe. *Politics & Society*, 20(1), 7–51.

Khmelko, I. (2010). The institutionalization of parliaments in transitioning nations. *Journal of East European & Asian Studies*, 1(4), 475–503.

Khmelko, I.S. (2011). Internal organization of post-communist parliaments over two decades: Leadership, parties, and committees. *Journal of Legislative Studies*, 17(2), 193–214.

Khmelko, I. (2019). Decline in legislative powers and rise of authoritarianism. *PS: Political Science & Politics*, 52(2), 267–280.

Khmelko, I., & Pigenko, V. (2010). Committee system development in Eastern European legislatures: The case of Ukraine. *Journal of East European & Asian Studies*, 1(3), 383–399.

Khmelko, I.S., Pigenko, V.A., & Wise, C.R. (2007). Assessing committee roles in a developing legislature: The case of the Ukrainian Parliament. *Journal of Legislative Studies*, 13(2), 210–234.

Khmelko, I.S., Wise, C.R., & Brown, T.L. (2010). Committees and legislative strengthening: The growing influence of committees in Ukraine's legislative process. *Journal of Legislative Studies*, 16(1), 73–95.

Khmelko, I., Bruslyk, O, & Rakhimkulov, E. (2019). The rise of powerful executives: Comparing the Ukrainian and Russian Legislatures. *PS: Political Science & Politics*, 52(2), 269–270.

Khmelko, I., & Bonnal, M. (2020). Corruption and legislatures: Exploring perceptions of Ukrainian legislators. *Public Integrity*, 22(4), 344–359.

Khmelko, I., Stapenhurst, R., & Mezey, M.L. (eds.). (2020). *Legislative decline in the 21st Century: A comparative perspective*. Routledge.

Kuzio, T. (ed.). (1998). *Contemporary Ukraine: dynamics of post-Soviet transformation*. ME Sharpe.

Olson, D.M., & Mezey, M.L. (eds.). (1991). *Legislatures in the policy process: The dilemmas of economic policy* (Vol. 8). Camridge: Cambridge University Press.

Pigenko, V., Wise, C.R., & Brown, T.L. (2002). Elite attitudes and democratic stability: analysing legislators' attitudes towards the separation of powers in Ukraine. *Europe-Asia Studies*, 54(1), 87–107.

Whitmore, S. (2006). Challenges and constraints for post-Soviet committees: exploring the impact of parties on committees in Ukraine. *Journal of Legislative Studies*, 12(1), 32–53.

Wise, C.R., & Pigenko, V. (1999). The separation of powers puzzle in Ukraine: sorting out responsibilities and relationships between President, parliament, and the prime minister. P. D'Anieri, R.S. Kravchuk & T Kuzio (eds.), *State and Institution Building in Ukraine*, New York: St. Martin's Press, 25–55.

17 Still deviant?

The development and reform of the UK House of Commons committee system (1979 to present)

Stephen Holden Bates, Louise Thompson, Mark Goodwin, and Stephen McKay

The UK committee system has idiosyncrasies that have led to it being described as a 'deviant case' in comparison to committee systems elsewhere (Mattson & Strøm 1995). The most important element of this deviancy is the operation of two distinct committee systems: select committees (SCs) mainly carry out scrutiny and hold government to account, while general committees, of which the most important are public bill committees (PBCs), work on legislation. A second element is the weak formal powers of committees and, particularly with regard to PBCs, their lack of independence from government. Neither type of committee is able to initiate legislation and SCs cannot propose legislative amendments; neither can they compel witnesses to attend (although most do attend in practice); membership of PBCs is determined by party managers; both types usually have an in-built government majority; the government is not required to act on SC reports and sometimes does not respond to them; and, despite some recent gains in this area, the time available for PBCs and for debate on SC reports in the main chamber of the Commons is restricted and mainly controlled by government. As a consequence, the UK Parliament has most often been viewed as a chamber-driven, rather than a committee-driven, legislature (Arter 2002).

As the two systems have quite different functions, powers, and processes, we discuss each committee system separately in the first three sections concerning formalities and structure, actors, and interactions. In the fourth section concerning committees in the policy process, we discuss each of the systems in turn and only when relevant to the different stages of the policy process. In the conclusion, we consider whether the UK committee system remains an outlier by evaluating the reforms implemented over the past two decades with the aim of strengthening the influence, effectiveness, and independence of committees. We argue that, while recent reforms have added to the independence and resources of committees and while committees do often exercise influence both through visible, formal mechanisms and informal persuasion, the weaknesses resulting from the division between the legislative and scrutiny function and the lack of coercive powers with respect to government

DOI: 10.4324/9781003106579-17

remain. As such, in terms of the strength of parliamentary committees, while the UK may well be playing catch-up with other countries around the world, it is far from becoming a committee-driven legislature.

Formalities and structure

The two main and distinct classes of committees in the UK system are select committees and general committees.[1] SCs are (semi-)permanent committees whose main business is to scrutinize and hold government to account. Their membership is renewed after each election but the committees themselves are established for an indefinite period. General committees (including public bill committees) are legislative committees. In the House of Commons (HoC), they are established on an ad hoc basis (with, therefore, a non-permanent membership) in response to the introduction of legislation on the floor of the House. They are dissolved once their scrutiny of the bill in question is concluded. In the House of Lords (HoL), general committees comprise the whole House, meaning that all peers may participate. The vast majority of legislative work done by committees in the UK takes place in PBCs. Due to issues of space, we focus below mainly on SCs and PBCs in the Commons.

Select committees

Although SCs have existed in some form for centuries, the present system is a relatively recent innovation, having been established in 1979. Since 1979, there have been three main types of SCs: *departmental*, which are installed to scrutinize a particular government department (e.g. the Treasury SC scrutinizes the Treasury, etc.); *administrative/domestic*, such as Procedure and Backbench Business, which focus on matters internal to the running of the HoC; and *cross-cutting scrutiny*, such as Public Accounts and Science and Technology, which deal with specific aspects of government activity or issues which cut across government portfolios. The HoC has committees of all three types; the HoL only has cross-cutting scrutiny committees and administrative committees. HoC SCs are established following a general election for the duration of a Parliament. In the Lords they are established only for one parliamentary session, although by convention the renewal of committees during the course of a parliament is a formality, meaning that Lords SCs also tend to endure for a full parliament.

The number of HoC SCs has grown over time from 33 full committees in the 1979–1980 parliamentary session to 44 in the 2015–2016 parliamentary session (with a peak of 50 in 2009–2010 when regional SCs were also in existence).[2] The number of departmental SCs is determined by the shape and size of the government, and in recent times has been around 20 in number. The House of Commons Standing Order 152 states that there will be a SC for each of the principal departments of government (2017: 193). Beyond departmental SCs, the number of other SCs is determined by those established by the standing orders published at the start of each parliament. As a result, these numbers remain relatively stable over time, although the government can amend the standing orders to modify, create, or abolish a SC.[3]

In 2010 there were a number of reforms of the HoC SC system (usually labelled the Wright Reforms). One of these reforms, introduced because of a concern that the size of committees was creeping upwards to unsustainable levels, was to set the number of departmental SC members at 11 (with the exception of the Northern Ireland Affairs SC which has a membership of 13 to accommodate members from the small Northern Irish parties). The size of other SCs is again determined by the standing orders with membership numbers usually ranging from eight to sixteen. Lords SCs usually have 12 members, with some variation.

Meetings of SCs are typically public although private sessions are also held, including for consideration of draft reports. Over the nine parliamentary sessions covering the period 2007 to 2017, there was an average of 38.5 meetings per session per committee. Of these 38.5 meetings, 28 (73 percent) were oral evidence meetings, or what might be called hearings, 98 percent of which were public meetings and 2 percent private. 27 percent of the committee meetings were private meetings for members (and clerks) only.[4] Minutes of both public and private meetings are made available and public sessions are televised or streamed via the internet.

The formal powers and responsibilities of SCs are set out in the standing orders. For those committees shadowing government departments, the role is described as follows in Standing Order 152:

(1) Select committees shall be appointed to examine the expenditure, administration and policy of the principal government departments ... and associated public bodies.
(4) Select committees appointed under this order shall have power (a) to send for persons, papers and records, to sit notwithstanding any adjournment of the House, to adjourn from place to place, and to report from time to time.

Yet, despite the presence of standing orders relating to SCs, their precise role and function at Westminster is not always absolutely clear. Since 2002, the rather broad requirement outlined above has been supplemented by a list of core tasks drawn up by the Liaison Committee – a committee made up of the chairs of the main SCs. The current five core tasks concern scrutinizing policy, implementation, administration, expenditure, and matters of public concern. In the main, the latest iteration is simply a restructuring of previous iterations, the exception being the introduction of a new core task related to matters of public concern. This addition is a formal codification of trends witnessed in (some) SCs over the past decade or so.

In practice, the main task of SCs is to undertake inquiries on specific topics by gathering evidence and producing reports. Most SC meetings are 'evidence sessions', or what might be labelled 'hearings' – meetings at which witnesses are invited to answer questions put to them by the committee in relation to a specific topic of inquiry. SCs invite government ministers, senior officials, policy experts, interest group representatives, and other figures of public importance to attend. Alongside the oral evidence given by these witnesses, SCs also invite submissions of written evidence from these groups and the wider public. The combined evidence is then compiled into a report with recommendations for government, to which the government must respond within a specified period, and that may also be debated by the HoC as a whole. SCs also hold pre-appointment hearings for public appointments within the area of competence of the committee. Committees may make recommendations on candidates, but these are not binding on the government, which retains final discretion over public appointments.

Public bill committees

Legislative committees in the HoC were introduced by Liberal Prime Minister William Gladstone in 1882. Although associated today with the scrutiny of legislation, their introduction was based on the grounds of efficiency and the avoidance of parliamentary obstacles. Gladstone's legislative agenda was being delayed by obstructive behaviour from Irish MPs. Legislative committees were intended to expedite the passage of the government's legislative programme and to free up time on the floor of the House for other parliamentary business. From 1906 all bills, apart from finance and appropriations bills, were sent to a bill committee following their second reading on the floor of the HoC, and this was confirmed through changes to the standing orders.

Contemporary bill committees bear little relation to their predecessors in terms of size or appointment (Thompson 2015: 31–44). Early standing committees were very large, with up to 80 members, and only covered specific policy areas. In the mid-20th century, membership consisted of two tiers: a core of specialist, permanent members, and an outer circle of ad hoc members. Today, PBCs are central to the legislative process and are responsible for scrutinizing around 30 to 50 pieces of government legislation each session. All bills which pass their second reading debate and vote in the HoC will have a committee stage, which, for most, will take place in a small ad hoc PBC of around 14 to 19 members.[5] In all parliamentary sessions, the committee stage accounts for more parliamentary time than any other stage of the legislative process (Thompson 2015: 1).

The principal work of a PBC committee is to scrutinize the bill before it on a 'line by line' basis to ensure that it is generally acceptable and has no unintended consequences. MPs may attempt to add, amend, or remove any words, phrases, clauses, or schedules within the bill, though any changes require either the acquiescence of the government minister or the assent of the majority of the committee. Committee debate proceeds through amendments and what are called 'stand part' debates on particular (sets of) clauses. In the

1980s, bill committees gained an additional capacity to take oral evidence, though these evidence-taking powers were very rarely used. It became a much more comprehensive procedure from 2006 when the legislative committee system underwent a major reform. Bill committees were given the power to send for 'persons, papers and records' (Standing Order 83A) and could therefore take oral or written evidence at the start of the committee stage of any bill. Committees typically hold three or four oral evidence sessions, bringing government ministers, officials, and representatives from business, charities, lobby groups, and other external organizations before them. Oral evidence cannot overlap with line-by-line scrutiny; the latter cannot begin until the former has been completed. When the whole bill has been scrutinized or when the time set aside for scrutiny in the programme for the bill has elapsed, the bill will be reported back to the House. MPs will then debate and amend the bill again at report stage.

As ad hoc bodies, the membership and duration of PBCs are tailored to the piece of legislation being scrutinized. A committee is appointed each time a bill completes its second reading stage and is disbanded when the bill is reported back to the House. The number of bill committees in operation at any one time, or indeed in any one parliamentary session, is dependent upon the frequency, size, and complexity of the government and private members' legislation being introduced and is therefore highly changeable. There is no limit on the number of committees which may sit at any given time, though only one private members' bill may have its committee stage at any one time.

The membership of PBCs mirrors the party balance of the HoC. Therefore, committee size varies partly due to the need to maintain party proportionality. Mirroring the party balance in the HoC means that the government will ordinarily have a clear majority.

Just as PBC membership mirrors the composition of the House, the layout of the committee room takes shape according to the Commons chamber. MPs sit facing each other in an adversarial fashion, with government MPs on one side and opposition MPs on the other. Seating at the back of the committee room is allocated to members of the public and anyone can attend, although public attendance at committee sessions is very low (usually just a handful) and these seats tend to be filled by representatives from lobby groups, officials, and the staff of committee members.

Actors in committees

Select committees

Before 2010, members were assigned to SCs by party leaders. Since 2010 and the Wright Reforms, committee chairs and members have been elected, the former by all MPs in the HoC through a secret ballot, the latter by party caucuses. This has reduced the ability of government to either appoint loyalists or to block the appointment of 'troublemakers' to SCs. The greater independence of committees from government following these reforms has been credited with raising the profile and effectiveness of SCs, although Bates et al. (2017) suggest some of these claims may be lacking empirical support.

The turnover rate of departmental SCs between 1979 and 2015 ranges from a low of 1 percent during the 2004–2005 parliamentary session to a high of 39 percent in 2010–2012. The mean average of turnover per parliamentary session for departmental SCs is 13 percent, with turnover tending to be lower at the beginning and end of a parliament, especially when turnover is weighted to take into account the length of parliamentary session (Bates et al. 2017). As reported in McKay et al. (2019), the median duration of committee membership for an individual member is a little under two years for each type of committee. About a quarter of MPs only remain members of a committee for about a year, while another quarter stay on their committees for at least three and a half years. Of all MPs elected since 1979, 69 percent have sat on a departmental committee at some point during their parliamentary career (with 16 percent not sitting on any SC during their time in the House of Commons). Twenty-seven percent of MPs have only ever sat on a departmental SC, 15 percent have sat on at least one departmental SC and at least one domestic/administrative committee, 14 percent have sat on at least one departmental SC and at least one other scrutiny committee, and 13 percent have sat on all three kinds of committee at least once during their parliamentary career.

MPs will normally only sit on one departmental SC at a time but may well also sit on other scrutiny or domestic and administrative committees. Chairs of departmental SCs also automatically sit on the Liaison Committee. SCs are intended to represent the voice of backbench MPs, scrutinizing and holding government to account so MPs with a government or opposition frontbench position, however junior, do not serve on SCs.

The four main roles in SCs are: (i) chair, (ii) member, (iii) witness,[6] and (iv) clerk[7] – civil servants who support the work of parliamentary committees. The chair has significant powers over agenda-setting, chairing meetings, allocating media work, choosing witnesses and drafting reports. In the HoC, chairships are distributed between parties either by convention (for example, the Treasury SC is always chaired by an MP from the main party in government and the Public Accounts Committee is always chaired by an MP from the main opposition party) or through discussion between party whips at the beginning of the parliament. The distribution of chairs is in proportion to the strength of parties in the House. Since chairs are designated for a particular party, elections are only ever contests between members of the same party, although members of all parties may vote.[8]

The role of chair has become more prominent since the 2010 Wright Reforms and many believe it has become more powerful too (Fisher 2015; Goodwin et al 2016; Kelso 2016). One of the aims of the Wright Reforms was to create a career path for MPs outside of government and for the position of HoC SC chair to be a sought-after career destination. Whether this is now the case is a moot point: witness for example the resignation in 2019 of Nicky Morgan from the position of chair of the Treasury SC, one of the most prestigious and high-profile committees, to take up a relatively low-profile ministerial position in the Johnson government. However, it is certainly the case that SC chairs have received a higher media profile since the Wright Reforms and, due to the introductions of elections and the subsequent legitimacy bestowed on incumbents, it is probably the case that chairs have increased independence and authority since 2010 in terms of how their committees are run and the choice of inquiries that are made (Kelso 2016).

Other committee members may advise, make proposals, vote, and amend the recommendations of the chair on the committee agenda, reports, and recommendations. Committee memberships besides the chair are distributed among parties according to the party composition of the House. As a result, the majority of members of any given SC will nearly always be members of the governing party. While nominations and results of elections for chairs are made public, this is not the case for the internal processes by which parties nominate their committee members. As with elections for chairs, contests for committee memberships are always among members of the same party, although in this case, only members of the relevant party may vote.

Membership of departmental SCs is gendered.[9] Goodwin et al. (2020) find that, over a near 40-year period since 1979, some committees have consistently had disproportionately fewer or more female members than would normally be expected given the overall gender balance of MPs. For example, the Treasury, Foreign Affairs, and Defence SCs are consistently very disproportionately male and the Home Affairs, Education, and Health are consistently very disproportionately female. Moreover, while there has been some improvement in the proportion of female chairs since the 2010 reforms (see also O'Brien 2012), the available evidence on candidacies for chair suggests that women do not put themselves forward as often for committees which cover high-status, traditionally masculine policy areas.

Public bill committees

In contrast to the SC appointments system, members of PBCs are not elected, nor do MPs necessarily put themselves forward for membership. Whereas SC membership is considered by many to afford high status to MPs, bill committee membership is traditionally seen as something to be avoided. Indeed, MPs themselves have described PBC work as 'enforced labour' (Wright 2010: 302).

At least one government minister will be required to take the bill through each committee, but this number may increase to three depending on the size and nature of the bill. Spokespersons from the two main opposition parties will also have a guaranteed place and at least one government whip will join, as will the minister's parliamentary private secretary (PPS). The frontbench membership may be constant for bill committees which fall under the same broad policy area, but the backbench membership will change. Opposition MPs will be appointed in line with party size in the Commons, but given the size of committees, small opposition parties rarely receive a place unless the larger party whips agree to forego one of their own members.

Backbench appointments are made formally by the Committee of Selection which is, on paper at least, required to take members' qualifications into account (SO 86). In practice, the Committee of Selection is composed of party whips, whose appointment criteria are more strategic. While some MPs do request to be appointed to the committee stage of a bill on the basis of their particular interest and expertise, particularly if the minister handling the bill is amenable (Thompson 2016: 40), many appointments made by government whips have the aim of facilitating a clean and easy passage. Newly elected government MPs will usually find a bill committee to be one of their first tasks, particularly if they have contributed to the second reading stage debate on the floor of the house. Though party loyalty may be the chief criterion for appointment, this does not mean that committees possess no policy expertise. Indeed, Thompson found that around two-thirds of committee members hold some form of specialization in the policy area under discussion (2016: 40). This is particularly true if an MP also serves on a relevant SC, which is a not uncommon occurrence, especially for opposition members. Furthermore, collecting evidence can boost the knowledge of appointed backbenchers and ensure a more level playing field compared to the better resourced frontbench team (Thompson 2014).

Interactions in committees

Select committees

The dominant culture operating in SCs is one of consensus-seeking and non-partisanship. The existence of SCs, and the support they enjoy, undoubtedly owes much to the belief that some of the work of Parliament is better undertaken in a more consensual mode of operation, rather than the adversarial, partisan style that otherwise dominates (Wollaston 2019).

The relative absence of cross-party modes of working within Parliament was a key theme of Anthony King's 1976 study of executive–legislative relations, and a feature that distinguished Westminster from other governing models. For King, the relationships within and between parties was the key to understanding British government, rather than the relationship between the executive and legislative branches understood as discrete corporate entities. While party relationships dominate according to King's schema, parliamentary committees can operate on a non-party basis, providing a venue for Parliament to act corporately in relation to the executive, in the way that standard models of executive-legislature relations posit (incorrectly, according to King). Committees would then allow members of the legislature to cast off their partisan role (principally to support or to oppose the government) and adopt a non-party, or private members, role (principally to check and hold the government to account or to represent citizens for example). Ideally, committees would create an environment wherein: those who participate in the work of non-party committees (usually SCs) change their perception of their own roles. They cease to see themselves as members of the Conservative Party or the Labour Party, concerned with scoring points off the other side, and come to see themselves simply as backbench Members of Parliament, concerned with investigating the quality of the performance of the executive (of whichever party), with protecting the rights of the citizen against the executive (of whichever party) and with asserting the prerogatives of backbench MPs (irrespective of party) (King 1976: 19).

While King was discussing a very different committee system to the one that exists today, much of his analysis remains apt. The self-image of present-day SCs is that they are non-party bodies owing their primary loyalty to 'Parliament' as a corporate entity. Yet due to the combined effect of committees' lack of resources, and the dominance of partisanship in British politics, the importance and influence of committees is limited. For example, SCs are (mainly) excluded from some of the key aspects of the work of Parliament, such as legislation, by virtue of their non-party character. Furthermore, as Hindmoor et al. (2009) note, these non-party committees do not exercise any delegated powers on behalf of Parliament.

Russell and Cowley (2016) revisit King's work and identify the SC system as a direct attempt to overcome the weakness of the 'non-party' mode in the British system. Alongside other measures such as the creation of the Backbench Business Committee and the Wright Reforms to membership and selection of committee members, Russell and Cowley point to the much-increased institutionalization of the non-party mode since King's paper. These institutions have become established with a norm of non-partisanship and a strong presumption towards consensus and the presentation of a united front among the membership. For example, official minority reports are not produced by SCs (although unofficial ones sometimes are, usually in the form of alternative drafts that are proposed in committee and then, if a division takes place, are included in the minutes), and divisions (formal votes) are not especially common and are decreasing (Holden Bates et al., 2019). *Contra* King, 'it can therefore no longer be said that the non-party mode in the House of Commons is underdeveloped', as Russell and Cowley (2016: 6) argue. They go further, claiming that, in relation to SCs, this is a direct consequence of their separation from legislative work (i.e. this separation is a positive attribute of the system and not a deficit).

Public bill committees

The strategic nature of the appointments system for bill committees and the way in which the layout and conduct of committee proceedings largely seek to mirror business on the floor of the Commons chamber, promotes adversarial interactions and militates against explicit bargaining and deal-making in the committee rooms themselves, although backroom bargaining does take place informally elsewhere. Such bargaining usually involves individual MPs and the government minster, with interest groups sometimes being involved also. The nature of the parliamentary system means that any changes will be introduced by the government, usually (but not always) with credit given to the MP involved.

Line-by-line stages are far more adversarial than the oral evidence-taking stage (Russell et al., 2013: 14). Government ministers generally feel a sense of ownership of the legislation in question and will stoically resist its amendment. Opposition appointments aim to ensure that controversial elements of the bill are opposed and that both the legislation and the minister are properly scrutinized. This scrutiny process is dominated by the opposition frontbench given the very detailed nature of legislation and the lack of any additional resources for backbench members, however active and knowledgeable. Contrastingly, government MPs are encouraged not to table amendments and not to speak and, if they do, to make sure that they support the bill. Whips and PPSs rarely speak, preferring to work behind the scenes to ensure that business runs as planned. This is not to say that all committee appointments are successful; government backbenchers do occasionally cause trouble for their ministers (Russell & Gover 2017: 139).

This general set-up does not mean that discussions are not constructive. Debate in the vast majority of committees proceeds congenially, with a recognition from most participants that formal changes will not be accepted by the government minister in this particular parliamentary venue. Ministers are regularly pressed for clarifications and explanations of aspects of the bill and often commit to writing to MPs if their queries cannot be answered without further discussion and clarification with officials. We can also see ministers making informal concessions or commitments to MPs at committee stage. Ministers may agree to make changes to the guidance or explanatory notes which accompany the legislation in question, they may promise to 'look again' or 'reconsider' an amendment, or a particular section of the bill, or they may make a firmer commitment to table an amendment at the bill's report stage, on the floor of the House. This enables the minister to come back to the House, often with the very same amendment proposed by an MP in committee, but without the humiliation of being seen to capitulate to the opposition. Finally, ministers may agree to a meeting with MPs or outside groups to discuss issues of concern (Thompson 2015: 79; Kalitowski 2008: 698). All four of these types of commitments will be noted by ministerial officials attending the committee (Cabinet Office 2017: 224), but, as they necessitate bargaining outside the committee room itself, there is no public record of them beyond the printed transcript of committee proceedings and, as such, they often go unnoticed.

Committees in the policy process

Problem definition and agenda-setting (select committees)

As their pattern of work is not dictated by legislative programmes, SCs have a great deal of autonomy over their own agenda and assignments, especially since their core tasks have been updated to include reference to investigating 'matters of public concern'. Inquiry subjects may be chosen by members without reference to, or interference from, the government, while the timing, style, and duration of inquiries is also at the discretion of the committee. Sometimes committees will be encouraged to undertake a particular assignment by government (for example, the Science and Technology SC was asked to look at developments in assisted reproductive technologies by the then government (Goodwin and Bates 2016)) but, in general, committees (in discussion with the clerks), and especially the chair, have considerable leeway in choosing topics for investigation.

A small number of committee tasks are, however, automatic and non-negotiable. These mainly pertain to pre-appointment hearings. For example, the Treasury SC will automatically hold pre-appointment hearings for any nominee to the Bank of England's Monetary Policy Committee. SCs are also obliged to scrutinize departmental accounts as part of their work and, although not dictated by a formal rule, some SCs will produce a report on regular government events and processes (for example, the Treasury SC will produce a report on every budget). On balance, then, SCs enjoy strong agenda control as a function of their separation from the legislative process.

This discretion over the agenda can express itself in quite different forms of scrutiny across SCs. There are arguably two ideal types with regard to how SCs approach assignments: a systematic, *police patrol* model of scrutiny whereby SCs scrutinize a specified range of areas repeated at regular intervals. Under this model, the committee's actions are predictable and regular. The alternative is to understand SC scrutiny as a *fire alarm* model, with committees responding to unpredictable events and developments. Of course, all committees fit somewhere between these two ideal types but certain committees, for example, the Defence SC, are consistently closer to the police patrol model and others, for example, the Digital, Culture, Media & Sport (DCMS) SC is consistently closer to the fire alarm model (at least in the recent past). The difference in style between the committees could also be understood as a difference in interpretation of the SC role. 'Inward-looking' committees like Defence work principally to oversee government ministers and officials and engage few outside interests. They are more likely to interpret their role as 'critical friends' seeking to hold the government to account rather than exerting influence over the agenda of their corresponding ministry. 'Outward-looking' committees like DCMS place more emphasis on incorporating interest groups, raising the profile of matters of public concern through their work, and influencing the public agenda or moving issues of public concern on to, or up, the government's (legislative) agenda.

SCs do indeed move issues on to the government's legislative agenda but not necessarily consistently and possibly only when certain conditions apply. Goodwin and Bates (2016) suggest that this agenda-setting power of SCs may be facilitated by a combination of five conditions: a long legislative timeframe, dedicated pre-legislative scrutiny by SCs (and outside PBCs), proactive and sustained involvement by SCs including the synchronization of their work with legislative timetables, the low political salience of the issues under consideration, and high scientific or technical content of legislation.

However, the (formal) links connecting backbench institutions such as SCs with government policy and legislative work remain very weak and clear agenda-setting by committees is likely to be exceptional. Nevertheless, Russell and Benton (2011, 2013) and Russell and Gover (2017) have demonstrated that recommendations made in SC reports are taken up in legislation relatively often. Russell and Benton (2013) found that 40 percent of Commons SC recommendations were accepted by government with a similar proportion going on to be implemented.[10] However, they also report that the impact of committees in this area is often indirect, non-linear, and reliant on 'soft power' or anticipated reaction rather than any more assertive, formal mechanism.

Policy formulation (public bill committees)[11]

Unlike some legislatures, UK legislators must consider and vote on all legislation in plenary before it is sent to committee. Therefore, the appointment of a PBC after the passage of a bill at second reading on the floor of the House inhibits any real form of control or agenda-setting and, of course, by the very nature and timing of their appointment, PBCs cannot initiate legislation. PBCs cannot reject the bill as a whole and they cannot put forward amendments which do not fit within the bill's long title or which go against the general principles which have been agreed at second reading. These limitations are firmly expressed within *Erskine May*, the book of parliamentary procedure. In practice, the limitations go much further than this. Goodwin and Bates (2016: 248) argue that once a bill has been presented to Parliament the opportunities for amendment are 'drastically reduced'.

Formal changes to the text of the bill do occur – approximately 88 percent of bills leave committee stage in an amended form (Thompson 2015: 52) – but the overwhelming majority of these amendments originate with the government. The in-built government majority means that defeats on government amendments are rare. Non-government amendments (those from government backbenchers or opposition MPs) occur in less than 20 percent of committees and typically concern very minor issues. Government ministers are prohibited from agreeing to any amendments at committee stage without collective agreement from the bill team (Cabinet Office 2017: 224).

PBCs also find themselves constrained in terms of time. While they can, if they wish, scrutinize every line of a bill, a programme motion debated and voted upon by the whole House after the bill's second reading vote sets out the date by which the committee must report the bill back to the House as a whole. There is no capacity for a PBC to delay a bill (indefinitely), or to veto it. If scrutiny of the bill has not been completed by the end date, the bill will simply move to its next legislative stage with whole sections being left unscrutinized by the committee (Brazier et al. 2005: 16).

Despite these formal constraints, PBCs do remain important to shaping policy, although this may only become apparent later in the process, at the bill's report stage or beyond. For example, ministerial commitments made in PBCs (as described above) are important for considering the effectiveness of policy change in legislative committees. Around two-thirds of the commitments made by ministers during committee stage find their way into legislation at report stage (Thompson 2015: 80). Moreover, a behavioural change has occurred among PBC members lately, with fewer amendments being pushed to a vote in committee to ensure that they can be tabled again at report stage (Thompson 2015: 91). MPs want to maximize their chances of success and ensuring that a formal decision has not been made in PBCs heightens the likelihood of the same amendment being selected by the Speaker for discussion at report.

Measuring policy impact on the basis of committee stage alone is thus ineffective. Stages of the legislative process should not be considered as discrete entities; PBC influence can extend much further than this.

Implementation and evaluation (select committees)

One of the core tasks of SCs refers to post-legislative scrutiny but, as noted by the Liaison Committee (2019), this is something that is often ignored or undertaken neither systematically nor particularly successfully by departmental SCs in the Commons. Norton (2019) argues that Commons committees are not well suited to post-legislative scrutiny; the HoL is better placed to conduct this kind of work both because of the level of expertise within the Lords and because its non-elected character means that its role in the policy-making process is more detached, reflective and, generally, has a greater independence from party concerns (see also Caygill 2019a, 2019b).

Conclusions

The UK system of parliamentary committees has been described as a deviant case due to its separation of legislative and scrutiny work into two distinct committee systems, and due to the weakness and lack of independence of committees in relation to government. Both of the main committee systems have undergone substantial reform during the 21st century. In each case, the aim has been to go some way towards strengthening the ability of committees to challenge and hold the government to account.

The system of membership assignment for SCs in the Commons was changed from appointment to election. Along with other reforms implemented at the same time, the purpose of this change was designed to loosen the grip of party managers over SC membership by curbing their ability to install government placeholders or to reward the loyalty of reliable party-line supporters. Whether this has been sufficient to overcome the historic weakness of the UK committee system is, however, moot. The reforms have certainly met with strong approval from parliamentarians and analysts; one of the main conclusions of the Liaison Committee's 2015 Legacy Report is that 'Public opinion, commentators and academic critics have all recognized that select committee work is the most constructive and productive aspect of Parliament' (2015: 40). SCs are often and increasingly viewed as Parliament at its best.

One of the reasons for this view of SCs in comparison to other parliamentary scrutiny mechanisms such as Question Time, and Urgent and Written Questions, lies in the abilities of SCs to send for persons, papers, and records in a way that other parliamentary institutions cannot. SCs can be considered a more effective way of achieving the scrutiny function of Parliament than chamber-based activities such as debates or Question Time, as the latter tend to be organized around elaborate procedural conventions that reduce the intensity of scrutiny of ministers and allow them to evade and avoid questions, as well as tending to exhibit a greater degree of partisanship. These activities are, of course, also restricted to questioning ministers, rather than officials, representatives of public bodies, or other external actors, as can routinely occur in SC hearings.

Yet research evidence concerning the efficacy of SC reforms is mixed and should temper any sweeping conclusions on this point. Bates et al. (2017) find that the impact of the reforms on MPs' engagement with SCs has been minimal to non-existent. Dunleavy and Muir (2013) argue that the Wright Reforms contributed to a substantial growth in media visibility for SCs. However, Gaines et al. (2019), focusing on a longer time frame, conclude that, while SCs have become more visible in the media over time, it is not yet clear whether the Wright Reforms and the 2012 changes to the core tasks caused an increase in this media visibility, or simply helped to codify a focus on work within the SC system that would garner more media attention that was already on an upwards trend pre-Wright Reforms (see also Kubala 2011). O'Brien (2012) finds that the new system of selecting members has favoured the election of chairwomen but Goodwin et al. (2020), while confirming O'Brien's finding, also find that the reforms have had little if any impact on making SCs more gender balanced at a membership level. Furthermore, the reforms did not make any substantive changes to the powers or responsibilities of SCs, which still rely on persuasion rather than power to influence the course of events and must continually battle to have their voice heard by government.

Turning to the other committee system, the key change to PBCs was the introduction in 2006 of oral and written evidence-taking as standard committee procedure. This has enhanced the scrutiny capacity of PBCs, acting as an information provider as well as assisting MPs with the identification of errors and inconsistencies in legislation. Thompson (2014, 2015) argues that this reform has helped to overcome some of the key criticisms of the legislative committee system as being filled by generalists. Russell et al. (2013) suggest that other significant reforms are needed to inject greater permanence and specialization into the system. For example, there is a broad consensus that more transparency is required in the method of appointment. Moreover, the novelty of minority government in recent years has generated discussion around whether there should be the presence of a government majority on PBCs. However, the PBC system remains overshadowed by that of SCs and, as such, the work and importance of the legislative committee system is still often overlooked. This means that further changes to the PBC system are not necessarily a priority for parliamentary reformers.

One source of the UK's deviancy – the separation of the legislative and scrutiny functions of committees into two discrete systems – clearly remains. While this may have some advantages, particularly in terms of allowing committees control of their own agenda, and fostering a non-partisan ethos among SC members (if non-partisanship is deemed beneficial), it can also be viewed as contributing significantly to the weaknesses of the UK parliamentary committee system in toto. The separation of the scrutiny and legislative functions, as well as the ad hoc nature of PBCs, impedes the development of specialization and of institutional memory, and contributes to the legislative function being overshadowed by the scrutiny function. This may all be seen as (potentially) detrimental to UK public policy. Moreover, despite reforms regarding evidence-taking for PBCs and increasing independence for SCs, both systems retain weak formal powers. Therefore, while both committee systems can and do influence government, policy, and legislation both formally and informally, this is perhaps *despite* their institutional architecture, rather than *because of* it. While recent reforms may have narrowed the gap with other countries in terms of committee strength, the deviant, outlier status of the UK almost certainly remains.

Notes

1 The other kinds of committee in the UK Parliament are: (i) grand committees, which focus on the regions of the UK; (ii) joint committees, which are made up of members from both Houses, can be both permanent or ad hoc, and which operate in a very similar manner to other SCs; (iii) ad hoc draft bill committees; and (iv) statutory instruments committees which are SCs but which differ from other SCs in being primarily legislative committees that consider secondary legislation.

2 Much of the data on SCs used for this chapter is taken from Goodwin et al. (2019).
3 There are currently six main SCs in the HoL – a figure which has remained relatively stable over time – and also approximately six cross-cutting joint committees with members from both Houses.
4 Data taken from HoC sessional returns and compiled by the authors and Wang Leung Ting.
5 Bills which are either very minor or considered to be of major constitutional importance will have their committee stage in a Committee of the Whole House. Occasionally, a bill will be scrutinized partly in a bill committee and partly in a Committee of the Whole House. In the HoL, the committee stage takes place in a grand committee (away from the main chamber) or in the chamber through a committee of the whole House. All peers can participate in these proceedings.
6 On witnesses, see Beswick & Elstub (2019), and Geddes (2017).
7 On committee clerks, see Geddes (2019).
8 Lords committees nominate a chair from among their membership.
9 As is the profile of witnesses (see Bates et al. 2019).
10 Although the authors of this chapter have been told anecdotally that 'good' clerks will seek to include 'recommendations' in SC reports that they know have already been looked at and accepted by departments.
11 SCs may also take on this legislative scrutiny role at times, whereby draft bills are sent to them for scrutiny (Kalitowski 2008: 695). Occasionally a SC may be convened for the specific purposes of legislative scrutiny, as happened in the House of Lords during the scrutiny of the Trade Union Bill (2016) but this is rare.

References

Arter, D. (2002). On assessing strength and weakness in parliamentary committee systems: some preliminary observations on the new Scottish Parliament. *Journal of Legislative Studies*, 8(2), 93–117.
Bates, I., Geddes, M., Goodwin, M., Holden Bates, S., & McKay, S. (2019) Why can't some Select Committees get a female witness? Retrieved from https://psaparliaments.org/2019/01/24/select-committees-female-witnesses/ (access: 16.07.2021).
Bates, S., Goodwin, M., & McKay, S. (2017). Do UK MPs engage more with select committees since the Wright Reforms? An interrupted time series analysis, 1979–2016. *Parliamentary Affairs*, 70(4), 780–800.
Beswick, D., & Elstub, S. (2019). Between diversity, representation and 'Best Evidence': rethinking Select Committee evidence-gathering practices. *Parliamentary Affairs*, 72(4), 945–964.
Brazier, A., Flinders, M.V., & McHugh, D. (2005). *New politics, new parliament?* Hansard Society.
Cabinet Office (2017) *Guide to making legislation*. London: Cabinet Office.
Caygill, T. (2019a). A tale of two houses? Post-legislative scrutiny in the UK Parliament. *European Journal of Law Reform*, 21(2), 87–101.
Caygill, T. (2019b). Legislation under review: an assessment of post-legislative scrutiny recommendations in the UK Parliament. *Journal of Legislative Studies*, 25(2), 295-313.
Dunleavy, P. & Muir, D. (2013). *Parliament bounces back – how Select Committees have become a power in the land*. Democratic Audit UK.

Fisher, L. (2015). The growing power and autonomy of House of Commons Select Committees: causes and effects. *Political Quarterly*, 86(3), 419–426.

Gaines, B.J., Goodwin, M., Holden Bates, S., & Sin, G. (2019). A bouncy house? UK Select Committee newsworthiness, 2005–18. *Journal of Legislative Studies*, 25(3) 409–433.

Geddes, M. (2017). Committee Hearings of the UK Parliament: who gives evidence and does this matter? *Parliamentary Affairs*, 71(2), 283–304.

Geddes, M. (2019). *Dramas at Westminster*. Manchester: Manchester University Press.

Goodwin, M., & Bates, S. (2016). The 'powerless parliament'? Agenda-setting and the role of the UK parliament in the Human Fertilisation and Embryology Act 2008. *British Politics*, 11(2), 232–255.

Goodwin, M., Bates, S., & McKay, S. (2016). *Elected chairs do not seem to have brought a new kind of parliamentarian to Select Committees*. Democratic Audit UK.

Goodwin, M., Holden Bates, S., & McKay, S. (2019) UK House of Commons Select Committee data archive. *osf.io/ywgh5* (access: 04.10.2020).

Goodwin, M, Holden Bates, S. & McKay, S. (2020). Electing to do women's work? Gendered divisions of labour in UK Select Committees, 1979–2016. *Politics and Gender*, First View, 1–33.

Hindmoor, A., Larkin, & Kennon, A. (2009). Assessing the influence of Select Committees in the UK: the Education and Skills Committee 1997–2005,' *Journal of Legislative Studies* 15, 71 89.

Holden Bates, S., Goodwin, M., McKay, S., & Ting, W.L. (2019) *Consensus and division(s) in departmental Select Committees*. Retrieved from https://parliamentsandlegislatures.wordpress.com/2019/07/24/consensus-and-divisions-in-departmental-select-committees/ (access: 04.10.2020).

House of Commons (2017). *Standing Orders (HC4)*, London, TSO.

Kalitowski, S. (2008). Rubber stamp or cockpit? The impact of parliament on government legislation. *Parliamentary Affairs*, 61(4), 694–708.

Kelso, A. (2016). Political leadership in parliament: the role of select committee chairs in the UK House of Commons. *Politics and Governance*, 4(2), 115–126.

King, A. (1976). Modes of executive-legislative relations: Great Britain, France, and West Germany. *Legislative Studies Quarterly*, 1(1), 11–36.

Kubala, M. (2011). Select committees in the House of Commons and the media. *Parliamentary Affairs*, 64(4), 694–713.

Liaison Committee (2013) *Select committee effectiveness, resources and powers: second report of session 2012–13*. HC 697, London, TSO.

Liaison Committee (2015) *Legacy report: first report of session 2014–15*, HC 954, London, TSO.

Liaison Committee (2019) *The effectiveness and influence of the select committee system: fourth report of session 2017–2019*, HC 1860, London, TSO.

Mattson, I., & Strøm, K. (1995). Parliamentary committees. In H. Döring (ed.). *Parliaments and majority rule in Western Europe*. Frankfurt: Campus, 249–307.

McKay, S., Goodwin, M., & Holden Bates, S. (2019). A means to an end and an end in itself: Select Committee membership, parliamentary roles and parliamentary careers, 1979–Present. *Parliamentary Affairs* 72(4), 799–820.

Norton, P. (2019). Post-legislative scrutiny in the UK Parliament: adding value. *Journal of Legislative Studies*. 25(3), 340–357.

O'Brien, D.Z. (2012). Gender and Select Committee elections in the British House of Commons. *Politics & Gender*, 8, 178–204.

Russell, M., & Benton, M. (2011). *Selective influence*. London, Constitution Unit.
Russell, M., & Benton, M. (2013). Assessing the impact of parliamentary oversight committees: the Select Committees in the British House of Commons, *Parliamentary Affairs* 66, 772–799.
Russell, M., & Cowley: (2016). The policy power of the Westminster parliament: the 'parliamentary state' and the empirical evidence. *Governance*, 29(1), 121–137.
Russell, M., Morris, B., & Larkin, P. (2013). *Fitting the bill*. London, Constitution Unit.
Russell, M., & Gover, D. (2017) *Legislation at Westminster*. Oxford: Oxford University Press.
Thompson, L. (2014). Evidence taking under the microscope: how has oral evidence affected the scrutiny of legislation in House of Commons committees? *British Politics*, 9(4), 385–400.
Thompson, L. (2015) *Making British law*. Basingstoke: Palgrave Macmillan.
Thompson, L. (2016). Debunking the myths of bill committees in the British House of Commons. *Politics*, 36(1), 36–48.
Wollaston, S. (2019). *How to make the select committee system more effective and influential*. Retrieved from https://constitution-unit.com/2019/10/15/how-to-make-the-select-committee-system-more-effective-and-influential/ (access: 04.10.2020).
Wright, T. (2010). What are MPs for? *Political Quarterly*, 81(3), 298–308.

18 'Specially commissioned minorities'
Committee governance and political parties in the United States Congress

Anne Marie Cammisa

> The House sits, not for serious discussion, but to sanction the conclusions of its Committees as rapidly as possible. It legislates in its committee-rooms; not by the determinations of majorities, but by the resolutions of *specially-commissioned minorities* [emphasis added].
> —Woodrow Wilson, *Congressional Government*, 1885

Woodrow Wilson called congressional committees 'specially-commissioned minorities', because Congress created them to delegate its workload to smaller numbers of legislators. As such, Wilson considered committees to be specialized 'little legislatures'. Committees in the United States Congress can be a tool for party leaders to consolidate their party's power; they can also be a tool for individual members of Congress to assert their power vis-à-vis their party. Committees were tools of the party until the early 20th century, when rank-and-file members demanded more control over the committee and its chair; by the end of the century, parties were asserting control. This chapter will examine committees as working groups within the partisan structure of Congress. It begins with an investigation into the history and background of committee governance in the United States, including trends towards centralization and decentralization, and eras of reform. Then the chapter turns to specifics of committee governance today, including sections on rules and procedures, format and function, and composition and membership of committees. The chapter concludes with a discussion of committees as specially commissioned minorities within the party system.

History and background

Before delving into committees in Congress, let us take a moment to describe the presidential (rather than parliamentary) environment in which they operate. The US Congress is part of a separated system, where the president is elected separately from Congress and the executive branch operates somewhat independently of Congress (e.g. the president appoints cabinet members and other agency officials, though the Senate must approve many of these appointments). Power is divided, not only among the three branches of

DOI: 10.4324/9781003106579-18

government but also within Congress itself. The two chambers of Congress, the House (with 435 members, elected in single-member districts every two years) and Senate (with 100 senators, elected every six years, and two senators per state, regardless of state size) operate independently of each other, and yet for any bill to become law, it must be passed in the same form by both the House and the Senate and signed by the president. The framers of the Constitution, fearful of both a powerful government and tyranny of the majority, purposely set up a system that makes it difficult to enact laws (Madison, Federalists 10 and 51),[1] and privileges minority rights within majority rule. Over time, a process for passing legislation has evolved which relies heavily on committees for consideration of bills.

In the earliest Congress, which convened in 1789, there were many fewer issues, and thus many fewer bills to be considered. As each issue came up in the House, the entire chamber would debate it, and, when a consensus was reached, create an ad hoc committee to write the consensus into the form of a bill, which would then be reported back to the chamber for discussion and then a vote on the House floor. Committees disbanded when the bill was complete. The Senate was more likely in this era to consider House legislation than to initiate its own (see Welsh 2008). Throughout this chapter, the focus will be on House committees; there is a larger body of literature on House committees, as they are more numerous, populated by more members, and more integral to processes of the chamber than Senate committees. As Congress matured as an institution, two important extra-constitutional resources evolved to aid its members in organizing both the chamber and the workload: political parties and congressional committees.

Over time, as more – and more complicated – issues came before Congress, permanent, standing committees were formed (over the objections of Federalists, such as Hamilton, who thought legislative proposals should go directly to executive agencies [Goodwin 1970: 6]). These committees generally remained in place from one Congress to the next (after each even-numbered election year, a 'new' Congress begins, and is numbered sequentially; the First Congress comprised the years 1789 to 1790 while the 116th Congress assembled from 2019 to 2020). Committees became an important part of the legislative process, which begins with the introduction of a bill in each chamber, then passes to committee consideration, where committees may consider (or not consider) a bill, hold hearings on it, amend it, and send it to the floor for further discussions, further amendments, and (perhaps) a vote on final passage. Much of the entire legislative process is extra-constitutional. That is, the Constitution sets forth the basic parameters that a bill must pass both chambers of Congress and be signed by the president, but the intricate steps of the process and the rules guiding those steps have evolved and become institutionalized over time.

Political parties, also referred to as factions in the 18th century, were denounced by George Washington in his farewell address. He believed that, among other things, parties may 'distract the public councils and enfeeble the public administration' as well as arouse 'ill-founded jealousies and false alarms, ... and occasionally riot and insurrection' (Washington 1795). However, prescient his words may have been, without parties, there would be no organizing principle within Congress and little to no mechanism for presenting candidates for election. Parties became entrenched in the structure and organization of Congress, particularly in the House of Representatives. Each party puts forth a candidate for speaker of the House; the majority party's candidate usually handily wins in a two-party system. Parties developed structures such as caucuses and the whip system, which allow party leaders to identify legislative priorities, assist members in reelection and, most importantly in a system with little party discipline, count votes. As we have seen, with ever-increasing numbers of issues before Congress, a second mechanism was necessary to organize the volume of proposed legislative output. Thus, parties grew as a method to organize the chamber and its membership, and committees grew as a method of organizing its legislative workload: 'Absent any discussion of political parties in the Constitution, committees evolved as the practical mechanism by which parties exercised and even shared power in Congress' (Welsh 2008: 17).

Woodrow Wilson, the only president of the United States to also hold a PhD in political science, wrote in his dissertation, *Congressional Government* (later published in book form), that 'Congress in public is Congress on public exhibition, whilst Congress in its committee-rooms is Congress at work' (Wilson 1885: 79). Committees have long been considered the workhorses of Congress, and an essential part of the legislative process, as they are the place where laws may be created, debated, and modified on their way to passage. Though Wilson's line is oft quoted and appropriately 'ubiquitous in the literature' (Gaines et al. 2019), the broader context is often overlooked: Wilson's thesis is that committee government is unwieldy and unrepresentative.[2] He argues that a British-style parliamentary system would be preferable (see Welsh 2008: 17), particularly concerning the importance of deliberative debate on the floor of the House of Commons, which Wilson argues is absent in the US Congress. Nevertheless, his point about committees is still valid: they are 'specially-commissioned minorities' (Wilson 1885: 79) that contribute to the diffusion of legislative decision-making in Congress. As we shall see, the party leadership has attempted to rein in this diffusion over time, while still 'specially commissioning' committees to engage in legislative work. Strong committees take power away from parties by dispersing legislative duties. More powerful parties (as in a parliamentary system) are more likely to absorb and integrate legislative functions (see Aldrich & Rohde 2019).

Centralization and decentralization in Congress

One reason that committees are so important in the US Congress is that the institution itself is decentralized. As noted, members of Congress are not beholden to political parties and often act independently of them. Party platforms are not necessarily important to individual candidates in single-member districts who may differ on issues that are of primary importance to them and their constituents. When a new Congress convenes, there may be a sense of particular legislative priorities (as, for example, in 2008 when the election of Barack Obama and a Democratic House and Senate catapulted health care to the top of the agenda), but there is not necessarily a firm, party-driven agenda. Members are, for the most part, free to vote as they wish, and parties often need to negotiate and cajole their own members to vote on party priorities, as happened during passage of the Affordable Care Act (Cammisa & Manuel 2014).

In this context, committees may form a counterbalance to parties. Members may select committees based on their policy interests (or for other reasons, discussed later) and use these committees to pursue legislative agendas that are not priorities for the party or may even be at odds with party platforms. At times, committees have asserted themselves as almost mini-fiefdoms, where a small number of individual members can create their power bases vis-à-vis the parties. Parties, in turn, can assert their dominance by controlling committee chairs, and, as we shall see later, sometimes by making end-runs around them. Although power has gone back and forth between committees and parties, parties have the upper hand. Committees are creatures of the parties in ways that parties are not creatures of committees.[3]

'The US House of Representatives is organized by whichever party has a majority of its seats ... Controlling the organization of the House means that the majority party decides who will preside over its deliberations, who will set its policy agenda, and who will dominate its workhorses: the standing committees'

(Jenkins & Stewart 2013: 17)

During the first century of the American government, parties gradually took on more and more control until rank-and-file members revolted in the second century of American government. Two time periods of 'revolt' occurred during the 20th century: in the first decade, in response to powerful Democratic Speaker Joe Cannon, and again in the 1970s when young, progressive Democrats attempted to wrest party control from the 'old bulls', many of whom were not only conservative but actively working against civil rights legislation. In the 1910 revolt against the autocratic Speaker 'Uncle' Joe Cannon, rank-and-file members stripped him (and therefore the Democratic Party) of power. Cannon was removed from the powerful Rules Committee he had chaired, and his power to appoint committee chairs was revoked; instead, the selection of chairmen reverted to seniority. Party power was decentralized, devolving to committees. Committee power, in turn, was centralized in the hands of the chair, whose position was based solely on the length of time in office, rather than party or committee member preferences.

The 1920s saw the development of the modern committee system, which, according to Deering and Smith (1997: 30) has six characteristics: (1) a structure that includes subcommittees, (2) specified and rule-bound jurisdictions for each committee, (3) committee power and influence over legislation,

(4) specified methods to appoint membership, (5) defined leadership positions and methods to recruit for them and, finally, (6) resources such as funding and staff. The importance of committees was highlighted by the passage of the Legislative Reorganization Act (LRA) of 1946, which helped institutionalize committees in a variety of ways. First, it streamlined the committee system by reducing the number of committees in both the House and Senate (and consequently, increasing the numbers of subcommittees). The Act supported seniority in the selection of committee chairs and gave those chairs control over legislative agendas and output. The LRA also gave committees staff and funding, in part to help them exercise their oversight function regarding executive agencies (Deering & Smith 1997: 29).

The middle of the 20th century, from the 1940s to 1964, became known as the 'Era of Committee Government' (Deering & Smith 1997: 30). Committees gained ascendancy, and control over the legislative agenda rested with committee chairs. Party power was decentralized to committees, while committee power was centralized in the chair. As the chairs consolidated their power in their individual committees, rank-and-file committee members became increasingly dissatisfied; it reached a peak in the 1960s and 1970s. By this time, many of the committee chairs were conservative Southern Democrats, who aligned with conservative Republicans in opposition to civil rights legislation. A second period of 'revolt' occurred, this time against the committee chairs and the system of seniority. Rank-and-file Democrats on committees moved to wrest power from the chairs

Unable to make broader changes to House rules, the younger, more progressive Democrats decided to make changes in the party rules (Aldrich & Rohde 2019). Because the Democrats were the majority party, rule changes could significantly impact the committees and their chairs. Changes in party rules lessened the stranglehold of seniority, by instituting a secret ballot for the committee to vote for its own chair. New Democratic Party rules further restricted the chairs' power by stripping them of the ability to select subcommittee chairs and allowing subcommittee chairs to control their own staffs and budgets. The House adopted legislation called the 'subcommittee bill of rights', that, among other things, fixed legislative jurisdiction for subcommittees and required committees to refer bills to subcommittees (Deering & Smith 1997: 38). While the reforms in the earlier part of the century had decentralized party power by increasing that of committee chairs, the 1970s reforms further decentralized power by decreasing the power of the chairs and increasing the power of rank-and-file committee members as well as subcommittees.

In addition to these decentralizing changes, party reformers also made changes that restored some aspects of the speaker's power that had been decentralized in the earlier reform period. The speaker is both the constitutional leader of the House and the leader of his party, and, as such, is subject to both party rules and House rules, as discussed later in the chapter.[4] In this case, the party rules gave some powers over the all-important Rules Committee back to the speaker: the power to appoint both the chair and the

Democratic members of the committee (as opposed to relying on seniority or having the party caucus vote for the chair and members). While House rules create committees, committee appointments and chairs are controlled by the parties. A new 'steering and policy committee' was established in the Democratic caucus, made up of Democratic leadership, to appoint members to committees (Aldrich & Rohde: 2018). Previously that role had belonged to Democrats on the Ways and Means Committee (Evans 2011: 404). The speaker was also given expanded powers such as the ability to refer legislation to multiple committees and to require that committees report out legislation by a particular date. It is remarkable that these changes, increasing the party (and speaker's) power, came from the rank and file, who simultaneously were decentralizing power in committees. In throwing off the yoke of the committee chairs, Democratic members realized that the party could be an ally.

> 'In the changed environment, most committee leaders came to think of themselves as part of a team with the majority leadership. In turn, they expected party leaders to provide adequate staff support and assistance in moving bills to passage on the floor'
> (Aldrich & Rohde 2018: 174)

In fact, Aldrich and Rohde see this as an example of their 'conditional party government' (CPG) theory. They argue that the more homogeneous a party's membership is, the more likely those members are to see the party as a useful tool for achieving their goals. Thus, leaders of homogeneous parties are likely to be granted more power by their members (Aldrich & Rohde 2018: 173). And, by the 1970s, the Democratic Party had indeed become more homogeneous. Not only were the Southern Democrats losing their hold on committee leadership, but voting patterns in the South were substantially changed with the passage of the Voting Rights Act of 1965, which increased the franchise of African-Americans. The South began electing more liberal members, and Southern Democrats began looking more like Northern Democrats. According to Aldrich and Rohde (2018), it is no surprise that Democratic party members would choose this time to award more authority to their leadership, and that is exactly what the party did. Similarly, the Republican Party gave more power to its leaders during the Republican revolution of the 1990s, seeing party unity as a powerful tool in throwing off the hegemony of the Democrats.

Other reforms

Revolts were not the only time when reform occurred. For example, the Legislative Reorganization Act (LRA) of 1946, discussed earlier, was an attempt to trim back statutorily the overgrown nature of committees. The number of Senate committees was reduced from 33 to 15. In the House, the number dropped from 48 to 19. Many of the committees that were eliminated became subcommittees instead. The LRA also allowed committees to hire staff (four professional and six clerical), 'formalized the legislative oversight functions of committees' and provided more staff positions for the Legislative Research Service (Welsh 2008: 8). A second Legislative Reorganization Act was passed in 1975, increasing the number of professional committee staff to six, and requiring that one-third of those be assigned to the minority. The Act also allowed the minority to call some witnesses at hearings, changed the name of the Legislative Research Service to the Congressional Research Service, giving it additional resources as well. The 1975 LRA also opened the committee process by requiring roll-call votes and allowing televised broadcasts of committee proceedings (Welsh 2008: 80).

The result of these periods of change was a House of Representatives in which committees and parties had complementary and symbiotic roles. Committees elected their leadership, created their subcommittees and still controlled much of the legislative process, while the party controlled the all-important Rules Committee and now had expanded referral powers. Republicans were frustrated that the Democratic Party, which held the majority in the House of Representatives for much of the 20th century, gave them little room to maneuver. Republican Party leaders felt doubly stymied: by their minority status and by their lack of control of committees and the legislative process. It is no surprise, then, that when the Republicans gained majority status in 1995 (for the first time in 40 years), the party leadership sought to consolidate its power – not just over the Democratic Party, but over the committee system as well. 'The importance and operating autonomy of standing committees are inversely related to the extent of partisan polarization within the parent chamber' (Evans 2011: 398). One might also say that standing committees have less independence as congressional parties act more like parliamentary parties.

Centralizing and decentralizing tendencies since 1994

The election of 1994 and the subsequent 104th Congress merit special attention in a volume about parliamentary committees, for in some ways, that election served to move the US Congress in the direction of a parliamentary system, albeit an American-style version of it. Although nothing in the basic election process changed, Republicans ran on a party platform called 'The Contract with America', which outlined both legislative priorities and rule changes in the House to make it easier to get legislation passed, including significant changes to the committee structure. Republican candidates held a signing ceremony and many candidates ran in their usual single-member districts in a most unusual way: on a party platform. The House voted on most planks of this Republican platform in the first 100 days of the 104th Congress, but due to the vagaries of the separated system, most of the legislation passed by the House died in the Senate, or was vetoed by the president, or overturned by the courts. For all the talk of a (somewhat) parliamentary-style election, the US Congress was not a parliament after all.[5] However, the 104th Congress created rule changes that had a large effect on committees in the House, in particular, making them less autonomous and thus centralizing power in the majority party.

While Democratic Party reforms in the 1970s simultaneously gave more power to committee members *and* the party (Rohde 1991), the Republican majority in Congress was more intent on strengthening the power of the latter. Republican reforms increased party power at the expense of committees. They gave control of the Rules Committee to the party. This is important because the Rules Committee can (and does) use its special rules to change the content and legislative language of committee bills as they are brought to the floor (Aldrich & Rohde 2018: 174). Subcommittee control was again centralized in the committee chairs, who could appoint subcommittee chairs. House Speaker Newt Gingrich (R-GA) believed 'that chairs should control their committees, but he also believed that the party should control the chairs' (Aldrich & Rohde 2018: 174). The Republicans also bypassed seniority in selecting committee chairs 'in favour of a loyalty-based system' (Stewart 2018: 8) and established six-year term limits for them. Each House committee was also limited to five subcommittees (with exceptions for the Appropriations, Government Reform, and Transportation Committees) (Welsh 2008: 12).

Republican reforms also took legislative power away from committees. Party leadership became more involved in drafting legislation, a task that was once considered primarily the domain of committees. Leadership also threatened committees who did not follow party priorities in legislation (for example, with restrictive rules, see Aldrich & Rohde 2018), and, if the committee reported out legislation that the party did not like, the party might form a task force, composed of loyal Republicans, to act as a committee and develop legislation in keeping with party priorities, acting almost as a shadow committee outside of the regular committee structure. The task-force legislation would move to the Rules Committee and the floor without input from the original committee of jurisdiction or the Democratic Party, undermining both rank-and-file members and the minority. In effect, a task force is a different type of 'specially commissioned minority', more fully controlled by the speaker as leader of the majority party. 'Pursuing a party agenda outside the committee system ... represents the application of parliamentary practice to governance' (Welsh 2008: 16), a practice generally frowned upon in the US system.

The Republicans also streamlined the committees in the House, eliminating several and renaming others (for example, the committee the Democrats called Education and Labor became Education and the Workforce). The Republican revolution retrenched committee power, and control over committees was returned to the Republican Party. Deviations from party priorities would be punished (even going so far as to threaten abolition of a committee, see Aldrich & Rohde 2018: 176). Power had shifted back to a strong speaker with a centralized party.

When Democrats regained the majority with the election of 2006, they did not seek to give back power to the committees. Instead, both learning from the Republicans and consistent with her authoritative leadership style, Speaker Nancy Pelosi (D-CA), sought to integrate power in her speakership. She decided to maintain the six-year term limit for committee chairs, writing it into the Democratic rules herself; however, the term limit was eliminated in the next Congress (Stewart 2019). While the Republicans had a goal of passing legislation in the first 100 days of the 104th Congress, Pelosi's Democratic caucus vowed to pass six priority bills in the first 100 hours of the 110th. These bills, including such items as raising the minimum wage, cutting interest rates on student loans, and lowering prescription drug costs, were written by the Democratic leadership, and like legislation from the earlier Republican Party task forces, bypassed committees and had no input from the minority party (Aldrich & Rohde 2018: 181). This trend, begun in the 104th Congress, creates a more closed legislative process than Americans have come to expect from their system. Not only does it limit or eliminate minority voices, but it also 'moves effective decision-making ... behind closed doors' (Welsh 2008: 17).

The 2018 election brought a return to the Democratic majority in the House after eight years of Republican rule, and also a bit of decentralization back to committees. On 'opening day' in January each new Congress votes on a set of rules proposed by the majority party to govern the legislative process. Democrats in 2019 proposed a rules package that opened up the process, giving more power to committees and members. Incoming Speaker Pelosi faced challenges from the more progressive members of her party's caucus such as Alexandria Ocasio-Cortez (D-NY), as well as from a centrist group, the 'Problem Solvers Caucus', composed of both Republicans and Democrats. The rules package is generally a party-line vote, but for the first time in 20 years, the package received a bipartisan vote (Problem Solvers 2019). The Problem Solvers Caucus had advocated for reforms that would allow members from both parties to have a broader voice in the legislative process (McPherson 2019). Consistent with conditional party government theory (Rohde 1991), a more heterogeneous party membership is less likely to centralize power in party leaders. Pelosi's rather fractious caucus included both progressives and moderates, and factions from either side threatened to vote against her. Though Pelosi was able to pull together enough votes to win the speakership, to do so, she had to promise to limit herself to two terms in the position.

The House rules changes for the 116th Congress returned some power back to committees and rank-and-file members. The rules changed the name of the Education and Workforce Committee back to Education and Labor (the name that Democrats prefer), required, among other things, that some types of legislation receive committee consideration and markup before floor consideration, removed term limits for committee chairs, and required that each committee hold 'Member Day' hearings, in which any member of Congress can testify about any legislative matter before that committee. The rules also required that the chair of a committee develop oversight plans in conjunction with the ranking member, giving some power back to the minority party. It also established two new select committees: Climate Crisis, and Modernization of Congress (Hudiberg, 2019). According to Rules Committee chairman James McGovern (D-MA),

> 'In a sign that we intend to run this place differently, these ideas were developed from the bottom up, not the top down. We asked every member for their ideas, from the longest-serving to the newly elected, Democrats and Republicans alike'
>
> (McGovern 2019)

Rules and procedures governing committees

Procedures for committee governance in the House come from four separate sources: legislative statutes (the LRAs of 1946 and 1975, discussed earlier), the Rules of the House of Representatives,[6] party rules and each committee's own rules. 'Shortly after each quadrennial election, each party caucuses to make several important decisions: leadership for the party, its nominee for the leadership of the chamber (each party nominates a candidate for speaker), and its slate of committees and their chairs' (Jenkins & Stewart 2013: 17). At the beginning of each new Congress (elected in an even year, convening in an odd year), the House passes a resolution approving the rules and procedures governing business in the chamber. The rules from the previous Congress are amended (and the amendments may be more or less extensive, depending upon whether there is a change in majority party). In addition, each party meets in caucus to amend its own rules for the new Congress. Finally, as directed by House rules, each committee has its own set of rules governing procedures, meetings, membership and subcommittees.

Committees in Congress are of three main types: standing, special/select, and joint. Table 18.1 contains a list of House and Senate committees in the 116th Congress and Table 18.2 a sample listing of a standing committee's jurisdiction.

In practice, House rules govern the overall makeup of committees within the basic guidelines of the relevant statutes. House Rule X lists the standing committees and delineates their jurisdiction. The House rules do not mention the party makeup of the committees (i.e., what proportion of committee membership is allotted to each party); that is done by the majority party leadership and reflects the proportion of each party in the chamber. Parties then make their own decisions as to which of their members will serve on each committee. For example, while the Democratic Party does not have term limits, the Republican Party limits committee chairs to only three terms, or six years (House Republican Conference Rule 15e). Finally, the committees themselves determine (within House and party guidelines) how the committee will be structured, what subcommittees it will have and how often and when to meet.

Table 18.3 shows the sources of authority for committee action and illustrates the complexity of the rules structure for committees. The Legislative Reorganization Act sets out the broad parameters of committee organization,

Table 18.1 Committees in the 116th United States Congress (2019–2020)

House	Senate
Standing Committees	
Agriculture	Agriculture, Nutrition, and Forestry
Appropriations	Appropriations
Armed Services	Armed Services
Budget	Banking, Housing, and Urban Affairs
Education and Labour	Budget
Energy and Commerce	Commerce, Science, and Transportation
Ethics	Energy and Natural Resources
Financial Services	Environment and Public Works
Foreign Affairs	Finance
Homeland Security	Foreign Relations
House Administration	Health, Education, Labor, and Pensions
Judiciary	Homeland Security and Governmental Affairs
Natural Resources	
Oversight and Reform	Judiciary
Rules	Rules and Administration
Science, Space, and Technology	Small Business and Entrepreneurship
Small Business	Veterans' Affairs
Transportation and Infrastructure	
Veterans' Affairs	
Ways and Means	
Select and Special Committees	
House Permanent Select Committee on Intelligence	Ageing (Special)
	Caucus on International Narcotics Control
Select Committee on the Climate Crisis	
Select Committee on the Modernization of Congress	Ethics (Select)
	Intelligence (Select)
Joint Committees	
Joint Committee on Printing	
Joint Committee on Taxation	
Joint Committee on the Library	

Source: Committees of the U.S. Congress, retrieved from: www.congress.gov/committees (access: 29.06.2021).

requiring that committees have jurisdiction over a particular topic area and that they must hold open committee hearings. Looking at the first row in the table, one can see, for example, that the LRA does not specify what jurisdiction each committee will have; jurisdiction is established by House Rule X, while general rules for the hearing process are outlined in House Rule XI. Party rules do not cover jurisdiction. On the other hand, the LRA does not provide limits for how many committees a member may join, or how many terms a chair may serve; those regulations are set forth under Republican and Democratic party rules. House Rule XI specifies that each committee must set forth its own rules and establish its quorum; therefore, the House Education and Labour Committee holds meetings on the second Wednesday of each

Table 18.2 Legislative jurisdiction of the US House Committee on Education and Labor

Committee on Education and Labor

(1) Child labor
(2) Gallaudet University and Howard University and Hospital
(3) Convict labor and the entry of goods made by convicts into interstate commerce
(4) Food programs for children in schools
(5) Labor standards and statistics
(6) Education or labor generally
(7) Mediation and arbitration of labor disputes
(8) Regulation or prevention of importation of foreign laborers under contract
(9) Workers' compensation
(10) Vocational rehabilitation
(11) Wages and hours of labor
(12) Welfare of miners
(13) Work incentive programs
(14) Organization, administration, and general management of the Department of Education
(15) Organization, administration, and general management of the Department of Labor

Source: House Rule X 'organization of committees', clause 1e, www.govinfo.gov/content/pkg/HMAN-116/pdf/HMAN-116-pg445.pdf (access: 05.01.2021).

month, and its quorum is set at one-third of its membership, according to its own rules. If the rules and regulations governing committee organization and structure seem to be a complicated web, that is because they are!

The fact that committees face four separate power sources – five, if Republican and Democratic party caucuses are counted separately – constrains their actions and also illustrates their importance in the legislative process. Taking the second point first, committees in Congress are essential to the work of Congress. Not only do these specially commissioned minorities subdivide the work into subject matter jurisdiction, but they provide fora for discussion of issues, agenda-setting, and consideration and amendment of bills, while also fulfilling electoral and legislative needs of members of Congress. Without committees, it would be extremely difficult to vet the large number of bills that come before the House of Representatives, and almost equally difficult to schedule legislation on the floor. And committees allow members to achieve their reelection goal by credit-claiming, position-taking and advertising (Fenno 1973, Mayhew 1974). It is no wonder that a variety of entities, including political parties, the House chamber, and committees themselves, want to exert control over committee actions. But committees are also rule-bound and their actions are limited by decisions of all of these actors. Complex and complicated, yes, but a system that is in keeping with the American goal of distributing power, allowing for minority voices to be heard and setting up systems that limit the power of government.

Table 18.3 Sources of authority for selected aspects of committee governance in the US House of Representatives, 116th Congress (2019–2020)

	Legislative Reorganization Act of 1970 (LRA) (applies to House and Senate)	House Rules X and XI (applies to House only)	Democratic Party Caucus Rules*	Republican Party Conference Rules*	Individual Committee Rules** (applies to committee members/chairs)
Committee jurisdiction	Requires that committees consider bills in their jurisdiction, but does not set the jurisdiction	House Rule X establishes the number of committees, names them and delineates their jurisdiction	Not covered under party rules	Not specifically addressed in published rules	Each committee establishes its own subcommittees and their jurisdiction (within the jurisdiction of the committee)
Limitations on the number of committees on which a member may serve	Not discussed	Not discussed	Appropriations, Rules, Ways & Means and Financial Services committees are considered exclusive; members can only serve on the one committee		n/a
Committee assignments and selection of chairs	Not discussed	Rule X specifies that committee membership is contingent upon party membership; also directs each committee to select a chair	The Democratic Caucus Steering and Policy Committee nominates, and the Caucus votes on committee members and chairs	The Republican Party Steering Committee nominates and the Caucus votes on committee members and chairs	Not discussed

How many committees may a person chair	Not discussed	An individual member is generally limited to chairing only one committee or subcommittee	n/a
Term limits for chairs	Not discussed	No term limits on chairs (though membership on the Budget Committee is limited to 3 terms out of any 5)*	Not mentioned; committee chairs follow party rules
Hearings and witnesses	Requires open committee hearings and published hearing reports; requires witnesses to submit testimony ahead of time	Rule XI requires open hearings according to LRA, sets out rules for calling witnesses/ testifying	The hearing process is not discussed in party rules	Example: Education and Labor Committee Rules 7 and 8 set forth specific procedures for hearings and the calling of witnesses.
Other	Requires public voting and hearing broadcasts, provides for staff /funding, requires committee reports be submitted at end of a Congress	Rule XI Specifies how committee reports should be submitted to the Clerk of the House. Directs committees to set rules, establish quorums	Both parties include rules about misconduct (e.g. what to do if a chair is convicted of a crime).	Example: Education and Labor holds meetings on the second Wednesday of each month at 10:00 AM; Sets its quorum at 1/3 of its members

* Some rules are only applicable when the party is in the majority.
** House Rule XI requires committees to establish their own rules.

Sources: House Rule X, www.govinfo.gov/content/pkg/HMAN-116/pdf/HMAN-116-pg445.pdf
House Rule XI, www.govinfo.gov/content/pkg/HMAN-116/pdf/HMAN-116-pg557.pdf, Legislative Reorganization Act of 1970, www.govinfo.gov/content/pkg/STATUTE-84/pdf/STATUTE-84-Pg1140.pdf, Democratic Party Rules, www.dems.gov/caucus-rules-of-116th-congress, Republican Party Rules, www.gop.gov/conference-rules-of-the-116th-congress/ (access: 05.01.2021).

While the committee system is an important tool for the parties (particularly the majority party), committees are not the only organizational structure available. Each party meets in its caucus or conference (i.e. gathering of all its members) and each caucus has its own organization to help get its business done. Parties have steering and policy committees to appoint party membership to committees and decide on party priorities, they have campaign committees to help reelect current membership, and they have whip systems, to count votes and facilitate communication between membership and leadership.

Format and function

As mentioned, committees in Congress are of three main types: standing, special/select, and joint. Standing committees in both the House and Senate are permanent, existing from one Congress to the next, though they can be changed or removed by changes to the chamber's rules. They are the central legislative committees of Congress. They have jurisdiction over particular policy areas and generally also have one or more subcommittees. Select or special committees are non-permanent committees (which may also be joint) put together temporarily to address a current issue or problem. Joint committees are committees that have members from both chambers of Congress. Standing committees are the basic 'workhorses' of Congress, and are generally the focus of discussion and research on congressional committees. In the US Congress, most standing committees are 'authorizing' committees, which create governmental programmes that 'appropriating' committees must fund. Standing committees can be further subdivided according to the categories developed by Lees and Shaw (1979): legislative, financial, investigative, administrative oversight, and parliamentary housekeeping. The authorizing committees are legislative ones, e.g. Transportation, Energy and Commerce, and Education and Labour. Several committees fall into the financial category: the House and Senate budget committees, which are responsible for the overall budget and budget resolution, the Senate Finance Committee, and the House Ways and Means Committee, tasked with taxation, and finally, the House and Senate Appropriations Committees, responsible for funding government programmes. Of these, both the Senate Finance Committee and the House Ways and Means Committee also have jurisdiction over policies beyond tax, and are thus legislative committees as well. Investigative functions occur according to the jurisdiction of standing legislative committees in the House and Senate. In addition, the House Oversight and Reform Committee serves as an investigative committee, and select committees in either chamber may be created for the purpose of investigating a specific matter. Parliamentary housekeeping committees include the House Administration Committee and the Senate Rules and Administration Committee, as well as the House Rules Committee, which also has an important role in the legislative process.

The Rules Committee in the House plays a unique role. It has as its main function overseeing the rules of the House for each Congress (generally voted on during the first day's meeting of the new Congress) and deciding on recesses and adjournments in the House (see House Rule X, Clause 1, section [o][2]). The committee is extremely important in the legislative process, however, because it writes and considers the 'special rules' which are attached to House legislation, laying out the procedures by which the legislation will be considered on the floor of the house. The Rules Committee has long been controlled by the majority party. As we have seen, at one time, the speaker was automatically a member of the Rules Committee; now the speaker generally asserts control by appointing a loyalist to chair the committee. The committee has a disproportionate number of majority party members, currently, nine Democrats and four Republicans in a ratio of 'two to one, plus one'. The reason the majority party keeps such close control over the rules committee is because of its function as the gatekeeper of legislative activity on the floor. For most major legislation, floor consideration does not begin until the Rules Committee attaches a special rule to the legislation that comes out of the originating committee (or, in some cases, a majority-party-constituted task force). The rule sets the parameters for debate, including the length of time for discussion and numbers and types of amendments. Controlling the Rules Committee means controlling the floor access of legislation that has been reported out from standing committees.

The House has one further committee to be mentioned: the Committee of the Whole, actually a parliamentary procedure which is not widely used outside of the former British empire. This is not a committee per se, but a legislative mechanism by which the House may consider legislation. When the House convenes as the Committee of the Whole (formally, the Committee of the Whole House on the State of the Union), it operates under different parliamentary procedures from its usual sessions and requires only a 100-person quorum, rather than the usual 218. The Committee of the Whole is used frequently and is the primary mechanism by which major bills are considered on the floor of the House. The purpose of the committee is to make it easier for the House to consider bills. When bill consideration is complete, the Committee of the Whole dissolves itself, and the House votes on the bill under its usual parliamentary rules and with a quorum of 218 (CRS 2013).

Committees in Congress have three general types of meetings: business meetings, markups, and hearings. According to House rules, each committee must have a business meeting at the start of Congress (and Republicans require that their party members first meet separately when their party is in the majority) and must have regularly scheduled business meetings throughout the following two years. Hearings are a major function of congressional committees and can be held for legislative, investigative, oversight, or confirmation purposes. The latter occur only in the Senate as part of the constitutional process by which the Senate must 'advise and consent' on presidential appointments, including both public ministers and federal judges. Such hearings may be perfunctory or quite adversarial (witness recent confirmation hearing on Supreme Court justice appointments). Oversight hearings are opportunities for members of Congress to inquire into the status of legislative programmes and their implementation by bureaucratic agencies. These too can be adversarial (especially if the majority in Congress is of a different party than the presidential administration) or collegial. Investigative hearings delve into a crisis, problem or scandal and may include investigations into bureaucratic action or inaction (in such case these hearings could also be classified as an oversight), or they may investigate business or economic problems more broadly.

Legislative hearings are held to draw attention to an issue or policy that is, or may result in, a legislative proposal. These hearings follow a particular format, with the chair and ranking member introducing the hearings with opening statements, after which witnesses testify and are questioned by members of the committee. Witnesses are called by the majority party with some input from the minority party and can be government officials, constituents, members of interest groups, individual businesses affected by the proposed legislation, or celebrities (boosting media attention of the hearing), and sometimes other members of Congress. Witnesses testify in panels that may include one person (an agency head or cabinet member) or several individuals (members of interest groups or constituents). The majority party controls the witness list though House rules require that the minority party be allowed some witnesses as well. This practice may seem inconsistent with majority rule, but it is in keeping with the American system's tendency to value minority rights. Even during the House Judiciary Committee's 2020 impeachment hearings on President Trump, the Republicans were allowed one witness to the Democrats' three.

The formal committee process begins with an announcement of the hearing, listing the witnesses. Each witness is required to submit written testimony prior to the hearing. His or her oral testimony is limited to five minutes, after which the witness is questioned by the committee members. The order of questioning is generally by seniority and moves back and forth between the majority and minority parties. The word 'questioning' is used loosely here. Members of Congress often appear to be making speeches rather than asking questions of the witness. Hearings are a way in which members present themselves to the public (Fenno 2003) by taking positions, advertising or claiming credit (Mayhew 1974). Their witness questions often turn into speeches, usually with the hope of a pithy soundbite that their constituents will hear on the local news that evening. Witnesses often do not have a specific question to answer, but usually take the opportunity to press home whatever message they would like to convey. Hearings themselves are political theatre.

Legislative hearings do not necessarily result in legislation. They are sometimes used as a trial balloon, to see how the public responds to an issue, or they may simply be an effort to demonstrate that the committee is paying attention to an issue. The real legislative work occurs during the markup, which is generally open to the public. It is here that the committee actually considers and debates a bill and its amendments. The process by which a bill becomes a law begins with an introduction in the chamber (in the House, any member can simply place a bill in the hopper, a little box next to the speaker's podium). Once introduced, the bill is referred to the committee by the speaker, in conjunction with the party leadership (and there can be some competition and turf wars among committees regarding jurisdiction). The committee chair runs the markup and members of the committee propose amendments, which are debated and then voted on. The committee then votes on the bill as amended. The next step in the process is floor consideration. In order to be scheduled on the floor of the House, the bill must first go to the Rules Committee to receive a special rule governing floor procedure on amendments and debate. Once the Rules Committee passes a rule, the rule and the legislation go to the floor, with the rule voted on first before the legislation can be considered. The Senate operates under a different procedure involving agreements made between majority and minority leadership.[7]

Hearings draw attention to an issue and let members put down a marker on legislation. They are a method by which members may make a statement for the record which outlines their position on an issue, their priorities for legislation, and their objections to other legislative provisions. This is an important part of the legislative process for the members of Congress and their party, but it is not the primary legislative work. Markups are a more direct way to have an impact on legislation. It is during markup that members may suggest changes to the legislation and debate policy alternatives with one another. They may also make their legislative and policy positions known through recorded votes on amendments that they either approve or disapprove. Again, these are important parts of the legislative process. However, both committee hearings and markups are open to the public, and not all issues will be debated in such a public forum. Members will do much of their work behind the scenes – discussing legislative strategies, negotiating and bargaining over specific legislative provision, and otherwise doing the 'sausage-making' for which legislative bodies are famous. Not all the work of the committee is visible to the public.

The committee is also important in floor consideration of bills. First, when the rule for the legislation is being discussed, committee members themselves act as witnesses in the Rules Committee hearings. In particular, the majority members are an important source of information to the Rules Committee. As it is tightly controlled by the majority party, its decisions about floor consideration are effectively party leadership decisions. Also, when a bill is considered on the floor, the chair of the originating committee generally acts as the floor manager, overseeing the process of consideration, organizing with the whip system and party leadership and otherwise working to ensure passage of a bill that is consistent with party and committee priorities.

The final stage of the process is often a conference committee, an ad hoc committee with members from both the House and the Senate that will resolve differences between the bills passed by both chambers. Each party selects its membership on the conference committee, and generally, conference committee membership is made up of members of the committee(s) that originally considered the bill. Since the speaker appoints the conference committee, she has some control over its outcome (Smith 2018: 152). The conference committee disbands when it has reached a compromise on the bill and sends it back to each chamber (alternatively, when it decides that it cannot agree on a compromise, the bill is killed). In recent years, conference committees have often been abandoned in favour of a 'ping pong' approach, in which the bill is sent back and forth as each chamber makes amendments (Sinclair 2012).

Finally, committees are also involved in the implementation of policies. Though the executive branch has the primary responsibility for carrying out the laws that Congress passes, committees monitor implementation in a variety of ways. They may hold oversight hearings to investigate how well agencies are implementing the programmes that Congress has authorized. In the hearings, the committee may request testimony from agency heads or bureaucrats. The legislation is often written with a requirement for the executive branch to submit evaluation reports to the committees. Members of committees and their staff may consult with executive agencies as reauthorization is being considered. Finally, Congress has additional resources at its disposal. The Congressional Research Service, at the request of a member, will write a neutral, non-partisan report on an issue, giving both sides where appropriate. The Government Accountability Office, another arm of Congress, will research and write evaluations of legislative agencies or programmes.

Composition and membership

Membership on committees is determined by the majority and minority parties in each chamber. At the start of each Congress, members make their committee preferences known, and the Steering and Policy Committees of each party in each chamber decides on membership for each committee. (Note that Steering and Policy Committees are extra-legislative committees, part of the party system, rather than the legislative committee system). Members in the House are limited to no more than two committees, and are likely to devote much of their energies to a single committee, giving them expertise in a particular issue area. Senators have to spread their attention more thinly since they are members of more committees. Senators generally serve on at least three committees, often four or even five. There are only 100 senators (as opposed to 435 House members) to be assigned to a similar number of committees as in the House. Thus, senators are more likely to be generalists who do not have the depth of knowledge on a single policy, but a breadth of knowledge over several areas.

Committee membership often aligns with member goals, as demonstrated in Richard Fenno's classic work, *Congressmen in Committees* (1973). Fenno says that members make their decisions on committees in accordance with three goals that may or may not conflict with one another. This is the basis of the distributional theory of committee memberships: that committees distribute benefits to their members. Members may desire to achieve prestige within the chamber, and certain committees are considered more prestigious than others. Those committees have changed over time. Prestigious committees include Ways and Means, Energy and Commerce, Rules, and Appropriations, though Appropriations has lost some of its cachet in an era of budget-cutting. Similarly, Foreign Affairs was once considered prestigious, though with an inwardly focused policy agenda this prestige has declined (see Davidson & Oleszek et al. 2014: 174, Stewart 2018: 12–14, Deering & Smith 1997: 79). Members may also desire to focus on the goal of public policy, making a name for themselves in a particular policy domain, such as education, the environment, or business. Members may come to a policy committee with some expertise in the area, but they will certainly develop more as they make a career on the committee. They will not only immerse themselves in the issue, they will also have interactions with interest groups and agency experts who may bring different perspectives to the table.

Finally, members of Congress usually want to be reelected to their chamber. There are several committees that Deering and Smith refer to as constituent committees, in which members focus on policy concerns of interest to their constituents, in the hopes of winning their votes in the next election. The possibility of 'bringing home the bacon' was more limited when earmarking (project-based funding for specific legislative districts) was banned by the Republican majority in 2011. Democratic efforts to bring earmarks back in the 117th Congress serve to help the reelection goal. Either way, constituents still want to know that their concerns are at the centre of their members' activities in Congress.

Conclusion: specially commissioned minorities at work

Committees can be important arenas for parties and members of Congress to act in all stages of the policy process. Though the president and political parties generally set the political agenda, committees can use hearings to help bring attention to an issue. Certainly committees, in concert with interest groups, play a large role in formulating policy alternatives to various problems in society. Committees can also be integral to the adoption of legislative measures, though, as we have seen, the Rules Committee and party leadership can sometimes undermine or even usurp their role in that phase. Implementation is obviously a role of executive branch agencies, but congressional oversight is a way that committees participate in the implementation process.

Committees are still 'specially-commissioned minorities', though perhaps not in the exact sense that Wilson meant. When Wilson was writing, and for much of American history, congressional committees, led by powerful chairs, dominated the legislative process. Chairs acted independently of political parties and had a great deal of control over legislation. Wilson was advocating for strong political parties and a Congress that acted more like a European parliament. He wanted floor sessions to be the focal point of the legislative process, and he lamented the parties' tendency to delegate authority to committees. Today, parties have a great deal more control over committees than they have had in the past, but the legislative process still occurs largely in committee. Wilson's dream of parliamentary parties in Congress has not been realized. Instead, parties still 'specially commission' committees to work on legislation, but they also exercise more control over committees and have developed ways to ensure that committee actions on important issues are consistent with party goals.

As the quote at the beginning of the chapter suggests, committees are small subsets of congressional membership that allow members to specialize in a policy area and facilitate legislative work. They have been commissioned by the institution through its parties both to streamline the workload of Congress, and to give benefits to members. 'When members found that they lacked the time and the detailed knowledge to make many decisions, they placed great powers in the hands of their standing committees' (Goodwin 1970: 9). Starting from ad hoc groups, formed to address one legislative issue at a time, committees have become an integral part of the policy process. Their roots are intertwined with the work of Congress at all levels, and while party leadership may at times attempt to control committee governance, it is not possible, nor desirable, for parties to weed them out. Instead, a variety of rules and norms have grown around the committee system. Parties have learned to rely on committees and work around them when necessary. Individual members continue to use committees to further their own needs. These 'specially-commissioned minorities' are not only integral to the congressional process, but they are also consistent with the intention of the framers of the American system, who created a system specifically designed to give minorities power.

Power has shifted among committee chairs, committee members, and political parties. Currently, the party is ascendant, but that could change, as succeeding generations develop their own ways of controlling the legislative process. Even now, there is some movement, however slight, to take committee control back from the party: rules changes in the 116th Congress gave some power back to committees and members in an effort to rein in the party's ability to bring legislation to the floor outside the committee process. Committees are tools for political parties and their members to gain control, power, and influence within the chamber. Whether the party, the committee chair, or committee members dominate committees has fluctuated over time. Rank-and-file members used committees to wrest power away from the majority party leaders in the early part of the 20th century. By the end of the century, however, rank-and-file Democrats learned that they could profit from giving power back to the party, which could dole out benefits to committees such as increased staff or funding. Committees are, for the time being, firmly in the hands of the party. This is not to say that parties have complete control; indeed, committees often act independently of the parties. However, when committees act independently *in a way that is inconsistent with majority party goals*, the party will pull in the reins. This has happened under both Republican and Democratic speakers, who, for example, may turn to the use of task forces to create legislation when committees are uncooperative or rebellious. As political parties have become more externally polarized, parties seek greater control over legislative output, most of which still occurs within the committee. Though history shows that party control of committees can vary depending upon member needs and the relative homogeneity of party membership, at this point, the majority party uses committees or bypasses them to achieve policy goals.

Indeed, to paraphrase Wilson, Congress in committee is parties – and party members – at work.

Notes

1 The Federalist Papers were written in the late 18th century to defend the US Constitution as it was sent to the original 13 states for ratification. They are frequently used to determine the intent of the framers in setting up the Constitution. Federalist 10 and 51, written by James Madison, explain, respectively, that a representative government avoids the mob rule that may ensue from a direct democracy, and that separating and blending powers (for example, by giving the president the power to veto legislation) ensures that no one branch of government may become tyrannical. Taken together, these two papers provide a justification for a system of government that makes it difficult to get things done.
2 The quote in its entirety is this: 'The House sits, not for serious discussion, but to sanction the conclusions of its Committees as rapidly as possible. It legislates in its committee-rooms; not by the determinations of majorities, but by the resolutions of *specially-commissioned minorities*; so that it is not far from the truth to say that Congress in session is Congress on public exhibition, whilst Congress in its committee-rooms is Congress at work (Wilson 1885: 78-79) (emphasis mine).
3 There are some exceptions. In the early days of the Senate, for example, the majority party had no control over committees, and the minority party in some instances controlled the members and chairs of committee (Welsh 2008: 5).
4 'Thus, the modern Speaker sits at the top of two powerful institutions: the House of Representatives *and* the legislative party of which he or she is leader' (Jenkins & Stewart 2012: 21).
5 For further discussion of the Contract with America and its meaning in the American context, see Manuel and Cammisa 1998 and Cammisa and Manuel 2014.
6 The House rules are published in a manual whose official title is *The Constitution, Jefferson's Manual and Rules of the House of Representatives*. The document is published every two years. The manual includes, as stated, the Constitution of the United States as well as Thomas Jefferson's manual regarding parliamentary rules for the chamber, the text of the Legislative Reorganization Act and, finally, the rules

for the Congress. The entire document runs more than 1,500 pages, and includes rules regarding everything from the speaker and other leadership, to broadcasting floor proceedings, and keeping records of proceedings.
7 The Senate uses a 'Unanimous Consent Agreement' to bring legislation to the floor. The majority and minority parties work out ahead of time what the parameters for debate will be, and if they cannot come to agreement, the legislation will not come to the floor. The Senate has only 100 senators compared to 435 representatives in the House. The House has more rules to control its large membership; the Senate gives its members more leeway. In the Senate, for example, rules allow any Senator to 'talk a bill to death'; this legislative 'filibustering' is not allowed under House rules. For further explanation, see Davidson et al. (2014: 230).

References

Aldrich, J. & Rohde, D. (2019.) Congressional committees in a continuing partisan era. In S. Kernell & S. Smith (eds.) *Principles and Practice of American Politics*, 7th ed. Washington, D.C.: CQ Press.
Cammisa, A.M. & Manuel, P. (2014). *The path of American public policy: comparative perspectives*. Lanham, MD: Lexington Books.
Congressional Research Service (CRS). (2013). *Committee of the Whole: An Introduction*. Washington, DC: Congressional Research Service.
Davidson, R., Oleszek, W., Lee, F., & Schickler, E. (2014) *Congress and its members*, 14th ed. Washington, D.C.: CQ Press
Deering, C.J. & Smith, S.S. (1997). *Committees in Congress*. Washington, D.C.: CQ Press.
Evans, C.L. (2011). Congressional Committees. In G.C. Edwards, F. Lee, & E. Schickler (eds.). *The Oxford handbook of the American Congress*. Oxford, UK: Oxford University Press.
Fenno, R. (1973). *Congressmen in committees*. Boston: Little, Brown and Company.
Fenno, R. (2003). *Homestyle: House members in their Districts*. Revised and reprinted. London: Longman.
Gaines, B., Goodwin, M., Holden Bates, S., & Sin, G. (2019). The study of legislative committees. *Journal of Legislative Studies* 25 (3), 331–39.
Goodwin, G., (1970). *The little legislatures: committees of Congress*. Boston, MA: University of Massachusetts Press.
House Rule X, Clause 1, section [o][2]. Retrieved from https://rules.house.gov/sites/democrats.rules.house.gov/files/117-House-Rules-Clerk.pdf (access: 27.05.2021)
Hudiberg, J. (2019). *House rules procedures affecting committee procedure in the 116th Congress (2019–2020)*. Washington, D.C.: Congressional Research Service.
Jenkins, J. & Stewart, C. (2013). *Fighting for the speakership: the House and the rise of party government*. Princeton, NJ: Princeton University Press.
Lees, J.D. & Shaw, M. (eds.) (1979). *Committees in legislatures: A comparative analysis*. Oxford: Martin Robinson.
Madison, J. (1787). Federalist 10 and 51.
Manuel, P. & Cammisa, A.M. (1998). *Checks and balances: how a parliamentary system could change American politics*. Boulder, CO: Westview Press.
Mayhew, D. (1974). *Congress: the electoral connection*. New Haven: Yale University Press
McPherson, L. (2019, January 3). House adopts rules package with few Democratic defections over PAYGO provision. *Roll Call*, Retrieved from www.rollcall.com/2019/01/03/house-adopts-rules-package-with-few-democratic-defections-over-paygo-provision/ (access: 29.10.2020.)

McGovern, J. (2019). *Chairman McGovern begins consideration of historic rules package to modernize the 116th Congress.* Washington. Retrieved from https://rules.house.gov/press-release/chairman-mcgovern-begins-consideration-historic-rules-package-modernize-116th-congress, (access: 28.10.2020.)

Problem Solvers Caucus. (2019). Problem solvers caucus breaks gridlock; rules reform passes the House. Press release. Retrieved from https://problemsolverscaucus-gottheimer.house.gov/media/press-releases/problem-solvers-caucus-break-gridlock-rules-reforms-pass-house. (access: 30.10.2021).

Rohde, D.W. (1991). *Parties and leaders in the postreform House.* Chicago, IL: University of Chicago Press.

Sinclair, B. (2012). Ping pong and other congressional pursuits: party leaders and post-passage procedural choice. In J. Strauss (ed.). *Party procedure in the United States Congress.* Lanham, MD: Rowman and Littlefield Publishers.

Smith, S. (2018). Congress, the troubled institution. In S. Kernell & S. Smith (eds.). *Principles and Practice of American Politics,* 7th ed. Washington, DC: CQ Press.

Stewart, C.S., III. (2018). The value of congressional committee assignments in the Republican Era. Paper presented at the 2019 annual meeting of the Midwest Political Science Association, Chicago, Illinois, April 5–8, 2018.

U.S. Congress, House. (2018). *Constitution, Jefferson's manual and rules of the House of Representatives of the United States, One Hundred Sixteenth Congress.* Washington: U.S. Govt. Print. Off. Retrieved from www.govinfo.gov/help/hman#about. (access: 02.11.2021).

U.S. Congress, House, Democratic Caucus. (2019). *Democratic caucus rules of the 116th Congress.* Retrieved from www.dems.gov/caucus-rules-of-116th-congress. (access: 03.11.2021).

U.S. Congress, House, Republican Conference. (2019). *Republican conference rules of the 116th Congress.* Retrieved from www.gop.gov/conference-rules-of-the-116th-congress. (access: 04.11.2021).

Welsh, M. (2008, July 28). An overview of the development of U.S. congressional committees. *Law Librarians Society of Washington, D.C.* Retrieved from www.gop.gov/conference-rules-of-the-116th-congress/ (access: 23.10.2021).

Wilson, W., *Congressional Government.* 1885. Boston & New York: Houghton-Mifflin.

Appendix: Parliamentary committees in the policy process

Based on the original research framework, the following list of questions was developed. The contributors were asked to used them as guidance in writing their chapters.

2.1 Formalities and structure – the institutional setting of committees

1. What is the format of the committee system, i.e. how many committees exist? What type of committee are they?
2. How many members do committees have?
3. Are ordinary committee sessions public or private by default? Can they be held in public by decision of the committee?
4. How high is the share of (ordinary) committee sessions held in public?
5. Do committees conduct public hearings? How has their number developed?
6. What types of committees exist and how do their tasks overlap?
7. Do committees 'mirror' the ministerial bureaucracy? How many committees handle matters from only one ministry or several ministries? How many matters from one ministry is handled by one or more committees?
8. How do committees contribute to the legislative, control, and communication functions of parliament as a whole?

2.2 Actors in committees

9. How are decisions about committee assignment made? What say do MPs have? What influence does the leadership of the parliamentary party – or others – have?
10. Are all MPs members of one – or more – committees? Can MPs be members of more than one committee? How many committee memberships do MPs have?
11. What is the turnover in committee membership, i.e. how long do MPs typically stay in one committee?

12. Does policy expertise lead to committee assignment or does committee assignment lead to policy expertise?
13. What are the relevant MP roles in committees? What influence do they have?

2.3 Interactions in committees

14. Do deliberation and discussion take place in committee sessions?
15. Do bargaining and deal-making occur in committee or outside the formal sessions?
16. Are differences between committees apparent? What kind of differences are they?
17. Are government officials regularly present in committees? May committees request their presence? If so, how often do they do that? Are these ministers or bureaucrats?
18. To what degree do the members of specific committees 'monopolize' contacts with interest groups and NGOs within their respective policy areas?
19. Who participates in public hearings?

3.1 Problem definition and agenda-setting

20. Do committees write general reports on current topics beyond legislation and oversight topics? Do they initiate matters to be dealt with by the government?
21. Can committees formally initiate legislation?
22. Can they take up topics in a non-legislative way and write a report or deliver recommendations about them?
23. Is it committees or individual MPs and party groups that define problems and set the agenda?
24. Can committees set and control their own agenda? Can they prioritize or delay issues on their agenda? Can they cut the agenda, for example by 'killing a bill'?
25. Can committees set the agenda for the government? What role do committees have in setting the agenda of political discussion? Or do individual MPs and party groups set these agendas?

3.2 Policy formulation

26. Do committees exercise substantial influence by transforming draft bills? Or do they have more of a formal role?
27. How substantial are the changes they make or recommend to be decided by the plenary?
28. Do committees have formal rights to make final decisions in place of the plenary?

3.3 Implementation and Evaluation

29. Do committees exercise oversight? To what degree?
30. Do committees regularly ask for implementation reports?
31. Are separate oversight committees installed?
32. Do committees decide on an oversight strategy or plan?

Index

accelerated legislation *see* urgency
ad hoc committees 10–12, 67, 99, 102, 118, 140, 169, 177, 193, 264, 321
agenda control 25, 101, 147, 173, 312
agenda-setting: committees 25, 182, 317–318; government 43–45, 150, 245, 269; parliament 109, 147, 182, 213; parties 62–75, 159, 239, 246
agricultural committees 23, 82, 124, 145, 230
amendments to legislation 98, 153, 183–184, 275, 296, 311
anticipation 29–30, 126, 130, 313
appropriations committees 11, 213–214, 327, 334, 339
Arab League 40, 58
Arab Spring 57
arenas, committees as 4, 29, 61, 73, 131, 216–217
artificial intelligence 119
Assemblée nationale 98 *see* France
assignment *see* committee assignment
auditing 155, 192, 238, 279
authoritarian regimes 57
autonomy: of committees 43, 101, 160, 257, 275; of parliament 112, 159, 161, 263; of MPs 85

backbenchers 105, 144, 309–310
bargaining 64, 70 *see also* negotiation
bicameral 98, 116, 189, 208, 263, 282
broadcasting committee meetings 194 *see also* television
budget committees 11, 170, 192, 200–201, 272
budget proposal 44, 213
Bundestag *see* Germany
business and commerce committees 83, 138, 147, 330

cabinet 44, 79, 161, 185, 193, 247
caucus 20, 150, 306
censure 160
centralization of power 161, 196, 201, 244
chamber-driven legislature 139, 302
checks-and-balances 9, 160, 263
Christian Democrats 121, 159, 161
Ciudadanos 245
civil servants 23, 69, 83, 180, 226, 307
civil service code 51
civil society organizations (CSOs) 20, 48, 57–58, 214, 269; *see also* Non-Governmental Organizations (NGOs)
classification of parliaments *see* arena legislature *and* working parliament
cleaning of a bill 28–29, 130
clerks 81, 304, 312
clientelism 31, 207, 217–219
coalition agreements 63, 118, 120, 160
coalition governance 63, 161, 290–291
Cold War 22, 199–200
colonialism 137–138, 208–209
commission of inquiry 280, *see* committees of inquiry
committee assignment 19, 43, 81–83, 143, 178–179, 195–196
committee chair 22, 68, 146, 185, 294, 324
committee competencies 5, 29, 79, 118
committee culture 85, 276
committee-driven legislature 139, 302–303
Committee for the Future 81, 91–93
committee mandate 50
Committee Manual 84
committee meetings, closed, *see* committee meetings, private

committee meetings, open, *see* committee meetings, public
committee meetings, private 16, 64, 67, 80, 105, 117, 304
committee meetings, public 16, 64, 67, 81, 104, 121, 163, 252
Committee of the Whole 335
Committee on Legislation 28, 163
committee reports 28, 43, 85, 128, 181, 215, 270
committee size 14, 19, 119–121, 140–141, 191, 247, 290, 306
committee staffers 44–51
committee termination 290
committees of inquiry 92, 181, 280
  see also investigating committees, study commissions, research committees
committees per MP 82, 165, 179, 247–248, 257
'common part' activities 73
communication: social media 39, 92, 105–108
comparencias 256
compromises 22, 44, 61, 146, 241
Comptroller 184
conditional party government 325
confidential information 49, 104
conference committee 338
conflict: committees and government 41, 91–92; committee meetings 22–23, 34–35, 104, 124; rapporteurs 109–11
Congressional Research Service 338
Congreso de los Diputados *see* Spain
consensus 82, 129–130, 146, 197
conservative parties 73, 121, 161, 189
constituencies 38, 82, 125, 195, 248
constitutional amendments 281
constitutional change 79, 100, 189, 209–210, 244, 263
constructive vote of no confidence 160–161
consultants 44, 49, 201
Contract with America, the 326
control 11–12; inquiry 80, 181, 247, 280; oversight 47–49, 185, 212, 216; scrutiny 47, 79, 89, 207, 217–218, 228
convocation 287–290
corporatism 123
correspondence between committees and ministries 33, 181, 228–231
corruption 206–207, 212, 281
crisis: COVID-19 9, 111–112, 118, 242; financial 90, 245
crisis management 86, 91, 98

'decline of parliament' thesis 62, 224
defence committees 13, 80, 117, 162, 228, 308
deferment rule 87
deliberation 3, 16, 104, 116, 184, 269
deliberative debate 322
Democrats (USA) 323–328
Denmark 14, 17, 29, 61
desirability of committees by MPs 82–83, 102, 231
deviant case 302, 314
digitalization: of committee subject matter 16, 91–92; of parliamentary functions 9, 46, 93, 104, 236
dilettante tactics 198, 204 *see also* obstruction of voting
discrimination 47, 251, 258
dissenting opinions 23, 85, 90, 272–276
distributional theory 9, 339
division of labour, 12, 43, 66–69, 241–244, 274
'do Arab states really have parliaments?' 56–58
draft bills 26, 53, 118, 150, 183, 247

earmarking 339
Earthquake, 2011 Great East Japan 193
education committees 67, 210, 270, 308, 327
Eduskunta *see* Finland
'effective majority' 189–190, 198–201
efficiency in procedures 11, 48–50, 207, 244, 274, 305
Egypt 14, 17, 29, 42, 52–56
elections 49, 80–84, 143, 182, 208, 266
electoral reform 161, 189, 196–202
electoral threshold 66, 163
emergency powers 111, 162, 263, 270
energy 71, 201, 230, 334
engine room of democracy 1, 94, 207
entrepreneurship committees *see* business and commerce committees
environmental issues 230, 339
'Era of Committee Governance' 324
Erskine May 313
ethics committees 181, 330
European Parliament 248
European Union Affairs 79, 89, 117, 247
evaluation 31, 127–130, 202, 238, 296, 314
evidence sessions 18, 305–306
experts 18, 83–84, 253, 269, 281, 305, 339

expertise, MP 9, 19–21, 82, 125, 144, 195, 231, 250 *see also* committee assignment
explanatory memorandum 54, 151, 311

faction 236–241, 287–289, 321–322
Fenno, R. F. 10, 20–21, 124, 217, 339
Fidesz 159–167
field hearing 18, 32, 46, 54
field trip *see* field visit
field visit 46, 54, 84, 130, 216, 276
finance committees 11, 80–81, 118, 145, 264, 334
Finland 14, 17, 29, 79
fire alarm model 312
'first past the post' 161, 189–190
first reading 26, 46, 67, 100, 179–183
Folketinget *see* Denmark
foreign affairs committees 90, 139, 162, 178, 192, 270, 339
fragmentation: committee system 10, 19; electoral 245; parliamentary 19, 127, 160, 245; party 178–179, 258
France 14, 17, 29, 98
Francoist regime 244
frontbenchers 249–250, 309–310
funding: committees 53, 207–209, 324, 341; parties 244

gatekeeping 163–164, 173, 299, 335
Germany 14, 17, 29, 116
gender 23, 40, 82, 201, 251, 266, 308
Ghana 14, 17, 29, 137
Gladstone, W. 305
government ministers in committees 53–54, 163, 200, 225, 252, 306
government statement 44–46
Grand Committee 89
Greens 69, 73, 121, 232
guillotine motion 276–278

health committees 43, 80, 142, 265–270, 308
hearings 18, 27, 31–32, 178, 229, 234, 253, 269, 304, 336–337; ministerial 88–90; private 83, 192, 304; public 5, 17, 47, 67, 104, 122–123, 269 *see also* televised hearings, field hearings
hiring practices 51, 68, 178
Hungary 14, 17, 29, 159

immunity of MPs 102, 117, 162, 166, 172, 282

implementation 12, 30–31, 44, 130, 183, 339
in camera *see* committee meeting, closed
informal bargaining 22, 107, 124, 180, 237–239, 302
information sharing 18, 54, 65–70, 180, 278
informational theory 9, 143–144, 249
innovation 21, 99, 169 *see also* digitalization *and* technology
inquiry 55, 101–102, 110, 155, 181, 202, 228, 247 *see also* investigating committees
'inquiry and report' 45 *see also* investigating committees
institutionalization 80, 159, 310
intelligence committees 80–81, 264–268, 330
interest group 18–24, 83, 123, 149, 226, 233–234, 311–312
interpellation 130, 163, 213, 236–239 *see also* questioning
interviews 19, 79–80, 129
investigating committees 10–12, 118–119, 169, 181, 280–281
'inward-looking' committees 312
iron triangle 23, 233
Islamic Development Bank 58
Israel 14, 17, 29, 177

Japan 14, 17, 29, 189
Jobbik party 165, 172
joint committees 41, 142, 181, 247, 264–265, 282
junior ministers 41, 63, 245, 274
justice committees 170–172, 183, 264, 282

killing bills 28, 100, 149, 182, 197, 236, 248
Kingdon, J. 25
Knesset *see* Israel
Kokkai *see* Japan

labour committees 175n6, 191, 229, 265, 330–333
Labour Party (UK) 310
Law on Committees 289
law spamming 295
leadership *see* committee chairs *and* speaker
legal advisors 184
legislative agreements 65–72

legislative initiative 26, 194, 295, 217
Legislative Reorganization Act, The 329
legislature vs. parliament 63, 116–117, 161, 207, 250
legitimacy 16, 123, 208, 253, 308
legitimizing assemblies 216
Liberal Democratic Party (LDP) 189, 195–200
Liberals 69–73, 232, 305
line-by-line scrutiny 294, 299, 305–306, 311
lobbying 24, 84, 180, 212, 306

Magles en- Nowwab *see* Egypt
majoritarian system 190, 195
majority party 109, 146, 197, 266, 290, 323
majority principle 237
mechanisms through which committees exercise influence 88–93
media, influence of 21, 32, 64, 105, 294, 336 *see also* social media
Member Day 328
Mezey, M. 138, 160, 177, 217, 263, 287
minority party 29, 62–69, 72–75, 202 *see also* opposition
mirroring 15, 43, 181, 247, 290
mixed-member majoritarian systems *see* majoritarian systems
monarchies 61, 224, 244, 302
motions 67–68, 179, 254, 275

negotiation 5, 19, 32, 68–69, 197–198, 227, 232
neo-corporatism 84 *see also* corporatism
NHK 194, 201 *see also* media, influence of
Nigeria 14, 17, 29, 206
No confidence, vote of 160–161, 246n1
Non-Governmental Organizations (NGOs) 16, 23, 84, 180, 253, 269
'non-party' mode 309–310
Nordic parliaments 61–79, 224–243
norms *see* socialization
Norton, P. 40–42, 139, 207, 217, 252, 314
Norway 14, 17, 29, 224
number of committees 14

obstruction of voting 22, 198–199 *see also* dilettante tactics
'old bulls' 323
Ombudspeople 11–13, 247, 282

omnibus law 276–278
opposition 22, 74, 93, 174, 203, 283
Országgyűlés *see* Hungary
Ottoman Empire 263, 280
outreach activities
oversight *see* control
oversight committee 11, 13, 30, 184, 214, 238, 279
oversight strategy 31, 130, 214, 257, 328

parliament size 14
parliamentarism 108, 117
parliamentary party group 22, 61, 112, 120, 244, 287
partisan theory 249
partisanship 51, 225, 310, 315
party affiliation 42–43, 163, 215, 232, 290
'party-centred' approach 143–144, 159, 161
party discipline 16, 110, 197, 244, 246, 266
party lists 161, 244
party loyalty 144, 309
party, small 67
party spokesperson 12, 66, 248 *see also* rapporteur
pass rate 194
patronage 210, 217 *see also* clientelism
PBC *see* public bill committees
permanent committees 14, 67–68, 80, 118, 177, 303
personalism 190, 195, 211
petition committees 11, 13, 264, 278, 282
petition, the right to 278–279
petitions 11–13, 46–48, 147, 278–279
'ping pong approach' 338
Plan and Budget Committee (PBC) 264, 272
plenary agenda 148, 272, 275, 281
plenary debate 3, 27–28, 45–46, 103, 228, 277
PMB *see* private members' bills
Podemos 245–246
polarization 298, 326
police patrol model 31, 130, 312
'policy advocate' 21
'policy communities' 1, 23, 25
policy cycle 6, 24–25, 85, 201, 216, 253
'policy kitchen' 59
'policy tribes' 200–203
political capital 46, 289
politiske forlig see legislative agreements

politicization 29, 91, 128, 225
populist parties 245
pork barreling 9, 16, 125, 195
portfolio 15, 117–118, 207, 211
post-colonialism *see* colonialism
post-communism 289
post-soviet 287 *see also* post-communism
poverty 141, 212
PPG *see* parliamentary party group
pre-legislative discussion 150
prestige of committees 19, 82, 238, 294, 308, 339
presidential system 63, 79, 102, 137, 263, 320
primary and secondary committees 270, 274–275
Prime Minister, role of 1–2, 88, 93, 111, 190, 305
private members' bills 147, 163, 173, 179, 225–228
problem definition 25, 127, 181–182, 201, 234, 312
Problem Solvers Caucus 328
procedural amendments 297
'profile' committee 295–296
professionalization 23, 290
proportional representation 161, 190, 278, 307
proportionality in committees 19, 67, 82, 103, 162, 195, 231–232, 278, 289, 306
'proto-deals' 61, 64
public bill committees 12, 302–303, 308–311, 313
public hearings *see* hearings

qualified majorities 263, 279, 281–283
qualified minorities 118
question time 30, 193, 200, 315
questioning 73–74, 163, 173, 194, 225, 256
questionnaires 39, 68, 74
quorum 26, 42, 185, 268, 281, 331
quotas 251, 289, 295

rapporteurs 2–3, 12, 27, 109–111, 125–127, 231; absence of 82
recall 20, 216, 295
recommendations, committee 23, 48, 214, 237, 239
reconciliation committee 57, 282–283
reconstruction: Germany 118; Japan 202
referral powers 148, 213, 326
reform: administrative 190, 200; electoral 161, 189, 195

'rehearsal for plenary', committees as 28, 107, 130
reprobation motion 254
Republican Revolution 327
Republicans (USA) 324–327, 336
research committees 193–194, 201
  see also committees of inquiry
research units 54–55
resource curse 209–210
roll-call vote 289, 326
RoP *see* rules of procedure
rubber-stamping 88, 137, 189, 209, 263, 287
rules committees 323, 335
rules of procedure 9, 15, 40, 80–81, 120, 183, 289

salary: MP 216; staff 56
sanctions 42, 145, 179
Sartori, G. 16, 19, 99, 119, 228, 237
Saudi Arabia 38–40, 43–44, 52, 54
'sausage-making' 337–338
scandal, political 110, 119, 212, 245, 294, 336
scrutiny *see* control
second reading 154, 182, 305–306, 313–314
Second World War 80, 118
secret ballot 266, 281, 306, 324
sectorization of MPs 33, 67, 127–128
segmentation of MPs 67, 85, 233
'segmented state' 23, 234
select committees 11, 19, 142, 302–304
selection: of candidate 244; of committees 125, 143–145, 309; of committee chairs 82, 264, 289, 327; of experts 83; of prime minister 190; of speakers 50, 299
separation of powers 34, 149, 160, 185, 269
shadow ministry 272
single-member districts 190, 199, 321, 326
Social Democrats 73, 82
Socialists 73, 110, 161, 167, 229, 232
socialization 3, 21, 34, 250
'soft power' 313
Spain 14, 17, 29, 202, 244
speaker 46–50, 141, 165, 179, 273
speaking time 124
specialization of MPs 43, 67–68, 131, 160, 195–196, 249
'specially-commissioned minorities' 339–340

split votes 225
spokesperson: committee 66, 70, 146, 231, 246, 275–276; party 66, 71, 146, 248–252, 258; *see also* rapporteur
staff, committee 50–53, 240, 258, 266: funding of 127, 208, 324–325; ratio to MPs 81, 266, 288; role of 46–50, 70
stakeholders 46–48, 139, 218, 253, 274
standing committees 99, 162, 170–174, 191, 229, 236
Standing Orders 44
Statements of Work (SoW) 51
steering committees 11, 191, 325, 332
Stortinget *see* Norway
strategic plan 44, 278
Strøm, K. 4, 61–63, 87, 122, 208, 224, 228, 239, 249, 302
strong committees 3, 32, 161, 183, 208, 224, 245, 257, 321
strong parliaments 6, 32, 217, 224, 240–241
Struck's Law 128
study commission 119
'subcommittee governance' 126
subcommittees 11–12, 116, 164, 247, 252–254, 270, 273, 274, 293, 324
success rate: committee-initiated bills 170–172; government-initiated bills 152, 170; private members' bills 246
sunset legislation 31, 131
supreme court 281, 336
surveys 39, 68, 83, 224, 232 *see also* questionnaires

technical assistance 51–54, 207, 217
technical drafting 46, 105, 153
technology committees 276, 303, 330
televised hearings 194–195, 200, 249, 269 *see also* hearings
television 74, 104, 194 *see also* media, influence of
temel kanun see guillotine motion
temperature of politics 128
term limits 329
termination: committee 290–293; examination and deliberation 194–197; MP powers 295; policy 24, 131
'testing ground for plenary', committees as 28, 107, 258 *see also* 'rehearsal for plenary', committees as

think tanks 23, 56–57
torba kanun see omnibus law
transformative parliaments 2, 5, 216
transparency 16–18, 84, 103–104, 124, 180, 316 *see also* closed committee meeting
troublemakers 307
Turkey 14, 17, 29, 263
Türkiye Büyük Millet Meclisi *see* Turkey
turnover 20, 145, 167, 195–196, 215, 231, 244, 249, 266–267, 307 *see also* volatility
types of legislatures 139, *see also* classification of legislatures
'tyranny of the majority' 198, 321

Ukraine 14, 17, 29, 287
unanimity 85, 237, 272
unicameral 52, 61, 79, 159, 263, 287
unitary systems 61, 79, 98, 159, 177, 287
United Kingdom 14, 17, 29, 302
United States of America 14, 17, 29, 320
urgency procedure 108, 138, 272

Verkhovna Rada Ukraïny *see* Ukraine
veto power 40, 65, 75, 101, 326
volatility 167
vote of no-confidence 160, 166, 259n11
voting 28; committee 192, 170–173, 200, 257–258; plenary 275, 282, 296
Voting Rights Act of 1965 325
Vox 245, 249–250

Washington, G. 321–322
websites: committee 13, 44, 46, 92, 104, 195; parliamentary 54, 163, 227, 300n7
whip 44, 110, 145, 307–309, 334, 337
Wilson, W. 1, 320, 322, 339–3411
'winnowing stage' 151
witnesses 23, 81, 184, 305, 333, 336 *see also* experts
'workhorses of parliament' 32, 117, 207, 226, 334
'working parliament' 2, 79 *see also* classification of parliaments
workload 102–103, 183, 210, 249, 289
Wright Reforms 304

zoku giin see 'policy tribes'
'zones of possible agreement' 64

9780367617950